DLP

A LANGUAGE FOR DISTRIBUTED LOGIC PROGRAMMING

Design, Semantics and Implementation

WILEY SERIES IN PARALLEL COMPUTING

Carey (ed.): Parallel Supercomputing: Methods, Algorithms and Applications

de Bakker (ed.): Languages for Parallel Architectures: Design, Semantics, Implementation Models

Axford: Concurrent Programming: Fundamental Techniques for Real-Time and Parallel Software Design

Gelenbe: Multiprocessor Performance

Treleaven (ed.): Parallel Computers: Object-oriented, Functional, Logic

Williams: Programming Models for Parallel Systems

Raynal and Helary: Synchronization and Control of Distributed Systems and Programs

Eliëns: DLP—A Language for Distributed Logic Programming: Design, Semantics and Implementation

Kacsuk and Wise (eds): Implementations of Distributed Prolog

DLP

A LANGUAGE FOR DISTRIBUTED LOGIC PROGRAMMING

Design, Semantics and Implementation

Anton Eliëns
Vrije University, Amsterdam
The Netherlands

JOHN WILEY & SONS
Chichester · New York · Brisbane · Toronto · Singapore

Other Wiley Editorial Offices

John Wiley & Sons, Inc., 605 Third Avenue,
New York, NY 10158-0012, USA

Jacaranda Wiley Ltd, G.P.O. Box 859, Brisbane,
Queensland 4001, Australia

John Wiley & Sons (Canada) Ltd, 22 Worcester Road,
Rexdale, Ontario M9W 1L1, Canada

John Wiley & Sons (SEA) Pte Ltd, 37 Jalan Pemimpin # 05-04,
Block B, Union Industrial Building, Singapore 2057

Library of Congress Cataloging-in-Publication Data

Eliëns, Anton.
DLP : a language for distributed logic programming : design, semantics, and implementation / Anton Eliëns.
p. cm.—(Wiley series in parallel computing)
Includes bibliographical references and index.
ISBN 0 471 93117 9
1. Logic programming (Computer science) 2. Electronic data processing—Distributed processing. I. Title. II. Series.
QA76.63.E45 1992
005.13—dc20 92-6775
CIP

British Library Cataloguing in Publication Data

A catalogue record for this book is available
from the British Library

ISBN 0 471 93117 9

Printed in Great Britain by Courier International Limited, East Kilbride

Contents

Preface

This book introduces the distributed logic programming language DLP. Distributed logic programming combines logic programming, object oriented programming and parallelism. The distinguishing feature of DLP with respect to other proposals is the support for distributed backtracking over the results of a rendez-vous between objects.

A leading interest behind this work has been the question of parallelism in expert system reasoning. Distributed logic programming is a suitable vehicle for the implementation of distributed knowledge-based systems, including expert systems, and systems for distributed problem solving. It is my conviction that the object oriented programming paradigm will grow in importance, both for knowledge representation and the implementation of knowledge-based systems. Parallelism, also, is a very desirable feature, in particular for AI applications.

Features of this book

- It covers the complete trajectory of the development of an experimental programming language in a coherent and integrated fashion, paying attention to the design, the semantics and the implementation.

- It introduces a concise, yet powerful, new multi-paradigm programming language for the implementation of distributed knowledge-based systems by means of small- to medium-size examples.

- It provides an introduction to logic programming, object oriented programming and parallel/distributed programming, and an evaluation of these paradigms from the perspective of software engineering.

- It provides an introduction to concurrency semantics and the semantics of languages with backtracking, leading to an elegant formal treatment of distributed backtracking.

- It presents a technique for deriving a prototype implementation from a semantic specification.

Intended readers The book is meant to address the following categories of readers.

Advanced students: The book treats the design, semantics and implementation of a multiple-paradigm programming language. It covers the application of object oriented modeling techniques in knowledge representation, and the implementation of a distributed knowledge-based system in the language DLP. It deals with formal concurrency semantics and the formal semantics of distributed backtracking. Also it describes the derivation of a prototype implementation from a semantic specification and discusses the problems that occur when combining the implementation models underlying logic programming, object oriented programming and parallel programming languages.

Young researchers: The book treats the complete trajectory of the development of an experimental programming language in a coherent fashion: the design, the semantics and the implementation. It thus provides a model for similar enterprises.

Knowledge engineers: The language DLP is a suitable vehicle for the specification and implementation of distributed knowledge-based systems. As such the book is of interest to the Artificial Intelligence community.

System developers: The book is of relevance to those interested in software engineering since it treats the application of object oriented modeling techniques in a distributed setting.

Organization This book covers the design, semantics and implementation of the language DLP. It is divided into twelve chapters distributed over three parts.

Part I: Design

1. *Introduction*: This chapter discusses the principles of object oriented modeling and introduces the concept of distributed logic programming. A brief characterization of the language DLP is given and its relation to other approaches is sketched. This chapter also contains an overview of the book.

2. *Paradigms of programming*: This chapter gives an introduction to the paradigms underlying distributed logic programming: logic programming, object oriented programming and parallel/distributed programming. An extensive introduction is given to the logic programming language Prolog, explaining its particular features and its use in typical programming examples.

3. *Extending Prolog to a parallel object oriented language*: The language DLP is introduced by means of exploring the extension of Prolog to a parallel object oriented language. After introducing objects, it is explained how objects communicate by means of a rendez-vous that allows backtracking over the exchanged results. Other features described include the acceptance of method calls, asynchronous communication and the distribution of objects and processes over a collection of processors. The constructs introduced will be illustrated by examples taken from the literature dealing with parallel programming. Among other celebrities the classic Dining Philosophers appear in our gallery.

4. *Object oriented modeling an distributed problem solving*: This chapter gives a number of examples that demonstrate how DLP may be applied in developing programs. Examples are given that show how inheritance and message-delegation

may be used to factor out control in searching a state space, and how these mechanisms may be used to solve problems of knowledge representation. To illustrate the role of object oriented modeling in distributed problem solving, the specification and implementation of a distributed medical expert system is described. The example shows how control may be distributed according to the hierarchic organization of knowledge by means of inheritance.

5. *Design perspectives*: In this chapter we will reflect on the motivations underlying our approach to distributed logic programming. Related work on integrating the paradigms of logic programming, object oriented programming and parallel/distributed programming will be discussed. The design choices made for DLP will be motivated during this discussion.

Part II: Semantics

6. *Process creation and communication in the presence of backtracking*: This chapter introduces the technical framework needed for our semantic enterprise. A self-contained introduction to (metric) concurrency semantics will be given, that includes a treatment of metric spaces, structured operational semantics, denotational (continuation) semantics and a general method to prove the equivalence between the operational semantics and a compositional denotational semantics. As an example, a semantic characterization is given of a very simple language. Further, three abstract languages will be introduced in order to study the major phenomena figuring in distributed logic programming in a more abstract setting and a semantic characterization is given for each of these languages.

7. *An abstract version of DLP and its operational semantics*: This chapter gives a detailed operational semantics of the core of DLP. This semantic characterization explains all the details of the behavior of DLP programs, in particular the behavior displayed during the rendez-vous between objects. This semantics is of a behavioral nature and must be regarded as complementary to a declarative semantics for the language.

8. *Comparative semantics for DLP*: Here the semantic study started in chapter 6 will be extended to the corresponding subsets of DLP. This chapter illustrates how equivalence proofs developed for uniform abstract languages carry over to their more complex non-uniform counterparts.

Part III: Implementation

9. *An implementation model for DLP*: This chapter describes how the computation models of logic programming and parallel object oriented programming are combined in our prototype implementation of DLP. An interesting feature of our solution is how the results of a method call by rendez-vous are communicated to the calling process.

10. *Deriving a Prolog interpreter*: The implementation of the Prolog part of DLP has been derived from a formal continuation semantics for Prolog. This semantics is described and it is shown how to derive the code for the interpreter from this semantics.

11. *The implementation of the prototype*: This chapter gives a detailed description of the implementation of the prototype implementation of DLP, including the way terms are handled, the implementation of objects and the communication protocols governing the communication between objects.

12. *Conclusions and future work*: We will comment on the current status of the language and its implementation. Further, some recommendations will be given for improving the efficiency of the DLP system and we will explore the possibility of providing a declarative semantics for a distributed logic programming language such as DLP.

History and motivations The starting point of this investigation of distributed logic programming was the development of a prototype system extending Prolog with primitives for parallelism. A leading interest behind this work has been the question of parallelism in expert system reasoning. As the system evolved, gradually a shift in emphasis occurred toward integrating object oriented features. Finally, the effort of developing a prototype has resulted in a language proposal, embodying the concept of a distributed logic programming language.

The final proposal has been rather influenced by the concepts developed for the parallel object oriented language POOL [America, 1987]. With some lenience one could speak of the language DLP, introduced in this book, as being a member of a family of POOL-like languages. The major difference between the distributed logic programming language to be presented here and the language POOL, as dealt with in [America and Rutten, 1989a], however is that the latter takes a Pascal-like language as its base language. The most obvious and perhaps important problem that arises concerns the (distributed) backtracking induced by the choice for a Prolog-like language as the base language. Nevertheless, with regard to the formal semantics, the resemblance with POOL enables in a significant degree to lean on the foundational efforts presented in [America and Rutten, 1989a]. In developing the formal semantics for distributed logic programming, another significant influence has been the research reported in [de Vink, 1989] and [de Bruin and de Vink, 1989], dealing with operational and denotational (continuation) semantics for Prolog with cut. A common (metric) framework that allows to integrate the topics of process creation, communication and backtracking is conceived in [de Bakker, 1991]. The work presented on the formal semantics of distributed logic programming may be regarded as a (non-trivial) application of the foundational results presented in the sources mentioned before. The primary concern here has been to use formal semantic techniques to elucidate the dynamics of distributed logic programming, notably process creation and communication in the presence of backtracking.

The design of a programming language is a delicate issue. Apart from the possibility of providing a formal semantics, there remains a rather subjective criterion of a more aesthetic nature. Is it pleasing to use the language? And for what applications? For the author the answer to the first question is naturally yes. Nonetheless, a first attempt has been made to convince the reader of the applicability and the expressiveness of the language by presenting a number of examples dealing with problems in parallel programming, knowledge representation and distributed problem solving.

A distributed medical (toy) expert system has been developed to illustrate the power of the language DLP.

How intricate the relation between formal semantics and actual systems can be is demonstrated by the fact that the core of the prototype consists of an interpreter based on a continuation semantics for sequential Prolog, adapted from [Allison, 1986]. It will be shown how the actual implementation of the Prolog interpreter is derived from this particular semantics; and also what extensions (read hacks, but positively) are needed to arrive at the full functionality of the prototype system. Many loose ends can still be detected in this transition from a formal semantics to an actual system. Perhaps the only valuable remark that can be made here is that the pleasure in experimenting with such a complex prototype system was definitely enhanced by taking a well-understood formal description of a constituent part of the final system as a starting point.

I regard this extension of Prolog to a distributed logic programming language as a first study in augmenting a logic based language with constructs for parallel object oriented programming. I am looking forward to similar extensions of, say, a resolution-based theorem prover like LMA/ITP [Wos et al, 1984].

Publications Parts of this book have been published elsewhere. Previous publications include

A. ELIËNS, *Extending Prolog to a parallel object oriented language*, in: Proc. IFIP W.G. 10.3 Working Conference on Decentralized Systems Lyon, M. Cosnard and C. Girault (eds.), North-Holland (1990) pp. 159-170

A. ELIËNS, *DLP – A language for distributed logic programming*, Dissertation University of Amsterdam, (1991)

A. ELIËNS, *Distributed Logic Programming for Artificial Intelligence*, AI Communications 4 (1), ECCAI (1991) pp. 11-21

A. ELIËNS, *Comparative semantics of a backtrackable rendez-vous*, in: Proc. CSN'91/SION Utrecht, Mathematisch Centrum, Amsterdam (1991) pp. 182-196

A. ELIËNS AND E.P. DE VINK, *Asynchronous rendez-vous in the presence of backtracking*, ISLP'91 Workshop on Asynchronous Communication, November 1991, San Diego (to appear by Springer Verlag)

Current status Recently, we developed Active C++, an extension of C++ with active classes and communication by rendez-vous [Eliëns and Visser, 1992]. We are now in the process of implementing DLP in Active C++. We hope to have a release both for Sun Sparc workstations and 486 personal computers by the end of 1992.

Information and source code For questions or comments contact the author at the *Vrije Universiteit, Department of Mathematics and Computer Science, De Boelelaan 1081, 1081 HV Amsterdam, The Netherlands*. Electronic mail messages should be addressed to `eliens@cs.vu.nl`.

Acknowledgements

I wish to acknowledge, first of all, those who actively took part in my scientific development, Paul Klint for his encouraging attitude during the writing of a first version of this book, and Jaco de Bakker for taking an early interest in my work and offering me the opportunity of this publication. Together with Jan Rutten, they discussed the subject of this book which was then to become my thesis. Their amiable scrutiny significantly improved the presentation of my ideas.

Acknowledgements are also due to Luis Monteiro, who has pointed out some critical issues in the language with respect to its declarative semantics, Peter van Emde Boas for common dilations on the subject, and Marc Bezem for continuous discussion on the topic of scientific standards.

I also wish to mention Carel van den Berg for giving invaluable technical support, Peter Lucas for sharing his knowledge of expert systems, Jan-Marie Jacquet for reading the first draft, Wouter Mettrop for bibliographical explorations, and, as dear friends and colleagues, Alban Ponse and Louis Kossen.

Further I wish to acknowledge Erik de Vink for deepening my semantic understanding of the phenomena at hand, Krzystov Apt for his benevolent criticism, Cees Visser for his willingness to invest his energy in an efficient implementation of the language, and Hans van Vliet for deepening my insight into the problems of software engineering.

Finally, I wish to thank Gaynor Redvers-Mutton for her encouraging editorial support, and the people at the Centre for Mathematics and Computer Science and the Computer Science Department of the Vrije Universiteit in Amsterdam for providing a congenial environment that allowed me to work on this book with the attention it required.

Anton Eliëns

Vrije Universiteit
Amsterdam, February 1992

Part I

Design

1

Introduction

- *The activity of the intuition consists in making spontaneous judgements which are not the results of conscious trains of reasoning ...* -
A. Turing, from Andrew Hodges, *The Enigma of Intelligence*

The use of object oriented techniques in the design and implementation phases of software development projects has resulted in a shift of emphasis in favor of the design phase since the effort of implementing a system in an object oriented programming language on the basis of an object oriented design may be regarded as a process of refining the decisions laid down in the design. The use of object oriented techniques has thus effectively reduced the gap between the concept-oriented world of design and the technology-oriented world of implementation. Cf. [Wirfs-Brock et al, 1990] and [Meyer, 1988].

This development may be taken a step further by proposing a logic-based object oriented language that allows to employ an abstract specification of an object oriented system as a prototype.[1] We will introduce a distributed logic programming language DLP that allows to specify an object oriented system in a highly abstract way. The language proposed extends logic programming with features specifically geared towards the specification of object oriented systems and thus corrects what has been commonly felt to be one of the major drawbacks of logic programming: *the lack of support for specifying large systems in a structured way.*

In addition to object oriented features, the language DLP supports parallelism, by

[1] In this context I may remark that, independent of the introduction of object oriented technology, the need for prototyping has arisen in software engineering practice to accommodate the difficulty of eliciting the proper requirements in the analysis phase. It is generally acknowledged that prototyping is well supported by object oriented programming languages.

allowing objects to have activity of their own. For many problem areas, concurrency or parallelism is a very natural phenomenon. Parallism and distribution fit in well with the object oriented paradigm since the actual (possibly concurrent) behavior or location of an object may remain hidden for the clients of an object.

An important application of DLP lies in the area of distributed knowledge based systems. We feel that the object oriented modeling approach may support a proper distribution of the various reasoning tasks that are involved, by taking the natural activity of the actors in a domain as the guideline in developing an intelligent system.

1.1 Principles of object oriented modeling

The philosophy of design underlying object oriented software development centers around *abstraction* and *information hiding*. Objects, encapsulating ***state*** and ***behavior***, support these notions. Moreover, objects provide a natural means to model a problem since the objects in a system may bear a close correspondence to the entities encountered in reality. As phrased in [Booch, 1986], each module in the system denotes an object or a class of objects from the problem space.

As a design method, the approaches treated in [Booch, 1991] and [Wirfs-Brock et al, 1990] have in common an emphasis on the identification of the objects that play a role in the system and on delineating the functionality of these objects, that is to assess what services are provided and how the objects interact in order to provide these services. As an heuristic guideline for finding the proper objects, often a 'linguistic' analysis of the documents stating the requirements is proposed. Nouns may suggest objects and verbs may suggest operations that are to be performed by objects.

Objects [Booch, 1986] characterizes objects as (clearly identifiable) entities that ***suffer*** and ***require*** actions. Operationally, an object may be defined as to comprise a ***state*** and ***behavior***. The actions an object suffers may be requests to give information on its state or may demand to change the state of the object. To provide a service an object may need to issue such requests to other objects.

In an object oriented system, computation amounts to sending messages between objects. Objects provide the means to encapsulate data and procedures and to hide the details of the implementation from the clients by specifying an external method interface. Apart from contributing to the modular structure of a program the encapsulation mechanism allows local changes to objects and thus enhances the maintenance of an object oriented system.

Objects may play a variety of roles, that is an object may be merely a passive server, awaiting requests to execute a message, or objects may autonomously control (parts of) a computation. The most usual case, however, is for an object to figure in both roles, and to collaborate with other objects in order to provide a service.

Inheritance There is some debate whether *inheritance* is to be considered an integral part of an object oriented development method. Cf. [Booch, 1986]. I share the view expressed in e.g. [Halbert and O'Brien, 1987] that inheritance is of major importance in the design and implementation of object oriented systems as a mechanism to suppress the complexity of a large collection of object descriptions by means of a hierarchical organization according to their functionality. Moreover, inheritance is of essential importance for the effective reuse of software. Cf. [Meyer, 1988] and [Wirfs-Brock et al, 1990]. In object oriented design, inheritance comes down to sharing specifications of behavioral properties of objects. In object oriented programming languages inheritance by code sharing has proven to be a very powerful mechanism.

Object oriented design The principal guideline in object oriented design is to find some meaningful decomposition, that allows to regard each of the components as an object providing certain services, reflecting the structure of the problem domain. Describing objects and characterizing their structural relations by means of inheritance are the two major components of an object oriented design methodology. Objects provide a mechanism to abstract from the details of how a service is provided. To make use of a service, it suffices to know what services an object offers and what messages must be sent to request for that service. Inheritance provides a means to create a hierarchy of objects and to separate the stable conceptual issues from more specific volatile details.

1.2 The concept of distributed logic programming

Distributed logic programming (DLP) may be characterized by the pseudo-equation

$$DLP = LP + OO + \|$$

stating that distributed logic programming combines logic programming (LP), object oriented programming (OO) and parallelism ($\|$).

Logic Programming has originally been used only in the context of Artificial Intelligence. Its most popular representative is Prolog. Because of its logical basis it allows to solve problems in a declarative way, that is by providing a logical description of the problem to be solved. See [Kowalski, 1979], [Bratko, 1990]. However, usually such specifications must be refined to become efficiently executable. Cf. [Hoare, 1987]. Prolog is a very suitable language for prototyping small systems. In software engineering practice, logic programming and in particular Prolog has been recognized as a potential aid in requirements engineering and design specification. See [Webster, 1988].

Object Oriented Programming has rapidly grown into a popular paradigm for developing complex systems. Objects integrate *data* and *methods* that operate on these data in a protected way. This allows to organize a program as a collection of objects, representing the conceptual structure of the problem. Part of the popularity of object oriented languages is due to the facilities for code sharing as offered by the inheritance mechanism. See [Wegner, 1987].

Object oriented programming allows to model problems in a very natural way. Its major promise for software engineering practice is in my opinion that it offers the opportunity of a close link between the various phases of the software life cycle, the engineering of requirements in the analysis phase and the design and implementation phases. Cf. [Wirfs-Brock et al, 1990], [Meyer, 1988].

Parallelism is somehow of independent interest. Most of the developments in parallel logic programming are based on exploiting the parallelism inherent in the computation model of logic programming languages. Parallelism in DLP is achieved by extending the notion of object to that of a process, in a similar fashion as the approach taken for POOL [America, 1987]. DLP, however, also supports multi-threaded objects, that have autonomous activity and may simultaneously evaluate method calls.

As [Booch, 1986] observes, objects provide a natural way to introduce concurrency, by associating (possibly multiple) processes with objects. Despite the fact that parallelism is often inherently part of the problem domain, not many design specification formalisms support concurrency. See [Webster, 1988].

A design goal in developing DLP was to provide a syntactically elegant language with a clear semantics that allows to express the conceptual structure of a program in a straightforward way and that may serve as a vehicle for prototyping. The next section summarizes the main ingredients of the language DLP. Readers not familiar with the language Prolog may wish to consult section 2.1 first.

1.3 The language DLP

The language DLP may be regarded as an extension of Prolog with *object declarations* and *statements* for the dynamic creation of objects, communication between objects and the assignment of values to non-logical instance variables of objects.

1.3.1 Object declarations

Object declarations in DLP have the form

object

```
object name {
var variables.
clauses
}
```

Both *object* and *var* are keywords. The variables declared by *var* are non-logical variables that may be assigned values by a special statement.

Objects act as prototypes in that new copies may be made by so-called *new* statements. Such copies are called *instances.* Each instance has its private copy of the non-logical variables of the declared object. In other words, non-logical variables act as instance variables.

Dynamically, a distinction is made between *active* objects and *passive* objects. Active objects must explicitly be created by a *new* statement. Syntactically, the distinction between active and passive objects is reflected in the occurrence of so-called *constructor* clauses in the declaration for active objects. Constructor clauses are clauses of which the head has a predicate name identical to the name of the object in which they occur. Constructor clauses specify an object's own activity. The other clauses occurring in an object declaration may be regarded as *method* clauses, specifying how a request to the object is handled. Passive objects only have method clauses.

1.3.2 Statements

DLP extends Prolog with a number of statements for dealing with non-logical variables, the creation of objects and the communication between objects. These statements may occur as atoms in a goal.

Non-logical variables For assigning a term t to a non-logical variable x the statement

- $x := t$

is provided. Before the assignment takes place, the term t is simplified. The non-logical variables occurring in t are replaced by their current values. In fact, such simplification takes place for each goal atom. DLP also supports arithmetical simplification.

New expressions For dynamically creating instances of objects the statement

- $O = new(c)$

is provided, where c is the name of a declared object. When evaluated as an atom, a reference to the newly created object will become bound to the logical variable O. For creating active objects the statement

- $O = new(c(t_1, ..., t_n))$

must be used. The activity of the newly created object consists of evaluating the *constructor* goal $c(t_1, ..., t_n)$, where c is the object name and $t_1, ..., t_n$ denote the actual parameters. The constructor goal will be evaluated by using the constructor clauses.

Actually, the expressions $new(c)$ and $new(c(t_1, ..., t_n))$ will be simplified to a reference to an object when they occur as a term in a goal. Both the statements introduced above may be regarded as special cases, in which the *new* expressions occur in a unification goal.

Method calls A method call is the evaluation of a goal by an object. To call the method m of an object O with actual parameters $t_1, ..., t_n$ the statement

- $O!m(t_1, ..., t_n)$

must be used. It is assumed that O is a logical variable referring to the object to which the request is addressed. When such an atom is encountered, the object O is asked to evaluate the goal $m(t_1, ..., t_n)$. If the object to which the call is addressed is willing to accept the request then the result of evaluating $m(t_1, ..., t_n)$ will be sent back to the caller. After sending the first result, subsequent results will be delivered whenever the caller tries to backtrack over the method call. If no alternative solutions can be produced the call fails.

Active objects must explicitly interrupt their own activity and state their willingness to accept a method call by a statement of the form

- *accept*$(m_1, ..., m_n)$

which indicates that any request for one of the methods $m_1, ..., m_n$ will be accepted.

1.3.3 The computation model of DLP

The computation model of DLP combines the computation model underlying Prolog and the model underlying a parallel object oriented language. Parallel object oriented processing must support objects, processes and communication between objects.

Objects contain non-logical data, persisting during the life time of the object, and clauses defining the functionality of the object.

Objects may be *active* or *passive*. The activity of an object is defined by so-called *constructor clauses* that describe the own activity of an object. Apart from constructor clauses, active objects may also contain so-called method clauses that are used when the object receives a method call. A *method call* is simply the request to evaluate a goal.

Processes are created when creating a new active object and for the evaluation of a method call. The process executing the own activity of an active object is called the *constructor process*. For each method call a process is created to enable backtracking over the results of a method call.

Passive objects have no activity but answering to method calls. Active objects must explicitly interrupt their own activity to indicate the willingness to answer a method call.

Communication with another object takes place by engaging in a (synchronous) rendez-vous. In order to achieve compatibility with the ordinary Prolog goal evaluation, DLP supports global backtracking over the results of a rendez-vous. With respect to backtracking, it is transparent whether a goal is evaluated remotely, by another object or locally, provided the necessary clauses are defined. This transparency holds for both passive and active objects.

Below is pictured what happens when a process issues a method call to an active object. Here we assume that *accept* statements may occur only in the constructor process associated with an (active) object.

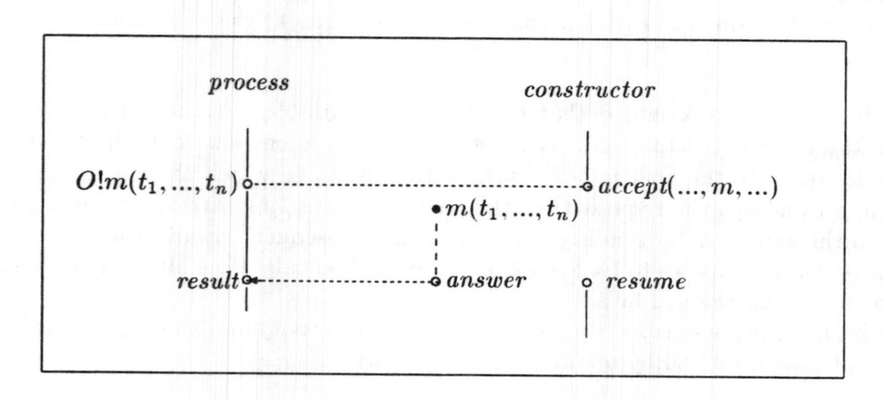

As soon as both the process calling the method and the constructor process of the object to which the call is addressed have synchronized, the activity of the constructor is interrupted and a process is created to evaluate the goal $m(t_1, ..., t_n)$. The constructor is interrupted for safety reasons, in order to guarantee that no other method call will be accepted.

The calling process waits for an answer. As soon as the caller has received a result, both the calling process and the constructor process resume their activity. On backtracking, the calling process may ask for alternative solutions.

Passive objects allow unlimited internal concurrency: in other words, an indefinite number of method calls may be active simultaneously. For active objects, mutual exclusion is provided to the extent that when a particular method call is accepted no other method call will be accepted until the first answer for that call is delivered. This protocol of mutual exclusion seemed more natural than either locking out the object until all answers have been delivered or providing no mutual exclusion at all.

An example As an example, consider the object declaration for a travel agency.

agency

```
object agency {
var cities = [amsterdam, paris, london].
agency() :-  run().
run() :-  accept(destination,add), run().
destination(X)  :-  member(X,cities).
add(X) :-  append([X],cities,R), cities := R.
}
```

A travel agency may be asked for a destination. The destinations an agency offers are contained in a list of cities. The non-logical variable *cities* storing this list is initialized to contain as possible destinations *amsterdam*, *paris* and *london*.

Creating a new agency, and subsequently asking it for a destination, is done as in the following goal.

```
?-
    O = new(agency()),
    O!destination(Y),
    ...
```

When evaluating the first component of this goal the logical variable O will become bound to the newly created *agency* that offers as destinations *amsterdam*, *paris* and *london*. Immediately thereafter the method call $O!destination(Y)$ will be evaluated, but the call will not be accepted until the accept statement expressing the willingness to accept a call is reached.

The evaluation of the method call will result in binding Y to *amsterdam* and when backtracking occurs, subsequently to *paris* and *london*. Then the call will fail. Backtracking over a *new* statement is not possible. This call will simply fail.

1.3.4 Inheritance

An essential feature of the object oriented approach is the use of inheritance to define the relations between objects. Cf. [Wegner, 1987], [Wegner and Zdonik, 1988], [Halbert and O'Brien, 1987]. Inheritance may be conveniently used to factor out the code common to a number of objects. For an untyped language, as DLP, inheritance is a facility to share code.

The declaration for an object inheriting from an object *base* is

inheritance

```
object name : base {
var variables.
clauses
}
```

This declaration will result in adding the non-logical variables and clauses declared for the object *base* to those of the declared object.

Any non-logical variables of the *base* object that occur also in the declared object will be overwritten by the non-logical variable of the declared object. This will be of significance only when at least one of the non-logical variables has an initializing declaration.

Such overwriting does not take place for clauses. When the declared object contains clauses similar to clauses in the base object, concerning the same predicate, then these will be treated as alternative choices for evaluating an atom.

As an example, consider the relation between a researcher and a professor, stated in the declaration below.

researcher

```
object researcher {
var field.
knowsof(X) :-   member(X,field).
}
object professor : researcher {
knowsof(X) :-   committee(Conference,X).
}
```

The intended meaning here is that a professor knows of the topics of the conferences for which he has been a member of the program committee, in addition to what he knows of as a researcher.

1.4 Relation to other work

The inspiration for this work comes from three directions: ***design representation technology***, ***multiple-paradigm languages*** and ***distributed problem solving***.

Design representation technology The idea of employing distributed logic programming as a tool for supporting the design of (object oriented) software systems is inspired by the survey of design representation techniques given in [Webster, 1988].

Because of its declarative nature, the language DLP may be used to specify an object oriented system in an abstract way. Due to the fact that DLP is a high level *programming* language, this specification may be used as a prototype embodying the behavior of the system.

Multiple-paradigm languages As related approaches in combining logic programming, object oriented programming and parallelism, I wish to mention first of all Delta Prolog that also supports distributed backtracking, but in the context of a less powerful communication mechanism. [Pereira et al, 1986]. Delta Prolog does not, however, provide any modularization construct.

Modularization in an object oriented style is offered by MultiLog, a multi-tasking object oriented Prolog developed to support prototyping embedded systems, that are (eventually) to be implemented in Ada. [Karam, 1988]. The distinguishing feature of DLP with respect to MultiLog however is that DLP supports backtracking over the answers of a method call by rendez-vous, whereas MultiLog proceeds from the assumption that such backtracking is not needed.

Other efforts at extending logic programming with object oriented features are reported in [Shapiro and Takeuchi, 1983], [Zaniolo, 1984] and [Davison, 1989].

Distributed problem solving Also related is the work on distributing (medical) reasoning tasks reported in [Gomez and Chandrasekaran, 1981]. A logical basis to this approach has been provided in [Kowalczyk and Treur, 1990].

The DLP approach to the issue of defining generic reasoning tasks comes from a programming perspective. In this respect DLP may be compared to the proposal in [Hynynen and Lassila, 1989], exploring the use of the object oriented programming paradigm in a distributed problem solver.

A more extensive discussion of related approaches is given in section 5.2.

1.5 An overview of this book

Our research covers the design, the semantics and the implementation of the language DLP.

1.5.1 Design

In part I we will introduce the language and present a number of examples that illustrate the use of the language. However, before this, an introduction will be given to the paradigms underlying distributed logic programming.

Logic programming Since, undeniably, logic programming lies at the heart of our approach, an extensive introduction is given to logic programming, and the language Prolog.

The notion of a *logic program* will be introduced and a thorough account will be given of the relation between the declarative, that is logical, interpretation and the procedural interpretation of a logic program, allowing logic programs to be used for computing. The nature of unification will be explained and the role of the logical variable therein.

For readers not familiar with the language Prolog, a treatment will be given of the basic constructs of the language as well as its particular features. Examples will be presented that explain the use of these features. Further, two typical search problems will be discussed for which Prolog may conveniently be used.

Object oriented programming To introduce object oriented programming, a brief account will be given of the developments that have contributed to the popularity of object oriented programming. Objects will be characterized as a device to *encapsulate* data and procedures that operate on these data. We will look at classes, as templates for creating objects. Then the notion of *inheritance* will be introduced, and the use of inheritance to factor out the functionality of a collection of objects or to create a specialization hierarchy will be explained. Further, we will discuss the role of object oriented modeling from the perspective of the requirements analysis and the design underlying a system.

Parallel/distributed programming Next, a characterization will be given of the major features of distributed programming and the three models underlying parallel/distributed programming will be introduced: *communicating sequential processes*, *object-based concurrency* and *concurrent logic programming*.

Communicating sequential processes provide a basic model to employ parallelism. Communication in this model may be characterized as synchronous transfer of values. Then it will be explained how objects may be combined with concurrency and we will take a closer look at the rendez-vous concept that is supported by Ada as a means to call remote procedures. The notion of active objects and method calls by rendez-vous will then be introduced. Lastly, we will discuss the computation model of concurrent logic programming and show how objects may be implemented using shared logical variables that act as channels between processes.

Software engineering We will conclude the introduction of the paradigms underlying distributed logic programming by reviewing the contributions of each of these paradigms to the practice of software engineering and we will assess their shortcomings. Briefly, we will discuss how distributed logic programming might provide a remedy.

The language DLP After introducing the paradigms out of which distributed logic programming originated, we will introduce the constructs of the language DLP by exploring how the language Prolog may be extended to support parallel object oriented programming. Objects will be introduced as a modularization construct that may contain non-logical (instance) variables, and it will be described how processes are created to evaluate method calls and to execute the own activity of (active) objects.

We will explore the use of synchronous bi-unification across channels as a mechanism to communicate between objects. Then *method calls by rendez-vous* will be introduced that allow synchronization by explicit *acceptance* statements and that support distributed backtracking over the results of a call. An extension of accept statements will be introduced that allows acceptance to depend on the parameters of the call.

Then, it will be shown how the communication primitives implementing the synchronous rendez-vous may be used for engaging in an *asynchronous* rendez-vous and how this mechanism allows the user to define (restricted) *and-parallelism*. We will further explain how the language supports the distribution of objects and processes over processors.

Finally, after summarizing the constructs by which DLP extends Prolog, we will distinguish three subsets of DLP of increasing complexity that will serve as a basis for our semantic study of DLP in part II.

Object oriented modeling To illustrate how DLP may be applied in developing actual systems it will be shown how inheritance and delegation may be used to factor out control in searching a state space. Also, an object oriented solution to the N-queens problem is presented that illustrates how to connect a number of active objects.

The use of inheritance for knowledge representation will be investigated and we will discuss the way that inheritance may be of influence on backtracking.

To demonstrate the role of object oriented modeling in developing systems for distributed problem solving we will describe the specification and implementation of a distributed medical expert system. The example shows how control may be distributed according to the hierarchic organization of the knowledge.

Design perspectives Having introduced the language DLP we will take a step back and reflect on the motivations underlying our approach to distributed logic programming. We will discuss the notion of distributed knowledge processing and our contribution to this area. We will then pay attention to related work aiming at the integration of logic programming, object oriented programming and parallel/distributed programming. A distinction will be made between these approaches according to their point of departure, that is whether they strive for an integration starting from a combination of logic programming and object oriented programming, logic programming and parallelism, or object oriented programming and parallelism. The design choices made for DLP will be motivated during this discussion.

1.5.2 Semantics

In part II, we will study the semantics of DLP. To characterize the behavior of programs, we will employ the technique of structured operational semantics introduced in [Plotkin, 1983]. In order to show that these semantics are well-defined in a mathematical sense, we will also provide a compositional denotational semantics.

The mathematical framework in which this semantic study takes place is the metric approach originally developed in [de Bakker and Zucker, 1982]. Chapter 6 provides a thorough introduction to the metric approach and its application to concurrency semantics.

In order to manage the complexity of our task, we have distinguished three subsets of the language DLP that allow us to study the various behavioral phenomena of distributed logic programming in a more isolated way. The simplest subset is a language that supports backtracking. We will extend this language with features for dynamic object creation and synchronous communication between objects with local backtracking that takes place within the confines of an object. Finally, our last subset represents a language that supports dynamic object creation and method calls by rendez-vous, allowing distributed backtracking over the results of a rendez-vous.

Before giving the semantics of (these subsets of) DLP, we will study the semantics of what we call uniform abstractions of these subsets, in which we will pay no attention to assignments to non-logical variables and the unification of logical variables. The results of this preliminary study carry over to our semantic study of DLP in a surprisingly smooth way.

It must be remarked that the semantics given are of a behavioral nature, that is characterizing the flow of control within objects and the communication between objects. These behavioral semantics must be regarded as complementary to a declarative semantics that clarifies the meaning of a program in terms of a logical model. It seems unlikely that such a declarative semantics is possible at all, without taking recourse to dynamic logic or *possible worlds semantics*. In chapter 12 some recommendations will be given of how to approach the problem of providing a declarative semantics for DLP.

1.5.3 Implementation

In part III, a detailed description is given of the implementation model employed in the prototype implementation of DLP. Our solution to integrating the computation models of logic programming and object oriented programming in a parallel/distributed setting has been to extend an imperative parallel object oriented language with logic programming capabilities.

Since our language DLP supports backtracking over the results of a rendez-vous, we had to make an explicit distinction between objects and processes. An interesting feature of our solution is the way the results of a method call are communicated to the calling process by means of so-called *resumptions*, which are goals that must be executed by the caller in order to effect the bindings resulting from the call.

In developing the prototype implementation of DLP, the code for the Prolog interpreter was derived from a formal continuation semantics of Prolog. Employing such a technique for implementing a protoype of an experimental language may be fruitful, since the resulting code will in general be rather compact. For an efficient implementation, however, an abstract machine approach such as the WAM for Prolog is an absolute necessity. See [Warren, 1983].

A detailed description is given of the implementation of the prototype of DLP, including the way terms are handled, the implementation of objects and the communication protocols governing the communication between objects.

We will then comment on the current status of the language and its implementation. Further, some recommendations will be given for improving the efficiency of the DLP system and we will explore the possibility of providing a declarative semantics for a distributed logic programming language such as DLP.

2

Paradigms of programming

- Perhaps a difference is to be sought in the opposite direction: perhaps expression is more direct and immediate than representation. -
Nelson Goodman, *Languages of Art*

The distributed logic programming language DLP that is introduced in this book is the result of combining notions of three distinct paradigms of computing: *logic programming*, *object oriented programming* and *parallel/distributed programming*.

This chapter is intended to introduce these paradigms of programming independently. In particular, an extensive introduction to logic programming is given, treating the general concepts underlying logic based computation. Also, a detailed description is given of the popular logic programming language Prolog, with examples that illustrate the use of Prolog in typical search problems.

The major features of object oriented programming such as *encapsulation* and *inheritance* will be introduced. Design decisions with respect to these features will be discussed by comparing their support in some of the most well-known object oriented languages, such as Smalltalk and C++. We also will discuss the mechanism of inheritance from the perspective of polymorphic types and behavioral refinement. Finally, we will comment on the impact of object oriented technology on the various phases of the software life cycle.

Further, an account is given of the three major computation paradigms underlying parallel/distributed programming: *communicating sequential processes*, *object-based concurrency* and *concurrent logic programming*.

We will conclude this chapter by looking at these distinct paradigms from a software engineering perspective, in order to establish the benefits and shortcomings of these paradigms of programming with respect to the actual development of software. We will then raise the question what contribution a combination of these paradigms might make to the practice of programming.

2.1 Logic programming

The primary virtue of logic programming is its declarative semantics. A *logic program* can be read as a theory stating relations between entities in a particular domain.

For a programmer, such an interpretation allows to separate the concerns for the logical structure of an algorithm from issues of control. The famous phrase

algorithm = logic + control

of [Kowalski, 1979] states this principle succinctly.

The idea of using predicate logic as a programming language arose from research in automated theorem-proving in the early 70s and resulted in the language Prolog. The first implementation was by Roussel/Colmerauer. Soon afterwards, efficient implementations became available which demonstrated the fruitfulness of this idea, at least for the kind of problems to be found in academic settings.

By now Prolog is a widely accepted programming tool which is applied in areas like databases, problem solving, natural language processing, compiler design and, not the least important, expert systems. According to [Butler Cox, 1983] Prolog has often been used to prototype small- to medium-scale expert systems in a business environment. As another indication of the potential of the paradigm, it may be mentioned that the Japanese Fifth Generation Computers project is based on logic programming.

The logical language used in logic programming is called *Horn clause logic*, which is a subset of predicate logic that enables an efficient computational interpretation. Cf. [Dowling and Gallier, 1984].

In this section, which is necessarily of an introductory nature, we will explore the notion of a *logic program* and its mathematical, logical foundations enabling a declarative reading of a program. Complementary to the declarative interpretation we will define a procedural interpretation that allows logic programs to be used for computing.[1] We will then describe the language Prolog, including the so-called *impure* or *extra-logical* facilities that are in practice considered necessary for using Prolog in actual programming tasks. We will defer a discussion of the merits of Prolog from a software engineering perspective to section 2.4.

2.1.1 Declarative versus procedural semantics

Logic is an excellent vehicle for reasoning about the state of affairs in a particular world. The advantage of logic is that it offers a natural formalism to express the facts and rules that pertain to that world. We will explain how such facts and rules can be stated in a *logic program*. Our treatment is based on [Lloyd, 1987].

[1] Readers not interested in the mathematical foundations of logic programming are advised to jump to section 2.1.3.

2.1.1.1 Logic programs

In a logic program terms are used to denote the entities that constitute the world that the program is about.

Terms Terms denote individuals. Terms are either constants or functional expressions. Constants are used as names for particular individuals. Numbers or names of persons are examples of constants. We will use the letter c, possibly subscripted, for indicating constants. To be able to refer to unspecified items we use logical variables, that we will write as capital X, Y, Z. We may also use compound terms to denote individuals. We use the letters f and g as function-symbols and write such functional expressions as $f(t_1, ..., t_n)$ where each t_i, for $0 \leq i \leq n$, is a term. In other words, if we define terms t by

$$t ::= c \mid X \mid f(t_1, ..., t_n) : n \geq 0$$

then a term can be either a constant, a logical variable or a compound term consisting of a function-symbol and zero or more argument-terms.

As an example from mathematical logic, we have the constant 0 and the compound terms $s(0)$, $s(s(0))$,..., which are commonly used to denote the natural numbers. As a hint, just count the number of function-symbols! To illustrate the use of a variable consider the term $s(X)$. This term may be regarded as denoting any number greater than zero, since whatever value X takes there is always at least one function-symbol.

Literals Having defined terms we may introduce *atoms* and *literals*. We use the letters p and q for predicate-symbols and write $p(t_1, ..., t_n)$ or $q(t_1, ..., t_n)$ for atoms. Atoms with zero arguments may be regarded as atomic propositions. A literal is either an atom or the negation of an atom. We will use the letters A and B, possibly subscripted to write literals. We will call literals with a negation sign negative literals, and literals without a negation sign positive literals.

Program clauses The constituents of a logic program are *clauses*. In general, clauses have the form

$$A \leftarrow B_1, ..., B_n$$

where A is commonly called the *head* of the clause and the literals $B_1, ..., B_n$ the body.

Informally such a clause may be read as stating that A holds if each of the literals $B_1, ..., B_n$ holds. In other words, the arrow pointing to the left may be read as an implication symbol relating the antecedent $B_1, ..., B_n$ to the consequent A. The antecedent $B_1, ..., B_n$ stands for the conjunction of the literals $B_1, ..., B_n$.

In case the number of literals in the body is zero as in the clause

$$A \leftarrow$$

the literal A may be regarded as unconditionally true.

The latter clause states a *fact*, whereas the former expresses an implication-like *rule*. These two kinds of clauses are called *program clauses*. A *logic program* is simply a collection of program clauses. We use the letter P to denote a logic program.

Goal clauses Apart from the program clauses, two additional kinds of clauses exist: *goal clauses* and the *empty clause.*

Goal clauses are of the form

$$\leftarrow G$$

where G is a conjunction of literals $B_1, ..., B_n$, just as the body of a program clause. In contrast with a program clause, a goal clause has an empty head.

A goal clause such as the one above can be regarded as a request to prove the conjunction of the literals $B_1, ..., B_n$. When also the right-hand side of a goal clause is empty we speak of the *empty clause*, which is usually written as $\Box$. For such a goal clause there is nothing left to be proven.

As an example, consider the clauses

number

$$number(0) \leftarrow$$
$$number(s(X)) \leftarrow number(X)$$

that define the natural numbers, including zero.

As a goal clause we may then state

$$\leftarrow number(s(s(0))$$

asking whether $s(s(0))$ is a natural number, which is obviously the case.

Clauses as logical formulas We have used an implication arrow, pointing to the left, to write clauses. To explain how a collection of clauses constitutes a logical theory, we will interprete the clauses introduced in terms of the other logical operators: conjunction, disjunction and negation.

When we have literals A and B we write $A \wedge B$ for the conjunction of A and B, which informally means that both A and B must be true. We write $A \vee B$ for the disjunction of A and B, with the informal meaning that either one of A and B must be true. And we write $\neg A$ for the negation of A, which informally is true only if A is not true.

From propositional logic we know that the implication $A \leftarrow B$ is true if and only if $A \vee \neg B$ is true, since when B is false it does not matter whether A is true. Using the logical operators introduced above, the general form of a clause is

$$A_1 \vee ... \vee A_m \leftarrow B_1 \wedge ... \wedge B_n$$

which, when it is written without the implication symbol, is equivalent to

$$A_1 \vee ... \vee A_m \vee \neg B_1 \vee ... \vee \neg B_n$$

that is a disjunction containing a number of positive literals A_i, for i ranging from 1 to m and negative literals B_j, for j ranging from 1 to n. That we may write the negation of $B_1 \wedge ... \wedge B_n$ as $\neg B_1 \vee ... \vee \neg B_n$ is due to the equivalence

$$\neg(B_1 \wedge ... \wedge B_n) = \neg B_1 \vee ... \vee \neg B_n$$

which is known as the *Morgan law*.

The clauses that we introduced previously correspond to disjunctive formulas in the following way:

rule	$A \leftarrow B_1, ..., B_n$	$A \vee \neg B_1 \vee ... \vee \neg B_n$
fact	$A \leftarrow$	A
goal	$\leftarrow B_1, ..., B_n$	$\neg B_1 \vee ... \vee \neg B_n$
empty	$\square$	*false*

For understanding this correspondence the reader must take into account that the empty conjunction, as occurs in the right hand side of the clause representing a fact, is always true. The empty disjunction on the other hand is always false since, intuitively, it is not possible to choose for a true literal.

A program P is a conjunction of program clauses. For convenience we write such a conjunction as a collection. We allow only Horn clauses that have only one positive literal, the literal representing the head of a clause, to occur in a logic program. Practically, this is motivated by the fact that proof procedures for general clauses are computationally very expensive. In addition, however, Horn clause programs have pleasant model-theoretic properties.

2.1.1.2 Declarative semantics

In this section we will investigate the model-theoretic properties of logic programs, that is how a logic program P is related to the world it is intended to describe.

Interpretations For giving an interpretation I to a logic program P we have to define a *domain of discourse* D that contains the individuals of the world about which our program speaks and over which the variables occurring in our program range. Formally, we then have to define an assignment that assigns to each constant name a specific individual. Moreover, we must define for each function-symbol f a corresponding mapping and for each predicate-symbol p a relation on the domain D. Finally, we must then define an assignment of variables to bind variables to elements of D.

Models A given interpretation I is a model for a clause if it makes the clause true. Now, when is a clause true for a given interpretation? A clause

$$A \leftarrow B_1, ..., B_n$$

is true for an interpretation I if A is true for I whenever $B_1, ..., B_n$ are true for I.

To establish the truth of a literal, for example

$$number(s(0))$$

we must relate the constant 0 to its intended interpretation, for which we take *zero*. Likewise we assign the functional expression $s(0)$ the value *one* and check whether *one* is a natural number, which is our interpretation of the predicate *number*.

Quantification When variables occur in a literal the situation is slightly more complicated. Since we are not able to find a model for a clause that contains free variables we assume that each clause is universally quantified, since clauses are meant to express general statements. So, for example, the clause

$$number(s(X)) \leftarrow number(X)$$

must be read as

$$\forall X.(number(s(X)) \leftarrow number(X))$$

which generalizes the clause to hold for all X. In order to establish the truth of the clause we have to check for all elements of our domain, which are the natural numbers in this case, whether the clause holds when substituting this element for X.

An extra complication arises when variables occur in the body of a clause that do not occur in the head of the clause. For example, the clause

$$p(X) \leftarrow q(X, Y)$$

stands for

$$\forall XY.(p(X) \leftarrow q(X, Y))$$

generalizing the clause to hold for all X and Y. However, by another law of logic, this may be rewritten to

$$\forall X.(p(X) \leftarrow \exists Y.q(X, Y))$$

where the variable Y that occurs only in the body of the clause is existentially quantified. This clause is true when for each assignment to X the literal $p(X)$ holds whenever there is some assignment to Y that makes $q(X, Y)$ true.

Hence, a goal clause of the form

$$\leftarrow G$$

must be read as being existentially quantified. To establish the falsity of a goal clause containing variables it suffices to find some assignment of values to variables that makes G true.

Logical consequence Having defined when a clause is true for a given interpretation we may characterize a *model* of a program P as an interpretation that makes each clause in P true. If there exists a model for P we say that P is *satisfiable*.

We call a formula G a logical consequence of P if every model of P is also a model of G. This is equivalent to saying that G is a logical consequence of P, if and only if $P \cup \{\neg G\}$ is unsatisfiable, which is equivalent to saying that there is no interpretation that makes each clause in $P \cup \{\leftarrow G\}$ true.

Hence, if we have a goal $\leftarrow B_1, ..., B_n$ with variables $Y_1, ..., Y_k$ then showing that $P \cup \{\leftarrow B_1, ..., B_n\}$ is unsatisfiable is exactly the same as showing that $\exists Y_1 ... Y_k.(B_1 \wedge ... \wedge B_n)$ is a logical consequence of P.

Herbrand models The basic problem that we are confronted with to establish that a conjunction of literals G is a logical consequence of a program P is to determine whether $P \cup \{\leftarrow G\}$ is unsatisfiable, which amounts to showing that every interpretation of $P \cup \{\leftarrow G\}$ is not a model! Since there are arbitrarily many interpretations for each logical theory this seems to be an infeasible task.

To manage the complexity of this task, we restrict our attention to a much smaller and more convenient class of interpretations, called Herbrand interpretations.[2] As our domain of discourse we take the so-called Herbrand universe of a program P which are all the *ground terms* that can be constructed from the terms occurring in P. Ground terms are variable-free terms. We construct these ground terms by substituting constants and already-created ground terms for variables. There may be infinitely many ground terms. In case the program contains no constant we use an arbitrary constant to construct the Herbrand universe.

As an example, the Herbrand universe of the program

number

$number(0) \leftarrow$
$number(s(X)) \leftarrow number(X)$

is the set

$$\{0, s(0), s(s(0)), ...\}$$

consisting of all the terms representing natural numbers.

For defining the relations that correspond to the predicate-symbols occurring in the program we introduce the so-called Herbrand base which is the collection of all *ground atoms* that can be constructed from the literals occurring in the program. An atom is just a positive literal, that is a literal without negation sign. A ground atom is a variable-free atom. These atoms may be regarded as representing all possible facts.

The Herbrand base corresponding to the program above, defining the natural numbers, is

$$\{number(0), number(s(0)), number(s(s(0))), ...\}$$

containing all possible atoms that express that a term is a number.

A *Herbrand model* for a program P is a Herbrand interpretation that is a model for P. An important property of Herbrand models is that if a program P has a model then P also has a Herbrand model, since in a way Herbrand models are the least committing models. Because of this property, showing that a collection of clauses $P \cup \{\leftarrow G\}$ is unsatisfiable reduces to the task of showing that $P \cup \{\leftarrow G\}$ has no Herbrand model.

Answer substitutions When a goal G contains variables we are not only interested in whether $P \cup \{G \leftarrow\}$ is unsatisfiable, but also in what variables must be assigned to the variables to achieve this.

[2] After the logician Herbrand. See [Robinson, 1965].

A *substitution* θ is a set of the form $\{X_1/t_1, ..., X_k/t_k\}$ that binds each variable X_i to a value t_i, for i ranging from 1 to k. We say that θ is a *ground substitution* if each t_i is a ground term. When we apply a substitution to a conjunction of literals G, which we write as $G\theta$, then each variable X_i occurring in G is replaced by the term t_i.

Now, if we find a substitution θ for which $\{P \cup \{\leftarrow G\theta\}\}$ has no Herbrand model then accordingly we have proven that $G\theta$ is a logical consequence of P. We call such a substitution a *correct answer substitution*. In general there may be more than one such substitution. From a logic programming point of view we are interested in all these bindings since they represent the output of evaluating a goal $\leftarrow G$.

Fixed points A Herbrand interpretation of a program P may be thought of simply as a subset of the Herbrand base for P, since typically ground terms are assigned to themselves.

The Herbrand models of Horn clause programs have a very special property, the so-called *model intersection property* that states: if $\{M_i\}$ is the collection of Herbrand models for P then the intersection $M_P = \cap_i M_i$ is also a Herbrand model of P. Moreover, M_P is the smallest model satisfying P. Herbrand models for programs consisting of general clauses do not have this property since, intuitively, the occurrence of multiple positive literals in a clause may give rise to multiple disjoint models.

The least model M_P represents all the positive information that can be derived from a logic program P. This intuition allows us to characterize the least model in a convenient way by means of the so-called *immediate consequence operator* T_P. Let I stand for Herbrand interpretations, that is subsets of the Herbrand base for a particular program P. Then the immediate consequence operator T_P is defined as

$$T_P(I) = \{A \mid \text{if } A \leftarrow B_1, ..., B_n \text{ is a ground instance of a clause in } P \text{ and } \{B_1, ..., B_n\} \subseteq I\}$$

Applying T_P to a Herbrand interpretation I results in all the facts that can be derived by applying rules for which the premises are contained in the given interpretation I.

We have that an interpretation I is a model of P whenever $T_P(I) \subseteq I$, that is I is a model when I already contains every fact that can be derived using I. We are looking for the least I satisfying this property or, which amounts to the same, for the least I satisfying $T_P(I) = I$, that is the least fixed point of T_P. The least fixed point of an operator T_P that is associated with a logic program P can intuitively be characterized by a bottom-up computation of all the (given and derivable) facts contained in the program P, that is by iterating the application of T_P, starting with the empty interpretation, until no more facts are added. The interested reader is referred to [Apt and van Emden, 1982] for a more detailed treatment. As a last remark, this bottom-up characterization of the declarative semantics of a logic program P provides a link with the procedural interpretation of P that characterizes how facts may be proven in a top-down manner. See also [van Emden and Kowalski, 1976].

2.1.1.3 Procedural semantics

Complementary to characterizing the meaning of a program, a more pragmatically oriented question is how we actually solve a goal, derive a conclusion or perform a computation in a logic programming system.

Refutation procedures In order to prove that a formula G is a logical consequence of P, which we may write symbolically as

$$P \vdash G$$

it suffices to show, as we have seen in the previous section, that the set of clauses that we get by adding the negation of G to P is inconsistent. Symbolically, we write

$$P \cup \{\leftarrow G\} \vdash \Box$$

to depict that we refute the assumption $\leftarrow G$, which is the denial of G, when added to P.

In [Robinson, 1965] *resolution* has been introduced as an efficient refutation procedure. Resolution knows a single inference rule. This rule allows to discard literals from clauses until the empty clause, containing no literals, results. Regarding clauses as sets, the resolution rule may be phrased as

$$\frac{\{A\} \cup C_1 \qquad\qquad \{\neg A \cup C_2\}}{C_1 \cup C_2}$$

stating that the clause $C_1 \cup C_2$ may be derived from the clauses $\{A\} \cup C_1$ and $\{\neg A\} \cup C_2$ by discarding the clashing literals A and $\neg A$ and merging the remainders of the clauses.[3] The resulting clause $C_1 \cup C_2$ is called the *resolvent*. Obviously, this procedure does not necessarily result in shorter clauses. Only if C_2 is empty the resulting clause will actually be shorter. The empty clause is derived whenever the set of clauses contains two clauses of the form $\{A\}$ and $\{\neg A\}$.

In addition to the resolution inference rule, a search strategy is needed to arrive at the empty clause in an efficient way. The resolution rule employed in logic programming systems, which is known as *SLD-resolution*, is a refinement of the general resolution rule that allows efficient search.

SLD resolution In a logic programming system, a goal consisting of a number of literals is evaluated by evaluating each of the goal literals. The evaluation of an atomic goal, that is a single literal, takes place by reducing the goal to its subgoals, that is by replacing it by the body of the clause of which the head matches with the goal literal. When that clause states a fact the resulting subgoal is empty, otherwise the subgoals are the literals contained in the body of that clause. An empty goal is trivially solved. A compound goal consisting of a number of literals is solved when each of its component literals is solved.

The *SLD-resolution rule*, with left-most literal selection built-in, may be phrased as follows.

[3] The justification for this inference rule lies in the fact that the resulting set of clauses, the original set with the derived clause added, is stronger than the original set.

When we have a goal G_j of the form

$\leftarrow B, \ldots$

and there is a clause C_{j+1} of the form $A \leftarrow G$, with no variables in common with G_j, for which we can find a substitution θ_{j+1} such that $A\theta_{j+1} = B\theta_{j+1}$ then we may derive the goal G_{j+1}, which is

$\leftarrow (G, \ldots)\theta_{j+1}$

that is the original goal with the body of the chosen clause replacing the selected literal, modified by the substitution θ_{j+1}.

The resulting goal G_{j+1} is the resolvent of the goal G_j and the clause C_{j+1}, with both the selected goal literal B and the head A of the chosen clause discarded. When the chosen clause represents a rule the literals of the body of that clause are put in front of the literals of the original goals, otherwise the resulting goal is the original goal minus the selected literal. In both cases, the substitution θ_{j+1} is applied. The proviso that the clause $A \leftarrow G$ has fresh variables, not occurring in the goal G_j, is needed to guarantee that the scope of the variables used in the clause is restricted to the clause itself. This requirement can easily be met by renaming the variables of a clause, if necessary.

An *SLD-refutation* of a set of clauses $P \cup \{\leftarrow G\}$ is a finite sequence $G_0, \ldots, G_k$ with $G = G_0$ the original goal literals and G_k the empty goal. If there is no such finite sequence or no finite sequence with G_k empty then the goal $\leftarrow G$ is not refutable. The set of ground goals that are refutable is called the ***success-set*** of a program.

As an example, let P be the program *number* given by

number

$number(0) \leftarrow$
$number(s(X)) \leftarrow number(X)$

and let $\leftarrow G$ be the goal $\leftarrow number(s(s(0)))$. The SLD-refutation of $\leftarrow G$ may then be depicted by the sequence of goals

$\leftarrow number(s(s(0)))$
$\leftarrow number(s(0))$
$\leftarrow number(0)$
$\square$

Each successive goal results from resolving its predecessor with the appropriate clause. It is easily verified that the success-set of the program *number* contains the atoms $number(0)$, $number(s(0))$, $number(s(s(0)))$,...

The ***computed answer substitution*** θ of a goal $\leftarrow G$ is the substitution obtained by restricting the composition of the substitutions $\theta_1, \ldots, \theta_k$ to the variables of G, where $\theta_1, \ldots, \theta_k$ is the sequence of substitutions used in the SLD-refutation of $P \cup \{\leftarrow G\}$.[4] Every computed answer substitution for $P \cup \{\leftarrow G\}$ is a correct answer substitution.

[4] Composing substitutions $\theta_1 = \{X_1/t_1, \ldots, X_n/t_n\}$ and $\theta_2 = \{Y_1/t'_1, \ldots, Yk/t'_k\}$ results in the substitution $\theta_1\theta_2 = \{X_1/t_1\theta_2, \ldots, X_n/t_n\theta_2, Y_1/t'_1, \ldots, Y_k/t'_k\}$ where $t_i\theta_2$, for $i = 1, \ldots, n$, is t_i modified by θ_2. The composition $\theta_1\theta_2$ exists only if θ_2 is *compatible* with θ_1. For further details see section 2.1.2.

The soundness of the SLD-resolution procedure may be established by noting that if there is an SLD-refutation of $P \cup \{\leftarrow G\}$ then $P \cup \{\leftarrow G\}$ is unsatisfiable. Also it holds that the success-set of a program P is contained in the least Herbrand model of P.

Search and backtracking The SLD-resolution rule is indeterminate with respect to the clause that will be chosen to reduce a goal literal. This non-determinism may lead to multiple refutation sequences and accordingly refuting a goal may result in a number of computed answer substitutions.

The search space of an SLD-derivation may be organized as a so-called *SLD-tree*. An SLD-tree for a goal $\leftarrow G$ and a program P is a tree consisting of nodes representing goals. The root node represents the goal $\leftarrow G$. The successor nodes of a non-empty goal node represent the goals that may be derived by resolving the goal with one of the clauses in P. We assume that successor nodes are ordered from left to right corresponding to the textual position in which the clauses occur in the program. The labels of the edges connecting a node with its successor nodes represent the substitution applied in the resolution step.

An example of an SLD-tree for the goal $\leftarrow number(X)$ is given below. The clauses used are those given in the *number* program above.

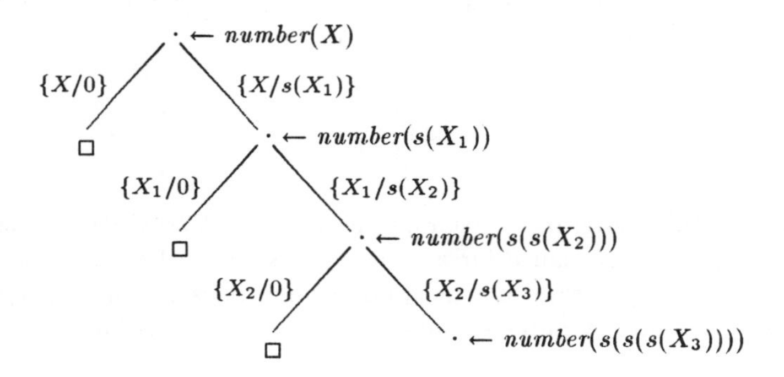

Each path in the tree ending in □ is a possible refutation of the goal $\leftarrow number(X)$. The computed answer substitutions corresponding with these refutations are obtained by composing the substitutions labeling the edges that occur on the path. There is an infinite number of possible solutions for the goal $\leftarrow number(X)$ and correspondly many bindings for X.

In actual logic programming systems, solutions are found by using some strategy to explore the search space of possible solutions as represented by the SLD-tree for a goal. For sequential systems that explore only one solution at a time (depth-first), the order in which solutions are found is determined by a so-called *search-rule* that prescribes the order in which the clauses that may be used are tried. Common practice is to try the clauses in the order they occur in the program. This leads to a left-to-right depth-first search of the SLD-tree. In the example above, all the paths represent a refutation, except the right-most path which is of infinite length. If clauses were selected in the reverse order, in this example the computation leading to the first solution would not terminate since the right-most path extends infinitely.

A path that is finite but does not end with an empty goal represents *failure*. These paths do not contribute to the possible answers for a goal. When failure is encountered in sequentially exploring the search space in a left-to-right depth-first manner, an alternative path may be found by backtracking to a previous choice, and trying the next clause in the nearest node above.

As an example, evaluating the goal $\leftarrow number(X), X = s(s(0))$ may be represented by the SLD-tree below.

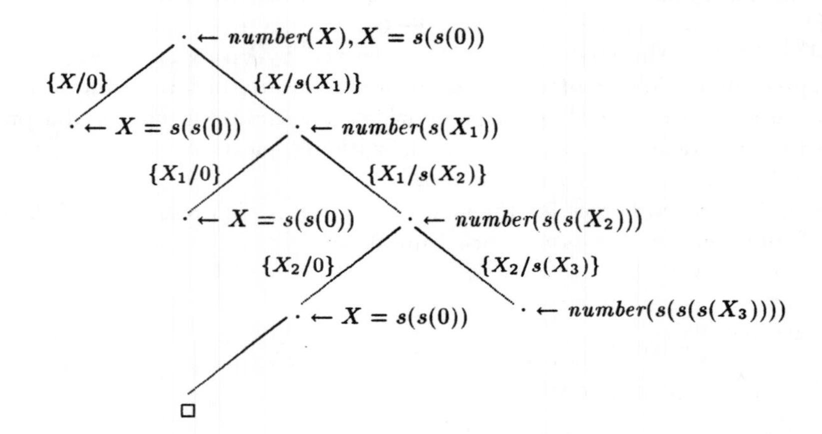

Note that the only acceptable solution is given by the binding $\{X/s(s(0))\}$.[5] Backtracking results in trying the next clause for a goal, by taking in the SLD-tree the right-neighboring edge of the edge resulting in failure. Such backtracking may also be used to generate all solutions, by inducing failure after a solution is found.

2.1.2 The logical variable

Apart from being a means to establish the satisfiability of a goal, the power of logic programming lies in the way values are computed during an inference. The output of a goal with variables is a substitution binding these variables to terms.

Terms are the elements of the universe a logic program deals with. As we have seen in section 2.1.1.1, defining logic programs, terms are either constants, variables or compound terms consisting of a function-symbol and zero or more argument-terms. We may use a logic program to define terms in a formal way.

The program

[5]The goal $X = s(s(0))$ will succeed only if there is a substitution θ for which $X\theta \equiv s(s(0))$. We will comment on the role of the logical variable, and how such a substitution can be found in the following section 2.1.2.

terms

$$\begin{aligned}&constant(0) \leftarrow\\&term(X) \leftarrow constant(X)\\&term(s(X)) \leftarrow term(X)\end{aligned}$$

assumes a constant 0 and a one-argument function-symbol s and defines terms in accordance with the definition given earlier.

The goal

$\leftarrow term(X)$

has as solutions all the possible bindings of X to the terms contained in the set

$\{0, s(0), s(s(0)), ...\}$

which represents the so-called Herbrand universe of the program *terms.*

The possible output that may result from evaluating the goal $\leftarrow term(X)$ is given by the substitutions

$\{X/0\}, \{X/s(0)\}, \{X/s(s(0))\},...$

binding X to the elements of the Herbrand universe. The question that we will answer in this section is how we are able to find these substitutions.

Substitutions Recall that a substitution θ is (represented by) a set of the form $\{X_1/t_1, ..., X_k/t_k\}$ that binds each variable X_i to a term t_i, for $i = 1, ..., k$. Applying a substitution θ to a term is recursively defined by

$c\theta = c$	for a constant c,
$X\theta = t$	for $\theta = \{..., X/t, ...\}$ and X otherwise, and
$f(t_1, ..., t_n)\theta = f(t_1\theta, ..., t_n\theta)$	for a compound term $f(t_1, ..., t_n)$

In other words, applying a substitution to a constant has no effect. Applying a substitution θ to a variable X results in the term t when the binding X/t occurs in θ. Applying a substitution θ to a compound term $f(t_1, ..., t_n)$ results in the term $f(t_1\theta, ..., t_n\theta)$ in which θ is applied recursively to the argument terms $t_1, ..., t_n$.

As an example, applying the substitution $\theta = \{X/s(0)\}$ gives

$0\theta = 0$, $X\theta = s(0)$, $Y\theta = Y$, and $s(X)\theta = s(s(0))$

The application of a substitution is easily generalized to literals, by applying the substitution to each argument of the atom, and to conjunctions of literals, by applying the substitution to each literal.

A substitution θ_2 is *incompatible* with a substitution θ_1 if there is a binding X/t_1 in θ_1 and a binding X/t_2 in θ_2 for which $t_1\theta_2 \neq t_2$. For θ_2 compatible with θ_1, the composition $\theta_1\theta_2$ of the substitutions $\theta_1 = \{X_1/t_1, ..., X_n/t_n\}$ and $\theta_2 = \{Y_1/t'_1, ..., Y_k/t'_k\}$ is given by the set $\{X_1/t_1\theta_2, ..., X_n/t_n\theta_2, Y_1/t'_1, ..., Y_k/t'_k\}$. If θ_2 is not compatible with θ_1, we say that the composition $\theta_1\theta_2$ does not exist.

For an arbitrary term t it holds that $(t\theta_1)\theta_2 = t(\theta_1\theta_2)$. Moreover, it is easy to check that the composition of substitutions is associative, that is that $(\theta_1\theta_2)\theta_3 = \theta_1(\theta_2\theta_3)$.

As an example, consider the composition of $\theta_1 = \{X/s(X_1)\}$ and $\theta_2 = \{X_1/s(X_2)\}$ which results in $\theta_1\theta_2 = \{X/s(s(X_2)), X_1/s(X_2)\}$.

Unification Substitutions are the result of unifying two terms. A substitution θ is a *unifier* of the terms t_1 and t_2 whenever $t_1\theta = t_2\theta$, that is when the terms become equal after applying θ.

The *most general unifier* of two terms is the smallest substitution unifying the two terms. For example, the substitution $\theta = \{X/s(0)\}$ is the most general unifier of the terms $f(X,Y)$ and $f(s(0),Y)$. However, the substitution $\theta' = \{X/s(0), Y/0\}$ is also a unifier, but clearly less general since it may be derived from θ by adding the binding for Y. in other words, a substitution θ is called the most general unifier of two terms, or *mgu* for short, if for each unifier σ of these two terms there is a substitution γ such that $\sigma = \theta\gamma$. A most general unifier can always be refined by another substitution to give an arbitrary unifier. Most general unifiers are not necessarily unique, but may be identified by renaming variables.

We will describe a simple recursive algorithm to decide whether two terms are unifiable and to compute the most general unifier if it exists. To indicate that two terms are not unifiable we use the value *fail*. We now write the composition of substitutions θ_1 and θ_2 explicitly as $\theta_1 \circ \theta_2$ and adopt the convention that $\theta_1 \circ \mathit{fail} = \mathit{fail}$ and $\mathit{fail} \circ \theta_2 = \mathit{fail}$. Also when θ_2 is incompatible with θ_1, because they disagree on the binding for a variable, we define the composition $\theta_1\theta_2 = \mathit{fail}$. We will use the constant ε to denote the empty substitution, for which it holds that $\theta \circ \varepsilon = \varepsilon \circ \theta = \theta$ for arbitrary θ. The algorithm is given by the following recursive equations

$$
\begin{aligned}
&\mathit{unify}(c_1, c_2) = \varepsilon \text{ if } c_1 = c_2,\\
&\mathit{unify}(X, t) = \{X/t\} \text{ if } X \text{ does not occur in } t,\\
&\mathit{unify}(t, X) = \mathit{unify}(X, t) \text{ if } t \text{ is not a variable},\\
&\mathit{unify}(f(t_1, ..., t_n), f(t'_1, ..., t'_n)) = \mathit{unify}(t_1, t'_1) \circ ... \circ \mathit{unify}(t_n, t'_n), \text{ and}\\
&\mathit{unify}(t_1, t_2) = \mathit{fail} \text{ otherwise}
\end{aligned}
$$

Unifying two constants results in the empty substitution whenever the constants are equal. In case one of the terms is a variable X, a substitution binding X to the other term is delivered, provided that X does not occur in that term. Unifying two compound terms is possible only when the two terms have the same function-symbol and the same number of arguments. The result is the composition of the substitutions resulting from the pairwise unification of the argument terms. This leads to failure whenever such unification proves to be impossible or an incompatibility arises. The unification function delivers *fail* when none of these cases apply.

As examples consider

$$
\begin{aligned}
&\mathit{unify}(p(s(X),0), p(Y,Z)) = \{Y/s(X)\} \circ \{Z/0\} = \{Y/s(X), Z/0\}\\
&\mathit{unify}(p(s(X),0), p(Y,X)) = \{Y/s(X)\} \circ \{X/0\} = \{Y/s(0), X/0\}\\
&\mathit{unify}(p(s(X),0), p(Y,s(Z))) = \{Y/s(X)\} \circ \mathit{fail} = \mathit{fail}\\
&\mathit{unify}(p(s(X),0), p(Y,Y)) = \{Y/s(X)\} \circ \{Y/0\} = \mathit{fail}
\end{aligned}
$$

In the last example *fail* results because an incompatibility arises between the substitutions resulting from unifying the argument terms, since they disagree on the binding of the variable Y.

The occur-check In the unification algorithm, a binding results whenever we encounter a variable X and a term t, provided that X does not occur in t. In actual logic programming systems this so-called *occur-check* is often omitted for reasons of efficiency. This may lead to anomalous behavior, as exemplified by the goal

$$\leftarrow X = s(X)$$

which succeeds, resulting in the binding $\{X/s(X)\}$, although it clearly has no solution.

Compound terms In logic programming systems, unification provides a uniform mechanisms for parameter passing, data selection and data construction. Terms can be used to package data in a way resembling records. For instance, the fields on a chessboard can be denoted by the terms

$$position(1,1),\ position(1,2), \ldots,\ position(8,8)$$

naming the index in respectively the row and the column of the board.

In a program the pattern of this structure can be used to select the wanted information, as illustrated in the clause that tests whether two positions occur on the same row.

row

$$same\_row(position(X,Y), position(X,Z)) \leftarrow$$

When evaluating a goal *same_row* containing two positions. the information concerning the rows is selected and the implicit constraint that the rows are equal, since they are both referred to by the variable X, is enforced by the unification procedure.

2.1.3 The language Prolog

Prolog is the most widely used logic programming language that exists today. It implements a logic programming system as treated in the previous sections, but in addition contains a number of features that are convenient when programming actual systems.

Syntax The syntax of Prolog programs resembles the syntax of logic programs as given before, except for some small notational differences such as the symbol separating the head from the body of a clause and the use of a dot to indicate the end of a clause. Below we list the BNF-grammar rules that describe the syntax of Prolog clauses. Terminal symbols are written bold-face.

terms

term ::= *constant* | *variable* | *compound*

compound ::= *functor* **(** *arguments* **)**

arguments ::= *term* | *term* **,** *arguments*

Terms are defined in the usual way. Prolog is, however, more liberal in what it considers as constants. Any quoted expression like 'AzY' or '*!&' is a constant. Prolog also allows the use of a so-called ***anonymous variable***, which is written as an underscore as for example in s(_). The anonymous variable is treated as an ordinary logical variable except that it will never become bound. Another difference is that arithmetical expressions, such as 1 + 2 and X * 5 may occur as terms. These expressions are read respectively as the terms +(1,2) and *(X,5) and are not interpreted unless they occur as arguments of the system-predicate ***is*** that may be used to evaluate these expressions.

clauses

literal ::= *predicate* | *predicate* (*arguments*)

fact ::= *literal* .

rule ::= *head* :- *body* .

head ::= *literal*

body ::= *literal* | *literal* , *body*

goal ::= ?- *body* .

clause ::= *fact* | *rule* | *goal*

Clauses represent either facts, rules or goals. When Prolog-systems are used interactively, which is often the case, the symbol ?-indicating a goal is usually given as a system prompt. A fact is written as a literal ended by a dot. However, a fact may also be written in a rule-format by substituting the literal *true* for the body.

Extra-logical features In the sections that follow, we will discuss the features that make Prolog a convenient programming language. Some of the features are rather harmless since they do not affect the logical semantics of a program. Examples of these are the list manipulation primitives and the *bagof* predicate that allows to collect a bag of items satisfying some predicate.

Other features however, such as the *cut* (section 2.1.3.4) and *negation by failure* (2.1.3.5), do not have a straightforward logical interpretation. These features are used to control the inference, that is the search for solutions and the amount of backtracking.

Features enabling *meta-programming* and *dynamic program modification* have a similar effect of obscuring the declarative semantics. Despite the obvious arguments against the inclusion of these features, they are nevertheless often used and are an essential part of Prolog as a programming language.

2.1.3.1 List manipulation

Lists may be used to store and manipulate sequences of items. Prolog offers a special syntax to deal with lists.

Examples of terms that denote lists are

[] – denoting the empty list,
[a,b,c] – denoting the list with elements a, b and c, and
[H|T] – denoting the list T with element H put in front.

Internally, non-empty lists may be thought to be represented as terms constructed with the function-symbol cons. We use [] to represent the empty list. To put an element a in front of the empty list we write cons(a,[]). The list [a,b,c] is represented by the term cons(a,cons(b,cons(c,[]))). Lists in Prolog are always ended by an empty list indicating an invisible last element.

The special notation [H|T] closely corresponds to the use of the constructor cons. The one-element list [a] may be written as [a|[]]. And similarly, the list [a,b,c] may be written as [a|[b,c]] or [a|[b|[c]]] or [a|[b|[c|[]]]]. The notation [H|T], which stands for a non-empty list with element H in front, is very convenient for performing operations on a list as illustrated by the clauses below.

The predicate *member* tests whether an item is an element of a given list.

member

```
member(X,[ X | _ ]).
member(X,[ _ | L ]) :-  member(X,L).
```

The first clause states that X is a member of the list $[X|\_]$ if X is identical to the first clause of the list, regardless of the contents of the rest of the list. The second clause proceeds by checking whether X is a member of the list excluding the first element.

The predicate *append* concatenates two lists.

append

```
append([],L,L).
append([H|T],L,[H|R]) :-  append(T,L,R).
```

Again, two cases are distinguished. When the first list is empty then the result is the second list. Otherwise, the front element of the first list is made the front element of the list that results from appending the second list to the rest of the first list.

Recursive definitions as exemplified by the clauses for *member* and *append* are typical of clauses dealing with lists or other recursive data-structures. The correctness of these definitions can be easily verified by looking at the declarative meaning of the clauses, taking account of the possible cases that may arise.

The definitions of both *member* and *append* may be read in a functional style. However, the predicate *member* can be used not only to check whether an element occurs in a list, but also to bind a variable successively to all the elements in a list. In a similar way, the predicate *append* may be used, perhaps somewhat surprisingly to generate all the sublists of a given list.

The predicate *sublist* checks whether a list S is a sublist of the list L.

sublist

```
sublist(S,L) :- append(L1,L2,L), append(S,L3,L2).
```

A list is a sublist of a given list when it coincides with a part of the given list, in other words when appending a list in front of the sublist and a list to the rear results in the given list. The lists appended in the front and to the rear of the sublist may be empty, and so may be the sublist itself. In this way all the possible sublists of a list may be generated, by backtracking over the possible combinations.

The predicates *delete* and *insert* may be used to delete or insert an element.

delete

```
delete(X,[X|L],L).
delete(X,[Y|L],[Y|R]) :- delete(X,L,R).
insert(X,L,R) :- delete(X,R,L).
```

The definition of *insert* reflects the fact that insertion is exactly the opposite of deletion.

The predicate *permutation* uses *insert* in a straightforward way.

permute

```
permutation([],[]).
permutation([H|T],R) :-
        permutation(T,L),
        insert(H,L,R).
```

Declaratively, the list R is a permutation of the list $[H \mid T]$ if R equals $[H \mid L]$ where L is a permutation of T. The permutation of an empty list is just the empty list.

Admittedly, these definitions may be hard to grasp at first, even if the structure is on the surface quite simple. The reader not familiar with this kind of definitions is advised to get hold of a Prolog system and to try to run these programs.

2.1.3.2 The *bagof* predicate

Many programs in Prolog rely on backtracking to get hold of the successive bindings that may arise from evaluating a goal. For instance, when evaluating the goal

```
?- member(X,[1,2,3]), member(X,[2,3,4]).
```

the variable X is first bound to 1 and only when the second goal fails the first goal will backtrack to the next solution and bind X to 2.

Most Prolog systems however provide a *setof* or *bagof* predicate that allows to compute a set or a bag of solutions.[6] For instance, to compute all the permutations of a given list L = [1,2,3] we may state the goal

[6] A *bag* differs from a set in that it may contain multiple identical elements. In Prolog *bags* and *sets* are represented by lists.

```
:- L = [1,2,3], bagof(X,permutation(L,X),R).
```

which results in a list R that contains all the permutations of L. Naturally, the *bagof* predicate may only be used when there are finitely many solutions, and for that matter not too many.

2.1.3.3 Built-in arithmetic

Prolog has several predefined numerical operators and relations. They include addition, subtraction, multiplication, division and the modulus giving the remainder of an integer division. Implementations may disagree on what symbols are used, but generally the operator + is used for addition, etc.

In most Prolog systems, arithmetical expressions are not evaluated.[7] To evaluate such expressions the system-predicate *is* is provided. As an example of its use, consider the goal

```
?- X is 2 * 2 + 3.
```

Evaluating this goal results in binding X to 7.

For being able to compare numerical values, Prolog provides a number of relational operators such as the *less-than operator* < . Also an operator to test the inequality of two terms is provided. We will write this operator as in

```
?- X ≠ 7.
```

This goal tests if the value of X is unequal to 7. The inequality operator can be used to test the syntactic (equality) of arbitrary terms.

Recall that the equality operator = results in unifying two terms. So, the goal

```
?- X = 2 + 3.
```

results in unifying X with the expression 2 + 3. Only if arithmetical expressions are automatically evaluated, as is the case in our implementation of Prolog underlying DLP, will X become bound to 5, otherwise X will be bound to the expression itself.

2.1.3.4 The cut operator

The *cut* operator may be used to reduce the amount of backtracking. As a manner of speaking, the cut is a means to make a program more determinate. Consider as an example the following definition of the predicate *member*.

member

```
member(X,[ X | _ ]) :- !.
member(X,[ _ | L ]) :- member(X,L).
```

The effect of the cut in the first clause, written as an exclamation mark, is to cut off the search for an alternative solution after encountering for the first time an element

[7] In our implementation of Prolog that is used to implement DLP, arithmetical expressions are automatically evaluated. Also, our notation of the arithmetical operators and relations differs somewhat from the notation encountered in for instance C-Prolog.

of the list that is equal to the given item. A drawback of the use of a cut in this example is that the clauses for *member* can no longer be used in a relational way to generate all the elements of a list in succession, since the search for further solutions will be stopped after binding the variable to the front element of the list.

Another example in which the cut is used to enforce functional behavior is given in the clauses computing the sign of a numerical value as either 1, 0 or -1.

sign

```
sign(X,1) :-  X >  0,!.
sign(X,0) :-  X = 0,!.
sign(X,-1).
```

In this definition the use of the cut could have been avoided by introducing a condition in the third clause, thus enforcing determinate behavior by explicit tests. The cut may be used for efficiency since once a clause for *sign* is successfully applied no further clauses will be tried.

The dynamic effect of using a cut can be best explained in terms of the SLD-search strategy. Recall that when a goal literal is evaluated, all the clauses whose head matches the literal may be tried to find a solution. However, if a cut occurs in the body of one of these clauses, all the alternative clauses following that particular clause will be forgotten as soon as that cut becomes the left-most goal literal. In other words, all the alternatives immediately to the right of that clause will be pruned from the SLD-tree. Apart from deleting these alternatives, the cut also results in abstaining from the search to alternative solutions for the literals immediately preceding the cut in the body of the clause.

As an example, consider the program

cut

```
p(0).
p(1).

q(X) :-  p(X), !, r(X).
q(X) :-  r(X).

r(1).
r(2).
```

The goal

```
?- q(X).
```

fails since after binding X to 0 by evaluating $p(X)$ in the first clause for q, the cut prevents finding an alternative solution for p(X) when $r(0)$ fails, and also prevents to try the second clause for q. In contrast, the goals

```
?- q(1).
?- q(2).
```

both succeed, as is easily verified.

2.1.3.5 Negation by failure

Prolog does not support ordinary negation. Instead Prolog supports what is called *negation by failure.* Some caution is necessary when using negation in Prolog, since when calling not(p(X)), for some predicate p with X unbound, X will remain unbound.

As an example of the use of negation consider the predicate *canfly.*

```
canfly(X) :- bird(X), not( penguin(X) ).
```

This definition states that an animal can fly if it is a bird but not a penguin.

A straightforward way to implement the use of *not* to check for an exceptional condition is given in the clauses for *canfly* below.

canfly

```
canfly(X) :- penguin(X), !, fail.
canfly(X) :- bird(X).
```

Dynamically, the occurrence of a cut in the first clause enforces that there is no alternative to failure once it is established that the animal in question is a penguin.

Making use of what we will introduce later as a meta-programming facility we can implement the (meta) predicate *not* according to the pattern outlined above as follows.

not

```
not(X) :- call(X),!,fail.
not(X).
```

In effect, these clauses state that the goal *not*(X) fails if the goal X is successfully evaluated and that the goal *not*(X) will succeed otherwise. Notice that the goal *not*(X) will not terminate if the goal X does not terminate.

2.1.3.6 Additional control structures

Despite the declarative semantics of logic programming, Prolog programmers often rely on control structures that are reminiscent of control structures encountered in traditional imperative languages.

Iteration Backtracking may be used to perform an operation iteratively. For instance, if we define the predicate *natural* by the clauses

natural

```
natural(0).
natural(X) :- natural(Y), X is Y + 1.
```

then the goal

```
?- natural(X), write(X), X = 100.
```

results in writing the first 101 natural numbers, including zero, to the screen. The iteration thus implemented is often referred to as a failure-driven loop and is in some cases a viable and efficient alternative to the use of recursion.

Conditional branching Just as we implemented the (meta) predicate *not*, we may implement a (non-logical) conditional operator.

cond

```
A → B :- A, !, B.
```

The clause defining the implication arrow enforces that the condition A is only evaluated once.

Likewise we may implement a disjunctive operator by the clauses

or

```
A ; B :- A.
A ; B :- B.
```

These clauses result in evaluating the first component of the disjunction and, only if the need arises, on backtracking the second component, as an alternative solution to the disjunctive goal.

Combined the conditional operator and the disjunctive operator may be used as in $A \rightarrow B; C$ to express the conditional *if* A *then* B *else* C .

2.1.3.7 Meta-programming

As in its famous predecessor Lisp, in Prolog programs may be treated as data. To this end Prolog offers a number of so-called *meta-predicates* that allow to inspect and manipulate terms and clauses. An example of a meta-predicate is the one-argument predicate *var* that may be used to check whether a term is a variable.

A quite powerful facility is offered by the meta-predicate *clause*. A goal of the form *clause*(A, B) may be used to select all clauses of which the head unifies with A and the body with B. When both A and B are variables the goal *clause*(A, B) results in enumerating all clauses, binding A to the head and B to the body of the clause currently pointed at. For clauses that represent facts, B will be bound to true.

A naive meta-interpreter An interesting application of meta-programming is a simple (meta) interpreter for Prolog written in only a few lines of Prolog.

backward

```
backward(true).
backward((A,B)) :-
    backward(A),
    backward(B).
backward(A) :-
    clause(A,B),
    backward(B).
```

The case analysis performed by the interpreter is straightforward. The goal *true* succeeds immediately. A conjunctive goal is split into parts which are successively evaluated. An atomic goal is solved by looking for a clause of which the head matches the goal, and solving the body of that clause.

The interpreter described above implements a so-called *backward chaining* inference procedure that is strongly analogous to the inference procedure of Prolog. The procedure described here does not, however, take account of cuts. A meta-interpreter of this kind is an excellent starting point for implementing an expert system since it is rather easy to adapt the inference procedure to particular cases or to extend it with explanation facilities, certainty-factors or a consultation component.[8] Cf. [Sterling, 1986].

2.1.3.8 Dynamic program modification

Another powerful feature that Prolog offers is the facility to assert or retract clauses dynamically. Asserting a clause results in adding the clause to the program. Retracting a clause effects the removal of that clause.

A example of the use of asserting clauses dynamically is given by the simple *forward chaining* inference procedure defined below. Cf. [Subrahmanyam, 1985].

forward

```
forward(G) :-  G.
forward(G) :-
    clause(A,B),
    B,
    assert(A),
    forward(G).
```

Forward chaining halts when the condition kept in the argument *G* of *forward* is satisfied. As long as the condition to stop has not been asserted, the forward chaining procedure asserts every fact that can be derived using one of the clauses. Clauses are tried irrespective of the goal that must be proved, which is reflected in the independence of the argument of *forward* representing the condition to halt and the variables used to select a clause.

[8] A similar backward chaining interpreter will be used in the distributed medical expert system described in chapter 4.

Forward chaining may be used to solve connectivity problems such as the one below.

connects

```
link(a,b).
link(b,c).
link(c,d).
link(d,e).

connects(X,Y) :- link(X,Y).
connects(X,Y) :- link(X,Z), connects(Z,Y).
```

The goal

```
?- forward( connects(a,e) ).
```

may now be used to check whether a is connected to e. A side-effect of evaluating this goal is the addition of the facts *connects*(a, b), *connects*(a, c),... Backward chaining, that may be used as well to solve this particular goal, will have no such effect.

2.1.4 Examples

Concluding our discussion of Prolog, two examples will be given that will illustrate how to use Prolog for implementing search in a finite search space.

The first example presents a solution to a problem in chess, the N-queens problem. Our solution is given for $N = 8$, but may be easily generalized to other values of N.

The second example illustrates depth-first search with a loop-check built-in to prevent non-termination.

2.1.4.1 The N-queens problem

A solution to the 8-queens problem is given by placing eight queens on a chessboard in such a way that no two queens attack each other. The N-queens problem is similar, with N queens on an N row and N column chessboard.

We can define a solution for an arbitrary number of queens recursively in the following way.

solution

```
solution([]).
solution([P|L]) :-
        solution(L),
        legal(P),
        noattack(P,L).
```

A list is a solution if no queen in the list attacks another queen in the list. The empty list clearly is a solution. A list $[P \mid L]$ is a solution if the list L is a solution and P represents a queen on a position on the board from where she does not attack any of the queens in L.

To represent the position of a queen on a chessboard we use terms of the form *pos*(X, Y) where X represents the row and Y the column number of the queens location on the board.

The predicate *legal* may be used to enumerate all the legal positions on a board.

legal

```
legal(pos(X,Y)) :-
        member(X,[1,2,3,4,5,6,7,8]),
        member(Y,[1,2,3,4,5,6,7,8]).
```

Finally, in order to check whether or not a queen attacks any of the queens in a list, we define the recursive predicate *noattack* as below.

noattack

```
noattack(_,[]).
noattack(pos(X,Y),[pos(A,B) | L]) :-
        X ≠ A,
        Y ≠ B,
        X-A ≠ B-Y,
        X-A ≠ Y-B,
        noattack(pos(X,Y),L).
```

A queen on a given position *pos*(X, Y) does not attack a queen on position *pos*(A, B) whenever the first four conditions in the body of the second clause are satisfied.[9] A solution to the 8-queens problem may be found by evaluating the goal

```
?- solution([X1,X2,X3,X4,X5,X6,X7,X8]).
```

which results in binding the variables $X_1, ..., X_8$ to the positions representing the queens on the chessboard.

2.1.4.2 The farmer, the wolf, the goat and the cabbage

An explicit representation of the state space is used in the problem of the farmer, the wolf, the goat and the cabbage.

A farmer has to carry a wolf, a goat and a cabbage across a river. The farmer has only a very small boat, so he can transport only one item at a time. However, when left alone, the wolf would eat the goat and the goat would eat the cabbage. The problem is to design an order in which this cannot occur.

In our solution, states will be represented by terms of the form

state(Farmer, Wolf, Goat, Cabbage)

[9] We assume here that the arithmetical expressions occurring on the left- and right-hand side of the inequality symbol are automatically evaluated. For Prolog systems that do not support such automatic evaluation the values of these expressions must be assigned to variables before testing their inequality.

where all arguments can take the values w or e, corresponding to the west and east side of the river, indicating the location of the actors in our play.

First, to be able to decide whether a state is safe, we define the following clauses.

safe

```
unsafe(state(X,Y,Y,C)) :-  opposite(X,Y).
unsafe(state(X,W,Y,Y)) :-  opposite(X,Y).

opposite(w,e).
opposite(e,w).

safe(X) :-  not(unsafe(X)).
```

For example, we can now derive that the *state*(w, e, e, w), where the wolf may eat the goat, is unsafe by using the first clause. Obviously, a state is safe if it is not unsafe.

Next, we define how to make the transition from a safe state to another safe state, that is a successor state of the given state.

move

```
move( state(X,X,G,C), state(Y,Y,G,C)) :-
        opposite(X,Y),
        safe( state(Y,Y,G,C) ).
move( state(X,W,X,C), state(Y,W,Y,C)) :-
        opposite(X,Y),
        safe( state(Y,W,Y,C) ).
move( state(X,W,G,X), state(Y,W,G,Y)) :-
        opposite(X,Y),
        safe( state(Y,W,G,Y) ).
move( state(X,W,G,C), state(Y,W,G,C)) :-
        opposite(X,Y),
        safe( state(Y,W,G,C) ).
```

The reader is invited to check that our description of safe state transitions is complete.

Having dealt with the preliminaries of defining safe states and transitions between safe states we define a predicate *depthfirst*(*Current*, *Path*, *Goal*, *Solution*) that enables us to find a goal state starting from an initial state. The first argument of the predicate *depthfirst* represents the initial or current state. The second argument represents the path, that is the sequence of states, traversed to reach the current state from the initial state. If the current state is the initial state then this path is empty. The path is stored in reversed order to be able to access it conveniently as a list. The third argument represents the goal state that must be reached for finding a solution, and the fourth argument is used to deliver the solution, that is the path traversed to reach the goal state. The following clauses implement such a depth-first search procedure.

depthfirst

```
depthfirst( Goal, Path, Goal, [Goal|Path]).
depthfirst( Current, Path, Goal, Sol ) :-
    move(Current,Next),
    not( member(Next, Path) ),
    depthfirst( Next, [Current|Path], Goal, Sol ).
```

The first clause of *depthfirst* states that a solution is found whenever the current state is identical to the goal state. When the current state is not identical to the goal state a transition is made to a successor state of the given state that does not already occur on the path leading to the current state. Then a recursive call to *depthfirst* is made with the selected state as the current state.

Evaluating the goal

```
?- depthfirst(state(w,w,w,w),[],state(e,e,e,e),Sol).
```

will bind *Sol* to the sequence of states connecting the initial $state(w, w, w, w)$ to the goal $state(e, e, e, e)$.

2.2 Object oriented programming

The contribution of object oriented programming to the practice of program development lies in the facilities it offers to specify in a declarative way the structure of a program as a collection of related objects. An object oriented program reflects the conceptual structure of a problem domain by specifying the proper data types, and their relation by means of inheritance. Object oriented programming can best be regarded as a methodology, the essence of which is captured by the directive implied by the phrase *object oriented modeling.*

Object oriented languages contribute to this methodology by providing the necessary technology. In this section, we will study the various mechanisms incorporated in object oriented programming languages and at the end we will come back to the more general issues that play a role in requirements analysis and the design of an object oriented system.[10]

A succinct formulation of the basic ingredients of object oriented programming languages is given by the equation

$$OOP = encapsulation + inheritance$$

These mechanisms, encapsulation by means of abstract data types and inheritance, allow to construct a declarative model of a given problem domain. When speaking of the *declarative nature* of object oriented programming, we do not intend to say that an object oriented program has a logical interpretation that is as strictly defined as the declarative interpretation of a logic program, but that in a rather loose sense an object oriented program may reflect part of the reality that it intends to model. The objects that we describe in an object oriented specification may thus partly

[10] See [Saunders, 1989] and [Blaschek et al, 1989] for an overview and comparison of object oriented programming languages.

correspond to entities in reality, although inevitably there will be objects for which such correspondence is not evident. These correspondences enhance our conceptual understanding of a program.

History Object oriented programming has its root in *simulation*. The first language supporting objects was Simula [Dahl and Nygaard, 1966]. Simula has been primarily used to simulate complex dynamic systems. Since Simula supported co-routining, objects could coexist in a quasi-concurrent fashion, exchanging messages in order to direct the flow of control.

The conception of computation as the exchange of messages between objects proved to be fruitful, as became apparent with the introduction of Smalltalk. Originally, Smalltalk was intended as a language for programming interactive graphic workstations. This intention has been realized, to the extent that similar languages are used nowadays to implement menu-driven, window-based user interfaces. Cf. [Linton et al, 1989], [Meyrowitz, 1986].

The introduction of Smalltalk meant both the introduction of a new language and the introduction of a radically different style of programming. Along with a new style came a new terminology, the now familiar terminology of objects, classes, methods, messages and inheritance.

Data abstraction Why has the introduction of object oriented programming resulted in such a radical change of our conception of programming? Differently, phrased, what have been the developments that have led to the acceptance of object oriented programming as a new paradigm?

These developments may be traced back to the introduction of *structured programming* in the 1970s. The advent of structured programming goes hand in hand with the dominance of what we may call the *procedural style* of programming. Developing a program by means of stepwise refinement was generally taken to consist of breaking up a problem into a number of abstract steps or procedures, that were then gradually refined by more detailed procedures. The effort went primarily into finding a proper algorithm and the procedures implementing it.

The major disadvantage of the procedural approach was its inadequacy with respect to the representation of data as structured entities. The theory of *abstract data types* offered a correction to these shortcomings and may be regarded as the most important constituent of object oriented programming, since it provides a mathematically well-founded notion of encapsulation as a means to specify the behavior of an entity in an abstract way.

An example of the abstract specification of a data type *stack* is given by the algebraic theory below.

stack

```
abstract data type stack

signature
  function new : stack;
  function push( x : element, s : stack ) → stack;
  function empty( s : stack) → boolean;
  function pop( s : stack ) → stack;
  function top( s : stack ) → element;

preconditions
  pre: pop( s : stack ) = not empty(s)
  pre: top( s : stack ) = not empty(s)

axioms
  empty( new ) = true
  empty( push(x,s) ) = false
  top( push(x,s) ) = x
  pop( push(x,s) ) = s
```

The algebraic specification of a stack has three components: a *signature* component that declares the functions needed to create and manipulate a stack, a component that specifies the *preconditions* that must be met when calling these (partial) functions, and a component that specifies the semantic constraints characterizing the behavior of a stack by means of equational *axioms*. The preconditions for applving the functions *pop* and *top* state that the stack may not be empty, otherwise the result of the function will not be defined.

The axioms fully describe the behavior of a stack. As an example, the composition of a *pop* and *push* operation, with *push* executed first, is evidently an identity operation for any conceivable stack.

Procedural abstraction In the specification of the abstract data type *stack* given above, the behavior of the stack has been characterized by means of equational axioms. We distinguish two ways to construct a stack, namely by using the constructor function *new* and by applying the function *push*. In addition to these constructors the operations *empty*, *top* and *pop* are specified.

A different way of characterizing the behavior of a stack is by a matrix relating the meaning of the various operations to the constructors.

	new	push(x,s')
empty(s)	true	false
top(s)	error	x
pop(s)	error	s'

We have omitted the preconditions for the operations *top* and *pop*, and instead defined the result as *error*.

Traditional ways of implementing abstract data types favor a horizontal partitioning of the matrix. This results in defining the operations on a concrete representation of the type by means of a case-statement distinguishing between the possible constructors of the type.

In contrast, the object oriented approach to implementing the abstract data types may be regarded as a vertical partitioning of the matrix. In this approach, the operations are grouped around the constructors. This method is referred to in [Cook, 1990] as *procedural abstraction*, since the operations defined for the constructors provide a procedural interface to the abstract type comprising these constructors.

The differences between these approaches come to light when extending an abstract type with either a constructor or operation.

Adding a constructor to a traditional abstract data type implementation requires to extend the definition of each operation with an additional case defining the result of the operation for the new constructor. In practice this means a modification of the source code. Using procedural abstraction, as in the object oriented approach, allows to add a new constructor incrementally. One merely has to add the new constructor defining the results of each operation.

When adding a new operation to an abstract data type implementation, it depends on the implementation language whether access to the source code is needed to add the operation (which must define the result for each possible constructor). In the object oriented approach, adding a new operation requires the use of inheritance, to create a variant that inherits the functionality of the original constructor while adding the new operation.

Data hiding An abstract data type specifies the behavior of a category of entities. Internal details of how such behavior is implemented remain hidden from the user of such entities. In this sense, the theory of abstract data types has certainly contributed to our awareness of the importance of *data hiding*.

These developments have been taken up by programming language designers and have resulted in the introduction of *modules* and a distinction between *specification* and *implementation* parts. An example of a language supporting such features is Modula-2 [Wirth, 1983].

The major disadvantage of modules, however, is that they do not constitute a type and may not be regarded as first class entities, however valuable they may be in providing a modularization mechanism. As argued in [Stroustrup, 1988] and [Meyer, 1988], objects may be regarded as implementations of abstract data types, since they encapsulate data and behavior. Moreover, an interface may be specified that hides all internal details of an object and prevents unprotected access to its data. Not all object oriented languages, however, provide such a protection mechanism. Smalltalk [Goldberg and Robson, 1983], C++ [Stroustrup, 1986] and Eiffel [Meyer, 1988] are languages that do provide such support.

Inheritance As a method of program development, the paradigm of *data abstraction* may be characterized as the activity of finding the right data types and specifying the appropriate behavior for these types.

Abstract data types alone, turn out to be rather inflexible and inconvenient for specifying large programs in a structured way. Cf. [Stroustrup, 1988]. Inheritance allows such specifications to be related in the sense that they may be shared or organized in a specialization hierarchy. In the view of most, with the exception of [Booch, 1986], inheritance is an integral part of the object oriented approach.

2.2.1 Encapsulation

The encapsulation mechanism offered by object oriented languages is embodied by the notion of an *object*. In most languages, objects are defined by a *class* declaration that characterizes the properties of the objects belonging to that class. In operational terms, a class may be regarded as a template for creating objects.

Objects may be thought of as structures that comprise both data and procedures that may operate on these data. Using Smalltalk terminology, we may write down the equation

$$object = data + methods$$

The variables that refer to the data contained by an object are often called *instance variables*, since such variables are privately owned by each instance of a class.

Methods, in Smalltalk, have exclusive access to the instance variables of the object for which they are defined. The methods of an object are, no more and no less, priviliged procedures that may operate on the data of an object. In other words, methods provide a functional abstraction mechanism that allows the contents of an object to remain hidden.

A pictorial representation of an object *counter*, containing an instance variable *n*, and supporting the methods *initialize*, *increment* and *value* is given below.

object *counter*	
instance variable	n
methods	initialize ← n := 0.
	increment ← n := n + 1.
	value ← result n.

Messages A method is executed for an object in response to a message. For a message to be a legal method call, the method must be defined in the *method interface* of the object. Methods that are private to an object may not be called.

Operationally, we may regard an object as encapsulating a *state* that is dependent on the values of the instance variables, and *behavior* that results from the functions embodied in the methods defined for the object. We may capture this operational view in the equation

$$object = state + behavior$$

that closely corresponds to our previous characterization of an object as encapsulating data and methods.

Computation in an object oriented system is sending messages. Sending a message to an object may result in a change of the state of the object and may possibly cause the object to send messages to other objects.

We may remark, following [Stroustrup, 1988], that an object oriented language supports data abstraction to the extent that access to the state of an object is effectively forbidden, except for the methods defined for the object.

To provide further protection, some languages allow to define an external *method interface* that states which methods are externally visible.

Responsibilities In addition to the syntactic and operational characterization given of objects, we may characterize an object from the perspective of program development as an entity with certain *responsibilities.* From this perspective an object can be regarded as providing a service in response to a message. We will refer to the object sending a message to ask for a service as a *client* of the object that supplies the service.

The external interface of an object, that comprises the methods visible to the clients of an object, may now be viewed as stating the responsibilities of an object, that is the services it is willing to supply.

As concerns the operations of an object (its responsibilities), a distinction can be made between methods to create and initialize an object (*constructors*), methods to dispose of an object (*destructors*), methods to change the state of an object (*modifiers*), methods to evaluate the current state (*selectors*) and methods to visit parts of the object (*iterators*). In a design, the description of an object will usually not contain a precise characterization of its constructor and destructor methods. However, when objects have activity of their own, the constructor characterizes this activity or may lay down the protocol for interaction with other objects. In these cases, the description of the constructor enhances a conceptual understanding of the functionality of the object.

2.2.2 Classes versus prototypes

Object creation may be *static*, in which case all objects are created at the beginning of a computation, or *dynamic*. Dynamic object creation allows objects to come into existence at the moment that they are needed. The three languages mentioned, Smalltalk, C++ and Eiffel, all support dynamic object creation.

Types An object is an instance of a class. A class acts as a template for creating objects. In a strictly typed language, where strictly typed means that each expression in the language may be assigned a type, the type of an object is determined by the class of which it is an instance.

Dynamically, an object may be regarded, using the characterization given in the annotated reference manual for C++, as a *region of storage, the meaning of which is determined by the type of the expression used to access it.* See [Ellis and Stroustrup, 1990]. Static typing allows to resolve the well-typedness of a program at compile-time and enables to deal in an efficient way with method calls, provided that these are not overridden in an inheritance hierarchy.

Smalltalk is an untyped language, that enforces no type checking. However, Smalltalk may be regarded as a dynamically typed language, since each computational entity created during the execution of a program is an object in the sense of being an instance of a class. Each object carries its own type information, telling to which class it belongs. When executing a method in response to a message, the object searches its method table, which is shared with the other instances of its class, for the appropriate procedure. When a method is not defined in the object's own method table, the method tables of the classes from which the object inherits are searched.

The language C++, in contrast, is statically and strictly typed, although it allows for exceptions to the type scheme. Calling a method, which is called a *member function* in C++, amounts to calling an ordinary function since the existence of that function may be assessed at compile-time. However, for a function declared *virtual*, which allows such a function to be overridden by inheriting classes, the appropriate binding cannot be resolved statically but must be computed at run-time.

Classes and instances Classes are templates for creating objects as instances of a class. Being an instance of a class, an object embodies the functionality of that class as well as the functionality inherited from the classes of which the object's class is a subclass. In other words, in a class-based system, we have two relations that determine the behavior of an object, the *instance* relation, denoting that an object is an instance of a class, and the *subclass* relation, indicating that a class is a subclass of a class. We may capture these relations pictorially by the arrows

$$C \xrightarrow{subclass} P$$

$$O \overset{instance}{\dashrightarrow} C$$

which must be read, respectively as, class C is a subclass of (the parent) class P, and object O is an instance of class C.

As an example, imagine the case that we have an object i that is an instance of a class *Integer*, which is a subclass of the class *Sortable*. Using inheritance allows to create an abstract superclass, such as the class *Sortable*, that contains the common properties of a number of subordinate classes. An example of such a property is the existence of the relation *less-than* by which instances of (subclasses of) *Sortable* may be compared and which can be used to define a generic sorting algorithm. As another subclass of *Sortable*, think of a class *String* that supports a lexicographical ordering among strings.

Having classes as a means to create objects, it is rather natural to introduce a mechanism that allows all instances of a certain class to share class-wide resources. Smalltalk, for example, allows to declare so-called *class variables* and *class methods* that are, in opposition to the common instance variables and methods, shared by all objects of that class. Class-variables are in other words a kind of global variable, with access restricted to the instances of the class.

Class-methods are procedures. These procedures are not allowed to access the instance variables defined for that class since these are private to each instance. Calling a class method is possible without creating an instance of the class. Class-methods are often used to create and initialize instances of a class.

In C++, variable or function members may be declared *static*. Static members are shared by all instances of a class, similar to class variables and class methods in Smalltalk. Like class methods, static member functions are not allowed to access ordinary member variables.

Prototypes The disadvantage of making a distinction between the functionality of classes (supporting class variables and class methods) and objects (that are instances of classes, supporting instance variables and ordinary methods), is that programmers are faced with the complexity of making a design choice with respect to where functionality must be put. The choice between class methods or (object) methods will not always be evident.

An alternative approach to creating objects is sketched in [Ungar and Smith, 1987], where *prototypes* are introduced as a unifying concept combining the functionality of classes and objects. Prototypes may be used as templates for creating objects, by cloning, and as computational entities that execute a method in response to a message. Cloning an object amounts to making a copy of an object, including its state at the moment the copy is made.

An interesting variant of cloning is to allow for *differential copying*, in which the differences with respect to certain attributes of the cloned object can be stated when creating the copy. In effect, the newly created object then inherits the functionality of the object from which it is created, possibly overriding or adding behavior by its differential specification. See also [Rodet and Cointe, 1991].

As an alternative way to share behavior between objects, inheritance may be implemented as *delegation* to a designated parent object. Using delegation instead of subclassing or differential cloning to effect inheritance allows to build inheritance structures dynamically, during the computation.

The advantage of using prototypes instead of classes to organize the conceptual structure of a program lies first of all in the simplicity that arises from the absence of classes. The primary relation supported by such an approach is the *inherits* relation, for which we have the choice to allow static inheritance by means of differential specifications or dynamic inheritance by making use of delegation.

An additional advantage of discarding classes is that *one-of-a-kind* objects are naturally supported, since no extra class for such an object needs to be introduced. Another advantage, mentioned in [Ungar and Smith, 1987] is that the problem of whether to support metaclasses, and to what extent, does not occur.

2.2.3 Metaclasses

In a class-based approach objects are organized in taxonomies along the class abstraction. A class describes the semantics of a set of objects and acts as a mould from which to create instances.

A class in itself is not an object but a syntactical construct used to describe objects. However, a number of class-based languages like Loops, Smalltalk, CommonLoops and Clos, allow a class to be characterized in a more abstract way by means of a metaclass. Metaclasses, in these languages, are used to implement the behavior of a class regarded as an object, behavior that is embodied in class variables and class methods. In addition, the implementation of a class by means of a metaclass allows the programmer to inspect the properties of a class dynamically. For instance a class may answer to a request whether it supports a particular method.[11]

From the perspective of object oriented modeling, metaclasses provide the means to capture general properties of the system on a higher level, by defining the appropriate metaclass for a category of classes.

Three-level architecture In Smalltalk and Loops, the dichotomy between classes and objects gives rise to a three-level architecture based on the distinction between objects, classes and metaclasses. The inheritance and instantiation structure of this architecture is pictured in the diagram below.

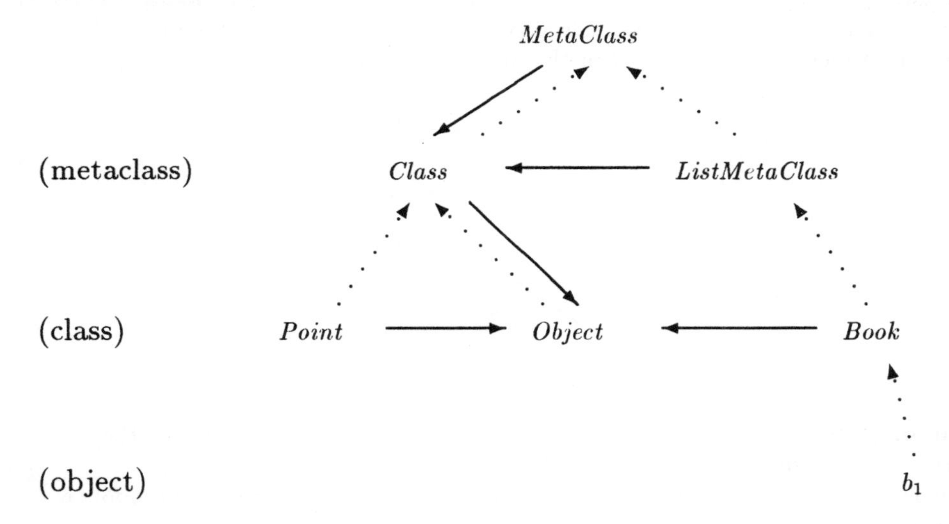

The diagram embodies two hierarchies, the hierarchy determined by the subclass relation (indicated by the solid arrows), and the hierarchy determined by the instance relation (indicated by the dotted arrows). The diagram contains three system-defined entities, namely *Object*, *Class* and *MetaClass*. Object is the root of the inheritance hierarchy, since every class (including metaclasses) must inherit the functionality of *Object*. Conversely, every ordinary class is an instance of *MetaClass*, or a subclass thereof.

Metaclasses, such as *Class* and the user defined *ListMetaClass*, are instances of the system-defined entity *MetaClass*. *MetaClass* has a quite peculiar status in this diagram since (the appropriate arrow is omitted) it must be regarded as an instance of itself. The capability of creating instances ultimately comes from *MetaClass*. This capability is inherited by both the (system-defined) metaclass *Class* and all user defined metaclasses.[12]

---

[11]Static members in C++ do not support such reflective capabilities, although library packages exist – as for example the NIHCL-library [Gorlen et al, 1990] – that do provide such features for C++.

[12]In Smalltalk, the user is not allowed to define own metaclasses. In Smalltalk, to each class

In the diagram, the object level contains a single object b_1 that is an instance of the class *Book*. Another user defined class is the class *Point*, which is an instance of *Class* and a subclass of the class *Object*.

The architecture sketched by this diagram has a fixed number of levels, corresponding to the distinct notions of object, class and metaclass. The disadvantage of such an architecture from the point of view of object oriented modeling is that generalizations with respect to the functionality of the system may be taken only one level up above the class level. In principle, one would like to allow an arbitrary number of levels at which such generalizations are possible.

Reflective architecture What we need is a view that unifies the notions of object, class and metaclass in a way that allows us to define metaclasses to an arbitrary level. In [Cointe, 1987] a solution is given that unifies these concepts by taking a class as an object defined by a *real* class. The key to this solution is to provide a reflective definition of a class, as illustrated in the diagram below.

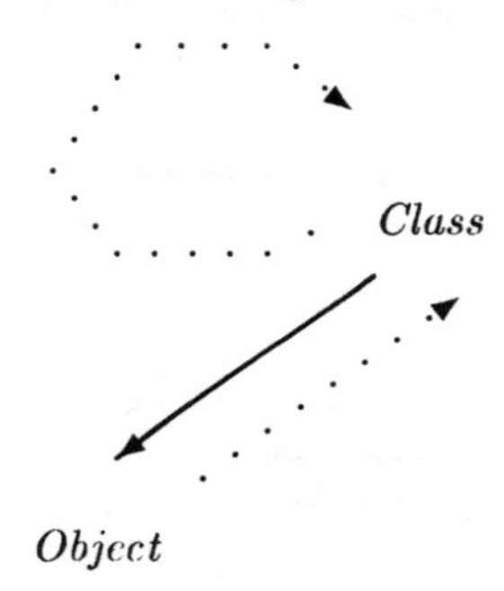

This diagram pictures that *Object* is an instance of *Class*. *Class*, on the other hand, inherits its behavior from *Object* but is an instance of itself.

The reflective model introduced in [Cointe, 1987] is fully described by the following postulates:

- An *object* encapsulates *data* and *procedures*.
- Objects are activated by *message passing*. A message specifies what procedure to apply by providing a *method selector* and the appropriate arguments.
- Every object belongs to a *class* that specifies the objects *attributes* (data) and *behavior* (methods or procedures). Objects are created as instances of a class.
- A class is also an object, instantiated by another class, called its *metaclass*. Consequently, to each class is associated a metaclass that describes its behavior as an object.
- A class can be defined as a subclass of one or many other class(es). The subclassing mechanism allows sharing of instance variables and methods, and is called *inheritance*. The class *Object* represents the most common behavior shared by all objects.

---

corresponds a metaclass that is hidden from the user.

- Instance variables of an object define a local environment. Class variables define a global environment shared by all the instances of a class. These class variables are defined at the metaclass level. It must hold that the class variable of an object is an instance variable of the objects class.

In other words, these postulates require that *Object* lies at the root of the inheritance hierarchy since every class is an object as well, and that *Class* lies at the root of the instantiation hierarchy as it provides the capability of creating new instances. Having *Class* at the root of the instantiation hierarchy entails a circular definition of *Class*, since *Class* must be its own instance.

In order to act as an object, a class must have an attribute *name* that records the class name, an attribute *supers* that tells from which classes attributes and methods are inherited, an attribute *iv* that records the local variables of the instances of the class, and an attribute *methods* that contains the methods defined for objects of the class.

In accordance with this discussion, we may instantiate the (metaclass) *Class* by the reflective pattern below.

Class

name	supers	iv	methods
Class	(*Object*)	(*name supers iv methods*)	(*new* ...)

Each class that displays such a reflective pattern may be regarded as a metaclass, since its instance variables reflect exactly the properties of a class. Minimally, a class must support the method *new* in order to create instances.

In the picture below, this scheme is illustrated by using *Class* as a metaclass for a *Point* class, that has two points as actual (object) instances.

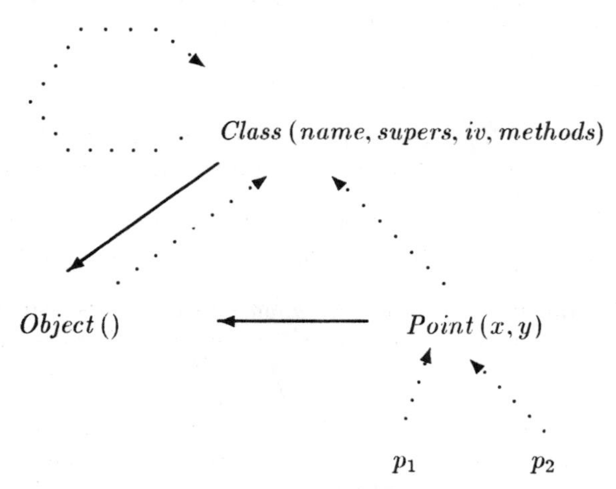

For each class the instance variables are given in brackets. The class *Point* is an ordinary instance of *Class* and need not contain the instance variables of *Class*. In contrast, a metaclass is created by inheriting from *Class*. It contains all the instance variables defined for *Class*. In addition, such a metaclass may contain the properties common to a category of classes.

The architecture described allows to define an arbitrary number of metaclasses on top of an ordinary class. It is doubtful, however, whether the use of such a tower of metaclasses will often occur in practice.

2.2.4 Inheritance

The popularity of the object oriented style of programming is to a large extent due to the possibility of sharing object (and class) specifications by means of inheritance.

Objects in themselves provide the means to encapsulate the implementation of behavior and to regulate the interactions between objects by defining an external interface that establishes the responsibilities of the object. In addition to the clients that request a service of an object by invoking one of the methods listed in the external method interface, inheritance introduces a new category of clients that make use of the functionality of (classes of) objects by sharing functional resources of these objects, that is instance variables and methods.

Inheritance may play a crucial role in object oriented modeling since it allows to factorize the properties common to a collection of classes in a common ancestor class. Because of this feature abstract classes may be specified to define the external interface of a collection of classes. The subclasses of an abstract class may then refine the definition provided by the abstract class by providing an implementation. From a software engineering perspective, inheritance promotes the reuse of software since when a class only captures part of the required functionality it may – using inheritance – easily be refined into a class that does capture all the functionality required.

Specialization hierarchies In its most simple form, the inheritance mechanism provides a way of sharing common attributes, and thus allows to create a specialization hierarchy among a number of concepts.

An example of such a specialization hierarchy is given in the tree below that depicts the relation between a variety of fruit.

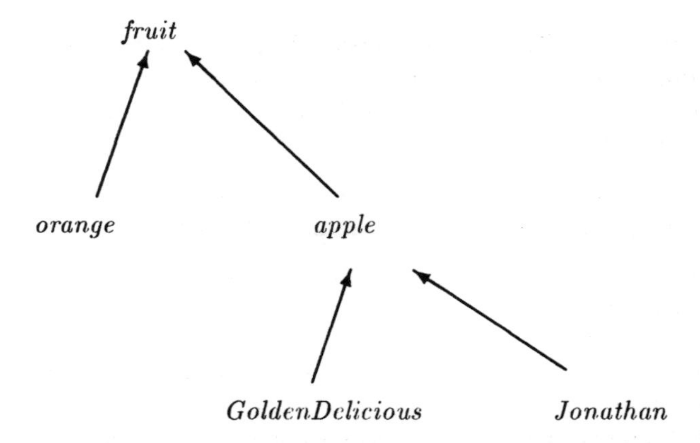

Since oranges are not the only fruit, we may encounter in this hierarchy a subtree that specifies some of the varieties of apples. As a common attribute of all the items in the tree we may think of the property of *being edible*. Specializations will occur with respect to the texture of their skin and the place of growth for example.

The most common interpretation of this kind of taxonomies is given by a predicate logic rendering of the relations expressed by the specialization tree. The hierarchy depicted above, for example, states that all apples are (a kind of) fruit, or in a predicate logic formula: $\forall x.apple(x) \rightarrow fruit(x)$.

Semantically, each node in the tree corresponds to a set of individuals (elements of a domain of discourse). This set is exactly the set described by the information provided by that particular node. In a specialization tree, each descendant of a node provides more specific information and thus restricts the number of individuals to which the description applies. In other words, taken as sets of individuals, the relation $apple \subset fruit$ holds.

Multiple inheritance Instead of one ancestor, as in the specification hierarchy above, a concept may as well have multiple parents from which it inherits. For instance, if we have a concept *edible* then we may make *apple* inherit from *edible* to express that all apples are edible. As another example, if we have an object (type) *machine* with attributes *age* and *fuel* and an object type *vehicle* with attribute *age* and *speed* then we may create the object type *car* with attributes *age*, *speed* and *fuel* by inheriting from both *machine* and *vehicle*, as pictured below.

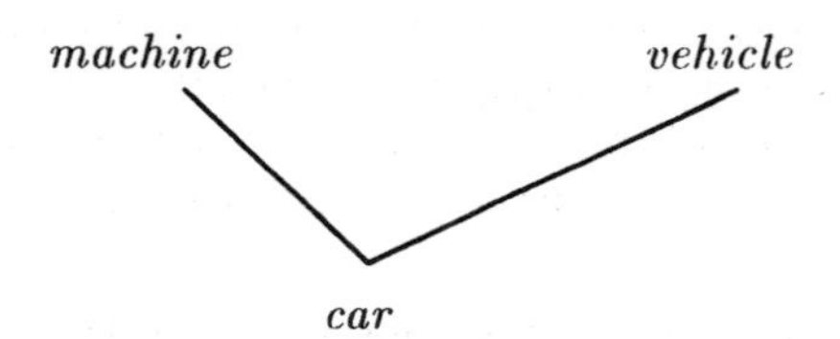

The meaning of the concept *car* is the set of individuals that is both a *machine* and a *vehicle*, in other words the cross-section of the sets corresponding to *machine* and *vehicle*. See [Cardelli, 1984].

Conformance Ideally, the inheritance relation in object oriented programming languages conforms to the notion of refining a description of a concept by providing more information. In that case we have a *substitution* property that states when a concept conforms to another concept:

> (Substitution) *whenever we may use an instance of a concept we may also use an instance of a refinement of that concept.*

This holds also in the case of multiple inheritance. For instance, if I am asked for a vehicle then I may hand over my car.

Technically, conformance may be checked by identifying concepts or classes with types. Regarding concepts as types, we speak of polymorphism since the inherited concepts may be taken to be subtypes of the original concept.

However, conflict may arise when properties are inherited that contradict each other. A famous example, illustrating the possibility of ambiguity in property inheritance systems, is the so-called Nixon-diamond.

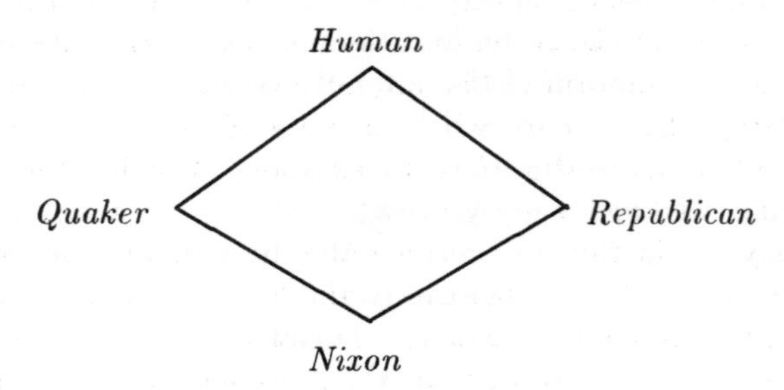

The inheritance diamond above states that *Nixon* is both a *Quaker* and a *Republican.* Knowing that Quakers are notorious pacifists and Republicans equally notorious non-pacifists, the question arises whether Nixon is a pacifist or a non-pacifist. Notorious, no doubt. With regard to the diamond, evidently the logical theory expressed by the inheritance graph is clearly inconsistent. Cf. [Touretzky, 1986].

If all the properties of the inherited concepts are preserved in the inheriting concept we say that the inheritance relation is *monotonic*. Otherwise, we say that the inheritance relation is non-monotonic. As observed in [Wegner and Zdonik, 1988], incremental system evolution often turns out to be non-monotonic, in practice. Non-monotonicity occurs when either exceptions or overridings are used to effect the desired behavior. In these cases we can no longer speak of *behavioral refinement* to characterize the inheritance relation employed.

2.2.5 Polymorphism

To decide on whether an object type conforms to another object type we need to have a notion of type and subtype, since then we may replace *conforms to* by *being a subtype*.

Pragmatically, we may regard a class inheriting from a class as a subtype of the type defined by the class, since the meaning of a class is operationally defined by the method lookup procedure employed by instances thereof. See [Wegner and Zdonik, 1988]. However, viewing classes as types is really overspecifying the notion of conformance and moreover such a view does not allow static type checking, since type errors are only dynamically detected as the result of a failing method lookup.

The procedure for dynamic method lookup (in the case of single inheritance) may be phrased recursively as follows.

lookup

```
procedure lookup(method, class)
    if method = localmethod then do localaction
    elsif inheritedclass = nil then undefined
    else lookup(method, inheritedclass)
```

Multiple inheritance gives rise to more complicated lookup algorithms. See [Ducournau and Habib, 1988]. With regard to polymorphism, whenever a method is defined for a superclass then no type error will occur when calling the method for an instance of a subclass since all methods of the superclass are inherited by the subclass. They may however be redefined, which involves the risk of specifying contradictory behavior that (intuitively) does not conform to the intended behavior of the inherited class.

The dynamic binding that occurs with virtual functions, for instance in C++, resembles the method lookup procedure sketched above. Conformance to a supertype however is statically checked in C++. Also, in C++ there are ways to use inheritance in a non-standard way, for instance to restrict the functionality of a class of objects. Cf. [Halbert and O'Brien, 1987]. A classical example of a nonstandard application of inheritance is to derive a *stack* from a *double ended queue* by disabling the ordinary *deque* operation (that delivers the first, that is oldest element of the queue). However, from the perspective of types, the relation

$$DQueue <_{subtype} Stack$$

holds, since a double ended queue may be regarded as inheriting all the behavior of a stack while adding a *deque* operation.

Objects as records In order to grasp the subtype relation between object classes we need to introduce a more formal notion of object types. To establish the type of an object, we may regard an object as a record containing attributes and functions that are accessible by labels. The notions employed here are due to [Cardelli, 1984]. An example of a record with values is the record

$$\{a = 1. b = true, c = \text{"}hello\text{"}\}$$

We will use type expressions of the form $e : \tau$ to denote that the expression e is of type τ. The conformance rule for arbitrary expressions may now be stated as follows.

$$(Conformance)\ \ if\ \ e : \tau'\ \ and\ \ \tau' \leq \tau\ \ then\ \ e : \tau$$

The rule expresses that an expression may always be regarded as being of an appropriate supertype.

For simple attributes a, say of type integer or subranges thereof, this property is easy to establish. For instance, when a : [2..5] then also a : [1..6], taking $[i..j]$ to be the interval ranging from i to j. The subtype relation for simple types corresponds to the subset relation with respect to the sets of individuals denoted by these types.

However, for functions $f : \sigma \rightarrow \tau$, where σ is the type of the domain and τ the type of the range of f, it is much more difficult to establish whether a function f' of type $\sigma' \rightarrow \tau'$ conforms to (the type of) f. In [Cardelli. 1984] the *function conformance rule* is given by

$$(Functions)\ \ if\ \ \sigma \leq \sigma'\ \ and\ \ \tau' \leq \tau\ \ then\ \ f' : \sigma' \rightarrow \tau' \leq f : \sigma \rightarrow \tau$$

The difficulty of applying this rule is brought about by the *contravariance* between the domain types, namely $\sigma \leq \sigma'$ whereas $f' \leq f$. We hope to give a more intuitive understanding of this rule in the next section by exploring the notion of *behavioral refinement* for functions.

In order to define a subtype relation for objects we state the following conformance rule for records.

$$(Records)\ \ if\ \ \tau'_1 \leq \tau_1\ \ and\ \ ...\ \ and\ \ \tau'_n \leq \tau_n\ \ then$$
$$\{a_1 : \tau'_1, ..., a_{n+m} : \tau'_{n+m}\} \leq \{a_1 : \tau_1, ..., a_n : \tau_n\}$$

In other words, a record type is a subtype of another record type if for each of the field $a_i : \tau_i$ (for $i = 1, ..., n$) there is a corresponding field $a_i : \tau'_i$ for which $\tau'_i \leq \tau_i$. The subtype may, however, contain additional fields.

As an example, defining the record types

$$vehicle = \{age : integer, speed : integer\}$$
$$machine = \{age : integer, fuel : string\}$$

we may establish that the record type *car* defined by

$$car = \{age : integer, speed : integer, fuel : string\}$$

is a subtype of both *vehicle* and *machine*.

We now have a (syntactic) notion of types that enables us to decide whether an object (type) conforms to – is a subtype of – another object (type).[13] In the next section we will provide a more intuitive notion of (behavioral) refinement based on the notion of *subtype conformance* introduced here.

2.2.6 Behavioral refinement

Designing an object oriented system requires to identify the objects needed to model the problem domain and to assess their *responsibilities* and (possible) cooperation with other objects. See [Wirfs-Brock et al, 1990] and also section 2.2.7.

From this perspective objects may be regarded as entities that provide a *service* in response to a message. The services an object is willing to provide are listed in the external method interface of (the class of) an object. The set of services provided by an object is called a *contract* in [Meyer, 1988]. A contract specifies the obligations of both the client and the server, that is when the client complies to the restrictions imposed by the server the server has the obligation to deliver the service.

Inheritance has been characterized as a means to specialize concepts or classes of objects. Viewing an object as an entity that provides a service, the question arises of what it means to specialize or refine a service. And *a fortiori*, what it means to refine a contract. The intuitive answer to this question, for a service, is that refinement means to provide a better service, a service that imposes less restrictions on the client and (yet) delivers better results. And for a contract, taken as a set of services, a better contract means a contract that comprises more services and with regard to the services already available, the individual services must be at least as good or better.

Perhaps somewhat surprisingly, these seemingly vague notions may be given a precise formal underpinning. In the following we will sketch the formal interpretation of the notions of refining a service and a contract (that is a set of services). We will start with a syntactic characterization of refinement, by showing how the subtype relation introduced previously may be regarded as characterizing the refinement of a service. Recall that to define the subtype relation between objects we took objects as records consisting of attributes and functions, and we characterized the subtype relation componentwise by defining a subtype relation for attributes and functions.

[13] In this treatment, we have not paid any attention to the recursive structure of object types. For a treatment of these aspects see [Cardelli and Wegner, 1985] and [Cook et al, 1990].

Attributes Each of the components of an object may be regarded as providing a service. An attribute may be regarded as providing the service of giving information about the state of an object. The type of the attribute tells what kind of information the attribute may provide. Taken as a service, an attribute (type) is improved upon by another attribute (type) if the latter gives more precise information concerning the state of the object. Hence the service refinement relation between attribute (types) is exactly the subtype relation between simple types, that we have characterized as the subset relation. As an example, the attribute $age : [0..120]$ gives less information than the attribute $age : [65..120]$. Applied to people, the latter simply tells more.

Functions The service provided by a function may be characterized by the input/output behavior of the function. Syntactically, the domain type (the types of the parameters of the function) specifies the restrictions imposed on the client – the user of the function; and the result type of the function specifies the restrictions to which the function delivering the service must conform.

Viewing a function as a service, a function f' is a better function then a function f if the result delivered by f' is better than the result delivered by f and if the restrictions imposed on the client by f' are less severe than the restrictions imposed by f. It is easy to see, this interpretation agrees with the subtyping rule for functions that states that $f' : \sigma' \rightarrow \tau' \leq f : \sigma \rightarrow \tau$ if $\sigma \leq \sigma'$ and $\tau' \leq \tau$.

As an example consider the functions

$$f : [9..11] \rightarrow [1..6]$$
$$f' : [8..12] \rightarrow [2..5]$$

We have that $f' \leq f$ since the domain of f' allows more freedom than the domain of f (because $[9..11] \leq [8..12]$) and the result of f' is more carefully delineated than the result of f (because $[2..5] \leq [1..6]$). It is left to the reader to think of a daily life interpretation for these functions.

Objects In a similar fashion, we may interpret the subtype relation between objects (taken as records) as a refinement relation between sets of services. Namely, a set of services may be improved by adding new services or by refining one or more of the already available services.

Having a purely syntactic notion of refinement however is not sufficient to characterize the behavior of objects in an adequate way, as the following example will show. Suppose that we have defined a class *Person* with an attribute *age* and a function *set_age*, and that we derive a class *Retiree* by restricting the range of the attribute *age*.

$$Person = \{age : [0..120], set\_age : [0..120] \rightarrow Person\}$$
$$Retiree = Person + \{age : [65..120]\}$$

According to our rules, the class *Retiree* refines the class *Person*. However, when we apply *set_age* with argument 40 to a *Retiree* we no longer have a *Retiree* since we are violating the restrictions imposed by the attribute *age* of a *Retiree*.

Now we could redefine *Retiree* as

$$Retiree = \{age : [65..120]. set\_age : [65..120] \rightarrow Retiree\}$$

but then we no longer have that $Retiree \leq Person$ since

$$set\_age_{Retiree} \not\leq_{subtype} set\_age_{Person}$$

because $[0..120] \not\leq [65..120]$. A solution to this problem is to introduce a function such as *inc_age* that allows to increment the age of a given person, be it a *Person* or a *Retiree*.

Contracts The example shows that the design of a hierarchy of classes is not altogether a trivial matter. Moreover, it shows that syntactic criteria are insufficient to decide on whether a hierarchy of classes provides the right abstraction. Type checking alone does not preclude such errors. The detection of a violation such as that exemplified by the function *set_age* will occur only at run-time.

In order to characterize the *contract* offered by an object in a more formal way [Meyer, 1988] proposes to use assertions to specify the behavioral characteristics of a method. The use of an assertion language to specify the pre- and post-conditions of a method provides a powerful means to lay down the restrictions to which the client of a method must conform and to characterize the obligations for the provider of the service (when these restrictions are met). In the actual development of systems, the use of pre- and post-conditions is of help in locating the source of errors. When a violated pre-condition is encountered the error must be looked for in the code of the client. Contrarily, the violation of a post-condition hints at a bug in the supplier.

Now, to establish what it means to refine a contract, recall that refining a service means to give better service while alleviating the restrictions imposed on the client. In accordance with the pattern established for the refinement of a function, to improve a method – of which the behavior is (partially) described by assertions – means to accept weaker pre-conditions and to guarantee stronger post-conditions. Refining a contract thus consists of adding new services or improving upon existing ones. See also [Helm et al, 1990] for contracts specifying behavioral compositions of objects.

2.2.7 Object oriented analysis and design

In the previous section we have given an inventory of the mechanisms provided by object oriented programming languages and we have indicated the possible use of these mechanisms in the enterprise of object oriented modeling. The question we wish to raise now is what influence object oriented technology may exert on the software life cycle and what issues play a role in object oriented analysis and design.

Object oriented analysis The main issue in the analysis phase is to extract the needs of the person or organization for which the software will be developed. Analysis is not so much concerned with the development of the system as with an adequate description of the problem domain, to enable the problem to be solved.

A basic requirement to any analysis method is that it provides the means to handle the complexity of the underlying problem domain. In [Coad and Yourdon, 1990] some currently used analysis methods, such as *functional decomposition*, the *data flow approach* and *semantic modeling* are discussed and compared with object oriented analysis. Functional decomposition amounts to breaking up the problem into functional steps that have to be carried out to complete the task. The data flow approach primarily models the flow of information and the events that are of influence on this flow. Information (or semantic) modeling comes closest to an object oriented approach, since it models the objects occurring in the domain, their attributes and their relationships.

Object oriented analysis may be regarded as extending the information modeling approach by providing the means to model not only the attributes but also the behavior of the entities occurring in the domain and by the use of inheritance to elucidate the conceptual relationships between these entities. Both the information modeling approach and the object oriented approach aim at modeling the problem domain, by identifying the objects that exist in that reality.

As a possible method to identify the proper objects, [Booch, 1986] and [Wirfs-Brock et al, 1990] suggest a linguistic analysis of a (written down) natural language account of the requirements. As a first attempt, objects are suggested by thinking of objects that correspond to the *nouns* occurring in the document and of operations or methods to correspond with the *verbs* used. Clearly, such a method provides only a first step towards a model or a design.

A major advantage of a modeling approach to analysis is that it facilitates the communication with domain experts, since these may be supposed to be well-acquainted with the objects that constitute the problem domain.[14] Another advantage of the modeling approach is that it allows for rapid prototyping. In particular in cases where there is a continual change of user requirements, prototyping may be helpful in establishing these requirements.

Object oriented design After completing the analysis phase, the next step is to design the system. Applying an object oriented approach. the transition between the analysis phase and the design phase may be rather smooth. The objects comprising the design may (to a certain extent) be thought of as refining the object identified during analysis. Similarly, when using an object oriented language, the objects actually implemented may be considered as a further refinement specifying the implementation details.

In addition, however, to the object identified in the analysis phase, objects will play a role in the design for which no clearly identifiable counterpart exists in reality. As an example of such objects, think of the objects that are needed to develop a (graphical) user interface. Also, objects may be present that embody hypothetical entities of the domain. For instance, in a medical expert system objects may be used to define the reasoning capabilities of the experts in a domain-independent manner. These objects do not exist in reality, but are artefacts needed to explain the functional behavior of the entities involved.

An example of a very elementary design method is the method introduced in [Beck and Cunningham, 1989]. The authors propose the use of so-called CRC-cards. An example of such a card (approximately the size of a small postcard) is pictured below.

[14]In contrast, domain experts are usually *not* well-acquainted with the methods used in functional decomposition or the data flow approach, nor are they generally willing to acquire that expertise.

Classname Responsibilities	*Collaborators*

The abbreviation CRC stands for *Class*, *Responsibility* and *Collaborators*. One such card may be used to describe the responsibilities of a particular class (of objects) and to indicate what kind of object classes are needed to provide the services listed under the responsibilities of the (object) class.

The design of a system consists of a collection of such cards, one for each class. The authors report that the use of these cards facilitates the design, in particular when working in groups; and, perhaps more importantly, that such a card design may be conveniently used to explain the design of a system to others. Using these cards, the dynamic operation of a system may be mimicked by selecting the appropriate card whenever a particular service is needed. Surprisingly simple, yet apparently quite effective. A similar method is proposed in [Coad and Yourdon, 1990].

As an example of the use of CRC-cards we will discuss the design of the classes underlying the user interface of Smalltalk programs. The approach taken by the designers of the Smalltalk system has become known as the MVC-paradigm. The basic postulate in this approach is that the classes describing the functionality that is needed to solve a problem must be separated from the classes that implement the interaction with the user.

The class describing the problem related functionality is known as the *model*. Smalltalk provides a class *Model* that incorporates the methods needed to specify the other classes in an independent way. A CRC-card describing the class *Model* is pictured below.

Model	
Maintain problem-related info.	...
Broadcast change information.	

A model class is defined as a subclass of *Model*. To enable the (graphic) display of a model, a *view* class must be associated with the model. To factor out the display, the model maintains a list of dependents of which the view object is a member. When the state of the model is changed, then the model notifies the objects in its list of dependents to allow these objects to update the information they have of the model.

The functionality of a view class is rendered by the CRC-card depicted below.

View	
Render the model.	Controller
	Model
Transform coordinates.	

Apart from the possibility of displaying its state, a model may need input from the user. In the MVC-paradigm, obtaining user input is delegated to a so-called *controller* object. A controller object in its turn cooperates with both the model and the view. An additional function of a controller object is to distribute the control in response to the input from the user. The functionality of a controller is summarized in the CRC-card depicted below.

Controller	
Interpret user input.	View
	Model
Distribute control.	

A model may allow for a variety of views and a variety of ways to obtain user input. Hence, to each model may correspond a multiple of view–controller pairs.

A design by CRC-cards may be regarded as a first attempt at modeling a real system. It presents, when properly documented, an overview of the design of the system that may be used to explain the decisions taken. However, it lacks the details needed to provide an adequate model that gives insight in the behavioral aspects of the system.

Object oriented modeling In an object oriented system, computation amounts to sending messages among objects. [Booch, 1986] identifies the roles that objects may play in such a system. An object may be an *actor* that operates by sending requests to other objects but provides no services. An object may be a *server* that may be requested to perform some task. The most usual case, however, is that an object both suffers and requires actions. These objects, called *agents* in [Booch, 1986], need as well as provide services. With regard to the distinctions made, we may want to phrase the design guideline '*minimize and localize dependencies among objects*' as a recommendation to maximize the number of actors and servers in a system, under the proviso that no more objects are introduced than necessary.

An important advantage of an object oriented approach is that objects allow for a natural introduction of concurrency. A client of an object does not have to be aware of whether the object has activity of its own or is passive and only activated to respond to a message. In contrast, when applying a functional decomposition method to design a system the introduction of concurrency requires to reorganize the modular structure of the program, since modules there represent the major computation steps.

The central guideline in developing an object oriented program comes down to the advice to construct an (object oriented) model of the problem domain. Object oriented modeling is hence the main activity in (an object oriented approach to) the requirement analysis and the design of a system.

2.3 Parallelism and distribution

One of the reasons for employing parallelism in a program is the need for efficiency. Preferably, the parallelism remains implicit, which means that the compiler takes care of how the concurrent execution of the program will take place. However, realizing implicit parallelism is in practice quite difficult and in most cases the programmer will have to indicate explicitly how to execute the program concurrently.

Another, equally valid motivation for employing parallelism is that it better fits the conceptual structure of the problem to be solved. As an example, to synchronize the behavior of objects it may be worthwhile to allow objects to have activity of their own. Cf. [Pelaez, 1989] and [Browne, 1986].

As an additional aspect, the processes that are involved in a concurrent computation may be geographically distributed, either because they need resources residing on distant processors or to attain an increase in execution speed. See [Chambers et al, 1984].

Programming languages that allow the computation to be spread over a number of distinct processors connected by a network are called *distributed programming languages.*

Computation models When classifying distributed programming languages we can distinguish between three distinct underlying computation models. The most basic of these is that of *communicating sequential processes*, first presented in the influential paper of [Hoare, 1978]. *Object-based concurrent languages* may be regarded as extending this basic model, by generalizing communication and providing additional features for synchronization and protection. Finally, the model underlying *concurrent logic programming languages* is perhaps the most flexible of these, since it allows to mimic the two previous ones. The languages that we will refer to in this section are listed in the table below.

Language	Reference
Ada	[DoD, 1982]
Concurrent C	[Tsujino et al, 1984]
Concurrent Prolog	[Shapiro, 1986]
CSP	[Hoare, 1978]
Emerald	[Black et al, 1987]
Linda	[Gelernter et al, 1986]
Occam	[Inmos, 1984]
Parlog	[Clark and Gregory, 1986]
POOL	[America, 1987]

Distributed programming languages may differ in what is employed as the *unit of parallelism*, the way they deal with *communication* and how *partial failures* are handled. In [Bal et al, 1989] an overview is given of a number of distributed programming languages, discussing the choices made with regard to these dimensions.

Parallelism There seems to be abundant choice in what to take as the unit of parallelism, to name a few: processes (CSP), tasks (Ada), active objects (POOL), multi-threaded objects (Emerald), clauses (Concurrent Prolog and Parlog), or even statements (Occam).

With respect to the *granularity* of computation, we encounter Concurrent Prolog and Parlog on the side of the spectrum of languages supporting small-grain parallelism and Ada or POOL on the other side, supporting large-grain parallelism. Large-grain parallelism means that, proportionally, the amount of computation significantly exceeds the time spent communicating with other processes.

Another important issue is whether a language supports the allocation of processes to processors. Allocation is supported for instance by POOL and Occam.

Communication Another decision that must be made concerns the way *communication* is dealt with. As alternatives we encounter data sharing and message passing. We mention Linda as an interesting example of data sharing.[15] Also Concurrent Prolog and Parlog, utilizing shared logical variables as the medium of communication, deserve to be classified among the distributed languages. Choosing for message passing we may employ point to point connections (CSP), channels (Occam, Delta Prolog) or broadcasting. Communication may to a certain extent be non-deterministic. For example, both the select statement of Ada and the guarded Horn clauses of Concurrent Prolog and Parlog result in a choice for a particular communication, ignoring alternatives.

Failures As an additional feature, some of the languages mentioned in [Bal et al, 1989] handle *partial failure* by offering exceptions, atomic sections or recovery mechanisms. Failure may be due to, for example, hardware errors or the violation of integrity constraints. We wish to remark that such failures are rather different from the failure encountered in a language such as Prolog. Failure in Prolog is one of the possible outcomes of a computation; it may even be used to generate all the solutions to a particular goal.

2.3.1 Communicating sequential processes

The basic model of a distributed programming language is that of a group of sequential processes that run in parallel and communicate by message passing. By a sequential process we mean a process with a single thread of control. Cf. [Wegner, 1987].

[15] The apparent contradiction between distribution and data sharing is resolved by making a distinction between *physical* data sharing and *logical* data sharing. Obviously, we mean the latter here. Logical data sharing provides the programmer with the illusion of common data by hiding the physical distribution of the data.

Processes The prime example of a language supporting communicating sequential processes is CSP. [Hoare, 1978]. In CSP we may create a fixed number of parallel processes by using a parallel operator. Each process consists of a name and a body, that is a sequence of statements. Communication between processes is achieved by using *send* and *receive* statements. As an example, consider the program

$$[p_1 :: p_2!3 \parallel p_2 :: p_1?n]$$

where process p_1 is about to execute the statement $p_2!3$, sending the value **3** to process p_2 and p_2 is about to execute $p_1?n$, to receive a value from p_1 that is assigned to the (integer) variable n. The proposal in [Hoare, 1978] also provides for pattern matching in communication. Also, a guarded command is offered, that allows to select a particular alternative dependent on the possibility of a communication. Due to its synchronous nature, communication in CSP is said to subsume synchronization mechanisms such as semaphores, events, conditional critical regions and monitors. Cf. [Andrews and Schneider, 1983].

Channels Occam is a language that embodies a number of the features of CSP. [Inmos, 1984]. A noticeable difference with CSP is that communication statements do not address processes, but that instead communication takes place over channels. Occam is the machine language of the transputer. Transputers may be connected into a network. The language provides a mechanism for mapping symbolic channels to the actual hardware channels implementing the network. In contrast to CSP, Occam also provides facilities for mapping processes on processing units.

Perhaps the major advantage of such a language is that it is efficiently implementable, giving the programmer full control over the hardware resources. Cf. [Bal et al. 1989]. From the point of view of program design, however, the necessity of such control may be considered a disadvantage. From this perspective, languages with inherent parallelism seem more suitable. As alternatives to languages supporting the basic model we have: object oriented languages, that support concurrently executing active objects; functional languages, that allow parallel evaluation due to the absence of side-effects; and logic programming languages, that enable to work in parallel on parts of the *and/or* proof tree.

2.3.2 Object-based concurrency

Conceptually, objects are independent entities and the paradigm of method call by message passing allows in a natural way for concurrency.

However, even when considering method calls as (synchronous) message passing, object based languages may fit well in a sequential model of computation, assuming that an object is passive except when answering a method call.

Extending the sequential object model to include parallelism may be achieved simply by allowing an object to be active on its own account, that is when not answering a message. As alternative ways to obtain parallelism, we mention the possibility to employ asynchronous communication as encountered in the Actor languages [Hewitt, 1977], [Agha, 1986]; or to add processes as an orthogonal concept to the language. A drawback of the last solution however is the need to provide extra facilities for synchronization and mutual exclusion. See also [Gehani and Roome, 1988]. Active objects seem in this respect to be a much more natural solution, since such protection is already offered by the method interface, assuming that only one method is answered at a time. Cf. [America, 1989b].

Active objects The notion of active objects, that may be created dynamically, has been adopted by the language POOL. For a more extensive description of POOL see section 9.5.1. Each object may have own activity, called the body of the object, that is started as soon as the object is created. The own activity of the object is interrupted to answer a method call when a so-called *answer statement* is encountered. The answer statement introduces a certain degree of non-determinism since, although a number of method calls may be considered acceptable, only one of these will be chosen.

The communication model of method calls in POOL has been derived from the *rendez-vous* as encountered in Ada. See below. The rendez-vous, as an interaction between processes, has a two-way nature. It generalizes in this respect the primitives provided by for example CSP, that allow only one-directional point-to-point communication. In the terminology of POOL, the rendez-vous model is based on three concepts: *a method declaration*, which is like the declaration of a procedure having the right to access the private data of an object; *a method call*, which is like a procedure call but with an object as an additional parameter; and an *answer statement*, to interrupt the own activity of an object and to state the willingness to accept a particular method call.[16] Answer statements allow to suspend the acceptance of a method call, dependent on the state of the object.[17]

The rendez-vous in Ada We will explain the rendez-vous concept in somewhat more detail by looking at some simple Ada program fragments, taken from [Perrott, 1987].

In Ada a process is called a *task*. As an example of the specification of a task, consider the declaration of a (single-element) buffer.

task

```
task buffer is
  deposit( c : in character );
  remove( c : out character );
end buffer
```

The declaration specifies that a buffer allows two operations, namely an operation to deposit a character and an operation to remove a character.

An implementation of the *buffer* is given by the following definition

[16] In the context of Ada one speaks of respectively an *entry declaration*, an *entry call* and an *accept statement*.

[17] Even stronger acceptance conditions may be imposed in Concurrent C that allows to inspect the actual parameters of a call to determine acceptance.

body

```
task body buffer is
   ch : character;
begin
  loop
    accept deposit( c : in character)  do   ch :=  c
   end
      accept remove( c : out character)  do   c :=
   ch   end
   end loop
end buffer
```

The *body* of a buffer specifies the own activity of a buffer, which is given by the succession of two accept statements, to accept subsequently a *deposit* call and a *remove* call, repeated indefinitely.

To illustrate the use of the buffer, we assume the existence of a *producer* task in which the statement

```
buffer.deposit(c);
```

for a character *c*, occurs and a *consumer* task in which a statement

```
buffer.remove(c);
```

occurs.

The first rendez-vous then takes place between the *producer* and the *buffer* when the buffer accepts the call for *deposit*. After that, the *buffer* has no other choice then to accept a *remove* call, which must come from the *consumer* task. It is important to note that the rendez-vous in Ada is of a *synchronous* nature. Only when the remote procedure call is completed may both tasks resume their activity.

From the implementation of the body of the *buffer* task, we can infer that the buffer actually is a one-element buffer. However, the implementation may be changed (without affecting the task specification) by using for example an array of characters. In that case we may wish to use a more sophisticated protocol for accepting a call, a protocol that allows to take into account the number of elements the buffer contains. Ada offers a so-called *select* statement and a construct enabling the conditional acceptance of a call by which such a protocol can be implemented. The non-determinism allowed by these constructs is local, since it is solely dependent on the internal state of the task.[18]

Multiple threads As another object-based distributed language, we wish to mention Emerald. Just as POOL, Emerald offers the possibility to create active objects dynamically. An important difference between POOL and Emerald however is that Emerald allows multiple threads of control: one object can be active answering a number of method calls. Moreover, the processes created for answering a method call

[18]In constrast, CSP supports global non-determinism by enabling a programmer to impose conditions with respect to the environment of the process, for instance to check whether a communication event may occur.

run in parallel with the process executing the own activity of the object. A monitor construct is provided to enable synchronization and protection when accessing local data shared by processes active for the object.

Allocation Object-based concurrency is most suitable for large-grain parallelism. Large-grain parallelism results in processes of considerable size. To the extent that these processes may run independently, speed-up can be obtained by allocating these processes to distinct processors.

The language POOL enables the programmer to locate a newly created object on a particular processor by so-called pragmas, listing the set of processors from which the system may choose.

In addition to a facility for mapping objects and processes to processors, Emerald supports the migration of objects and processes by allowing them to move, or to be moved, from one processor to another.

2.3.3 Concurrent logic programming

The model underlying concurrent logic programming forms a rather radical departure from the two previous models in that communication is essentially effected through shared logical variables. Parallelism is inherent in the computation model of logic programming languages, because of their declarative nature. Basically, two kinds of parallelism can be distinguished: *and*-parallelism that is due to the parallel evaluation of the atoms in a compound goal, and *or*-parallelism that arises from trying multiple clauses simultaneously for finding a solution to a goal atom.

Although there are a number of attempts at implementing parallel Prolog this way, the two major representatives of concurrent logic programming, Concurrent Prolog and Parlog, have based their approach on the additional assumption of committed choice non-determinism and restricted unification.

Committed choice Unlimited *or*-parallelism, required to find all solutions to a goal, may result in an uncontrollable amount of processes. To restrict *or*-parallelism, guarded Horn clauses were introduced. A guarded Horn clause is a clause of the form

$$A :\!- G_1, ..., G_n \mid B_1, ..., B_m.$$

where A is the head of the clause, $G_1, ..., G_n$ the guard goals and $B_1, ..., B_m$ the actual body of the clause. When a goal atom is evaluated, all clauses of which the head unifies with the atom are selected and the guards of these clauses are evaluated in parallel. The first clause of which the guard is evaluated successfully is committed to. The alternative solutions to the goal atom, embodied in the competing clauses, are thrown away. Since only one clause is chosen, backtracking over alternative solutions is impossible, once the commitment to that particular clause is made. What is allowed as a guard influences the expressiveness of the language in a significant degree, and for that matter the difficulty of implementing it. See [Shapiro, 1989] for an extensive discussion of this topic.

Restricted unification Unrestricted *and*-parallelism, that is the parallel evaluation of the atoms in a compound goal, may result in incompatible bindings of the logical variables involved. To handle this problem, both Concurrent Prolog and Parlog require to indicate which atom acts as the producer of a binding to a variable and which atoms are merely consuming the binding. Concurrent Prolog uses annotations to indicate the variables that must be bound to a term to enable the evaluation of the atom in which they occur to proceed. Parlog, on the other hand, uses mode declarations, indicating the input/output behavior of the arguments of a predicate.

Objects Concurrent logic programming languages offer a very versatile mechanism for implementing distributed systems. Cf. [Shapiro, 1989]. In particular these languages allow to implement active objects with state variables in a very elegant way. This is achieved by defining clauses for objects according to the scheme presented below.

object

```
obj(State, [Message|Messages]) :-
            handle Message,
            update State to State',
            obj(State',Messages).
```

An object is implemented as a tail-recursive process, that receives messages and updates its state if necessary. Cf. [Shapiro and Takeuchi, 1983]. As an example, consider the clauses implementing a counter in Concurrent Prolog.

ctr

```
ctr(N,[inc() | T]) :-  N1 = N + 1, ctr(N1,T).
ctr(N,[value(N) | T]) :-  ctr(N,T).
```

The first argument of *ctr* represents the state of the object, that is passed as an argument to the recursive call, appropriately modified if necessary. The second argument represents the stream of incoming messages, with the tail unspecified to await later binding.

Concurrent logic programming languages offer fine-grained parallelism. As an additional feature for dynamically mapping computations to processes [Shapiro, 1984] proposes a turtle notation for executing Concurrent Prolog programs on a grid of processors. See also section 3.7.

Extensions The primary advantage of using a concurrent logic programming language for implementing distributed systems is the declarative nature of these languages, allowing a logical interpretation of a program. This property is preserved when implementing objects in the way shown. To overcome the syntactical complexity of this approach, two languages combining logic programming and object oriented programming have been proposed, Vulcan and Polka, that preserve the declarative semantics of their underlying logic programming languages.[19] The drawback of this approach, however, is that the restrictions imposed by the requirement of efficiency – committed choice and restricted unification – do not allow for the occurrence of backtracking.

2.4 Software engineering perspectives

Of the various phases of the software life cycle, the design phase is perhaps the most interesting one since it aims at reconciling the requirements resulting from the analysis phase and the restrictions that are *a priori* imposed on the implementation phase. On the one hand a design must specify the structure and functionality of a system in a conceptually clear way and on the other hand it must take into account the feasibility of an implementation. To conclude this introductory chapter, we will investigate what support the three paradigms just treated provide with respect to the design of a system, that is to which problems they promise a solution and which questions they leave unanswered.

Logic programming The contribution of logic programming as a program design formalism lies primarily in its declarative nature. Designing a program in a logic programming formalism enables an easy transition to an actual implementation in a language such as Prolog. Prolog is a general purpose language based on first order logic with a simple semantics. It uses backward chaining inference as a computation mechanism. Due to its declarative semantics a Prolog program may be read as a logical theory concerning a particular domain. This aspect has contributed to the popularity of Prolog for AI-applications. It has been extensively used to implement expert systems. See [Butler Cox, 1983]. Further, it has been used to model British legislation, drug design and even systems programming.

In addition, in [Webster, 1988] Prolog is characterized as a potentially powerful design representation tool, since it may be used to specify the functionality of systems in a concise and formally precise way.[20]

For the representation of knowledge, however, Prolog has a number of drawbacks. It lacks first of all facilities to modularize knowledge, that is to partition the knowledge in module-like entities. It lacks, secondly, a means to construct hierarchies of concepts in a structural way. A number of extensions have been proposed to deal with these deficiencies, extensions with hierarchical frame-based representations, with inheritance hierarchies and object oriented features. According to [Subrahmanyam, 1985], none of these extensions have matured sufficiently to gain wide acceptance. Promising approaches seem to be those aiming at incorporating object oriented features in the logic programming paradigm, that allow to create logical theories dynamically as first-class entities.

[19] These languages will be discussed in section 5.2.2.

[20] In a similar vein, constraint logic programming languages can be thought of as providing an even more powerful formalism, since these languages have knowledge of a particular (formal) domain built-in, which allows them to solve equations over these domains.

Object oriented programming Object oriented software technology has major impacts on the traditional software life cycle. One of these impacts is the shift of emphasis brought about in the relation between the design and the implementation phases of a software development project. The design phase has become increasingly important since the availability of object oriented programming languages allows to regard the implementation as a process of refining the decisions made in designing the system.

The popularity of object oriented programming languages is partly due also to their successful use in prototyping systems of medium complexity. According to [Meyer, 1988] the introduction of object oriented programming has meant the beginning of a revolution in the program development process, since these languages allow to design a system bottom-up, instead of in the traditional way, top-down. The end result of developing a system, bottom-up or top-down, is a set of classes that specifies abstractly the functionality of the corresponding objects by means of external method interfaces. After a while, designing a system comes down to selecting a number of already existing components and assembling them according to the requirements resulting from analysis.

Although, undeniably, the object oriented approach promotes the reuse of software, there are many problems to be solved before this view becomes reality. See for example [Meyer, 1990] and [Booch and Vilot, 1990]. One of the major problems that we encounter here is the problem of *granularity*. In many cases, a class will be a too low-level entity to serve as the unit of reuse. A visual metaphor that illustrates this problem is given by the term *ravioli-code* to characterize a large collection of well-structured objects with highly complex interrelations. To overcome problems of granularity, one has to think in terms of application frameworks to capture the functionality of subsystems. Even then, the specification of a system in an object oriented programming language falls short of providing insight into the conceptual structure of the system, that is the design underlying the program.[21]

Experience has shown that prototyping is advantageous in situations where the requirements are likely to change. To enhance the conceptual understanding of the system embodied by the prototype, the language in which the prototype is implemented needs to be of a sufficiently high level to allow the code to be read as a formal specification of the system. An object oriented approach is only fruitful then, if the objects implementing the system provide an abstract view that corresponds with the way we perceive the problem domain.

Parallel/distributed programming The choice for a parallel or distributed implementation may be motivated either by the application domain, in which concurrency is a natural phenomenon, or by efficiency considerations. From either perspective, designing a distributed system involves a partitioning of the system into separate components and an allocation of these components to (possibly distinct) processes. See [Shatz and Wang, 1987].

In order to distribute the computation among a number of concurrently executing components, the design will have to indicate a partitioning of the functionality among

[21] The plethora of constructs that may be encountered in actual object oriented programming languages makes this insight even more difficult.

a number of distinct logical modules. Further, the design must specify the synchronization and possibly the communication that occurs between these logical modules. Logical modules, in the sense used here, may be active objects, single-threaded processes or even multi-threaded processes.

For the actual exploitation of parallelism, an allocation of these modular entities to processes must be given, taking into account possible precedence relations that may hinder the independent execution of these modules. Allocation may be done statically, before actually starting a system, or may be determined dynamically by an allocation algorithm that takes system parameters such as the workload and the availability of processors into account. Using a performance oriented cost function to determine an optimal allocation, further factors that may be taken into account are the amount of interprocessor communication and the total completion time.

One of the principal difficulties in designing a distributed system is to ensure the correctness of the program. Verifying a distributed system is difficult because of the non-deterministic behavior of such a system, that results from the independence of the concurrently executing components. This non-determinism makes dynamic testing almost infeasible. First of all, it is hard to reproduce the state of the system that has resulted in an error. Secondly, since there is no global state there is no way to freeze the execution in order to inspect the states of the individual components. Before freezing takes effect, the relevant components may already have changed their local state.

As a more fruitful approach, [Shatz and Wang, 1987] recommend to employ *static testing*, an analysis that may be performed without executing the program. In a static test all syntactically specified control-flow paths must be considered. Analysis may then reveal the potential for deadlock, or the occurrence of particular communication events. Given the difficulty of applying a verification method to ordinary sequential languages, the difficulty of applying such a method to a distributed program will be clear.

Distributed logic programming In the previous discussion we have indicated some of the problems that arise in designing a software system. Whatever formalism is used, the partitioning of a program into modules and the specification of the interaction between modules will always remain a non-trivial problem that can only be solved by creative thinking. Our effort of introducing a new language is not meant as a promise to make this task any easier but to provide the means to encode a solution in a high level formalism, including all relevant aspects of a system (including its physical distribution). Such a high level description promotes the conceptual understanding of the system specified and makes the task of verifying the program easier. In developing the language DLP, which will be the subject of the rest of this book, we have made choices to combine the paradigms introduced in this chapter. With this discussion we have made an attempt to motivate these decisions from a software engineering perspective.

3

Extending Prolog to a parallel object oriented language

- *A sceptical lady patient has a rather long dream, in which certain persons tell her of my book on Wit, and praise it highly. Then something is said about a 'channel', perhaps another book in which 'channel' occurs, or something else to do with 'channel'... she doesn't know; it is quite vague* -
Sigmund Freud, *The Interpretation of Dreams*

We will investigate the constructs that are needed for extending Prolog to produce a language suited for parallel and distributed computation, and which fit in the framework imposed by the object oriented programming paradigm. The constructs introduced are all incorporated in the language DLP, of which an overview is given in section 3.8. This chapter is of an exploratory nature. We will reflect on the design considerations in chapter 5.

In section 3.1 we will introduce objects as a means for providing modularization, and for encapsulating data. The information contained in an object is accessible by methods that are defined by clauses. We will briefly discuss inheritance among objects. We will make a distinction between passive, having no activity, and active objects, having own activity. Section 3.2 may be regarded as an intermezzo exploring communication between active objects via channels. In section 3.3 we treat a synchronous rendez-vous mechanism for handling method calls to active objects. A discussion of the distributed backtracking that may occur in a rendez-vous is given in section 3.4. Section 3.5 deals with a construct for the conditional acceptance of method calls. In section 3.6 we treat an asynchronous rendez-vous mechanism which gives the programmer additional control over the parallel evaluation of goals. In section 3.7 we deal with the constructs needed for the allocation of objects and processes. In section 3.8 we define the language DLP as the collection of constructs introduced. And, finally, in section 3.9 we will delineate a number of subsets of DLP that will be studied from a formal semantic perspective in part II.

Since the primary intention here is to give the intuition behind the mechanisms needed for parallel object oriented logic programming, and give motivations for the constructs proposed by means of examples, the description of the constructs will be informal.

3.1 Objects and processes

We start by introducing the notion of objects. Throughout, a program is a Prolog-like program and a collection of object declarations.

In its most simple form an object declaration looks as follows.

```
object name {
clauses
}
```

As we continue, we will gradually introduce features giving more functionality to an object.

3.1.1 Objects as modules

The first view that we will take of objects is simply to regard them as modules, containing a collection of clauses. As an example of such an object, look at the declaration for a library of list manipulation predicates.

lib

```
object lib {
member(X,[ X | _ ]).
member(X,[ _ | T ]) :-  member(X,T).
append([],L,L).
append([H|T],L,[H|R]) :-  append(T,L,R).
}
```

Clauses can be activated by a goal of the form

- *name*!*goal*

which is a request for the evaluation of *goal* using the clauses defined for the object with that *name*.

An example of the use of such a goal could be

```
?- lib!member(X,[amsterdam, paris, london]).
```

which, following ordinary Prolog evaluation rules, would bind the logical variable X successively to the cities mentioned in the second argument of *member*.

Method call The intended semantics for an object as declared above does not deviate in any significant way from the semantics of an ordinary Prolog program. In other words, evaluating the goal $lib!member(X, L)$ will give the same results as evaluating the goal $member(X, L)$ when the clauses for *member* are directly added to the program. This holds in particular for backtracking. When a goal has multiple solutions, these solutions will be tried just as for an ordinary goal.

Below we have pictured how communication with an object takes place.

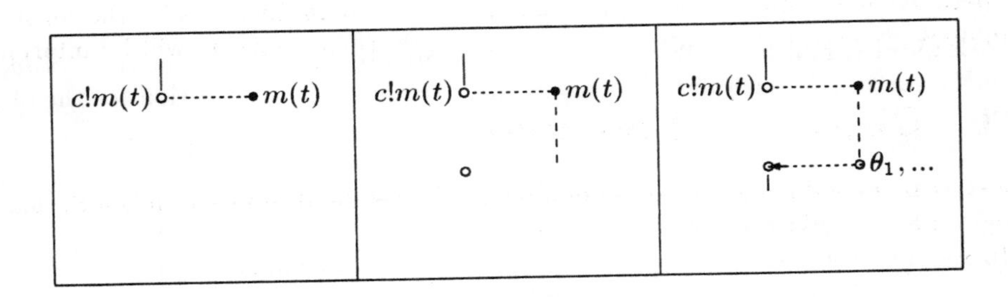

Assume that we have an object c. The goal $c!m(t)$ asks the object c to evaluate $m(t)$, where m is a predicate name and t represents the arguments of the call. We use a predicate name m since, adopting standard terminology, we will speak of the methods of an object, which in our case are ordinary clauses. While the goal $m(t)$ is being evaluated, the caller waits for an answer. Backtracking over the results, indicated by $\theta_1, \ldots$, may take place as long as there are alternative solutions. Backtracking is initiated by the object that called for the method.

The obvious advantage of having the clauses for a predicate assembled in a module-like object is that, when a different functionality for these predicates is required, another object can simply be asked to do the evaluation.

Use We may extend the facilities for modular programming by allowing an object to use the clauses of another object. For example, when defining a predicate $inboth(X, L_1, L_2)$, which checks whether X occurs both in list L_1 and L_2, it is convenient to be able to use the definition for *member* directly by using the clauses of *lib*, instead of explicitly addressing each call of *member* at the object *lib*. This is realized in the declaration for the object *check*.

check

```
object check {
use lib.
inboth(X,L1,L2) :- member(X,L1), member(X,L2).
}
```

The effect of a *use* declaration is that the clauses of the used objects become part of the object.

3.1.2 Objects with states

Modules of the kind treated above, however useful they may be, do not deserve to be classified as objects, since they do not contain any private data nor do they have an internal state. Below we will introduce *non-logical variables*, for which we allow destructive assignment.[1] In addition, we will introduce a facility to make instances, or rather copies, of declared objects. Furthermore, we will briefly discuss how objects may inherit non-logical variables and clauses from other objects.

Non-logical variables Objects may contain private data. We introduce *non-logical variables* for storing such data. As an example consider the declaration for the object *travel*.

travel

```
object travel {
use lib.
var city = [amsterdam, paris, london].
reachable(X) :-  member(X, city).
}
```

We may ask such an object to evaluate the goal *reachable(tokyo)* as in

```
?- travel!reachable(tokyo).
```

for which the answer is, perhaps unfortunately, no. When the goal *reachable(tokyo)* is evaluated we assume that the non-logical variable *city* is replaced by its value, the list of cities to which it is initialized. Moreover, because of the backtracking provided by Prolog, we could ask the object *travel* to list all reachable cities.

The advantage of overloading predicate names becomes apparent when we imagine the situation in which we have a number of travel agencies, implemented by the objects $travel_1, ..., travel_n$, similar to the object *travel* but with (possibly) different values for the non-logical variable *city*, which allows us to ask

?- lib!member(O,[$travel_1, ..., travel_n$]), O!reachable(tokyo).

that may after all get us where we want to be.

Non-logical variables, that allow to store persistent data and that enable search over these data by backtracking, are of relevance for the implementation of knowledge based systems. For a small example it may not seem worthwhile to introduce non-logical variables, but in a real life situation the data may be stored in a large database.

Only the clauses declared for an object have access to the non-logical variables. This justifies our speaking of clauses as methods, since the clauses provide an interface to the object encapsulating these data.

[1] Non-logical variables are usually called *instance variables* in object oriented terminology.

Assignment Having non-logical variables, the question immediately arises as to whether we may change the value of such a variable or not. It seems unnatural to have to answer no, since, for example, a travel agency may decide to change the service it offers now and again. We introduce a goal of the form

- *variable* := *term*

for assigning values to non-logical variables. The use of such a goal is illustrated in the following version of *travel.*

travel

```
object travel {
use lib.
var city = [amsterdam, paris, london].
reachable(X) :-   member(X,city).
add(X) :-   append([X],city,R), city  :=   R.
}
```

So, as an example, when we have as a goal

```
?- travel!add(berlin).
```

each successive request to *travel* includes *berlin* as a reachable city. For convenience we have assumed that the list of destinations always grows longer. In general, assignment to a non-logical variable is destructive, in that the previous value is lost.[2]

Instances of objects Objects with mutable states require to have the possibility to create instances of objects of a particular kind. For example, we might wish to have a number of instances of the object *travel*, which differ in the destinations they offer.

Each *instance* of an object contains both a copy of the non-logical variables of the object and a copy of its clauses. The non-logical variables of an instance are initialized to the current value of the non-logical variables of the object. Apart from the clauses declared for the object, a copy is also made of the clauses contained in the objects occurring in the *use* list.

To create an instance of an object we introduce a goal

- $O = new(name)$

that results in binding the newly created instance of the object to the logical variable O. Its use is illustrated by a goal like

```
?-
    O1 = new(travel), O2 = new(travel),
    O1!add(berlin), O2!add(antwerpen).
```

[2] We will discuss the protection needed in the presence of concurrency in section 3.3, where we treat the rendez-vous mechanism.

in which two instances of the object *travel* are created, which differ in that they respectively include *berlin* and *antwerpen* in their offer of reachable destinations. Notice that instances of objects are also objects.[3]

3.1.3 Inheritance

As we have seen, an object may use the clauses of the objects contained in its *use* list. We propose another feature to enable an object to inherit the non-logical variables of other objects. This type of inheritance is exemplified in the declaration

```
object travel {
var city = [amsterdam, paris, london].
}
object agency {
isa travel.
...
}
```

This declaration ensures that the object *agency*, and all its instances, will have a non-logical variable *city*, initialized to the list above.

In most cases the inheritance relation is such that the inheriting object contains both the non-logical variables and the clauses of the objects it inherits. We have introduced the notation

```
object a:b { ... }
```

as a shorthand for

```
object a {
isa b.
use b.
...
}
```

As an example, consider the declaration below.

agency

```
object travel {
use lib.
var city = [amsterdam, paris, london].
reachable(X) :-   member(X,city).
}
object agency : travel {
book(X)   :-   reachable(X), price(X,Y), write(
    pay(Y) ).
price(amsterdam,5).
...
}
```

[3] We have deviated from standard terminology, in not speaking of objects as instances of classes, since both the named object declared in the program and its instances (that is copies) may be used as objects.

The object *agency* may use all the clauses of *travel*, and in addition has access to the non-logical variable *city*.

Inheritance is effected by code-sharing, in a static way. Conceptually, the inheriting object contains a copy of the objects it inherits. We will discuss how we deal with clashes that may arise in multiple inheritance in chapter 4, where we will also provide some examples of how inheritance may be used for knowledge representation.

3.1.4 Active objects

So far, we have not given any clue as to how we will deal with concurrent programming in our (yet to be proposed) language. The first idea that comes to mind is to make passive (instances of) objects active, by letting them have activity of their own. Having a number of objects concurrently executing some activity of their own is, however, not of much help when there is no means to communicate with these objects. Thus, in addition to providing the means to create active instances of objects, it is also necessary to provide a way by which their activity can be interrupted in order to evaluate some goal.

An active object is created by a goal of the form

- $O = new(name(t_1, ..., t_n))$

where *name* is the name of the declared object, and $t_1, ..., t_n$ are arbitrary terms.

The term $name(t_1, ..., t_n)$ is called the *constructor*, since, when creating a new object, a process is started to evaluate the goal $name(t_1, ..., t_n)$. In order to avoid failure, clauses must be defined by which the constructor can be evaluated. The predicate name of the head of these clauses which, for obvious reasons we call *constructor clauses*, is identical to the name of the declared object.

Processes Multiple processes may refer to a single object. Apart from the constructor process, a process is created for each method call in order to keep track of the backtracking over the results of that call. We have pictured an object and some processes referring to it below.

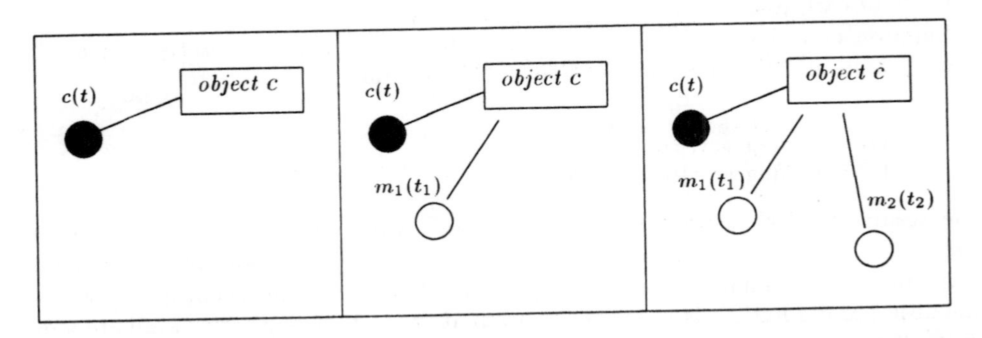

The call $O = new(c(t))$ results in a new instance of the object c together with a constructor process evaluating $c(t)$. Both the calls $O!m_1(t_1)$ and $O!m_2(t_2)$, which may come from different processes, result in a separate process for evaluating these calls.

Acceptance The constructor clauses specify what may be called the *body* of an object, which determines its own activity. To interrupt this own activity we provide the goal

- *accept*(*any*)

that forces the object to wait until it is requested to evaluate a goal.[4] When this has happened –that is when the goal is evaluated and an answer has been sent back– the accept goal succeeds and the object may continue with its own activity.

As an example, consider the object declaration for an *agency* that, in a naive way, implements the amalgamation of a number of travel agencies of the old kind.

agency

```
object agency {
use lib.
var city = [].
agency(L) :-
        member(O,L),
        O!reachable(X),
        add(X),
        fail.
agency(_) :-  run().
run() :-  accept(any), run().
reachable(X)  :-  member(X,city).
add(X) :-  append([X],city,R), city :=  R.
}
```

The declaration for *agency* differs from the declaration for the object *travel* only in having constructor clauses and an auxiliary clause for *run*(), that define the own activity of each instance of an *agency*.

Suppose now that we wish to combine four travel agencies, $travel_1, ..., travel_4$ of the old kind into two new agencies, then we may state as a goal

```
?-
   O1 = new(agency([travel₁, travel₂])),
   O2 = new(agency([travel₃, travel₄]))....
```

the result of which is that both agencies start with initializing their list of cities concurrently. The body of an agency consists, after initialization, of a tail-recursive loop stating the willingness to accept any goal. Each time the accept goal is reached, the object waits until it is requested to evaluate a goal. A request to evaluate a goal, in its turn, must wait until the object is willing to accept such a request.

[4]Later on we will encounter accept goals of a more complex nature.

3.1.5 Concurrency and synchronization

We have sketched here the simplest form of the evaluation of a goal by an object. We call this *remote goal evaluation* since we have not yet provided the means to be selective about what is acceptable as a request.

Clearly, apart from the initialization and the fact that the own activity of an object must explicitly be interrupted, the semantics of an active object must be similar to that of a passive object. Conceptually, we may regard a passive object *obj* to be executing its constructor *obj*(), defined by

obj() :- *accept*(any), obj().

In contrast with active objects, however, passive objects have unlimited internal concurrency as explained below.

Backtracking A question we have not addressed when treating the remote evaluation of a goal by an active object is how to deal with the possible occurrence of backtracking over the resulting answers. Our approach is colored by our intention to have a semantics which coincides with that for ordinary Prolog, as far as backtracking is concerned.

In our proposal we deal with the backtracking that may occur in a method call by creating a new process for each request to evaluate a goal. The backtracking information needed for finding all solutions for the goal is maintained by that process.

Internal concurrency When multiple processes referring to a single object are active concurrently we speak of internal concurrency. For active objects we provide mutual exclusion between method calls in order to protect the access of non-logical variables. Mutual exclusion, however, restricts the degree of internal concurrency of an object. We do not wish to impose any restrictions on the internal concurrency displayed by passive objects. The programmer must take care to provide the protection necessary for safely accessing non-logical variables. Active objects allow only a limited form of internal concurrency, namely for backtracking over multiple answers to a method call.

Synchronization We consider remote goal evaluation as an important means for objects to communicate with each other. Moreover, by requiring it to be stated explicitly whether an object is willing to accept a request, we have provided a means for synchronizing the behavior of objects.

However, we may wish to be more selective in what to accept as a request. For instance, what is acceptable may depend on the state of the object, or even on conditions imposed on the arguments of the call. When the object is selective in this sense, it seems more apt to speak of a rendez-vous, since both the object and the process that requests the evaluation of a goal participate in establishing the communication.

Summarizing, what we have described to this point is more or less a fully-fledged object oriented language. We may regard the clauses defined for an object as methods, having access to private data stored in the non-logical variables. Calling a method is to engage in a rendez-vous, when the object is willing to accept the call.

Before continuing our description of this approach, however, we wish to reflect on the possibility of realizing objects with states that communicate by means of message passing. Do we need non-logical variables to implement states? And, do we need a synchronous rendez-vous to communicate with objects? We will deal with these questions in the next section, where we explore the possibility of using channels as the medium of communication between active objects.

3.2 Communication over channels

We may implement objects as continuously running processes communicating with each other over channels. Cf. [Shapiro and Takeuchi, 1983], [Pereira and Nasr, 1984]. Before going into details we will present the language constructs involved. First of all we need a facility to create processes. We will use a goal of the form

- $new(c(t_1, ..., t_n))$

to create an active instance of the object c.

To create new channels we use a goal of the form

- $C = new(channel)$

which results in binding the newly created channel to the logical variable C.

Further we need, what we call an output statement of the form

- $C!t$

where C refers to a channel and t is an arbitrary term.

Also, we need an input statement of the form

- $C?t$

where C is assumed to refer to a channel and t is an arbitrary term.

Counter We will characterize the semantics of communication over channels by giving a simple example, adapted from [Pereira and Nasr, 1984], but originally given in [Shapiro and Takeuchi, 1983]. Assume that we wish to implement a counter that allows us to ask for its value and to increment its value. Clearly, we must have some means to store the state of the object, and also some means to send it the corresponding messages. With the constructs introduced, our implementation looks as follows.

ctr

```
object ctr {
ctr(C) :-  run(C,0).
run(C,N) :-
        C?inc(),
        N1 = N + 1,
        run(C,N1).

run(C,N) :-
        C?value(N),
        run(C,N).
}
```

The first clause encountered is the constructor for an instance of *ctr*. The argument C is assumed to refer to a channel. Evaluating the constructor results in calling $run(C,0)$, initializing the (logical) state variable holding the value of the counter to zero. The remaining two clauses define the body of the object. The first clause contains the input statement $C?inc()$ that is used to increment the value of the counter. The second clause contains the input statement $C?value(N)$ that is used to answer requests for the value of the counter. The value of the counter is maintained appropriately by passing it as an argument to the tail-recursive call to *run*.

A typical example of the use of such a counter is the goal

```
?-
   C = new(channel),
   new(ctr(C)),
   C!inc(),
   C!value(X).
```

that modifies the binding of X to one.

The example given illustrates the use of such objects to implement server processes. Let us now give a more detailed description of the semantics of communication over channels.

Bi-directional unification Communication over channels is synchronous, in that both sides wait until there are complementary communication requests for that channel. For the example above this means that the body of the counter will remain at the goal $C?inc()$ until the user process reaches an output statement. We call a communication successful if the term on the input side, or more briefly the input term, is unifiable with the output term, the term on the output side. When these terms do not unify, as in the case for $inc()$ and $value(X)$, the input side is allowed to backtrack until it finds another input statement for that channel and the procedure is repeated. As long as the input side is backtracking the output side waits with its request to communicate.

The asymmetry with respect to backtracking is exemplified above. We must remark, however, that Delta Prolog adopts a communication mechanism that is symmetric in its backtracking behavior but is rather complex.

We stress that both in Delta Prolog and in our proposal communication over channels is bi-directional, in the sense that variables in both the input term and the output term may receive a value through unification.

As an example consider the following object declaration

```
object a {
a(C) :-  run(C,0).
run(C,N) :-  C?f(N,Y), run(C,Y).
}
```

The body of the object a, which is defined by the clauses constructor $a(C)$, consist of executing *run*. An active object outputs a term $f(N,Y)$ over over channel C. Initially, N is zero. When evaluating the goal

```
?- C = new(channel), new(a(C)), C!f(X,1).
```

an object $a(C)$, that is initialized with channel C. The newly created object runs indepently of the process evaluating the original goal. Since both $C!f(N,Y)$ and $C?(X,1)$ share the same channel, an attempt at communication takes place, which results in binding X to zero and Y in the body of a to one.

Sieve We conclude this intermezzo with an example in which the number of processes can grow indefinitely large. Below we present our implementation of the solution to the problem of generating primes given in [Hoare, 1978].

The solution consists of a chain of processes, the first of which – called the *driver* – produces natural numbers and the others – representing the primes – check for divisibility by a prime. The definition of the *driver* process is as follows.

driver

```
object driver {
driver(I) :-
        C = new(channel),
        new(sieve(C)),
        drive(C,I).
drive(C,I) :-
        C!I, J = I+2, drive(C,J).
}
```

The body of the driver produces an infinite sequence of (odd) natural numbers which are sent to the first sieve process.

sieve

```
object sieve {
sieve(C) :-
        C?P,
        collect(P),
        Cout = new(channel),
        new(sieve(Cout)),
        run(P,C,Cout).

run(P,C,Cout) :-
        C?I,
        ( I//P ≠ 0 → Cout!I ; true ),
        run(P,C,Cout).

collect(I) :-  write(I).
}
```

A *sieve* contains a prime and checks all incoming numbers for divisibility by that prime. The first number received by a *sieve* process is known to be a prime. The process then creates a new *sieve* and checks all incoming naturals for divisibility by the prime it has stored. If the incoming natural is not divisible by the prime stored by the sieve it is sent to the successor process of that sieve.

The output is collected by sending each prime with which a new sieve is initialized to a special process. The goal $I//P \neq 0$ is evaluated by simplifying $I//P$ to I *moduloP* followed by a test as to whether the result is unequal to zero.

The program is started by the goal

```
?- new(driver(3)).
```

The structure of the collection of processes may be pictured as

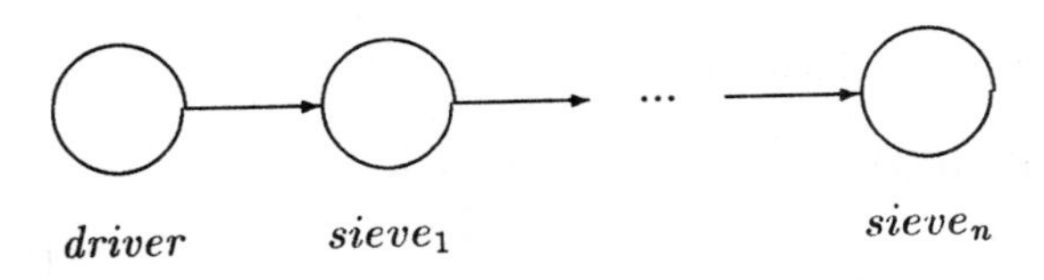

where each arrow represents a channel.

As sketched here, communication over channels offers a rather limited functionality. In particular, since we have not included guarded commands or annotated variables, synchronization must rely purely on the synchronous nature of communication. Another important limitation is that no backtracking over the results of a communication is allowed, once a successful communication is achieved.

3.3 Communication by rendez-vous

In the previous section we have seen how we may implement objects with states without the use of non-logical variables to store the state of such objects. The approach sketched there has a number of limitations. Instead of augmenting the proposal of the previous section, we will take up the main thread of this chapter and will investigate how we may achieve object oriented behavior by regarding clauses as methods.

Below we summarize the language features that we treat in this section.

- $x := t$ — to assign the value of a term to the non-logical variable x
- $O = new(c(t_1, ..., t_n))$ — to create an active instance of c, to which O will refer
- $O!m(t_1, ..., t_n)$ — to call the method m of the object to which O refers
- $accept(m_1, ..., m_n)$ — to state the willingness to accept calls for $m_1, ..., m_n$

States As we have indicated in the section introducing objects we may use non-logical variables to store persistent data. We rephrase the declaration of the counter presented in the previous section to recall its use.

ctr

```
object ctr {
var n=0.
ctr() :-   accept(any), ctr().
inc() :-   n :=  n + 1.
value(N) :-   N = n.
}
```

This solution differs from the previous one in that the state of the object is not maintained by keeping the value of the counter as an argument in a tail-recursive loop, but as an explicit non-logical variable that can be updated by assignment.[5] A typical use of such a counter is exemplified by the goal

```
?-
    C = new(ctr()),
    C!inc(),
    C!value(X).
```

In this a counter is created, which subsequently receives the method calls *inc*() and *value*(X). Despite the notational similarity with communication over channels, the calls *C*!*inc*() and *C*!*value*(X) are now method calls, that is goals that are evaluated by the object. The evaluation of these goals is taken care of by the clauses defined for *inc* and *value*.

[5] We allow for arithmetic simplifications both in the right-hand side of assignments to non-logical variables and in the left- and right-hand sides of an equality.

Mutual exclusion Method calls for an active object must be explicitly accepted by an accept statement. To answer a method call an active object must interrupt its own activity. To protect the access to non-logical variables, mutual exclusion between method calls is provided by not allowing any method call to be accepted as long as the evaluation of a method call has not led to an answer being returned.

An important question to answer is: when do we allow an object to continue with its own activity? In the absence of backtracking the natural choice is: immediately after the answer has been delivered. In the presence of backtracking we might wish to deliver all answers before allowing an object to continue its own activity. However this is overly restrictive since protection of non-logical variables is not really needed when backtracking over alternative solutions as shown in section 3.4.

Another thorny issue, which arises in the presence of backtracking, is what to do with non-logical variables that may be assigned values in an imperative way. Must these assignments be undone on backtracking or not? As the example of a counter shows, assignment to non-logical variables is of an imperative nature. Consequently, such assignments are not undone on backtracking!

Suspension The mutual exclusion provided by the counter is meant only to protect the access to non-logical variables. At any time, any method call is acceptable. It is conceivable, however, that whether or not a method call is acceptable depends on the state of the object, as expressed in its non-logical variables.

A typical example of such an object is the semaphore, given below.

sema

```
object sema {
var n = 0.

sema(N) :-  n :=  N, run.

p() :-  n :=  n- 1.
v() :-  n :=  n + 1.

run :-
        ( n == 0 → accept(v) ; accept(p,v) ),
        run.
}
```

The constructor for *sema* causes the semaphore to loop over a conditional that tests the value of the non-logical variable n. When the value of n is zero. calls to $p()$ will be suspended, because of the statement $accept(v)$; otherwise both $p()$ and $v()$ may occur, since when n is not zero the statement $accept(p, v)$ is evaluated.

A semaphore of the kind above may be used to regulate the concurrent evaluation of goals by passive objects. To illustrate this we present a modified version of the travel agency described in section 1.2.

travel

```
object travel {
use lib.
var s = new(sema(1)).
var city = [amsterdam, paris, london].
reachable(X) :-  member(X,city).
add(X) :-  s!p(), append([X],city,R), city := R,
    s!v().
}
```

The object *travel* implements a multiple readers/single writers protocol, since adding an item to the city list is embedded in the semaphore calls $p()$ and $v()$. The initialization of the non-logical variable s to an active instance of *sema* occurs exactly once for each instance of *travel*.

Semantics Let us now take a closer look at the semantics of the accept statement. We only allow accept statements to occur in active objects since we wish method calls for passive objects to be evaluated concurrently.[6]

Calling a method of an active object results in a rendez-vous, when that object is willing to accept the call. The interaction between the processes involved is pictured below.

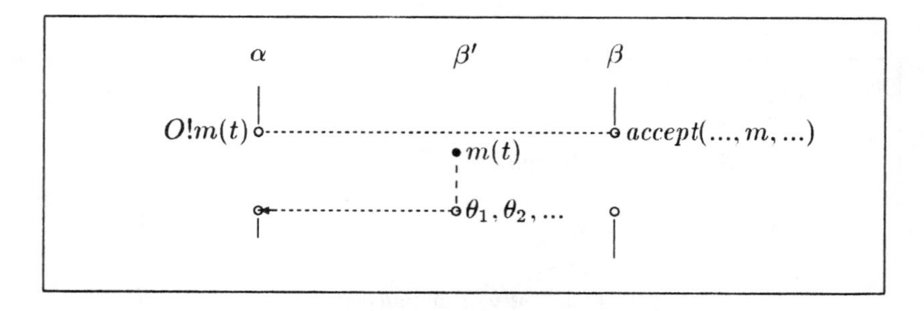

Suppose that we have a process α that calls $O!m(t)$, with O bound to the object of which β evaluates the constructor. When β reaches an accept statement the activity of β is interrupted, and a new process β' is started to evaluate $m(t)$ which refers to the same object as β. Process β resumes the evaluation of the constructor as soon as the first answer, say θ_1, is produced. Thereafter β' continues to produce alternative solutions, as may be requested by α.

Operationally, when an accept statement is reached, the evaluation of the current goal is suspended until a method allowed by the arguments of the accept statement is called for. We call the argument of the accept statement the *accept list*, and by

[6] In addition, for active objects we do allow accept statements to occur (possibly nested) in processes for evaluating method calls. In our semantic description, however, we impose the requirement that accept statements may occur only in the constructor process of an object.

convention take *any* to stand for all methods of the object. When a method not occurring in the accept list is called for, the call is suspended and the object waits until another call satisfying the accept list occurs. The suspended call will result in a process evaluating the method call whenever the accept list is changed in such a way that the call is allowed. To handle suspended calls the object maintains a so-called *accept queue.* All suspended calls join in the accept queue, in the order in which they arrive. When the accept list is changed, the object first searches the queue and takes the first call satisfying the new accept list. If no such call is present the object waits for other incoming calls. This procedure guarantees fairness in handling method calls since because of the FIFO behavior of the accept queue, no allowed call will be suspended forever. Cf. [America, 1989b].

Dining philosophers

Our pièce de résistance is an implementation of a solution for the problem of the *Dining Philosophers.* Cf. [Dijkstra, 1971], [Hoare, 1978].

Five philosophers must spent their time *thinking* and *eating.* When a philosopher wants to eat he must get hold of two forks. Since only five forks are available, each philosopher must await his turn. To avoid the situation where each philosopher sits waiting with one fork, only four philosophers at a time are allowed in the dining room.

Since a philosopher needs to know no more than his name, the dining room and his proper forks he may, after creation, proceed to enter the cycle of thinking, entering the dining room, picking up his forks, eating and leaving the dining room to start thinking again.

philopher

```
object philosopher {
var name.
philosopher(Name,Room,Lf,Rf) :-
        name := Name,
        proceed(Room,Lf,Rf).
think :-   write(thinking(name)).
eat :-   write(eating(name)).
proceed(Room,Lf,Rf) :-
        think,
        Room!enter(),
        Lf!pickup(), Rf!pickup(),
        eat,
        Lf!putdown(), Rf!putdown(),
        Room!exit(),
        proceed(Room,Lf,Rf).
}
```

A philosopher is admitted to the dining room when less than four guests are present, otherwise he must wait for one of his colleagues to leave.

room

```
object room {
var occupancy=0.
room() :-
        (
        occupancy == 0 → accept(enter) ;
        occupancy == 4 → accept(exit) ;
        accept(enter, exit)
        ),
        room().
enter() :- occupancy := occupancy + 1.
exit() :- occupancy := occupancy− 1.
}
```

Forks can only be picked up and then put down.

fork

```
object fork {
pickup().
putdown().
fork() :-
        accept( pickup ),
        accept( putdown ),
        fork().
}
```

The ceremony is started by assigning the philosophers their proper forks and showing them the dining room. We omit the details of their initiation.

The example demonstrates the synchronization enforced by accept statements. Such behavior could not be effected by using synchronous communication over channels. In fact, the synchronization and suspension capability of the rendez-vous mechanism makes communication over channels superfluous. However, communication involving accept statements and non-logical variables is semantically considerably more complex, and seems to preclude a declarative semantics. Apart from this, communication over channels is more efficient.

3.4 Distributed backtracking

Distributed backtracking is an important issue for systems that wish to support *don't know* non-determinism, in contrast to *don't care* nondeterminism where, once a choice is made, all alternatives are thrown away. The examples presented previously were deterministic in the sense that only one solution needed to be produced. The object presented in the following example, however, may produce an infinite number of solutions.

nat

```
object nat {
number(0).
number(s(X)) :-  number(X).
}
```

Its use is illustrated by

```
?- nat!number(X), write(X), fail.
```

which will print all natural numbers, eventually. Backtracking is done lazily, in that on backtracking the object evaluating *number* will start to produce the next solution. Note that the goal

```
:-  nat!number(X), X = s(s(0)).
```

differs from the goal

```
:-  nat!number(s(s(0))).
```

in that the latter only communicates success, whereas the former has to communicate three bindings for X.

Backtracking in the presence of non-logical variables In the presence of non-logical variables mutual exclusion is needed for reasons of protection. Mutual exclusion takes effect for active objects only. This protection, however, lasts until the first answer is requested and received. This procedure is motivated by the assumption that any important change of the state of the object can be achieved during the period that the first solution is produced. Backtracking over the second and remaining solutions can be done while other processes are active.

We will show how the state of an object can be fixed by binding it to a non-logical variable. Consider another variant of our, by now familiar, travel agency.

travel

```
object travel {
use lib.
var city = [amsterdam, paris, london].
travel() :-  accept(any), travel().
reachable(X) :-  L = city, member(X,L).
add(X) :-  append([X],city,R), city := R.
}
```

In the clause for *reachable* we have made explicit the binding of the second argument of *member* to the value of the city list. Since an instance of *travel* is now an active object the mutual exclusion mechanism prevents the city list from being changed while the first answer for *reachable* is being produced. After that, *member* may backtrack, but with the value of the city list bound to L, as it was at the time of the call.

Now suppose that we declare *travel* in the following, somewhat contrived, manner.

travel

```
object travel {
use lib.
var city = [amsterdam, paris, london].
travel() :-  accept(any), travel().
reachable(X) :-  length(city,N), get(N,X).
add(X) :-  append([X],city,R), city :=  R.
get(N,X) :-  element(N,city,X).
get(N,X) :-  N > 1, N1 = N- 1, get(N1,X).
length([],0).
length([H|T],N) :-  length(T,N1), N = N1 + 1.
element(1,[ X | _ ],X).
element(N,[ _ | T ],X) :-
        N > 1,
        N1 = N- 1,
        element(N1,T,X).
}
```

The reader may check that in this case the city list may be updated, by adding elements to the front, while the process evaluating *reachable* is backtracking over the possible solutions. In general such interference is not desirable but, as has been shown, this can easily be avoided by binding the state of an object to a logical variable.

Deterministic objects In many cases we do not need the full power of backtracking over the results in a rendez-vous. For instance, asking the value of a counter results in precisely one answer. Such deterministic behavior is obvious when the call contains no unbound logical variables, since the answer will then be either failure or success.

To cope with the cases in which this cannot so easily be decided we have provided a way of declaring an object to be deterministic. Our counter is clearly a deterministic object.

ctr

```
deterministic object ctr {
var n=0.
ctr() :-  accept(any), ctr().
inc() :-  n :=  n + 1.
value(N) :-  N = n.
}
```

The prefix *deterministic* enforces that only one solution will be returned for each method call.

3.5 Conditional acceptance

The accept statement that we have considered allows only the names of methods for which a call is acceptable. We will now introduce a much more powerful mechanism that allows, among other things, the imposition of arbitrary conditions on the arguments of the call.

The format of the *conditional accept statement* is

- $accept(..., m(t_1, ..., t_n) : guard \rightarrow goal, ...)$

The conditional accept statement is similar to the accept statement treated previously except that, instead of a method name m, expressions of the form

$$m(t_1, ..., t_n) : guard \rightarrow goal$$

and simplifications thereof, as listed below, may occur as arguments.

Semantics When an accept statement is encountered, for instance when evaluating the constructor of an object, the accept expressions occurring in the statement are stored in the so-called *accept list* of the object.

The accept list is consulted for each request to evaluate a method call. For simple accept statements the accept list consists of method names. Whether a method call is acceptable then only depends on the method name being a member of the accept list.

Checking whether a method call satisfies the acceptance condition imposed by an accept expression of the form $m(t_1, ..., t_n) : guard \rightarrow goal$ requires more effort.

When a method is called, say by $m(t'_1, ..., t'_n)$, then it is first tried whether the call can be unified with the expression $m(t_1, ..., t_n)$. If the unification is successful then, in addition, the *guard* will be evaluated, instantiated by the bindings that result from the unification of the call with the method template $m(t_1, ..., t_n)$. If the evaluation of the guard succeeds also, the call will be answered by evaluating *goal*, instantiated by the bindings resulting from unifying the call with the template and the evaluation of the guard.

It is easy to see that the conditional accept statement subsumes the original accept statement since the statement $accept(m)$ has meaning identical to

$$accept(m(t_1, ..., t_n) : true \rightarrow m(t_1, ..., t_n))$$

Both the *guard* and the *goal* of an accept expression may contain variables occurring in the method template $m(t_1, ..., t_n)$. The bindings computed to answer the caller are determined by the evaluation of the goal and, in addition, by both the unification with the template and the evaluation of the *guard*. Below we indicate what happens when an accept expression of a simpler form is encountered.

Accept expressions The arguments of the accept statement are called *accept expressions.* Accept expressions may take one of the following forms.

- m — accepts all calls for method m
- $m(t_1, ..., t_n)$ — accepts all calls that unify with $m(t_1, ..., t_n)$
- m : *guard* — accepts all calls for m if the *guard* holds
- $m(t_1, ..., t_n)$: *guard* — accepts all calls that unify with $m(t_1, ..., t_n)$ for which the *guard* holds
- m : *guard* → *goal* — executes *goal* for all calls to m if the *guard* holds

In addition we have

- $m(t_1, ..., t_n)$: *guard* → *goal*

that executes *goal* for all calls unifying with $m(t_1, ... t_n)$ for which the *guard* holds.

To illustrate the power of the generalized accept statement we re-express some of the examples presented earlier.

Examples We will first give an alternative declaration for the object *sema.*

sema

```
object sema {
var n = 0.
sema(N) :-  n := N, run.
p() :-  n := n− 1.
v() :-  n := n + 1.
run :-  N=n, accept(v:N ≥ 0, p:N> 0), run.
}
```

The behavior of an instance of *sema* is identical to the behavior of the object *sema* as defined before. The present declaration differs from the previous one in that the Prolog conditional goal

n == 0 → answer(v) ; answer(p,v)

is replaced by the conditional accept statement

accept(v:N ≥ 0, p:N> 0)

with N bound to n, in which the guards contain the conditions under which the method calls may be accepted.

States Perhaps somewhat surprisingly, we no longer need to use non-logical variables to maintain the state of an (active) object. We will illustrate this by (re) declaring our familiar counter.

ctr

```
object ctr {
ctr() :-  run(0).
run(N) :-  accept(
              inc():true →  N1 = N + 1,
              value(N):true →  N1 = N
              ),run(N1).
}
```

The state is passed as an argument in a tail-recursive call to *run*, which implements the body of the object.

In a similar way we can implement a semaphore, as shown below.

sema

```
object sema {
sema(N) :-  accept(
              v:N≥ 0 →  N1 = N + 1,
              p:N> 0 →  N1 = N− 1
              ), sema(N1).
}
```

which is a rather elegant way of coding a semaphore. Notice that we do not have to specify clauses for the methods but may specify the functionality of a method in the *goal* part of an accept expression.

Non-logical variables are no longer necessary to represent the state of an object because of the enlarged functionality of the accept statement. However, logical state variables, maintained as an argument in a tail-recursive loop, may not be inherited whereas non-logical state variables may be inherited among objects, thus allowing a rather concise description of the functionality of a collection of objects.

Another reason not to abandon non-logical variables has to do with efficiency. Passing a complex state as an argument after each method call is clearly less efficient.

Backtracking The generalized accept statement preserves backtracking over the possible answers delivered in a rendez-vous, as illustrated by our rephrasing of the declaration of a travel agency.

travel

```
object travel {
use lib.

travel() :-   run([amsterdam,paris,london]).

run(L) :-  accept(
             reachable(X): L1 = L →  member(X,L),
             add(X): true →  append([X],L,L1)
             ), run(L1).
}
```

As before we may generate all reachable cities by stating the goal

?- travel!reachable(X).

Since the *goal* in a conditional accept expression may fail, care must be taken to update the state variable in a proper way, as illustrated in the example above where the parameter for the tail-recursive call to *run* (L1) is bound to the original list L.

3.6 An asynchronous rendez-vous mechanism

The rendez-vous presented consists of two parts, the creation of a process to evaluate a method call and the request for an answer. For creation of the evaluating process, one may use the special statement

- $Q = O!m(t)$

to request the object to which O refers to create a process to evaluate the goal $m(t)$. The variable Q thereafter refers to that process. For the request of the result we introduce

- $Q?$

that asks the process, referred to by Q, for an (other) answer.

Informal semantics Using somewhat contradictory terminology, a call of the form $Q = O!m(t)$ may be regarded as an asynchronous method call, since receiving the (possibly multiple) answers requires an explicit request of the form $Q?$. The variable Q is bound to a pointer to the process evaluating $m(t)$. The method call $m(t)$ must explicitly be accepted by an accept goal of the object to which O refers. We call the goal $Q?$ a *resumption request*, since it delivers a resumption containing the answer substitutions that result from the call. Evaluating the resumption enables the possible variable bindings of these answers to take effect in the current context.

The decomposition of a method call in the request of evaluation and the request of a result allows the programmer to achieve extra parallelism, since the newly created process runs independently of the invoking process, which does not have to wait for an answer. Such overlapping of processes is expressed by a goal of the form

$$Q = O!m(t),\ G,\ Q?$$

Between the creation of the process evaluating the goal $m(t)$ and stating the resumption request to collect the answers to $m(t)$, the invoking process can perform any action whatsoever.

Below we have depicted the steps that are taken in evaluating a goal such as the one above.

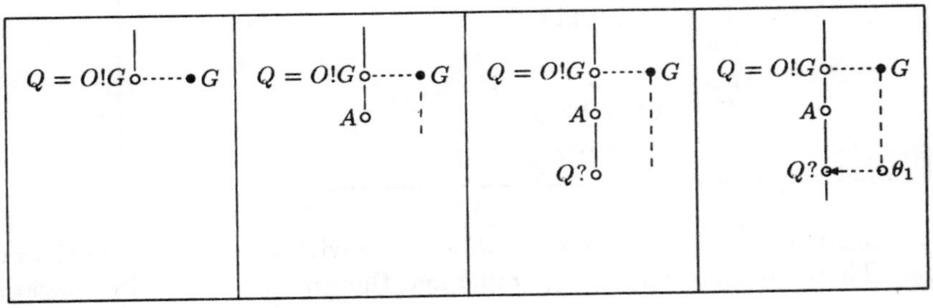

When the call $Q = O!G$ is accepted, a process for evaluating G is created. The caller may proceed with the evaluation of A, whereafter it must wait for an answer for G. The resumption goal $Q?$ succeeds when the answer is received.

The asynchronous rendez-vous preserves completeness in coupling the solutions produced by evaluating $m(t)$ with the bindings resulting from the evaluation of G. When backtracking occurs each alternative binding resulting from the evaluation of G must be coupled with all possible solutions of $m(t)$. However, if $m(t)$ has infinitely many solutions, G will never be tried for producing alternative bindings.

And parallelism The decomposition of the rendez-vous allows to define and-parallelism in a rather straightforward way, as

```
A&B :-  Q = self!B, A, Q?.
```

where *self* refers to the object evaluating the goal *A&B*. Such goals may however occur only in passive objects, since only passive objects allow internal concurrency.

An advantage of this approach is that the programmer may restrict the cases where parallel evaluation occurs by imposing extra conditions (cf. [DeGroot, 1984]) as in

```
A&B :-  ground(B),!, Q = self!B, A, Q?.
A&B :-  A, B.
```

where splitting of a new process is allowed only when B is ground. Note that the cut in the first clause is used to avoid unwanted backtracking over the second solution of A&B.

Example A typical example of the use of this kind of parallelism is the following, familiar, quicksort program.

qsort

```
qsort([],[]).
qsort([X|T],S) :-
  split(X,T,L1,L2),
  ( qsort(L1,S1) & qsort(L2,S2) ),
  append(S1,[X|S2],S).

split(X,[],[],[]).
split(X,[Y|T],[Y|L1],L2) :-
      X > Y,!,
      split(X,T,L1,L2).
split(X,[Y|T],L1,[Y|L2]) :-
      split(X,T,L1,L2).
```

Each non-empty list is divided into two sublists, one with values less than the values in the other. These are then sorted in parallel and the sorted sublists are concatenated.

3.7 Allocation of objects and processes

In the examples given, no attention has been paid to the issue of allocating (instances of) objects and the actual distribution of computation over the available resources.

When a new instance of an object is created, it can be allocated to a particular processor node by a statement of the form

- $O = new(obj@N)$

where N is a so-called *node expression* denoting a particular processor node and *obj* is either the name of an object or a constructor, that is an object name with arguments.

In addition it is possible to split off a process to evaluate a goal on a particular node by the statement $G@N$ where G is a goal and N is a node number. The meaning of a goal $G@N$ is given by the clause

```
G@N :-  O = new(self@N), Q = O!G, Q?.
```

Such a goal may be used only for passive objects.

Node expressions refer to a processor of the parallel machine on which the system runs. The parallel machine for which our system is intended is assumed to have a limited number of processor nodes that are connected with each other by a communication network. The programmer can refer to each of n processors by its number, $0, ..., n-1$. To permit a more refined strategy of allocating processes and resources, *node expressions* may be used, from which a processor number can be calculated. Apart from viewing the network as a linear sequence of processors, the programmer may regard the configuration as an (imaginary) tree, or as a grid of processors.

Tree organization A node expression of the form

$$I_0 : I_1 : ... : I_n$$

denotes, with the branching degree (by default) fixed to two, the processor associated with the node in the tree reached by following the path $I_1, ..., I_n$ from I_0. The association of processor numbers with nodes of the tree is done by counting the nodes of tree breadth first. For example the expression $0 : 1 : 2 : 1$. giving the path $1, 2, 1$ from 0, gives the processor number 9.

As an example of how such node expressions can be used to distribute the computation load over the available processors, consider the following variant of the quicksort program presented earlier.

qsort

```
qsort(L,R) :-   qsort(0,L,R).
qsort(N,[],[]).
qsort(N,[X|T],S) :-
  split(X,T,L1,L2),
  ( sort(N:1,L1,S1)@N:1 & sort(N:2,L2,S2)@N:2 ),
  append(S1,[X|S2],S).
```

When splitting off two processes for sorting the sublists, the processes are allocated on the successor nodes of the current node, as long as sufficient processors are available. More refined strategies may be encoded by including tests on the length of the lists.

Matrix organization The processor topology may also be viewed as a matrix with certain dimensions (say a square array of dimension 4 for 16 processors). The programmer can index this matrix by expressions of the form

$$N_1 \# N_2$$

which allows the distribution of the load over the available processors by moving, for instance, north from $N_1 \# N_2$ to $N_1 \# N_2 + 1$, over the matrix. Abbreviations such as *north*, *west* and so on are provided to facilitate these kinds of turtle movements over the matrix of processors. Cf. [Shapiro, 1984].

3.8 The language DLP

The constructs that we have explored in previous sections are part of the language DLP, a language for distributed logic programming, that has been the result of the research reported in this book. In this section we provide an overview of the language DLP. In the next section we will isolate the subsets of DLP chosen for studying the semantics of the language.

3.8.1 Declarations

A DLP program consists of a number of object declarations. The clauses occurring in the object declarations may contain special statements for updating non-logical (instance) variables, for creating objects and for communicating with other objects.

An object declaration is of the form

```
object name {
use objects.
var variables.

clauses
}
```

Among the clauses may be *constructor* clauses, that enable to create active instances of an object. The clauses of an object act as methods, in that they have exclusive access to the non-logical variables of an object. Clauses are ordinary Prolog clauses, except for the possible occurrence of *special forms* by which DLP extends Prolog.

Inheritance of the non-logical variables of objects is achieved by including the declaration

```
isa objects
```

in the object declaration. The declared object then contains a copy of all the non-logical variables of the objects mentioned in the *isa* list.

Clauses are inherited from objects by including the declaration

```
use objects
```

The declared object then adds the clauses of the objects mentioned in the *use* list to its own clauses.

A declaration of the form

```
object a:b { ... }
```

must be read as

```
object a {
isa b.
use b.
...
}
```

Inheritance is static. It is effected before an object starts to evaluate a goal. In other words, there is no interaction between objects, except on the occasion of an explicit communication.[7]

3.8.2 Statements

The core of DLP consists of the special forms

- $v := t$ — to assign (the value of) the term t to the non-logical variable v
- $O = new(c(t))$ — to create an active instance of the object c
- $O!m(t)$ — to call the method $m(t)$ for the object O

[7]See chapter 4 for a more precise characterization of inheritance, and the resolution of possible name conflicts.

- $accept(m_1, ..., m_n)$ — to state the willingness to accept methods $m_1, ..., m_n$

These are the extensions that play a prominent role in part II, treating the semantics of DLP. Moreover, the constructs listed above are sufficient to solve most of the knowledge representation problems presented in chapter 4.

Channels In addition, however, we have special forms that allow to communicate over channels.

- $C = new(channel)$ — to create a new channel
- $C!t$ — to put output term t on channel C
- $C?t$ — to put t as an input term on channel C

Conditional acceptance Apart from the regular accept statement we have introduced a generalized accept statement, that may contain *conditional accept expressions* of the form

- $method : guard \rightarrow goal$

that result in the *goal* being evaluated, if the *method* template matches the call and moreover the *guard* holds. (Cf. section 3.5)

Process creation and resumptions For those wishing to squeeze out the last drop of parallelism we have included the primitives

- $Q = O!G$ — to create a process to evaluate G
- $Q?$ — to ask for the results of process Q

These are the primitives that have been used to implement the synchronous rendezvous as

```
O!G :-  Q = O!G, Q?.
```

Allocation Lastly, since effective parallelism requires some strategy of allocating resources we have provided *node-expressions* that can be used to allocate an object or a process, evaluating a goal. The special forms

- $O = new(obj@N)$
- $G@N$

where *obj* is either an object name or a constructor, respectively allocate an object or a goal at the processor node denoted by N.

Remarks Since we have striven for full compatibility with Prolog, we have retained the backtracking behavior to the extent possible. We support both *local* backtracking, that occurs within the confines of a process, and *global* (or *distributed*) backtracking in which multiple processes are involved.

We have made a distinction between *active* objects, which have own activity that must explicitly be interrupted to answer method calls; and *passive* objects that may answer a method any time. Active objects are allowed to have a limited amount of internal concurrency, in that multiple processes may be active backtracking over the results of a method call. Passive objects, on the other hand, display full internal concurrency. Method calls may be evaluated concurrently. Providing the needed protection is in this case the duty of the programmer.

3.9 DLP as a family of languages

For studying the semantic aspects of the language, it has appeared profitable to isolate a number of subsets of DLP. Due to the static nature of the inheritance mechanism we may ignore inheritance. For all the sub-languages DLP_0 - DLP_2 (see below) we have provided both an operational and a denotational (continuation) semantics in chapter 8. We have not included a semantic characterization of conditional acceptance since, despite the elegance of the construct, this seems rather complex. Features such as allocation are omitted since they are simply not interesting from a semantic point of view. Neither have we included a treatment of the cut, nor a treatment of assert and retract statements. The reader not interested in semantic issues is advised to jump to the next chapter.

Backtracking and non-logical variables. We consider DLP_0 to be the base language of DLP. It extends Prolog (without cut) with a construct to assign values to non-logical variables.

DLP_0 = *Prolog + non-logical variables*		
non-logical variables	$v := t$	assigns the term t to the non-logical variable v

Moreover, in unification goals of the form $t_1 = t_2$, and in the right hand side of assignments, non-logical variables are replaced by their values and arithmetical expressions are simplified.

Communication over channels. The sub-language DLP_1 extends DLP_0 by a construct to create active instances of objects. Also, communication over channels is introduced.

$DLP_1 = DLP_0 + communication\ over\ channels$		
object creation	$new(c(t))$	creates an object executing $c(t)$
channels	$C = new(channel)$	creates a new channel
	$C!t$	output statement for term t over channel C
	$C?t$	input statement for term t over channel C

Communication over channels is relatively simple, since the backtracking that occurs during a communication is a local phenomenon, restricted to the process at the input side of the channel.

Communication by rendez-vous. Our next extension is called DLP_2. It extends DLP_0 by constructs for synchronizing on method calls.

$DLP_2 = DLP_0 + communication\ by\ rendez\text{-}vous$		
object creation	$O = new(c(t))$	creates an active instance of object c
rendez-vous	$Q :: O!m(t)$	asynchronous call of the method $m(t)$ for object O
	$Q?$	to request the resumption from process Q
	$accept(m_1, ..., m_n)$	states the willingness to accept the methods $m_1, ..., m_n$

As a restriction for DLP_2, which does not hold for DLP, we require that accept statements occur only in constructor processes.

We have given an operational semantics of DLP_2 in chapter 7. The backtracking that may occur during a rendez-vous is global. We speak of global or distributed backtracking, since the process calling the method may force the answering process to backtrack over any remaining answers.

4

Object oriented modeling and distributed problem solving

- It seemed easy when I thought of it... Not words. An act.
I won't write anymore. -
Cesar Pavese, *This Business of Living*

The language DLP introduced in the previous chapter is meant as a vehicle for the specification and implementation of distributed knowledge based systems. As an illustration of such an application, the specification and implementation of a distributed medical expert system will be described in section 4.4. Traditional problems encountered in software engineering, such as modularization and the distribution of control, reoccur when implementing knowledge based systems. Solving these problems becomes increasingly urgent when introducing parallelism in order to distribute the problem solving activity among distinct computing agents.

In this chapter examples will be given that illustrate how DLP may be applied to object oriented modeling and distributed problem solving. An important contribution of the object oriented approach to programming has been the use of inheritance for defining the behavior of objects in an incremental way. As an example of the use of inheritance it will be shown how to factor out control in searching a state space. Factoring out control is also achieved by regarding the state space as an object that is given as a parameter to the search procedure. Further, an object oriented solution to the N-queens problem will be presented, where each queen is modeled as an active object busy satisfying the constraints imposed by the problem. Inheritance also provides a convenient mechanism for representing the knowledge contained by an object, in terms of its relation to other objects. It will be shown how inheritance is used to create objects that may be considered as a specialization of the inherited object. Further, examples will be given that illustrate how inheritance may be effected dynamically by delegating messages, and how inheritance may affect the backtracking behavior of an object.

The specification and implementation of the distributed medical expert system illustrates that the object oriented paradigm provides a natural means of distributing the problem solving tasks following the hierarchical representation of the knowledge.

4.1 Factoring out control in searching a state space

The problem of the farmer, the wolf, the goat and the cabbage discussed in section 2.1.4.2 presented an example of searching in a state space.

Abstractly, a search problem can be specified by the predicates

$$move(Current, Next)$$
$$goal(State)$$

defining, respectively, the transitions from a state to its successor states and a goal state. More than one goal state may be given. In addition, an initial state s_0 must be specified from which the search is started.

A solution of a search problem is a sequence of states $s_1, ..., s_k$ such that s_1 is the initial state equal to s_0 and s_k is a goal state, for which $goal(s_k)$ holds. Moreover, for $i = 1, ..., k$, the state s_{i+1} must be a successor state of s_i, that is $move(s_i, s_{i+1})$ must hold. Variants of this scheme may be devised by specifying for each transition a cost which allows to search a path of minimal cost, or by specifying for each state a value which allows to search heuristically, by choosing the highest valued state as a successor to a given state.

Regarding a particular state space as an object defining both the predicates *move* and *goal*, control with respect to searching the state space can be factored out using inheritance or by making the state space a parameter of the search procedure.

Inheritance An example search procedure is defined in the object *search* below.

search

```
object search {
search(Node,Node) :-  goal(Node).
search(Node, Sol) :-
          move(Node,Next),
          search(Next,Sol).
}
```

As a solution only the goal state is delivered, when reached. The second clause of the predicate *search* specifies that each successor of the given state is tried for reaching a solution. The albeit trivial maze defined below inherits the search procedure by using the object *search* as a base class.

maze

```
object maze : search {
link(a,b).
link(b,c).
link(b,d).
link(d,e).
move(X,Y) :-   link(X,Y).
goal(e).
}
```

The maze can now directly be asked to search for a solution starting from the initial state *a* as in the goal

```
?- maze!search(a,S).
```

Evaluating this goal will result in binding the variable S to the goal state e.

The simple search procedure specified above can be used to search for a solution to the *8-queens problem* by defining the transition between states as the addition of a non-attacking queen to a (possibly empty) list of queens.

8-queens

```
object queens : search {
move(S,[Q|S]) :-   legal(Q), noattack(Q,S).
legal(pos(X,Y)) :-
        member(X,[1,2,3,4,5,6,7,8]),
        member(Y,[1,2,3,4,5,6,7,8]).
noattack(_,[]).
noattack(pos(X,Y),[pos(A,B) | L]) :-
        X ≠ A,
        Y ≠ B,
        X-A ≠ B-Y,
        X-A ≠ Y-B,
        noattack(pos(X,Y),L).
goal([X1,X2,X3,X4,X5,X6,X7,X8]).
}
```

The clause representing the goal state enforces that there must be eight queens in the final list, none of which attack any of the other queens.

The goal

```
?- queens!search([],S).
```

will result in the desired outcome.

Parametrization The simple search procedure specified above sufficed for the examples given because in both examples the search space contained no cycles. For a search space containing cycles, such as the maze defined below, we have to use a different search procedure, for example the depth-first search procedure used in solving the problem of the farmer, the wolf, the goat and the cabbage.

maze

```
object maze {
link(a,b).
link(b,c).
link(c,a).
link(c,d).
link(d,e).
move(X,Y) :-  link(X,Y).
move(X,Y) :-  link(Y,X).
goal(e).
}
```

The object *dfs* specifies a search procedure that has the state space as an extra parameter. As an object, the state space is known to have the methods *goal* and *move* defining the characteristics of the state space. The depth-first search procedure defined in *dfs* has a built-in check for cycles.

dfs

```
object dfs {
dfs(Space, C, P, [C|P]) :-  Space!goal(C).
dfs(Space, Current, Path, Sol ) :-
            Space!move(Current,Next),
            not( member(Next, Path) ),
            dfs(Space, Next, [Current|Path], Sol ).
search(Space, Start, Sol) :-  dfs(Space, Start, [],
    Sol).
}
```

We may now search the maze by stating the goal

```
?- dfs!search(maze,a,S).
```

The check for cycles prevents us from infinitely recurring in already visited states.

These examples demonstrate how a variety of search procedures may be used, dependent on the needs imposed by the characteristics of the search space. Examples of such search procedures are, apart from depth-first search, for instance breadth-first search and best-first search. The reader is referred to [Bratko, 1990] for a more detailed exposition of search procedures.

4.2 An object oriented solution to the N-queens problem

The example presented in this section is a case study in object oriented programming taken from [Budd, 1991]. The essence of this particular solution to the queens problem is that each queen is made an object endowed with the power to discover a solution in cooperation with the other queens. The definition of the object *queen* is given in figure 4.1.

To establish the functionality of a queen, we may observe that each queen must know about its position on the board, and hence must have non-logical instance variables *row* and *column* to record its positions. Since in no solution can any queen be in the same column as another queen, each queen is initially assigned a unique column number. Recall that in our previous solutions to the 8-queens problem a solution was found for n queens by extending a solution for $n - 1$ queens with a queen not attacking any of the queens already found. The empty list gave a trivial solution for n is zero and the list was extended until it contained eight mutually non-attacking queens. The principle of extending a solution for a smaller number of queens is reflected in the pattern of communication between the queens. Each queen, except the one positioned in the first column, needs to be able to ask the queen in its left neighboring column to provide a solution that it may extend. The queen in the left-most column simply responds to requests to position itself on a row or try another row. The data maintained by each queen are hence its *row* index, which may change in the process of finding a solution, its *column* index which is fixed when creating the queen, and a pointer to its neighbor, which has the constant *nil* as its value if the queen is the left-most queen (in column 1).

An acceptable position for a particular column n is a configuration of column 1 to n in which no queen can attack any other queen in those columns. The methods that a queen must have in order to support the *generate-and-test* procedure are the methods *first* to initialize the row and to find an acceptable solution for itself and its left neighbors, the method *next* to advance a row (modulo the number of queens) and find the next acceptable solution, and the method *can_attack* that is used to test whether the queen itself or any of its left neighbors can attack a position. Both the methods *first* and *next* make use of the predicate *test_or_advance*, which tests whether the queen can be attacked by any of its left neighbors and advances to the next row if this is the case.

A solution to the N-queens problem, for N is 4, will be printed by stating the goal

```
?-
        N = 4,
        Q1 = new(queen(N,1,nil)),
        Q2 = new(queen(N,2,Q1)),
        Q3 = new(queen(N,3,Q2)),
        Q4 = new(queen(N,4,Q3)),
        Q4!first(),
        Q4!print().
```

Calling the method *print* results in printing the positions of the queen and its neighbors.

Figure 4.1: *An object oriented solution to the N-queens problem*

queen

```
object queen {
var max, row, column, neighbor.
queen(N,C,Qn) :-
        max := N,
        row := 1,
        column := C,
        neighbor := Qn,
        run.
run :- accept(any), run.
first() :-
        ( neighbor ≠ nil → neighbor!first(); true),
        test_or_advance().
next() :-
        write(next_try(row,column)),
        (row == max →
                (neighbor ≠ nil → neighbor!next(); true);
                true),
        row := (row // max) + 1,
        test_or_advance().
can_attack(R,C) :-
        Cd = C- column,
        (
        row == R → true;
        row + Cd == R → true;
        row- Cd == R → true;
        neighbor ≠ nil → neighbor!can_attack(R,C)
        ).
test_or_advance() :-
        neighbor ≠ nil →
                ( neighbor!can_attack(row,column) → next() );
                true.
print() :-
        write(position(row,column)),
        (neighbor ≠ nil → neighbor!print(); true).
}
```

Each queen checks whether it occupies a legal position with respect to its neighbor. The last queen in the row does not have a neighbor as is indicated by the constant []. *The expression* row // max *delivers* row *modulo* max, *where* max *is the instance variable recording the maximum row number.*

4.3 Knowledge representation and inheritance

Inheritance provides a powerful means to organize a collection of objects. It may be used either to provide a conceptual model of the relations between the various objects that play a role in the system, as a mechanism to factorize code (as in the example showing how to factor out search control) or as a method of a stepwise refinement of object specifications. Cf. [Thomsen, 1987].

Static inheritance Inheritance may occur in a number of guises. Most simply, inheritance may be viewed as code-sharing. For the inheriting object, extra code must be specified such that the object in some sense specializes the inherited object. In a typed setting we would be tempted to speak of the inheriting object as belonging to a subtype of the type of the inherited object. However, in [America, 1987a] it is adequately observed that subtyping is a far more abstract notion, that encompasses inheritance by code-sharing.

Dynamic inheritance A rather different form of inheritance, found for instance in Actor languages [Agha, 1986], is achieved by delegating messages to the inherited objects, whenever the inheriting object does not provide any specific functionality for dealing with a method call. In contrast to code-sharing, inheritance by delegation is dynamic. See also [Ungar and Smith, 1987].

Inheritance in DLP is static. Objects in DLP may inherit non-logical variables from other objects as well as clauses, by code sharing. With respect to the clauses of an object, inheritance in DLP must be regarded as a mechanism to extend a logical theory. Semantically, extending a theory results in a more precisely defined model. Operationally, it allows to derive more goals – namely all the statements made true by the *combined* set of clauses.

In this section we will give a more precise description of the inheritance mechanism offered by DLP. We will discuss multiple inheritance, what to do with name clashes, and we will explain the difference between overriding already defined clauses and adding clauses to allow (more) backtracking. As an example of the use of inheritance to specialize a given object, a semaphore will be characterized as a special kind of counter, extending the functionality of a counter with the behavioral characteristics of a semaphore. Next, an example will be given illustrating how to deal with self-reference when delegating messages to other objects. Finally, we will give an example to illustrate how inheritance may be used to add knowledge to an existing object by extending the definition of a predicate.

4.3.1 Inheritance in DLP

In section 3.1.2 we have introduced the notation

```
object a:b { ... }
```

for indicating that object *a* inherits both the non-logical variables and the clauses of object *b*. Inheritance is static, in that the non-logical variables and the clauses of the inherited objects are just added to those of the inheriting object.

Multiple inheritance is allowed. We may put

```
object a:(b,c) { ... }
```

to effect that object a inherits both b and c. Moreover inheritance is recursively applied, in that also objects inherited by inherited objects are inherited. Cycles in the inheritance graph may occur. Nevertheless, each object is inherited only once, since it is checked whether it has already been inherited. We say that an object occurs earlier than another object in the inheritance list, if in applying inheritance recursively (depth first, in left to right order) it is dealt with before the other object. For dealing with cycles and possible clashes it is convenient to assume that the inheriting object itself occurs as the first object in the inheritance list. As an example, the declaration

```
object a:(b,c) { ... }
object b:(d,a) { ... }
object d:e { ... }
```

results in the list $a \cdot b \cdot d \cdot e \cdot c$ as the inheritance list for a, the list $b \cdot d \cdot e \cdot a$ for b and $d \cdot e$ for d.

Clashes may occur, when using such a copying method for inheritance, between non-logical variables with the same name, and between clauses defining a similar predicate.

Clashing non-logical variables are treated in a very simple-minded way. When encountering multiple non-logical variables with the same name, and possibly different initializations, the one belonging to the object occurring first in the inheritance list is chosen. Since the inheriting object is considered to occur as the first object in the inheritance list the initializing expressions for variables defined for the object itself take precedence over other initializations.

Overriding versus backtracking For clauses that define a similar predicate, occurring in different objects, there is the choice between inheriting them in an overriding fashion (by overwriting them) or to allow backtracking over all clauses occurring in objects in the inheritance list.

Overwriting clauses implies that whenever a clause from the inheriting object succeeds, no clause of the inherited objects is tried for solving the (sub)goal. Since DLP is intended for knowledge based applications the clauses of the inherited objects are added to the clauses defined for the object itself, in the order in which the inherited objects occur in the inheritance list (see also section 12.2).

4.3.2 Specialization by inheritance

An object may specialize another object by inheriting its code, and adding some specific functionality.

We may now define a semaphore, as respectively a specialization of a number and a counter, by declaring *semaphore*

```
object number {
var n = 0.
put(N) :-  n :=  N.
value(N) :-  N = n.
}
object counter : number {
inc() :-  n :=  n + 1.
dec() :-  n :=  n- 1.
}
object semaphore : counter {
semaphore(N)  :-  put(N), run.
p() :-  dec().
v() :-  inc().
run :-
        value(N),
        ( N == 0 →  accept(v); accept(p,v) ),
        run.
}
```

Hence a *semaphore* is a kind of *counter*, which itself is a kind of *number*. In this, somewhat artificial example, the only active object is a semaphore, active in the sense that it contains a constructor clause. The non-logical variable n is inherited from the object *number*, via the object *counter* which provides the methods for incrementing or decrementing n.

Conceptually, when creating an instance of *semaphore*, an object is created that contains n as a local non-logical variable and as clauses all clauses occurring in the objects involved. As a consequence, when calling the constructor for *semaphore*, the non-logical variable of the newly created object is assigned a value by the call to *put*.

4.3.3 Message delegation and self-reference

Extensive research has been invested in using Horn clause logic for querying and updating a database. Partly this research has been motivated by the flexibility of Horn clause logic for defining virtual attributes, the values of which are not given by actual data items but must be computed from the information stored. A somewhat radical extrapolation of these attempts is represented by approaches using objects to store information and to guide the retrieval. Such retrieval may partly take place by evaluating clauses. Cf. [Houtsma and Balsters, 1988].

As an example of an object oriented approach, to (for instance) modeling the hierarchical organization of a firm, consider the following program fragment, telling us that an employee has a manager, and that in his turn a manager is an employee.

firm

```
object employee {
var manager.
employee(M) :-  manager := M, run.
run :-  accept(any), run.
request(S,A) :-  manager!approve(S,A).
}
object manager : employee {
manager(M) :-  employee(M).
approve(S,approved) :-  unimportant(S).
approve(S,rejected) :-  unreasonable(S).
unimportant(domestic_trip).
unimportant(presentation).
unreasonable(double_salary).
}
```

For an employee to undertake any action he/she must request his/her manager for approval. This is implemented by asking the manager stored in the non-logical variable of the employee to approve of that particular action. Since the manager is an employee, he himself may have to ask for approval of his manager. Chaining upwards in the hierarchy a manager must exist that has no obligation to ask for approval. This manager may be created with *self* as an argument for the constructor, which makes asking for approval a local affair, depending on what the top manager himself considers reasonable and important. The goal

```
:-
  M = new(manager(self)),
  E = new(employee(M)),
  E ! request(domestic_trip, A).
```

provides an example of creating a one-level hierarchy.

4.3.4 Inheritance and backtracking

Applying inheritance in integrating *data* and *knowledge* may require that knowledge is used in an additive fashion. In other words, the pieces contained in the individual objects may all contribute to the solution. We have adapted the example given in [Houtsma and Balsters, 1988] to illustrate the need for using all knowledge available.

For convenience, we introduce an abbreviation for accessing the value of the non-logical variables of a particular object. We use the expression

- *O@name*

to stand for the value of the non-logical *name* of the object *O*.

The idea of the example is that there are two kinds of researchers: associates and professors. They have similar interests, in that they both know of a number of topics.

A researcher has a name and works in some field, that is given as a list of topics. A researcher knows of a topic whenever he has visited a conference that somehow concerns the topic. Naturally, a researcher knows all of his field.[1]

researcher

```
object researcher : environment {
var name, field.

researcher(N,F) :-
        name := N,
        field := F,
        work().

work() :- accept(any), work().

knowsof(Topic) :- member(Topic,field).

knowsof(Topic) :-
            visitor(name, Conference),
            Conference ! concerns(Topic).

}
```

The constructor for *researcher* stores the name of the fellow and his *field* of interest, and then calls for *work*() that is interrupted only to answer what he knows of. A researcher inherits a number of things from an *environment*. For instance, whether a researcher is a *visitor* at a conference is assumed to be known by its environment.

An associate is a researcher that works under a professor. Apart from what he knows of as a researcher he is also assumed to know of everything his professor knows of.

associate

```
object associate : researcher {

var prof.

associate(N,F,P) :-
        prof := P,
        researcher(N,F).
associate(R,P) :-
        prof := P,
        researcher(R@name, R@field).

knowsof(Topic) :- prof ! knowsof(Topic).

}
```

In case a new associate already is a researcher of some unidentified kind his non-logical variables of interest may simply be copied, as expressed in the second clause

[1] We assume that both *member* and *append* are available as system predicates.

for *associate*.[2] The other constructor explicitly takes his name and field of interest.

A professor is a researcher and apart from what he knows of as a researcher he also knows of the topics of all conferences for which he is a member of the program committee.

professor

```
object professor : researcher {
professor(R) :-  researcher(R@name, R@field).
professor(N,F) :-  researcher(N,F).
knowsof(Topic) :-
      committee( name, Conference),
      Conference ! concerns(Topic).
}
```

Similarly as for an associate, two constructors are provided to be able to cope with his past. In the clause for *knowsof*, the non-logical variable *name* comes from being a *researcher*. Being a researcher, a professor inherits the *environment* declared for researchers. Whether a professor is a member of a program committee must be known by the environment.

Next we define a conference, for instance one concerning parallel processing.

conference

```
object parallel_processing_conference {
var topics = [ computers , concurrency ].
concerns(Topic) :-   member(Topic, topics).
}
```

And all that remains to be done is to declare in what *environment* our actors live. We assume that an environment is just a collection of facts by which, among other things, it may be established that one is a member of a program committee or a visitor of a conference.

environment

```
object environment {
var conferences = [ parallel_processing_conference ].
committee(knuth, parallel_processing_conference ).
committee(turing, parallel_processing_conference ).
visitor(newman, parallel_processing_conference ).
visitor(overbeek, parallel_processing_conference ).
}
```

[2] Since inheritance is static we cannot take the object itself. Instead we must copy its contents. The resulting *associate* object is an object that contains both the non-logical variable *prof* and the non-logical variables of the *researcher* object.

The bag of topics associate *newman* knows of is delivered by evaluating the goal

```
?- P = new( professor( turing, [computing] ) ),
   A = new( associate( newman, [engineering], P )),
   A !bagof(X, knowsof(X), Topics).
```

As a remark, we may ask an associate for all topics he or she knows of, since being a researcher he or she is willing to accept anything that interrupts the work.

4.4 The specification and implementation of a distributed medical expert system

Designing an object oriented system involves modeling the problem domain by using objects. For many objects in the system there will indeed be an observable entity in the problem domain whose functionality is reflected in the object. But, in order to be able to design a working system, it will be unavoidable to introduce objects that can only be considered the counterpart of some inferred entities in the problem domain, entities that must be assumed to exist in order to explain some phenomenon or functional behavior. When designing a system, it is important to be able to separate those two kinds of objects, since our assumptions with regard to such behavior may change.

In modeling medical diagnosis, an example of the introduction of such artificial objects is provided by the objects implementing the reasoning capability of the diagnosticians. It seems valid to assume that a doctor comes to a conclusion concerning a certain disease by applying *knowledge* to *facts*. The assumptions with respect to how this takes place are embodied in the reasoning component that consists of the objects *infer* and *facts*. The *knowledge* that is needed to make inferences on the other hand is assumed to belong to the area of medical practice itself. The reasoning component, nevertheless, is dependent on the format of the knowledge.

An expert system may be characterized as a system having the capability of a human expert. A medical expert system has medical expertise. In the design of our (toy) medical expert system a distinction is made between the reasoning component and a component modeling the behavior of the various actors and entities in medical practice. The medical knowledge presented here is purely fictional. The knowledge we do have of this area comes from [Lucas, 1986].

4.4.1 The reasoning component

The reasoning component of a traditional expert system consists of two parts: a store of *facts* that, in the case of medical diagnosis, initially contains the observed symptoms and a so-called *inference engine* that deduces new facts by using knowledge rules embodying the expertise. See [Hayes-Roth, 1985], [Lucas, 1986].

Knowledge rules of the form

$$conditions \longrightarrow conclusion$$

are used by the system to add new facts when the given facts satisfy the conditions of the rule. The strategy by which new facts are derived may be characterized as *backward reasoning.* It proceeds by taking the conclusion of a rule, for example as a possible diagnosis, and checking the conditions of the rule. A condition is satisfied when it is either a fact, or it may be derived as a fact by applying some of the other rules.

Facts Facts are stored in the object declared below.

facts

```
object facts {
var data=[].
facts(D) :-  data := D, run.
run :-  accept(holds, add), run.
holds(X) :-  member(X,data).
add(X) :-
        append([X],data,R),
        data := R.
}
```

The object *facts* has a non-logical variable *data* containing an initially empty list of facts. When creating an active instance of *facts* the instance variable *data* is initialized to the given facts. The object may then be asked whether a particular fact holds, or it may be asked to add a new fact.

Inference engine The inference engine operates on a collection of facts, by applying knowledge contained in rules. A derivation is successful if the item that must be derived either holds as a fact or is derivable by recursively applying a knowledge rule.

infer

```
object infer {
var knowledge, facts.
derive(H) :-  facts!holds(H),!.
derive(H) :-
        knowledge!rule(P,H),
        test(P),
        facts!add(H).
test([]).
test([X|R]) :
        derive(X),
        test(R).
}
```

The object *infer* as presented is of an abstract nature. It has the non-logical variables *knowledge* and *facts* to store respectively knowledge and facts. However, these variables can only be given a value by an object inheriting the capabilities of *infer*.

4.4.2 Modeling medical practice

The actors (or in the terminology of [Booch, 1986], the agents) that play a role in our conception of medical practice are *doctors*, having general knowledge of diseases, and *specialists*, having knowledge of special diseases. We also have a *clinic* to assign doctors and specialists to patients for consultation.

Our medical knowledge is structured as an inheritance tree. At the top of this tree we find the most general knowledge concerning diseases. This knowledge is refined for specific diseases going down the tree. Cf. [Gomez and Chandrasekaran, 1981].

Doctor A *doctor* inherits the reasoning capacity needed to derive a diagnosis from the object *infer*. In other words, a doctor is a straightforward modification of an inference engine. Cf. [Wegner and Zdonik, 1988]. A doctor possesses knowledge about diseases as represented by the object *disease* described below. This knowledge is also used to suggest the possible diagnoses the doctor will look for.

doctor

```
object doctor : infer {

doctor() :-
        knowledge := disease,
        accept(diagnosis),
        doctor().

diagnosis(F,D) :-
        facts := F,
        member(D,knowledge@diagnoses),
        derive(D).
}
```

Before being able to accept the request for a diagnosis, the non-logical variable *knowledge*, inherited from *infer*, must be initialized to *disease*. The non-logical variable *facts* is updated when starting to search for a diagnosis. All possible diagnoses a doctor knows of will be tried.

Disease An object oriented modeling technique has also been applied in the hierarchical representation of knowledge about diseases. Our knowledge of diseases is structured as an inheritance tree. At the root of the tree we have the object *disease*, that represents the most general knowledge of diseases.

This knowledge is laid down in rules that enable to assess whether a patient has the symptoms of someone who is ill.

disease

```
object disease {
var diagnoses = [disease],
    causes = [liver,lungs].
rule([high_temperature],fever).
rule([fever],disease).
}
```

Note that *disease* is both a constant, indicating a diagnosis, and an object, representing domain knowledge. Apart from the rules that contain the knowledge needed to establish a diagnosis, the object contains also a list of possible *diagnoses*, which for the generic case simply states that a patient may have a disease. These diagnoses function as hypotheses when searching for the actual diagnosis. The rules inform us that a patient has a disease if he has fever, that is a high temperature.

In addition, the knowledge concerning a disease contains an indication of its possible *causes*. Such knowledge is included to allow specialists to give advice about the further examinations.

Other diseases are specializations of the generic object *disease*. The objects representing specific diseases share by inheritance the more general knowledge. This knowledge is, for each disease, augmented with a number of rules embodying the specific knowledge concerning that disease. Each specific disease contains also a list of possible diagnoses in order to direct the search for a diagnosis. This list overwrites the list of diagnoses pertaining to the more general case.

As an example of refining the generic object disease to a particular case consider the declaration for a liver disease.

liver

```
object liver : disease {
var diagnoses = [liver_disease],
    causes = [intrahepatic, extrahepatic].
rule([disease,yellow_skin],liver_disease).
}
```

Notice that, in accordance with our discussion of inheritance, the values of the variables *diagnoses* and *causes* are determined by the object containing the knowledge of a liver disease.

Before going to a specialist, let us see what a doctor can do.

```
?-
    F = new(facts([high_temperature,yellow_skin])),
    M = new(doctor()),
    M!diagnosis(F,D).
```

The diagnosis delivered will be *disease*, since the doctor is not assumed to know anything about liver diseases. The patient needs a (liver disease) specialist for a more refined diagnosis.

Before continuing we enlarge our body of knowledge.

lungs

```
object lungs : disease {
var diagnoses = [tuberculosis, asthma],
    causes = [].
rule([coughing,bleeding],tuberculosis).
rule([coughing,red_eyes],asthma).
}
```

The knowledge added contains some fictional rules concerning lung diseases. A lung disease allows for two possible diagnoses, which may give rise to backtracking during the consultation. Also we add some knowledge refining the knowledge about liver diseases.

hepatic

```
object intrahepatic : liver {
var diagnoses = [intrahepatic],
    causes = [].
rule([liver_disease,sweating],intrahepatic).
}


object extrahepatic : liver {
var diagnoses = [extrahepatic],
    causes = [].
rule([liver_disease,bleeding],extrahepatic).
}
```

Neither for lung diseases nor for the intrahepatic and extrahepatic variants of liver diseases are any causes known.

Specialist The hierarchical structure of medical knowledge suggests to distribute the search for possible diagnoses over a number of specialists. In the practice of doctors, sending patients to specialists is a natural phenomenon. A ***specialist*** is a doctor having specific knowledge of a certain class of diseases. Apart from giving a diagnosis, a specialist also gives advice for further examination. This definition of a specialist enables to search, following the hierarchy of possible diseases, for the most specific diagnosis, taking the most general disease as a starting point.

specialist

```
object specialist : doctor {

specialist(K) :-
      knowledge := K,
      accept(diagnosis),
      accept(advice).

advice(A) :- A = knowledge@causes.
}
```

The non-logical variable *knowledge*, inherited from *infer* (by being a *doctor*), is assigned the object representing a particular class of diseases. The constructor for a *specialist* further enforces that advice may be asked for only if a diagnosis has been given.

Clinic The distributed nature of our diagnostic system comes to light in the definition of a *clinic*, that handles the distribution of tasks among the specialists. A clinic receives patients and assigns to each patient a doctor. This doctor is a specialist knowing all about diseases in general. When the specialist comes to the conclusion that the patient has a disease, he gives advice for further examinations.

The advice given by a specialist is used to consult other specialists, having more specific knowledge of the diseases listed in the advice. An examination results in listing all the diagnoses that apply to the case. The advice given by a specialist consists of a list of possible causes. For each possible cause a specialist is created to examine the patient. Exploring the possible causes may occur in parallel, as indicated by the use of the parallel *and*-operator introduced in the previous section. The specialists created to explore the possible causes of a disease may be allocated to some processor by using the allocation primitives mentioned in section 3.8.2. The result of exploring the possible causes is a possibly empty list of diagnoses.

clinic

```
object clinic {

case(C,D) :-
      F = new(facts(C)),
      examine(disease,F,D).

examine(K,F,[D|R]) :-
      M = new(specialist(K)),
      M!diagnosis(F,D),
      M!advice(A),
      explore(F,A,R).

examine(K,_,[]).

explore(F,[],[]).

explore(F,[K|T],[D|R]) :-
      examine(K,F,D) & explore(F,T,R).

}
```

Below I present the worst case that I can imagine.

```
?- clinic!case([high_temperature,yellow_skin,sweating,coughing,bleeding],D).
```

The reader is invited to compute the appropriate diagnoses by hand.

5

Design perspectives

- I have a commission for you... A literary matter. I know my limitations; the skill of rhymed malice, the arts of metrical slander, are quite beyond my powers, You understand. -
Salman Rushdie, *The Satanic Verses*

The primary motivation in developing DLP was to provide an environment suited for implementing distributed knowledge-based systems, such as expert systems and systems for distributed problem solving. Questions arising with respect to the design of a language that supports distributed knowledge processing are to what extent the language needs to be *declarative*, how *parallelism* is incorporated and what constructs are provided for the *representation of knowledge*.

Declarative languages It is widely recognized that, for modeling a domain of expertise or problem solving, preference should be given to a declarative language for knowledge representation. Cf. [Apt et al. 1987], [Wos et al, 1984]. Nevertheless, although we have clearly stated such a preference by taking Horn clause logic as a base language for DLP, it is our (strongly held) opinion that a mere declarative language does not provide sufficient means to control search and inference to the extent necessary for building systems with non-trivial functionality. Cf. [Hayes-Roth, 1985]. Partly, this control can be effected by relying on a standard way of evaluation, such as the left-to-right evaluation of Prolog goals, or by defining a strategy adequate for the problem at hand as described in [Wos et al, 1984]. A language such as Prolog, however, allows more drastic means for effecting control, notably by means of the cut and the *assert* and *retract* statements, the use of which is justifiably frowned upon by those taking a strictly declarative stand. See also [Bobrow, 1984], [Meltzer, 1982], [Rabin, 1974], [Goguen, 1984], [Padawitz, 1988].

Parallelism When thinking about parallelism the ideological gap between a pragmatic approach and what is theoretically justifiable inevitably seems to widen. Serious difficulty in exploiting the parallelism inherent in the computation model of logic programming languages has been caused by the need to restrict the number of processes created for evaluating a goal, and to avoid excessive communication between processes. Cf. [Conery, 1987]. Moreover, for reasons of synchronization several ad hoc solutions have been proposed, such as the *wait* statement in Parlog, and the annotated variable in Concurrent Prolog. Cf. [Ramakrishnan, 1986]. Rather than adhering to some established conception of concurrent logic programming (cf. [Ringwood, 1988]), we have decided to investigate what, to our mind, is needed for distributed problem solving, and more specifically for distributed logic programming. See also [van Emden and de Lucena Filho, 1982], [Fahlman, 1985], [Lusk and Overbeek, 1984], [Hasegawa and Amamiya, 1984], [van den Herik and Henseler, 1986], [Lipovski and Hermenegildo, 1985], [Monteiro, 1981], [Monteiro, 1984].

Knowledge representation With respect to issues of knowledge representation we have taken the stand that, although we wish to support a declarative language, we also wish to provide a programmer with sufficient means for programming a suitable solution, even if this would mean leaving the declarative realm. For efficiently exploiting parallelism, this seems unavoidable; for knowledge representation, although not unavoidable, the provision of non-declarative constructs inspired by the paradigm of object oriented programming simply means following a trend, that is giving in to the need expressed by programmers in the field of knowledge-based systems. Cf. [Ait-Kaci and Nasr, 1986], [Hynynen and Lassila, 1989], [King, 1989], [Tello, 1989], [Ohsuga and Yamauchi, 1985].

5.1 Distributed knowledge processing

To delineate the notion of distributed knowledge processing, let us look at a characterization of distributed programming languages:

> Distributed programming languages support computation by multiple autonomous processes that communicate by message passing rather than shared variables and may be implemented by geographically separated networks of communicating processes [Bal et al, 1989].

To arrive at a definition of distributed knowledge processing we have to refine the notion of computation into the notion of *reasoning*. Common parlance in the context of distributed knowledge processing, moreover, requires us to speak of *agents* instead of processes. We may thus characterize distributed knowledge processing languages as

> ... languages that support reasoning by multiple autonomous agents that communicate by message passing ...

From a software engineering perspective the issues that arise in developing a distributed knowledge-based system are no different than in developing any distributed system: the distribution of *data* and *control*. The distribution of data involves decisions concerning shared resources and protocols that enable a safe use of these resources. To properly distribute control requires partitioning of the reasoning process into appropriate subtasks that may be distributed over the agents participating in this process. Cf. [Butler and Karonis, 1988], [Fox, 1981], [Gomez and Chandrasekaran, 1981], [McArthur et al, 1982], [Smith and Davis, 1981].

5.1.1 Distributing data

In characterizing the architectural properties of knowledge based systems, and in particular expert systems, a distinction is usually made between a (static) knowledge part and a (dynamic) store of data. Cf. [Hayes-Roth, 1985]. The knowledge part, for instance a collection of inference rules describing the properties of a particular domain, may be considered static since it is not likely to change during the execution of a system. The data, or facts, representing some actual situation, however, will likely change dynamically. The collection of shared facts may change, either because of events occurring in the environment or by the derivation of new facts as a result of applying the knowledge to the known facts. The distinction between static and dynamic has implications for how we approach the distribution of data.

Static knowledge The actual distribution of static knowledge may be suggested by the way the knowledge is structured for domain experts. As an example, in the realm of medical diagnosis systems an early attempt at distributing knowledge can be found in [Gomez and Chandrasekaran, 1981]. They propose to structure the knowledge as a hierarchy of medical concepts. They moreover suggested to associate with each concept a process that is busy checking whether the observed symptoms justify the diagnosis of the disease represented by that concept. Another approach at distributing knowledge can be found in [Aikins, 1980], where a frame-like system supporting prototypes is used to model the diagnosis of lung diseases.

Dynamic facts Both the systems described above employed a common store of facts, shared by all the agents, to record the state of the reasoning process. This kind of architecture is also known as a *blackboard system*. Blackboard systems allow a number of agents to work concurrently, synchronizing only when interacting with the blackboard. Interaction with the blackboard occurs, either to retrieve information or to store information. New information may activate other agents to review their results.

5.1.2 Distributing control

Apart from solving problems in a certain domain of expertise, a distributed system must somehow decide how to decompose a complex task in subtasks. A possible solution to this problem is to designate *specialists*, that are special agents, for particular subtasks. In many cases, subtasks must cooperate in order to construct an answer from the (partial) answers resulting from the subtasks.

Subtasks Several metaphors exist that characterize the different solutions to the problem of how to arrive at a proper division of a (reasoning) task in subtasks. Cf. [Fox, 1981]. These metaphors range from the image of a hierarchic (military-like) organization to a heterarchic (market-like) organization of processes. In a hierarchic organization control is fixed and we may expect the results of the subtasks to contribute in a uniform way to the end result. In a heterarchic organization, the flow of control will be much more unpredictable and likewise the contribution of each subtask to the end result may be of a non-deterministic nature. An example of an architecture supporting a heterarchical form of organization is a blackboard system that does not coordinate the creation, activity and interaction of the agent except by means of the blackboard. To constrain the non-determinism of such a system, agents may be assigned more specific tasks according to their expertise.

Specialists In the medical expert system described in section 4.4 we introduced *specialists* (in its literal meaning) to explore classes of diagnosis. In contrast with the approach described in [Gomez and Chandrasekaran, 1981], that allows each concept to search for symptoms fitting its diagnosis, our specialists are general purpose problem solvers capable of generating diagnoses within a particular medical area. An instance of a specialist, with knowledge of a specific field, is created in order to explore a subtree of the hierarchy embodying the static knowledge, the medical concepts applying to that field. Specialists are created only when during the diagnostic process the need arises to refine a particular diagnosis. The specialists operate quasi-independently. They cooperate implicitly, however, by virtue of sharing the dynamic data storing the observed symptoms and the derived intermediate diagnoses. An important feature of this approach is that the creation and activity of the agents cooperating to find a solution is governed by the structure of the static knowledge concerning that domain. See also [Davis, 1980], [Smith and Davis, 1981].

5.2 DLP = LP + OO + ||

Having sketched the motivation for developing the language DLP, we wish to take a step back, in order to reflect on the origins of DLP in the design space of computer programming languages. See for analog studies [Davison, 1989a], [America, 1989b]. At the end of this chapter we will ask ourselves whether or not there really is a need for such a language.

Before justifying our own decisions we may well look at the alternatives we have in combining the three components of our language: logic programming, object oriented programming and parallelism. The diagrams below suggest three possible ways of arriving at such a combination.

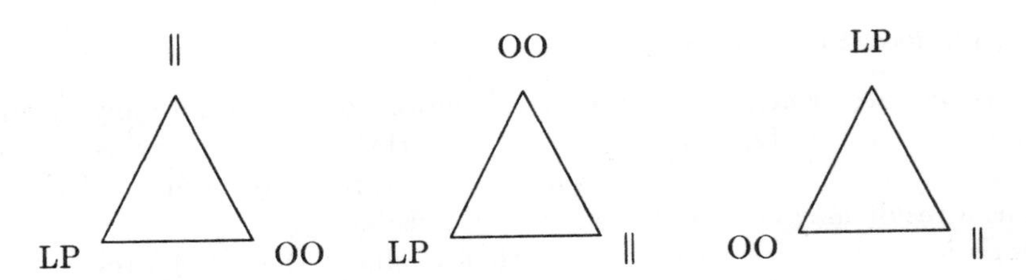

Either we may start from a combination of logic programming and object oriented programming (LP + OO) and add concurrency to it; or we may take a combination of logic programming and concurrency (LP + ||) and extend this to include object oriented programming; or we may take a concurrent object oriented language (OO + ||) and lift this in order to support logic programming.

According to this scheme we may classify a number of related approaches as in the table below.

	Language	LP	OO	||	References
LP + OO	Logical Objects	+	+	−	[Conery, 1988]
	SPOOL	+	+	−	[Fukunaga and Hirose, 1986]
	Communicating Prolog Units	+	+	+	[Mello and Natali, 1986]
LP + ||	Vulcan	+	+	+	[Kahn et al, 1986]
	Polka	+	+	+	[Davison, 1989]
	Delta Prolog	+	−	+	[Pereira and Nasr, 1984]
OO + ||	MultiLog	+	+	+	[Karam, 1988]
	Orient84/K	+	+	+	[Ishikawa and Tokoro, 1986]

To indicate where DLP must be located in the table above, we may remark that our language is very much like MultiLog. In contrast to MultiLog, however, DLP supports backtracking over the results of a method call, a property it shares with the languages falling under the heading LP + OO, combining logic programming and object oriented programming.

In the sections that follow, we will investigate the merits of DLP with respect to our classification scheme. For each of the combinations LP + OO, LP + || and OO + || we will try to delineate the central issue tackled and the problems encountered in completing the triangle. After describing the related approaches that exemplify that particular combination we will discuss the solutions provided in DLP.

5.2.1 Logic programming and objects

The central question in combining logic programming and object oriented programming is how to implement objects with internal states. Such states must be hidden. An object, in other words, must guarantee a certain protection with respect to the access and modification of its state by providing a suitable method interface.

Logical Objects provide an extension of Prolog with so-called *object clauses*. [Conery, 1988]. An object clause is a generalized Horn clause of the form

$method(X), object(S) :- ..., object(S_1).$

Such a clause is activated when a compound goal contains both a literal unifying with $method(X)$ and a literal unifying with $object(S)$. In this way, after having created an object with an initial state, goal literals may be interpreted as method calls to an object, that as a result may change its state in an invisible way.

A characteristic feature of this proposal is that it allows the usual Prolog backtracking over method calls. The advantage of the approach sketched is that 'it does minimal damage to the pure logic programming foundations'.

As a drawback, we may mention that *referential transparency* is lost: the meaning of an atom is no longer a fixed relation but relative to all possible states of the object for which the atom is a method.

Two implementations exist. The first is a meta-interpreter, which maintains a list of object states. The second exists in the form of a preprocessor translating object clauses to Prolog clauses. An implementation based on an extended version of the Warren Abstract Machine is planned.

SPOOL is a Prolog based object oriented language. See [Fukunaga and Hirose, 1986]. It extends Prolog with classes, instance variables, and message passing to enable the communication between instances of clauses.

The clauses defined for a class act as methods. In a method call of the form

send(Receiver, Message)

both the *Receiver* and the *Message* may be variables, thus allowing backtracking both with respect to the destination of the message and the method that will be applied. This rather unwieldy backtracking behavior is made possible by embedding methods in Prolog clauses representing a class of objects. See [Yokoi, 1986] for the details of the compilation of SPOOL to Prolog.

The advantage of this approach is that it combines the expressiveness of a logic programming language with the organizational capabilities of object oriented programming.

To our mind, the backtracking that may arise from anonymous method calls, where the destination is a variable, seems somewhat extravagant.

In [Fukunaga and Hirose, 1986] an application of SPOOL for producing program annotations is described.

Communicating Prolog Units extend Prolog with object oriented programming constructs by employing meta-programming techniques to define and handle the interaction between *units* of Prolog clauses. [Mello and Natali, 1986].

Communication between units is possible by using a meta-predicate of the form

send(Destination, Goal, Answer)

where *Destination* represents the unit by which the *Goal* must be evaluated. The results are collected in the *Answer* argument.

Units act as objects, since an internal state may be represented by clauses, and modified by asserting or retracting clauses.

A process, that is an instance of a unit, may influence the way external requests are handled by providing synchronization clauses of the form *entry*(...), *accept*(...) :- *body*(...).

When a goal in a *send* statement unifies with the *entry* part of the head of the clause, the evaluation of the *body* is postponed until the *accept* part of the head is satisfied. The functionality of these synchronization clauses resembles that of a rendez-vous.

The approach followed here has resulted in a number of constructs with great expressive power, due to the application of meta-programming techniques. A clear advantage is that the backtracking behavior of Prolog is retained.

Currently, there exists only a prototype implementation in Prolog.

In comparison with the approach taken for Logical Objects, that remains within the logic programming framework, the language SPOOL is of a more hybrid nature. A common characteristic of the three approaches sketched above is that they allow backtracking over method calls, which seems partly to be a result of embedding object oriented constructs in Prolog. The extent to which this is a deliberate design decision or an accidental quality due to the implementation is not altogether clear.

Both Logical Objects and SPOOL are sequential languages. For Communicating Prolog Units, concurrency is introduced by allowing units, that are like objects, to be active.

DLP supports objects with states primarily by what we have called non-logical variables. Passive objects merely respond to method calls, that may be regarded as the evaluation of a goal by an object. With respect to the backtracking behavior of such method calls we have decided to strive for full compatibility with Prolog. In other words, it must make no difference whether a goal is evaluated by means of a method call or in the ordinary way, provided the clauses needed for evaluating the goal are available.

Having objects with non-logical variables complicates matters a bit. We have decided that backtracking over the results of a method call does not undo any modification to the non-logical variables of the object to which the call was addressed. This decision needs some justification.

As a first observation, we wish to state that from the outside the non-logical variables of an object are invisible. Calling a method results in binding logical variables to some value, possibly in a number of alternative ways, or in failure. How these results are computed is the responsibility of the object.

Secondly, we may remark that we conceive of non-logical variables as an abstract representation of entities such as a database. Undoing modifications to such entities at every attempt at backtracking over a method call may lead to serious problems, in particular since in a logic programming context failure is a natural outcome of a computation.

We have already made clear that we wish to distinguish between partial failure in the sense of hardware errors or the violation of integrity constraints and failure in the logic programming sense. To our mind, automatically undoing modifications to non-logical variables may be better handled by additional features such as atomic sections or recovery mechanisms. Cf. [Klint, 1985].

In the third place, we wish to point out that, although automatic recovery on backtracking may seem a feasible solution for a sequential language, when introducing concurrency a number of problems arise due to the interaction with other objects. What is the scope for which we must guarantee protection? And, how do we handle the possible interference by other method calls?

5.2.2 Logic programming and concurrency

In section 2.3 we have introduced concurrent logic programming as one of the paradigms of distributed computing. We have also sketched how to use a concurrent logic programming language to implement objects. In this section we will treat two languages that provide object oriented extensions to a concurrent logic programming language.

Vulcan provides linguistic support for object oriented programming based on the computation model of concurrent logic programming. [Kahn et al. 1986].

To accommodate the need of programmers to use convenient program cliches, a preprocessor has been built that allows to dispose of the verbosity adhering to programming object oriented programs directly in Concurrent Prolog.

A program in Vulcan consists of clauses for classes and clauses for methods, possibly mingled with plain Concurrent Prolog clauses. The object oriented features supported include message sending, class inheritance and inheritance by delegation.

The advantage of such an approach is that it allows to offer the programmer a variety of constructs, that are nevertheless based on a simple and clean semantics. Another advantage may lay in the concurrent nature of the language.

As a drawback, in comparison with the two previous approaches, we may mention that backtracking is not supported; more specifically backtracking over method calls is not possible due to the committed choice character of Concurrent Prolog.

Polka is a hybrid language, combining the paradigms of concurrent logic programming and object oriented programming. [Davison, 1989]. Based on Parlog, it introduces object oriented constructs such as classes, instance variables, inheritance and self-communication. These abstractions enable to write a 'higher level Parlog', reducing the verbosity of ordinary Parlog.

A very powerful mechanism is provided by the incorporation of meta-level programming constructs that allow to treat classes as first order entities. In terms of expressiveness, this last feature may be considered an advantage of this particular approach at combining logic programming and object oriented programming. The operational semantics provided for the language suggests that the semantic complexity of this hybrid language is still manageable.

It is observed that the absence of backtracking, due to the committed choice character of Parlog, may be considered an advantage or a disadvantage, dependent on the needs of the application. Polka has been used to implement, among other things, a blackboard expert system. The implementation of Polka is described in [Davison, 1989].

A restriction adhering to both languages is the absence of backtracking over the results of a method call. As a remedy one could re-introduce backtracking by integrating a concurrent language with Prolog. Cf. [Shapiro, 1989]. Merely providing an interface between the two languages is not satisfactory, simply because it does not provide an integration of the two computation models underlying these languages. Embedding Prolog in a concurrent logic programming language, although feasible for non-flat versions allowing arbitrary goals in the guard, leads to efficiency problems. Moreover, as [Shapiro, 1989] observes, the implementation techniques for concurrent logic programming languages lag far behind those developed for sequential Prolog. Cf. [Hermenegildo, 1986]. Another option might be to extend Prolog to a language combining logic programming and concurrency. An example of such an approach is the language Delta Prolog.

Delta Prolog is a distributed logic programming language that extends Prolog to include *and*-parallelism and synchronous communication with two-way pattern matching. Cf. [Pereira and Nasr, 1984], [Pereira et al. 1986]. Parallel processes may be created by using the operator || for the parallel composition of goals. Processes may synchronize and communicate with each other by means of so-called *event goals*, a construct based on the notion of event of the distributed logic described in [Monteiro, 1984].

Event goals are goals of the form $T?E$ or $T!E$, where E represents an event and T a term, the event pattern. As an example, the compound parallel goal

$$T_1!E \parallel T_2?E$$

succeeds if T_1 and T_2 unify.

Delta Prolog supports fully distributed backtracking, that occurs when one of the components of a parallel goal does not succeed. The backtracking order is then just as in ordinary Prolog. Another occasion on which globally controlled backtracking occurs is when two compatible event goals fail to result in a communication.

The advantage of Delta Prolog is, first of all, that it includes full Prolog as a subset, and secondly, that it supports backtracking on the results of a communication. As a disadvantage, we may note that it does not provide modular features that may be of help in program design. In comparison with the rendez-vous construct, communication via events is less general, since the suspension of attempts at communication is not supported.

An implementation of Delta Prolog exists, as an extension to C-Prolog partly written in C and partly in Prolog, that allows to execute Delta Prolog programs on a network of processors.

When we compare Delta Prolog with the object oriented languages based on the concurrent logic programming model, the most obvious difference is that communication in Delta Prolog must be stated explicitly, whereas communication in the concurrent logic programming languages is mediated by shared logical variables. Another difference is that processes created for executing a concurrent logic program are usually fine-grained, whereas Delta Prolog gives rise to coarse grain parallelism.

We note that Delta Prolog allows to implement objects in a similar way as the concurrent logic programming languages. We do not consider Delta Prolog to be object oriented, however.

DLP supports concurrency in basically two ways. The first, perhaps most natural way, is to create active objects that execute their own activity in parallel with the activity of other objects. The second way is to let an object evaluate a number of method calls simultaneously.

To implement this, a notion of processes has been introduced, distinct from objects. Each active object has a so-called constructor process associated with it, that handles the evaluation of the body of the object, as expressed in the constructor clauses. Moreover, for each method call a process is created to handle the backtracking information needed to generate all answers to the call, and to communicate these to the invoking process.

When multiple processes are active for some object, we speak of internal concurrency, or multi-threaded objects. Passive objects allow unlimited internal concurrency. On the other hand, for active objects we have allowed such internal concurrency only for backtracking over alternative answers, after having delivered the first answer. The reason for this policy is that we wish to guarantee mutual exclusion between method calls for the time needed to produce the first answer. That is to say, no two method calls will be active similtaneously with producing their first results. A method call may however become active when other processes are still busy backtracking over the answers of a call.

The language DLP provides primitives for synchronous communication over channels, that are rather similar to those offered by Delta Prolog. However, the backtracking that may arise during communication over channels in DLP is much more limited than the distributed backtracking supported by Delta Prolog, in that it occurs locally within the confines of the process stating the input goal. The rendez-vous supported by DLP does not suffer from such a restriction. Moreover, we claim that our rendez-vous allows to impose synchronization constraints that cannot be expressed in Delta Prolog.

Additional parallelism may be achieved in DLP by using the primitives for process creation and resumption requests directly. These constructs allow to join the results of two independently running processes sharing logical variables. We have not encountered any such mechanism in the literature! We remark that these primitives have been used to implement the synchronous rendez-vous arising from a method call.

To enable active objects to engage in a rendez-vous we have provided an accept statement for interrupting the own activity and to state the willingness to answer particular method calls. This construct has been inspired by languages combining the object oriented programming paradigm with concurrency.

A notable difference between DLP on the one hand and Delta Prolog and the two object oriented languages based on the concurrent logic programming model on the other hand is that states of objects in DLP are kept in non-logical (instance) variables whereas in the three other approaches states are maintained as the argument of a tail-recursive predicate. We note that the conditional accept statement introduced in section 3.5 allows a similar implementation of objects.

5.2.3 Objects and concurrency

A radically different approach at combining logic programming, object oriented programming and concurrency is to take an existent parallel object oriented language as a starting point and to attempt to lift it to a language supporting logic based computation. Such an approach is exemplified by the language MultiLog. As another example we wish to mention the language Orient84/K.

MultiLog is a multi-tasking, object oriented Prolog [Karam, 1988]. It is intended to be used for prototyping concurrent, embedded systems. MultiLog supports both passive and active objects, instance variables, methods, classes and inheritance.

Active objects are large-grain sequential processes, that may communicate with each other by a *rendez-vous*-like method call. To engage in such a rendez-vous an active object must interrupt its activity by an Ada-like accept statement.

Once a rendez-vous is successfully completed, that is when an answer has been delivered, all contact with the object to which the call was addressed is broken off. When the invoking process backtracks, no 'hidden communication' takes place to generate alternative solutions. Instead, the logical variables that have been bound in evaluating the method call simply become unbound.[1] MultiLog, however, does support local backtracking, that may be needed to select the appropriate clauses for answering a method call. This design decision, for not supporting global or distributed backtracking, is motivated by the intended use of the language for prototyping embedded systems: an equivalent mechanism does not exist in target languages such as Ada!

Currently, research is being done to improve the efficiency of the MultiLog system, and to provide a suitable user interface.

Orient84/K combines the paradigms of object oriented, logic based, demon oriented and concurrent programming. [Ishikawa and Tokoro, 1986].

Concurrency is achieved by having active objects executing their own behavior. Apart from a *behavioral* part, each object contains a *knowledge-base* part consisting of clauses, and a *monitor* part specifying the synchronization conditions of the object.

Orient84/K supports instance variables. classes, inheritance, prioritized execution of objects, prioritized answering of method calls and *trigger* predicates, that become activated when certain conditions are met.

In [Ishikawa and Tokoro, 1986] considerable attention is paid to the design of a virtual machine for efficiently executing concurrent objects. The issues considered include the management of concurrently and sequentially executable objects, and the compilation of Orient84/K programs into an efficient intermediate code.

Both MultiLog and Orient84/K support single-threaded objects only. One of the possible advantages of lifting a parallel object oriented language may be that the mechanisms for process creation and communication are to a certain extent available. However, implementing a Prolog interpreter is not altogether a trivial matter.

DLP is, apart from a number of notational differences, quite similar to MultiLog. A notable exception to this similarity, however, is that, unlike MultiLog, DLP does support global backtracking over the results of a rendez-vous.

In a sense our language DLP may be regarded as the result of lifting the language POOL to a logic programming language. See section 9.5.1 and [America, 1987]. The problem we had to solve was to find the proper constructs for process creation and communication between processes. As a consequence, our initial design goal has been

[1] In [Davison, 1989] MultiLog is incorrectly classified among the languages that support backtracking over the results of a communication.

the extension of Prolog to a parallel object oriented language. Unlike MultiLog and the object oriented languages based on concurrent logic programming, we did not wish to give up compatibility with Prolog. DLP therefore supports the *don't know* non-determinism of backtracking.

5.3 Who needs distributed logic programming?

Now that the reader has become familiar with the language DLP, we may well try to assess what contribution DLP offers to the programming community. It is easy to observe that a number of the examples given are equally well implementable in at least one of the other languages mentioned. For example, competing implementations of the Dining Philosophers exist in Parlog and MultiLog. See [Ringwood, 1988] and [Karam, 1989]. The merit of DLP with respect to the examples encountered is that DLP is sufficiently expressive to provide a natural solution to all of these. Alas, the notion of a *natural* solution is rather subjective.

In this section we will attempt to establish what benefits DLP carries for the practice of software engineering, what use it has as a implementation vehicle for AI applications, and what it offers as a specification formalism for distributed systems.

5.3.1 Software Engineering

From a software engineering perspective, adopting the object oriented approach entails that *object oriented modeling* becomes the central activity in the process of design. We propose DLP as a high level specification language that supports such a methodology.

Specification Objects in DLP may be regarded as logical theories that specify the behavior of a component in a declarative way. The encapsulation mechanism provided by DLP allows to regard the answers to a method call as statements that are true for that component.

Design representation technologies are classified in [Webster, 1988] along the axes of *formality* and *conceptual complexity*. With regard to *formality* distributed logic programming (as embodied in DLP) lies, in our estimate of this classification, between Prolog and knowledge representation formalisms such as KEE and ART. It is not as formal though as ordinary first order (mathematical) logic or algebraic specification formalisms. This lack of formality is primarily due to the facilities offered for parallelism and the distribution of processes.

The expression of *conceptual complexity* is definitely enhanced by the introduction of object oriented features that allow to structure a system in semi-independent entities, and a fair estimate is that distributed logic programming is comparable in this respect to frame-based languages such as KL-ONE and the methods commonly employed in object oriented design.

Both distributed logic programming and the above mentioned knowledge representation formalisms have in common that their specifications are *executable*. In contrast to these formalisms, I wish to stress that the proposed approach is logic-based, thus allowing for a declarative interpretation of its components, insofar as these are implemented in a pure logic programming style. See [Padawitz, 1988] for examples of specifications of computational problems in Horn clause theories. However, see also [Hoare, 1987] for a more sceptical view.

Object oriented modeling In designing DLP we have chosen for a rather simple object model, and we have not provided a class construct, let alone a metaclass construct. An example of a language, similar to ours in that it also supports a kind of backtrackable method call, is the language ObjVProlog described in [Malenfant et al, 1989]. This language offers a reflexive object/class model derived from the model described in [Cointe, 1987]. See section 2.2.3. However, the language does not support active objects but instead supports a kind of and-parallelism, resulting from the concurrent execution of methods for distinct objects. Its computation model allows only single-threaded objects and thus offers limited parallelism.

In order to serve as a flexible vehicle for the specification and implementation of object oriented systems, the language DLP needs to be embedded in a suitable programming environment, including facilities for interactive use and documentation support. An extension of DLP incorporating hypertext features, along the lines sketched in [Parsay et al, 1989], is conceivable. As references to hypertext, consult [Conklin, 1987] and [Meyrowitz, 1986].

Combining multiple paradigms Despite the fact that Smalltalk has (re) introduced the concept of object oriented programming, the idea of extending a given language (such as Pascal, C, Lisp or Prolog) with object oriented features seems unavoidable, regarding the numerous reports on these efforts. Less common is to extend a given language with features that enable parallel/distributed programming, but also in this respect our effort is far from unique. In the previous section, we have motivated our design choices by a comparison with other similar approaches, and we have shown that our approach is unique in so far that it supports global backtracking over the results of a rendez-vous in a distributed context. Another contribution of our language lies in its computation model, where we make a distinction between objects (embodying a state) and processes associated with an object, that carry out the activity of that object – its own activity and the evaluation of method calls – partly concurrently.

The last issue, we wish to discuss is to what extent we should support an interface to a more efficient (imperative) language such as C++ or Eiffel. For actually implementing systems, such an interface would offer the opportunity to arrive at an efficient implementation in an evolutionary way. It is at present, however, difficult to conceive of how such an integration should take place, that is how to specify an interface between the two levels in a sufficiently abstract way. For examples of such an integration see [Butler et al, 1986] and [Talukdar et al, 1986].

5.3.2 Artificial Intelligence

In the area of Artificial Intelligence, Prolog has proven to be a powerful tool for implementing intelligent or knowledge-based systems. Cf. [Bratko, 1990].

Applications of object oriented technology to AI problems are described in [Tello, 1989]. Currently, there is a debate as to what contributions an object oriented approach offers to AI. See [OOPSLA 91]. Apart from solving a number of software engineering issues, we regard the power of the object oriented approach to lie primarily in its imperative to attain a natural model of the problem domain. Such an approach has been successful in developing expert systems and is promising, to my mind, for the development of other complex systems as well. Cf. [Aikins, 1980], [Hynynen and Lassila, 1989], [Kowalczyk and Treur, 1990].

The contribution of DLP to AI is clearly its potential to implement distributed knowledge-based systems, whereby it inherits all the advantages of its base language Prolog. Since DLP is a general purpose language it allows to implement a variety of protocols for reaching a conclusion in distributed reasoning. An example of such a protocol is sketched below.

Contract negotiation A very interesting solution to the effective mating of tasks and capabilities is provided in [Davis, 1980] where the active participation of both processes needing and processes offering a certain capability is described as *contract negotiation*. The idea is that a process that needs some task to be performed broadcasts a message, inviting processes to subscribe to the task and state their price. After a certain time then the process that initiated the subscription decides what offer, if any, is the most suitable. Further negotiation may follow if the process does not accept the task after all, or if it needs some further information or capability to perform the task effectively. In the latter case the initiating process may send the required information or capability.

Broadcasting Our language DLP does not in its turn support features that are offered by other languages. For example, DLP does not offer facilities for broadcasting messages. It may be worthwhile to consider incorporating a restricted broadcast facility, for instance to send a message to all instances of a named object. However, how to deal with shared instantiations of logical variables is not immediately obvious. A restricted broadcast facility can however be quite easily programmed in DLP as it is. Moreover, DLP allows to assert clauses dynamically, hence the required functionality may be sent to the selected processes in the form of clauses.

5.3.3 Distributed Systems

Distributed systems have a high degree of non-determinism, due to the assumption that each component in such a system may have its own behavior. The verification of such systems is a difficult problem.

Verification Verifying a distributed system is a difficult task. Evidently, this task is even harder when the system is specified by means of low-level concurrency and communication constructs. The introduction of an object-based approach, based on tasks and communication by rendez-vous, was motivated by the wish to make the verification of such systems more amenable. However, for languages such as Ada and POOL (embodying this approach), the number of details that must be taken into account make such a verification an almost infeasible task.

Prototyping The language Multilog (see section 5.2.3) was explicitly developed as a prototyping tool for Ada-like programs with the intention to make the verification of such programs easier. In [Karam, 1988a] an example of this is reported, demonstrating how the use of a high level language facilitates the reasoning about the synchronization and communication aspects of a complex system. In a similar vein we propose DLP as a language for prototyping distributed systems, to enable the specification of process creation and communication in an abstract logical way.

Partial failure Also, although we have provided primitives for allocating objects and processes, we have not provided support to deal with partial failures due to hardware errors and the like. Instead, we have relied on the failure mechanism of Prolog to deal with cases of this sort. In specifying the communication mechanism, however, we have laid down the requirements that must be met for reliable communication. These requirements are formalized in the appropriate sections in part II, by providing a mathematically well-founded description of the interaction between objects and processes.

Applications An example of modeling an interaction protocol in a high level language is given in [Armstrong et al, 1986], discussing the issues that arise in telecommunication systems. Another interesting area of application is the development of musical (composition and sound synthesis) systems, that are of an intrinsically concurrent and distributed nature. In this area also, the object oriented approach has proven to be fruitful. See [Pope, 1991].

Part II

Semantics

Part II

6

Process creation and communication in the presence of backtracking

- I shall offer you
the rich burnt fat
of a white goat.
Yes, I shall leave it behind for you. -
Sappho

A formal semantic analysis provides a touchstone by which to judge the validity of the constructs proposed in a language design. For our language DLP, or rather abstract versions thereof, we will provide both an operational semantics, characterizing the behavior of a program, and a denotational semantics, giving the meaning of a program in terms of a mapping to some domain of mathematical objects. We use the phrase *comparative semantics* for our effort to prove these characterizations equivalent.

The semantics given here is of a *behavioral* nature – intended to study the operational characteristics of the language – and must be regarded as providing a preliminary to the study of the declarative semantics of DLP, which is only briefly explored in section 12.2.

Before studying the operational and denotational semantics of our language DLP in any detail, we wish to provide the reader with an introduction to the techniques used in our semantic description. In particular we wish to treat in this chapter the mathematical background to (metric) denotational semantics, in order to be able to concentrate in following chapters on issues concerning the language rather than on the tools used in the analysis. Our treatment, here and in subsequent chapters, owes in a considerable extent to the foundational work presented in [America and Rutten, 1989a], notably [America and Rutten, 1989b] and [Kok and Rutten, 1988]; as well as the work on analyzing flow of control in logic programming languages reported in [de Bakker, 1991]. For any details omitted in our sketch of it, we refer the reader to the various sources. For alternative approaches see [Jones and Mycroft, 1984] and [Debray and Mishra, 1988].

Another, equally important, reason for including this introductory chapter is to give the reader some feeling for the way we tackle the problems in providing a semantics for the distributed logic programming language DLP — problems caused by the complex interaction between communication and backtracking. To this end we define three abstract languages $\mathcal{B}_0$, $\mathcal{B}_1$ and $\mathcal{B}_2$ that illustrate the creation of processes, communication and backtracking that may occur in DLP. These languages are similar to the languages $\mathcal{L}_0$, $\mathcal{L}_1$ and $\mathcal{L}_2$ used in chapter 8 for giving the comparative semantics of DLP, except that they abstract from all details having to do with the logic programming aspects of DLP, such as the renaming of logical variables and unification.[1] What we are primarily interested in here is an analysis of the flow of control and the communication behavior displayed by programs in DLP-like languages, omitting as many details as possible.

First, we will sketch the mathematical background of our semantic enterprise. We define metric spaces, and we characterize the kind of mathematical domains we use in defining our semantic models. Next, after having briefly described the structure of the equivalence proofs that we use to relate an operational and a denotational characterization, we will provide the semantics for the language $\mathcal{A}$, a simple language with choice, illustrating the techniques introduced.

To meet our second goal, of giving an introductory account of the problems encountered in a distributed logic programming language, we define the languages:

$\mathcal{B}_0$ - a simple language with backtracking,

$\mathcal{B}_1$ - the language $\mathcal{B}_0$ extended with dynamic object creation and communication with local backtracking, and

$\mathcal{B}_2$ - the language $\mathcal{B}_0$ extended with dynamic object creation and communication with global backtracking.

For these languages we give both an operational and a denotational semantics, and relate these by proving their equivalence. We encourage those interested only in the operational semantics of DLP to jump to chapter 7.

6.1 The metric approach

We will model the behavior of our language(s), denotationally, on a so-called process domain. Process domains may be given by reflexive equations of the form $\mathbb{P} \cong \mathcal{F}(\mathbb{P})$, stating the equivalence between $\mathbb{P}$ and a composite domain derived from $\mathbb{P}$. The

[1] An overview of DLP and the variants introduced for studying the semantics aspects of the language is given in section 3.8.

framework of complete metric spaces has proved very useful for solving equations of this kind. The technique for solving reflexive domain equations introduced in [de Bakker and Zucker, 1982] has been generalized in [America and Rutten, 1989b] in order to cope with the need to solve equations of the form $\mathbb{P} \cong \mathbb{P} \to \mathbb{P}$ that arose in developing a semantics for POOL. Cf. [America et al, 1989].

6.1.1 Metric spaces

A *metric space* is a pair (M, d) with M a non-empty set and d a mapping $d : M \times M \to [0,1]$ that assigns to each two elements from M a distance in the range $[0,1]$. The *metric* d must satisfy for arbitrary elements $x, y \in M$ the properties that

(a) $d(x,y) = 0 \Longleftrightarrow x = y$

(b) $d(x,y) = d(y,x)$

and for each $z \in M$,

(c) $d(x,y) \leq d(x,z) + d(y,z)$

When instead of (c) d satisfies

(c') $d(x,y) \leq max\{d(x,z), d(y,z)\}$

then d is called an *ultra-metric.*

As an example, for A an arbitrary set, the so-called discrete metric on A is defined by $d(x,y) = 0$ if $x = y$ and 1 otherwise. As a second example, for A an alphabet and $A^\infty = A^\star \cup A^\omega$, the set of finite and infinite words over A, we may put $d(x,y) = 2^{-sup\{n \mid x(n)=y(n)\}}$, where $x(n)$ denotes the prefix of length n when the length of x exceeds n and equals x otherwise. By convention $2^{-\infty} = 0$. Now (A^∞, d) is an ultra-metric space.

We are interested primarily in *complete* metric spaces. Let (M, d) be a metric space, and let $(x_i)_i$ be a sequence in M, then $(x_i)_i$ is a Cauchy sequence whenever for every $\varepsilon > 0$ there is a $N \in \mathbb{N}$ such that $\forall n, m > N. d(x_n, x_m) < \varepsilon$. In other words, past a certain point the distance between two elements in the sequence is smaller than this arbitrary ε. We call an element $x \in M$ the limit of a sequence $(x_i)_i$ whenever for arbitrary ε we can find an $N \in \mathbb{N}$ such that $\forall n > N. d(x_n, x) < \varepsilon$. We call such a sequence convergent and write $lim_{i\to\infty} x_i = x$. A metric space (M, d) is called complete whenever each Cauchy sequence converges to an element of M.

The importance of complete metric spaces derives from the possibility to characterize unique fixed points of functions within such a space. Let (M_1, d_1), (M_2, d_2) be metric spaces. For a function $f : M_1 \to M_2$, we call f continuous whenever we have that $lim_i f(x_i) = f(x)$ for an arbitrary sequence $(x_i)_i$ in M_1 with limit x. We write $f : M_1 \to^\varepsilon M_2$, for arbitrary constant ε whenever, for all $x, y \in M_1$, it holds that $d_2(f(x), f(y)) \leq \varepsilon \cdot d_1(x,y)$. We call f *non distance increasing (ndi)* when $0 \leq \varepsilon \leq 1$. The function f is called *contracting* when $0 \leq \varepsilon < 1$. We will write $f : M_1 \to^1 M_2$ for f *ndi*. Note that each contracting function is *ndi*.

Theorem 6.1.1

a. *Let* (M_1, d_1) *and* (M_2, d_2) *be metric spaces, then each ndi* $f : M_1 \rightarrow^1 M_2$ *is continuous.*

b. [Banach] *For* (M, d) *a complete metric space, each contracting* $f \in M \rightarrow M$ *has a unique fixed point which equals lim* $f^i(x)$ *for arbitrary* $x \in M$*, where by definition* $f^0(x) = x$ *and* $f^{i+1}(x) = f(f^i(x))$.

Having characterized complete metric spaces, we provide the means to construct complete metric spaces from given complete metric spaces. Let (M_i, d_i) be complete metric spaces, for $i = 1, ..., n$. We may construct the (complete) function space $(M_1 \rightarrow M_2, d_{M_1 \rightarrow M_2})$ by defining

$$d_{M_1 \rightarrow M_2}(f_1, f_2) = sup_{x \in M_1}\{d_2(f_1(x), f_2(x))\}$$

that is as the supremum of the distances of the function values in M_2. The (complete) union space $(M_1 \cup ... \cup M_n, d_{M_1 \cup ... \cup M_n})$ is obtained by defining

$$\begin{aligned} d_{M_1 \cup ... \cup M_n}(x, y) &= d_i(x, y) \ \text{ if } x, y \in M_i \\ &= 1 \ \text{ otherwise} \end{aligned}$$

assuming that $M_1, ..., M_n$ are disjoint. Similarly, we obtain the (complete) product space $(M_1 \times .. \times M_n, d_{M_1 \times ... \times M_n})$ by letting

$$d_{M_1 \times ... \times M_n}((x_1, ..., x_n), (y_1, ..., y_n)) = max_i\{d_i(x_i, y_i)\}$$

For (M, d) a metric space, we call a subset X of M closed whenever each converging sequence with elements in X has its limit in X. Let $\mathcal{P}nc(M) = \{X \mid X \subset M, X$ non-empty and closed $\}$. From (M, d) a complete metric space, we may construct the (complete) power space $(\mathcal{P}nc(M), d_{\mathcal{P}nc(M)})$ by defining

$$d_{\mathcal{P}nc(M)}(X, Y) = max\{sup_{x \in X}\{d(x, Y)\}, sup_{y \in Y}\{d(y, X)\}\}$$

where $d(x, Y) = inf_{y \in Y}\{d(x, y)\}$. The distance $d_{\mathcal{P}nc(M)}$ is usually called the Hausdorff distance and is written as d_H. By convention $sup\ \emptyset = 0$ and $inf\ \emptyset = 1$. A similar construction holds for compact power sets, defined by $\mathcal{P}co(M) = \{X \mid X \subset M, X$ compact $\}$. Finally, for (M, d) a metric space, we may define the complete metric space $id_\varepsilon(M, d)$, for $0 < \varepsilon < 1$, as (M, d') where $d'(x, y) = \varepsilon \cdot d(x, y)$ for $x, y \in M$. In all the cases above we may uniformly replace *metric* by *ultra-metric*.

6.1.2 Domains

The mathematical domains for our denotational semantics are complete metric spaces satisfying a reflexive domain equation of the form $\mathbb{P} \cong \mathcal{F}(\mathbb{P})$, where $\mathcal{F}(\mathbb{P})$ is an expression composed of some given fixed spaces by applying one or more of the constructions for obtaining complete metric spaces. [America and Rutten, 1989b] show that such an equation is solvable if $\mathcal{F}$, taken as a functor on the category of metric spaces, is contracting in the sense that the elements of the image of the functor, including (category-theoretically speaking) both objects and arrows, are in some sense nearer to each other than the elements from which they were derived. They also show that the completion procedure described in [de Bakker and Zucker, 1982] can be generalized to a direct limit construction for the sequence obtained by applying $\mathcal{F}$ to an arbitrary one-point space. The requirement that $\mathcal{F}$ is contracting, as a functor on complete metric spaces, is essential for the existence of such a limit.

We will illustrate our notion of domains by giving some examples.[2] For A an arbitrary set, with typical elements a, the domain $\mathbb{P}_1$, defined by

- $\mathbb{P}_1 \cong A \cup A \times \mathbb{P}_1$

consists, intuitively speaking, of all sequences over A. As examples of elements from $\mathbb{P}_1$ we have a, $< a_1, a_2 >$ and $< a_1, < a_2, \ldots >>$. For notational convenience we use an infix pairing operator $\cdot$ to be able to write pairs of the form $< a, \rho >$, with $\rho \in \mathbb{P}_1$, as $a \cdot \rho$. Our examples above may now be written as a, $a_1 \cdot a_2$ and $a_1 \cdot (a_2 \cdot \ldots)$.

We may use elements of $\mathbb{P}_1$ to describe sequences of action labels, with each label denoting an action by which a computation goes from one state to another. From this perspective, the expression $< a_1, < a_2, \ldots >>$ corresponds to the (deterministic) computation

$$\cdot \xrightarrow{a_1} \cdot \xrightarrow{a_2} \ldots$$

The domain $\mathbb{P}_1$ is isomorphic to A^∞, the set of strings over A, defined by $A^\infty = A^\star \cup A^\omega$. To prove this we may define a concatenation operator $\hat{\circ} : A^\infty \times A^\infty \to A^\infty$ for strings w over A, by the equations $w_1 \hat{\circ} w_2 = w_1 w_2$ if w_1 is of finite length and w_1 otherwise. We will denote the empty string by ε and state $\varepsilon w = w = w\varepsilon$.

To solve the equation for $\mathbb{P}_1$ we must, technically speaking, write

$$\mathbb{P}_1 \cong A \cup A \times id_{\frac{1}{2}}(\mathbb{P}_1)$$

and construct the corresponding metric, which can then be proven equal to the metric on A^∞. The functor implicitly defined by the right-hand side of the isometry equation above is contracting, which is (intuitively) a consequence of the fact that the occurrence of $\mathbb{P}_1$ is preceded by a factor $id_{\frac{1}{2}}$. In the following we will leave this factor out.

An example of a domain that allows to model non-deterministic computations is the domain $\mathbb{P}_2$, with typical elements ρ, defined by

- $\mathbb{P}_2 \cong \mathcal{P}_{co}(A \cup A \times \mathbb{P}_2)$

The domain $\mathbb{P}_2$ exemplifies a branching structure, that may be regarded as consisting of rooted trees, of which the branches are labeled with elements from an alphabet A. As examples of elements of $\mathbb{P}_2$ we have $\{a\}$, $\{a, a \cdot \{a_1 . a_2\}\}$, and $\{a_1 \cdot \rho_1, a_2 \cdot \rho_2\}$, the latter of which may be depicted as

[2]In the following, we will omit brackets as much as possible. The product operator will always bind stronger then the (set) union operator. For example $\mathbb{P}_1 \cong A \cup A \times \mathbb{P}_1$ must be read as $\mathbb{P}_1 \cong A \cup (A \times \mathbb{P}_1)$

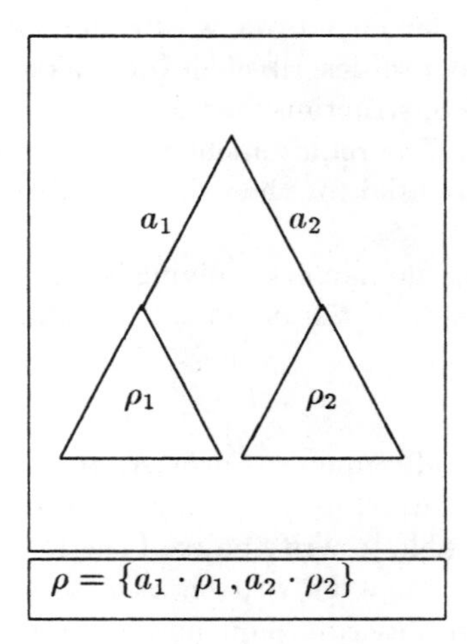

A tree such as the one above models non-deterministic behavior in that either a_1 may be chosen after which ρ_1 follows, or a_2 followed by ρ_2. These trees satisfy the additional properties of being commutative, in the sense that the order of the elements in the set representing a process is unimportant, and absorptive, in the sense that multiple occurrences of an item in such a set are collapsed. The condition requiring $\mathbb{P}_2$ to contain only compact sets corresponds, intuitively, with the requirement that the tree is finitely branching, or in other words that the non-determinism in the computation is bounded.

Our motivation to use a branching structure, instead of a domain consisting of sets of strings over an alphabet, may be elucidated by means of our next example domain given by

- $\mathbb{P}_3 \cong \mathcal{P}_{co}(A \cup C \cup A \times \mathbb{P}_3 \cup C \times \mathbb{P}_3)$

where, in addition to A we have a set C, with elements c, consisting of what we like to call communication intentions. The branching nature of our domain allows us to distinguish between the processes $\{a_1 \cdot \{a_2, c\}\}$ and $\{a_1 \cdot \{a_2\}, a_1 \cdot \{c\}\}$, as depicted below.

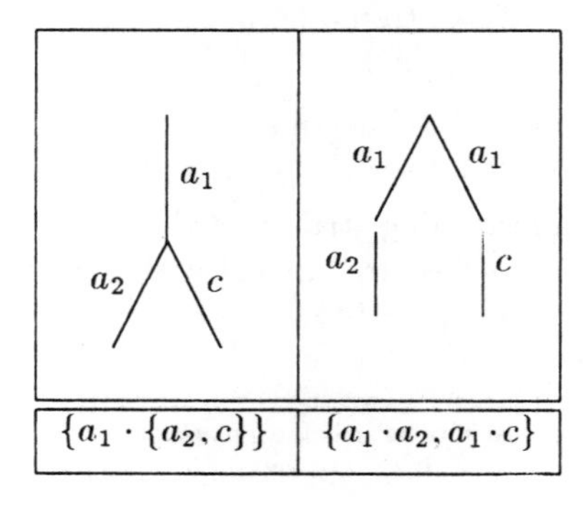

Now, if we have a choice between an action a and a failure due to an unresolved communication intention c, obviously we would like to choose for the action, and forget about the communication. If however we have no other choice then we must admit that we have reached a dead-end. Naively, using a function $trace : \mathbb{P}_3 \to \mathcal{P}((A \cup C)^\infty)$, the sets of traces resulting from these processes would be

$$trace(\{a_1 \cdot \{a_2, c\}\}) = \{a_1a_2, a_1c\} = trace(\{a_1 \cdot \{a_2\}, a_1 \cdot \{c\}\})$$

However, putting the considerations above in effect we obtain a function $trace^\star$ that yields the traces not ending in an unresolved communication intention:

$$trace^\star(\{a_1 \cdot \{a_2, c\}\}) = \{a_1a_2\} \neq \{a_1a_2, a_1c\} = trace^\star(\{a_1 \cdot \{a_2\}, a_1 \cdot \{c\}\})$$

We cannot make such a distinction in a structure, such as $\mathcal{P}_{nc}((A \cup C)^\infty)$, which is a linear structure. See also [de Bakker et al, 1984].

What we have treated thus far are domains for modeling so-called *uniform* languages, i.e. languages that may be modeled without the use of a state parameter. In contrast, non-uniform languages need a state for modeling the effect of actions, as for example assignments in an imperative language. The next two example domains correspond with respectively $\mathbb{P}_1$ and $\mathbb{P}_3$, except that they depend on elements of a set Σ:

- $\mathbb{P}_4 \cong \Sigma \to (A \cup A \times \mathbb{P}_4)$
- $\mathbb{P}_5 \cong \Sigma \to \mathcal{P}_{co}(A \cup C \cup A \times \mathbb{P}_5 \cup C \times \mathbb{P}_5)$

In the present chapter we will not use these domains; we will do so, however, when modeling the languages $\mathcal{L}_0$, $\mathcal{L}_1$ and $\mathcal{L}_2$ that also cover the (logic) programming aspects of DLP in chapter 8.

We may remark that we do not actually need to use an equation of the form

$$\mathbb{P} \cong \mathbb{P} \to \mathbb{P}$$

for which the generalization in [America and Rutten, 1989b] was intended. However, in giving the semantics of global (distributed) backtracking, we have avoided its use only at the expense of a quite intricate operator, as we will see in section 6.5.3.

6.1.3 Using contractions in proving the equivalence of semantic models

The use of contractions to characterize a variety of models has been advocated in [Kok and Rutten, 1988], and has proven its usefulness in proving the equality of operational and denotational semantics. In short, when we succeed in proving that both the operational semantics and the denotational semantics are a fixed point of a higher order mapping, then by the uniqueness of fixed points, as stated in theorem 6.1.1 they are equal.

In somewhat more detail, when we have, say, a language $\mathcal{L}$ we may specify a (labeled) transition system describing the possible computation steps of a program in $\mathcal{L}$. With $\mathbb{R}$ a set containing the possible results, for instance sets of strings of action labels, we may define an operational semantics $\mathcal{O}[\![\cdot]\!] : \mathcal{L} \to \mathbb{R}$ as the fixed point of a higher order mapping $\Psi : (\mathcal{L} \to \mathbb{R}) \to (\mathcal{L} \to \mathbb{R})$, collecting all possible computation sequences. Next we define $\mathcal{D}[\![\cdot]\!] : \mathcal{L} \to \mathbb{P}$ for a domain $\mathbb{P}$. Now taking a projection $\pi : \mathbb{P} \to \mathbb{R}$, mapping elements from $\mathbb{P}$ to $\mathbb{R}$, we must show that $\pi \circ \mathcal{D}$, the composition of π and $\mathcal{D}[\![\cdot]\!]$ is a fixed point of the mapping Ψ, and by theorem 6.1.1 we are done.

We have used this technique for structuring our equivalence proofs, following [de Bakker, 1991].

6.2 A simple language with choice

In order to illustrate the technical notions introduced in the previous section we will treat a simple language $\mathcal{A}$ that, basically, may be used to execute actions from a set of actions A. Statements in the language $\mathcal{A}$ are goals, either to execute an action, to evaluate a recursively defined goal, or to evaluate a compound goal. We speak of goals here for conformity with the languages $\mathcal{B}_0$, $\mathcal{B}_1$ and $\mathcal{B}_2$. We may note that $\mathcal{A}$ is a context-free language.

Syntax We assume the set A of actions, mentioned above, with typical elements a, and a set *Pvar* of procedure variables, with typical elements p.

We may then define *goals* $g \in Goal$ by

$$g ::= a \mid p \mid g_1; g_2 \mid g_1 + g_2$$

A goal of the form $g_1; g_2$ stands for sequential composition and a goal of the form $g_1 + g_2$ represents a choice between goal g_1 and g_2.

We define *procedure declarations* as being of the form $p \leftarrow g$ for $p \in Pvar$ and $g \in Goal$. We call g the *body* of the procedure p.

We let *declarations* D take the form

$$D = \{p \leftarrow g \mid p \in Pvar, g \in Goal\}$$

A *program* in $\mathcal{A}$ is a tuple $< D \mid g >$, with D a declaration and g a goal.

6.2.1 Operational semantics

We will define the operational semantics of the language $\mathcal{A}$ in terms of the behavior that may be observed when executing a program. We define a set of labels Λ, with typical elements η, such that

$$\Lambda = A \cup \{\star\}$$

contains the actions $a \in A$ and the special label $\star$. The label $\star$ will be used to denote behavior that is visible, but silent in the sense that it cannot further be inspected. The empty label, denoted by the empty word ε, will be used to denote invisible behavior and consequently will disappear in the operational semantics. We take $\Lambda^\infty = \Lambda^\star \cup \Lambda^\omega$ as the set of finite and infinite strings over Λ. The concatenation operator $\hat{\circ} : \Lambda^\infty \times \Lambda^\infty \to \Lambda^\infty$ is defined as the usual string concatenation for strings in Λ^∞, which satisfies $\varepsilon \mathbin{\hat{\circ}} w = w = w \mathbin{\hat{\circ}} \varepsilon$. We moreover define

$$\mathbb{R} = \mathcal{P}_{nc}(\Lambda^\infty)$$

and extend the concatenation operator for strings in Λ^∞ by defining $w \hat{\circ} X = \{w \hat{\circ} x : x \in X\}$.

We will specify the computation steps that may occur when executing a program by means of a Plotkin-style transition system, defined by a number of transition rules. Our transition rules are axioms of the form $\Gamma \xrightarrow{\eta} \Gamma'$, stating that the configuration Γ may be taken to Γ' while displaying η. The label η may be empty, denoting the fact that the transition to which the rule gives rise is unobservable. We will call transitions with the empty label as being unlabeled.

Configurations Γ represent, in a rather straightforward way, the part of the goal that still must be evaluated. In order to deal with termination we define syntactic continuations $S \in \mathit{SynCo}$ by

$$S ::= \surd \mid g; S$$

and let a configuration Γ be an element of $\mathit{Conf} = \mathit{SynCo}$.

The transition rules below specify a transition system $(\mathit{Conf}\ \Lambda, \longrightarrow)$, where the relation $\longrightarrow$ ranges over the product $\mathit{Conf} \times \Lambda \times \mathit{Conf}$. The rules are specified relative to some declaration D.

$\mathcal{A}$

$a; S \xrightarrow{a} S$	*Action*
$p; S \xrightarrow{\star} g; S$ for $p \leftarrow g$ in D	*Rec*
$(g_1; g_2); S \longrightarrow g_1; (g_2; S)$	*Seq*
$(g_1 + g_2); S \longrightarrow g_1; S$ $\longrightarrow g_2; S$	*Choice*

As an explanation, the axiom for *Action* states that a configuration that has an action a as its first goal may be taken to that configuration without the action, while displaying the label a. The axiom *Rec* states that a call for p is replaced by the body for p, while displaying the special label $\star$. Applying the axiom *Seq* enables a further analysis of the first goal, simply by changing the brackets. The axiom *Choice* allows to continue with either one of the goals g_1 or g_2. Both the axioms *Seq* and *Choice* give rise to unlabeled transitions.

As an example, starting with the goal $a_1; a_2$ we have the computation

$$(a_1; a_2); \surd \longrightarrow a_1; (a_2; \surd) \xrightarrow{a_1} a_2; \surd \xrightarrow{a_2} \surd \qquad \text{(a)}$$

As another example, a possible computation resulting from the goal $(a_1; a_2) + (a_1; a_3)$ is

$$((a_1; a_2) + (a_1; a_3)); \surd \longrightarrow (a_1; a_3); \surd \longrightarrow a_1; (a_3; \surd) \xrightarrow{a_1} a_3; \surd \xrightarrow{a_3} \surd \qquad \text{(b)}$$

As the observable behavior of the goal evaluated in (a) we take the set $\{a_1a_2\}$, and for the one evaluated in (b) we take $\{a_1a_2, a_1a_3\}$. We formalize our notion of observability below.

Computation sequences Since we are interested only in the labeled transitions, which represent steps in which non-trivial computation occurs, we must in some way abstract from the unlabeled transitions. We define two configurations Γ and Γ' to be related by $\longrightarrow\!\!\!\!\!\rightarrow$, notation $\Gamma \longrightarrow\!\!\!\!\!\rightarrow \Gamma'$, if there is a (possibly empty) sequence of unlabeled transitions from Γ to Γ'. Next we define $\Gamma \xrightarrow{\eta}\!\!\!\!\rightarrow \Gamma'$ to hold if there is a configuration Γ'' for which $\Gamma \longrightarrow\!\!\!\!\!\rightarrow \Gamma''$ and moreover $\Gamma'' \xrightarrow{\eta} \Gamma'$ for a non-empty label η. In other words $\Gamma \xrightarrow{\eta}\!\!\!\!\rightarrow \Gamma'$ whenever there is a transition with label η preceded by zero or more unlabeled transitions. We will say that Γ *blocks* if there is no label η and configuration Γ' for which $\Gamma \xrightarrow{\eta}\!\!\!\!\rightarrow \Gamma'$. An alternative way to deal with empty transitions would be to define transition rules with non-empty premises, allowing to ignore the empty labels. We prefer to use axioms, however, for their conciseness.

Now we can define the *operational semantics* of a program $< D \mid g > \in \mathcal{A}$ as a mapping $\mathcal{O}[\![\cdot]\!] : \mathcal{A} \to \mathbb{R}$.

Definition 6.2.1 $\mathcal{O}[\![< D \mid g >]\!] = \mathcal{T}[\![g; \surd]\!]$ *where* $\mathcal{T}$ *is given by*

$$\mathcal{T}[\![\Gamma]\!] = \begin{cases} \{\varepsilon\} & \text{if } \Gamma \text{ blocks} \\ \bigcup\{\eta \,\hat{\circ}\, \mathcal{T}[\![\Gamma']\!] : \Gamma \xrightarrow{\eta}\!\!\!\!\rightarrow \Gamma'\} & \text{otherwise} \end{cases}$$

Above we have defined $\mathcal{T}$ by a reflexive equation. As it stands it is not clear whether $\mathcal{T}$ exists. Before showing that, we will illustrate our approach by defining the function computing the factorial. The function $fac : \mathbb{N} \to \mathbb{N}$ may be written as

$$fac(n) \equiv \;\; if \;\; n = 0 \;\; then \;\; 1 \;\; else \;\; n \star fac(n-1)$$

The proof that fac is well-defined proceeds by induction on n. An alternative way to characterize the function fac is to define a higher order mapping $\Phi : (\mathbb{N} \to \mathbb{N}) \to (\mathbb{N} \to \mathbb{N})$, taking functions over the natural numbers to functions over the natural numbers, by

$$\Phi(\phi) = \lambda n.\, if \;\; n = 0 \;\; then \;\; 1 \;\; else \;\; n \star \phi(n-1)$$

and state that $fac = fix\Phi$. We may obtain the fixed point of Φ by iterating the application of Φ to an arbitrary function f an indefinite number of times. As an example $\Phi^2(f)$, the two-fold application of Φ to f, looks as

$$\lambda n.\, if\; n = 0 \; then \; 1 \; else \;\; n \star (\lambda n'.\, if \; n' = 0 \; then \; 1 \; else \; n' \star f(n'-1))(n-1)$$

We may check that $\Phi(fac) = fac$ by observing that $\Phi(fac)(n)$ equals $if\; n = 0 \; then \; 1 \; else \; n \star fac(n-1)$ which clearly equals $fac(n)$.

In order to show that $\mathcal{T}$ exists we define a higher order mapping $\Psi : (Conf \to \mathbb{R}) \to (Conf \to \mathbb{R})$ by

$$\Psi(\phi)[\![\Gamma]\!] = \begin{cases} \{\varepsilon\} & \text{if } \Gamma \text{ blocks} \\ \bigcup\{\eta \mathbin{\hat{\circ}} \phi[\![\Gamma']\!] : \Gamma \xrightarrow{\eta} \Gamma'\} & \text{otherwise} \end{cases}$$

and define $\mathcal{T} = fix\Psi$.
We state that Ψ is well-defined, in that it takes *ndi* functions to *ndi* functions. Also Ψ is contracting since, intuitively, with each application a label is added.[3] Hence Ψ has a fixed point, which moreover is unique due to theorem 6.1.1. As a remark, we must note that we have suppressed the dependency of $\mathcal{T}$ and Ψ on the declaration D.

6.2.2 Denotational semantics

The distinguishing feature of a denotational semantics is its compositionality. A compositional semantics allows to give mathematical meaning to parts of a program, that may be glued together by semantic operators to yield the meaning of the composite program.

Instead of giving a direct denotational semantics we take a slightly devious route in assigning mathematical meaning to the language $\mathcal{A}$, by giving a continuation semantics instead.

We will use semantic continuations $R \in SemCo = \mathbb{R}$. Semantic continuations are introduced here for the reader to become familiar with the kind of continuation semantics used for analyzing the languages with backtracking, not because they are more convenient for this particular case. The usefulness of continuation semantics for modeling a variety of (more or less) exotic language features has been eloquently defended in [de Bruin, 1986], to which we refer the reader for a more extensive account of this brand of denotational semantics.

Without further ado we define the function $\mathcal{D}[\![\cdot]\!] : Goal \to SemCo \to \mathbb{R}$.

$\mathcal{A}$

(i) $\mathcal{D}[\![a]\!]R = a \mathbin{\hat{\circ}} R$

(ii) $\mathcal{D}[\![p]\!]R = \star \mathbin{\hat{\circ}} \mathcal{D}[\![g]\!]R$ for $p \leftarrow g$ in D

(iii) $\mathcal{D}[\![g_1; g_2]\!]R = \mathcal{D}[\![g_1]\!](\mathcal{D}[\![g_2]\!]R)$

(iv) $\mathcal{D}[\![g_1 + g_2]\!]R = \mathcal{D}[\![g_1]\!]R \cup \mathcal{D}[\![g_2]\!]R$

The difference with a direct denotational semantics comes to light in the equation (iii) for sequential composition, where we put the result of evaluating g_2 in the continuation.

[3]Since recursive procedure call results in a label, we do not have to impose the requirement that bodies of procedures are guarded to prevent the occurrence of infinite sequences of invisible transitions.

Those familiar with denotational semantics may have frowned upon the equations for recursive procedure call in $\mathcal{D}[\![\cdot]\!]$. We take the opportunity to remark that the metric setting developed thus far may also be profitably used in characterizing functions such as $\mathcal{D}[\![\cdot]\!]$ as the fixed point of a higher order mapping $\Phi : (Goal \rightarrow SemCo \rightarrow \mathbb{R}) \rightarrow (Goal \rightarrow SemCo \rightarrow \mathbb{R})$.
We define Φ by

$$\Phi(\phi)[\![a]\!]R = a \;\hat{\circ}\; R$$

$$\Phi(\phi)[\![p]\!]R = \star \;\hat{\circ}\; \phi[\![g]\!]R \text{ for } p \leftarrow g \text{ in } D$$

$$\Phi(\phi)[\![g_1; g_2]\!]R = \Phi(\phi)[\![g_1]\!](\Phi(\phi)[\![g_2]\!]R)$$

$$\Phi(\phi)[\![g_1 + g_2]\!]R = \Phi(\phi)[\![g_1]\!]R \cup \Phi(\phi)[\![g_2]\!]R$$

and must now prove that Φ is contracting and well-defined in the sense that it maps *ndi* functions to *ndi* functions. Although by no means necessary, this approach is convenient since we no longer have the need for an environment parameter, as traditionally encountered in denotational semantics, to cope with recursion.

Definition 6.2.2 *For a program* $< D \mid g >$ *the meaning* $\mathcal{M}[\![< D \mid g >]\!] = \mathcal{D}[\![g]\!]\{\varepsilon\}$.

We give two examples.

$$\mathcal{M}[\![a_1; a_2]\!] = \mathcal{D}[\![a_1; a_2]\!]\{\varepsilon\} = \mathcal{D}[\![a_1]\!](\mathcal{D}[\![a_2]\!]\{\varepsilon\}) = a_1 \;\hat{\circ}\; (a_2 \;\hat{\circ}\; \{\varepsilon\}) = \{a_1 a_2\}$$

$$\begin{aligned}\mathcal{M}[\![(a_1; a_2) + (a_1; a_3)]\!] &= \mathcal{D}[\![(a_1; a_2) + (a_1; a_3)]\!]\{\varepsilon\} \\ &= \mathcal{D}[\![a_1; a_2]\!]\{\varepsilon\} \cup \mathcal{D}[\![a_1; a_3]\!]\{\varepsilon\} \\ &= \{a_1 a_2, a_1 a_3\}\end{aligned}$$

6.2.3 Equivalence between operational and denotational semantics

We wish the observable behavior of a program $< D \mid g >$ assigned to it by the operational semantics $\mathcal{O}[\![\cdot]\!]$ to be adequately characterized by the mathematical meaning given by the function $\mathcal{M}[\![\cdot]\!]$.

Theorem 6.2.3 $\mathcal{O}[\![< D \mid g >]\!] = \mathcal{M}[\![< D \mid g >]\!]$

We will give an outline of the proof and promise to fill in the details later.

$$\begin{aligned}\mathcal{O}[\![< D \mid g >]\!] &= \mathcal{T}[\![g; \surd]\!] && \text{by definition 6.2.1} \\ &= \mathcal{R}[\![g; \surd]\!] && \text{by corollary 6.2.7} \\ &= \mathcal{D}[\![g]\!]\{\varepsilon\} && \text{by definition 6.2.4} \\ &= \mathcal{M}[\![< D \mid g >]\!] && \text{by definition 6.2.2}\end{aligned}$$

In the proof we make use of an intermediate semantic function $\mathcal{R} : SynCo \to SemCo$ mapping syntactic continuations to semantic continuations.

Definition 6.2.4

a. $\mathcal{R}[\![\surd]\!] = \{\varepsilon\}$

b. $\mathcal{R}[\![g; S]\!] = \mathcal{D}[\![g]\!]\mathcal{R}[\![S]\!]$

We may state the following property.

Lemma 6.2.5 $\mathcal{R}[\![(g_1; g_2); S]\!] = \mathcal{R}[\![g_1; (g_2; S)]\!]$

Proof: The proof amounts to repeatedly applying the definition of $\mathcal{R}$ and D as shown. We have that

$$\begin{aligned} \mathcal{R}[\![g_1; (g_2; S)]\!] &= \mathcal{D}[\![g_1]\!]\mathcal{R}[\![g_2; S]\!] \\ &= \mathcal{D}[\![g_1]\!](\mathcal{D}[\![g_2]\!]\mathcal{R}[\![S]\!]) \\ &= \mathcal{D}[\![g_1; g_2]\!]\mathcal{R}[\![S]\!] \\ &= \mathcal{R}[\![(g_1; g_2); S]\!] \text{ as desired} \end{aligned}$$

□

The key step in the proof that $\mathcal{O} = \mathcal{M}$ consists of showing that the function $\mathcal{R}$ is a fixed point of the operator Ψ that characterizes the operational meaning of a program (see section 6.2.1).

Lemma 6.2.6 $\Psi(\mathcal{R}) = \mathcal{R}$

Proof: In order to be able to use induction we define a complexity measure c on configurations of the form $g; S$ by stating

$$c(g; S) = c(g) \text{ with } c(a) = c(p) = 1$$

and

$$c(g_1; g_2) = c(g_1 + g_2) = c(g_1) + c(g_2) + 1$$

We must now prove for each Γ that $\Psi(\mathcal{R})[\![\Gamma]\!] = \mathcal{R}[\![\Gamma]\!]$. As induction hypothesis we assume that whenever $c(\Gamma) > c(\Gamma')$ then $\Psi(\mathcal{R})[\![\Gamma']\!] = \mathcal{R}[\![\Gamma']\!]$. When $\Gamma = \surd$ the result is immediate. For Γ of the form $g; S$ the proof proceeds by a case analysis on g.

- If $g \equiv a$ then

$$\begin{aligned} \Psi(\mathcal{R})[\![a; S]\!] &= a \mathbin{\hat{\circ}} \mathcal{R}[\![S]\!] \text{ (by the definition of } \Psi(\mathcal{R})) \\ &= \mathcal{D}[\![a]\!]\mathcal{R}[\![S]\!] \text{ (by the definition of } \mathcal{D}) \\ &= \mathcal{R}[\![a; S]\!] \text{ (by definition 6.2.4)} \end{aligned}$$

- If $g \equiv p$ then

$$\begin{aligned}\Psi(\mathcal{R})[\![p;S]\!] &= \star \mathbin{\hat{\circ}} \mathcal{R}[\![g';S]\!] \quad (\text{for } p \leftarrow g' \text{ in } D)\\ &= \star \mathbin{\hat{\circ}} \mathcal{D}[\![g']\!]\mathcal{R}[\![S]\!] \quad (\text{by definition 6.2.4})\\ &= \mathcal{D}[\![p]\!]\mathcal{R}[\![S]\!] \quad (\text{by the definition of } \mathcal{D})\\ &= \mathcal{R}[\![p;S]\!] \quad (\text{again by definition 6.2.4})\end{aligned}$$

- If $g \equiv g_1; g_2$ then

$$\begin{aligned}\Psi(\mathcal{R})[\![(g_1;g_2);S]\!] &= \Psi(\mathcal{R})[\![g_1;(g_2;S)]\!] \quad (\text{by the definition of } \Psi(\mathcal{R}))\\ &= \mathcal{R}[\![g_1;(g_2;S)]\!] \quad (\text{by induction})\\ &= \mathcal{R}[\![(g_1;g_2);S]\!] \quad (\text{by lemma 6.2.5})\end{aligned}$$

- For $g \equiv g_1 + g_2$ we have

$$\begin{aligned}\Psi(\mathcal{R})[\![(g_1+g_2);S]\!] &= \Psi(\mathcal{R})[\![g_1;S]\!] \cup \Psi(\mathcal{R})[\![g_2;S]\!]\\ &= \mathcal{R}[\![g_1;S]\!] \cup \mathcal{R}[\![g_2;S]\!] \quad (\text{by induction})\\ &= \mathcal{D}[\![g_1]\!]\mathcal{R}[\![S]\!] \cup \mathcal{D}[\![g_2]\!]\mathcal{R}[\![S]\!] \quad (\text{by definition 6.2.4})\\ &= \mathcal{D}[\![g_1+g_2]\!]\mathcal{R}[\![S]\!] \quad (\text{by the definition of } \mathcal{D})\\ &= \mathcal{R}[\![(g_1+g_2);S]\!] \quad (\text{again by definition 6.2.4})\end{aligned}$$

□

Our corollary follows from the fact that the fixed point of Ψ is unique.

Corollary 6.2.7 $\mathcal{T} = \mathcal{R}$

The proof of the equivalence $\mathcal{O} = \mathcal{M}$ given above hinges on finding a semantic counterpart for the syntactic continuation employed in giving the operational semantics. In the sections that follow we will apply this proof technique to the semantics of considerably more complex languages.

6.3 A language with backtracking

In the previous section we have illustrated the major ingredients of our semantic approach by giving the comparative semantics for a very simple language. We will apply these techniques now to languages that become progressively more complex with respect to their backtracking behavior.

We will start with the language $\mathcal{B}_0$, a simple language with backtracking.[4] The language $\mathcal{B}_0$ differs from the language $\mathcal{A}$ in that we have replaced the choice construct $g_1 + g_2$ by a construct $g_1 \Box g_2$, for alternative composition, that instead of choosing between g_1 and g_2 enforces to backtrack over the alternatives.

[4] Our treatment closely follows the treatment of a very similar language given in [de Bakker, 1991].

Although backtracking may be used for mimicking non-deterministic computation, the behavior of backtracking itself is deterministic in the sense that the order in which the evaluation of alternative goals takes place is completely determined. The determinate nature of backtracking is reflected in the fact that the behavior of a program in $\mathcal{B}_0$ may be characterized by a single string of action labels, instead of a set of such strings as for programs in $\mathcal{A}$.

Another difference with the language $\mathcal{A}$ is that actions in $\mathcal{B}_0$ may fail. Failure, as determined by an abstract interpretation function, gives rise to backtracking.

Syntax Again we assume to have actions $a \in A$, and procedure variables $p \in Pvar$. As special actions we assume to have an action *skip* and an action *fail*.

We define *goals* $g \in Goal$ by

$$g ::= a \mid p \mid g_1; g_2 \mid g_1 \square g_2$$

and let *declarations* D take the form

$$D = \{p \leftarrow g \mid p \in Pvar, g \in Goal\}$$

A *program* is a tuple $< D \mid g >$, with D a declaration and g a goal.

6.3.1 Operational semantics

We will characterize the behavior of a program in $\mathcal{B}_0$ as a string over a set of labels Λ that we define by

$$\Lambda = A \cup \{\star\}$$

with $\star$ given the interpretation of a silent action. We also use ε for an unobservable action, as explained previously. Since the behavior of a program in $\mathcal{B}_0$ is determinate we may map its meaning to an element of $\Lambda^\infty = \Lambda^\star \cup \Lambda^\omega$.

As for $\mathcal{A}$ we use syntactic continuations in specifying the transition rules. In order to deal with backtracking, however, we must distinguish between syntactic success continuations and syntactic failure continuations, as explained below. A success continuation represents the part of the program that must be executed to find a solution. Success continuations $R \in SuccCo$ are similar to the syntactic continuations used for $\mathcal{A}$. We define

$$R ::= \surd \mid g; R$$

Success continuations R correspond to the sequential evaluation of a goal, without backtracking. They are used as in $g; \surd$, for an arbitrary goal g. When g is successfully evaluated then the empty success continuation $\surd$ is reached.

Evaluating a choice in the language $\mathcal{A}$ allowed us to forget about the alternative. Backtracking, however, requires to keep account of what alternatives remain to be evaluated. For this purpose we use so-called failure continuations $F \in FailCo$ defined by

$$F ::= \Delta \mid R : F$$

The empty failure continuation Δ represents the situation that all possible solutions have been explored. Intuitively, a failure continuation, that we write as $R : F$, is a stack having a success continuation R on top. If R for some reason fails then the failure continuation F, which is the remainder of the stack, may be used to find a solution. The evaluation of a goal g is started by the failure continuation $g; \surd : \Delta$. When during the execution an alternative goal, say of the form $g_1 \Box g_2$ is encountered, as represented by $(g_1 \Box g_2); R : F$, then the resulting failure continuation is $(g_1; R) : (g_2; R) : F$, having the success continuation $g_1; R$ on top of the stack and $g_2; R$ as the first alternative to be explored.

As configurations we now take failure continuations and let Γ range over $Conf = FailCo$. We assume to have an abstract interpretation function $I : A \rightarrow \{true, false\}$ defining for each action whether it is successful or fails. The function I must satisfy $I(skip) = true$ and $I(fail) = false$.

$\mathcal{B}_0$

$a; R : F \xrightarrow{a} R : F$ if $I(a)$ $\longrightarrow F$ otherwise	*Action*
$p; R : F \xrightarrow{\star} g; R : F$ for $p \leftarrow g$ in D	*Rec*
$(g_1; g_2); R : F \longrightarrow g_1; (g_2; R) : F$	*Seq*
$(g_1 \Box g_2); R : F \longrightarrow (g_1; R) : (g_2; R) : F$	*Alt*
$\surd : F \longrightarrow F$	*Tick*

Notice that whenever an action fails, as expressed in the axiom for *Action*, the failure stack is popped in order to search for an alternative solution. Since we like to find all solutions, when a solution is reached as indicated by the occurrence of a $\surd$, the stack is also popped in order to evaluate the remaining alternatives.

As an example, consider the goals $a_1 \Box a_2$ and $a_1; a_2$ that give rise to the computations

$$(a_1 \Box a_2); \surd : \Delta \longrightarrow (a_1; \surd) : (a_2; \surd) : \Delta \xrightarrow{a_1} \surd : (a_2; \surd) : \Delta$$
$$\longrightarrow a_2; \surd : \Delta \xrightarrow{a_2} \surd : \Delta \longrightarrow \Delta$$

$$(a_1; a_2); \surd : \Delta \longrightarrow a_1; (a_2; \surd) : \Delta \xrightarrow{a_1} a_2; \surd : \Delta \xrightarrow{a_2} \surd : \Delta \longrightarrow \Delta$$

Both computations result in the same observable behavior. Consider however the goal $(a_1 \Box a_2); a_3$ for which we have

$$((a_1 \Box a_2); a_3); \surd : \Delta \longrightarrow (a_1 \Box a_2); (a_3; \surd) : \Delta$$
$$\longrightarrow (a_1; (a_3; \surd)) : (a_2; (a_3; \surd)) : \Delta$$
$$\xrightarrow{a_1} (a_3; \surd) : (a_2; (a_3; \surd)) : \Delta \xrightarrow{a_3} \surd : (a_2; (a_3; \surd)) : \Delta$$
$$\longrightarrow a_2; (a_3; \surd) : \Delta \xrightarrow{a_2} a_3; \surd : \Delta \xrightarrow{a_3} \surd : \Delta \longrightarrow \Delta$$

The behavior of this computation is characterized by the string $a_1 a_3 a_2 a_3$ which is clearly different from the behavior resulting from the evaluation of $(a_1; a_2); a_3$.

Finally we give some examples of failing actions.

$$\mathit{fail}; \mathit{skip}; \surd : \Delta \longrightarrow \Delta$$

$$\mathit{skip}; \mathit{fail}; \surd : \Delta \xrightarrow{\mathit{skip}} \mathit{fail}; \surd : \Delta \longrightarrow \Delta$$

$$\mathit{fail} \Box \mathit{skip}; \surd : \Delta \longrightarrow \mathit{fail}; \surd : \mathit{skip}; \surd : \Delta \longrightarrow \mathit{skip}; \surd : \Delta \xrightarrow{\mathit{skip}} \surd : \Delta \longrightarrow \Delta$$

$$\mathit{skip} \Box \mathit{fail}; \surd : \Delta \longrightarrow \mathit{skip}; \surd : \mathit{fail}; \surd : \Delta \xrightarrow{\mathit{skip}} \surd : \mathit{fail}; \surd : \Delta$$
$$\longrightarrow \mathit{fail}; \surd : \Delta \longrightarrow \Delta$$

Using the relation $\stackrel{\eta}{\twoheadrightarrow}$ as given for $\mathcal{A}$ we may define the operational semantics of a program $< D \mid g >$ in $\mathcal{B}_0$ as a function $\mathcal{O}[\![\cdot]\!] : \mathcal{B}_0 \rightarrow \Lambda^\infty$. as below.

Definition 6.3.1 $\mathcal{O}[\![< D \mid g >]\!] = \mathcal{T}[\![g; \surd : \Delta]\!]$ *where for*

$$\Psi : (\mathit{Conf} \rightarrow \Lambda^\infty) \rightarrow (\mathit{Conf} \rightarrow \Lambda^\infty)$$

and

$$\Psi(\phi)[\![\Gamma]\!] = \begin{cases} \varepsilon & \text{if } \Gamma \text{ blocks} \\ \eta \mathbin{\hat{\circ}} \phi[\![\Gamma']\!] \text{ if } \Gamma \stackrel{\eta}{\twoheadrightarrow} \Gamma' & \text{otherwise} \end{cases}$$

we let $\mathcal{T} = \mathit{fix}\Psi$.

6.3.2 Denotational semantics

As the domain for our denotational semantics we take Λ^∞, and let ρ range over it.

With respect to the semantic continuations we must make a distinction, similar to the one made when specifying the transition rules, between semantic success continuations and semantic failure continuations. We define the set of semantic failure continuations to be Λ^∞ itself, by defining

$$\mathit{Fail} = \Lambda^\infty$$

Semantic success continuations are defined as the function space

$$\mathit{Succ} = \mathit{Fail} \rightarrow \Lambda^\infty$$

We use typical elements $R \in Succ$ and $F \in Fail$, not to be confused with their syntactic counterparts. The idea of applying (semantic) success continuations to failure continuations to model backtracking behavior is due to [de Bruin, 1986].

Our denotational semantics $\mathcal{D}[\![\cdot]\!] : Goal \rightarrow Succ \rightarrow Fail \rightarrow \Lambda^{\infty}$ is defined by the equations below.

$\mathcal{B}_0$

(i) $\mathcal{D}[\![a]\!]RF = I(a) \rightarrow a \mathbin{\hat{\circ}} RF, F$

(ii) $\mathcal{D}[\![p]\!]RF = \star \mathbin{\hat{\circ}} \mathcal{D}[\![g]\!]RF$ for $p \leftarrow g$ in D

(iii) $\mathcal{D}[\![g_1; g_2]\!]RF = \mathcal{D}[\![g_1]\!](\mathcal{D}[\![g_2]\!]R)F$

(iv) $\mathcal{D}[\![g_1 \Box g_2]\!]RF = \mathcal{D}[\![g_1]\!]R(\mathcal{D}[\![g_2]\!]RF)$

As a comment, the expression $I(a) \rightarrow a \mathbin{\hat{\circ}} RF, F$ must be read as

$$\textit{if } I(a) \textit{ then } a \mathbin{\hat{\circ}} (R(F)) \textit{ else } F$$

where $R(F)$ denotes the application of R to F. Note that only in (i) R must be applied to F. In the other equations R and F are just taken along, the brackets are used there only for disambiguation.

The difference between success continuations and failure continuations comes to light in the equations for the goals $g_1; g_2$ and $g_1 \Box g_2$. For the latter, the meaning corresponding to the second component is put in the failure continuation, while for the first it is put in the success continuation.

Definition 6.3.2 *Let* $R_0 = \lambda\rho.\rho$ *and* $F_0 = \varepsilon$ *then* $\mathcal{M}[\![< D \mid g >]\!] = \mathcal{D}[\![g]\!]R_0F_0$.

Again some examples. We assume that no action fails.

$$\mathcal{D}[\![a_1; a_2]\!]R_0F_0 = \mathcal{D}[\![a_1]\!](\mathcal{D}[\![a_2]\!]R_0)F_0 = a_1 \mathbin{\hat{\circ}} (a_2 \mathbin{\hat{\circ}} \varepsilon) = a_1a_2$$

$$\mathcal{D}[\![a_1 \Box a_2]\!]R_0F_0 = \mathcal{D}[\![a_1]\!]R_0(\mathcal{D}[\![a_2]\!]R_0F_0) = a_1 \mathbin{\hat{\circ}} (a_2 \mathbin{\hat{\circ}} \varepsilon) = a_1a_2$$

We also have

$$\begin{aligned}\mathcal{D}[\![(a_1 \Box a_2); a_3]\!]R_0F_0 &= \mathcal{D}[\![a_1 \Box a_2]\!](\mathcal{D}[\![a_3]\!]R_0)F_0 \\ &= \mathcal{D}[\![a_1]\!](\mathcal{D}[\![a_3]\!]R_0)(\mathcal{D}[\![a_2]\!](\mathcal{D}[\![a_3]\!]R_0)F_0) \\ &= a_1 \mathbin{\hat{\circ}} (a_3 \mathbin{\hat{\circ}} (a_2 \mathbin{\hat{\circ}} (a_3 \mathbin{\hat{\circ}} \varepsilon))) \\ &= a_1a_3a_2a_3\end{aligned}$$

6.3.3 Equivalence between operational and denotational semantics

We state our objective in giving the comparative semantics for $\mathcal{B}_0$ as a theorem.

Theorem 6.3.3 $\mathcal{O}[\![< D \mid g >]\!] = \mathcal{M}[\![< D \mid g >]\!]$

The proof has a structure similar to the one given for $\mathcal{A}$. (section 6.2.3)

$$\begin{aligned} \mathcal{O}[\![< D \mid g >]\!] &= \mathcal{T}[\![g; \surd : \Delta]\!] && \text{by definition 6.3.1} \\ &= \mathcal{F}[\![g; \surd : \Delta]\!] && \text{by corollary 6.3.7} \\ &= \mathcal{D}[\![g]\!] R_0 F_0 && \text{by definition 6.3.4} \\ &= \mathcal{M}[\![< D \mid g >]\!] && \text{by definition 6.3.2} \end{aligned}$$

In the actual proof we will use the intermediate semantic functions

$\mathcal{R} : SuccCo \rightarrow Succ$
$\mathcal{F} : FailCo \rightarrow Fail$

mapping syntactic success and failure continuations to their semantic counterparts.

Definition 6.3.4

a. $\mathcal{R}[\![\surd]\!] = \lambda\rho.\rho$

b. $\mathcal{R}[\![g; R]\!] = \mathcal{D}[\![g]\!]\mathcal{R}[\![R]\!]$

c. $\mathcal{F}[\![\Delta]\!] = \varepsilon$

d. $\mathcal{F}[\![R : F]\!] = \mathcal{R}[\![R]\!]\mathcal{F}[\![F]\!]$

The following lemma states that unobservable transitions do no harm.

Lemma 6.3.5 *If* $\Gamma \longrightarrow \Gamma'$ *then* $\mathcal{F}[\![\Gamma]\!] = \mathcal{F}[\![\Gamma']\!]$

Proof: Consider first the case that $\Gamma = a; R : F$ and assume that $\Gamma \longrightarrow \Gamma'$, which occurs when $I(a)$ is *false*. Now

$$\begin{aligned} \mathcal{F}[\![a; R : F]\!] &= \mathcal{R}[\![a; R]\!]\mathcal{F}[\![F]\!] \\ &= \mathcal{D}[\![a]\!]\mathcal{R}[\![R]\!]\mathcal{F}[\![F]\!] \\ &= \mathcal{F}[\![F]\!] \end{aligned}$$

simply by applying the definitions.

As a second case we give the proof for *Alt*. Let $\Gamma = g_1 \square g_2; R : F$. Then

$$\begin{aligned}\mathcal{F}[\![(g_1 \Box g_2); R : F]\!] &= \mathcal{R}[\![(g_1 \Box g_2); R]\!]\mathcal{F}[\![F]\!] \\ &= \mathcal{D}[\![g_1 \Box g_2]\!]\mathcal{R}[\![R]\!]\mathcal{F}[\![F]\!] \\ &= \mathcal{D}[\![g_1]\!]\mathcal{R}[\![R]\!](\mathcal{D}[\![g_2]\!]\mathcal{R}[\![R]\!]\mathcal{F}[\![F]\!]) \\ &= \mathcal{R}[\![g_1; R]\!]\mathcal{F}[\![g_2; R : F]\!] = \mathcal{F}[\![g_1; R : g_2; R : F]\!]\end{aligned}$$

□

Again, the key step in the proof that $\mathcal{O} = \mathcal{M}$ consists of showing that the function $\mathcal{F}$ is a fixed point of the operator Ψ that characterizes the operational meaning of a program (section 6.3.1).

Lemma 6.3.6 $\Psi(\mathcal{F}) = \mathcal{F}$

We introduce a complexity measure c on $\Gamma \in \mathit{FailCo}$ such that whenever $\Gamma \longrightarrow \Gamma'$ we have that $c(\Gamma) > c(\Gamma')$, by defining

$$c(\Delta) = 0 \text{ and } c(g; R : F) = c(g) + c(F)$$

$$c(a) = c(p) = c(\surd) = 1$$

$$c(g_1; g_2) = c(g_1 \Box g_2) = c(g_1) + c(g_2) + 1$$

As an illustration

$$\begin{aligned}c((g_1 \Box g_2); R : F) &= c(g_1 \Box g_2) + c(F) \\ &= c(g_1) + c(g_2) + 1 + c(F) \\ &> c(g_1) + c(g_2) + c(F) \\ &= c(g_1; R : g_2; R : F)\end{aligned}$$

We must prove for each Γ that $\Psi(\mathcal{F})[\![\Gamma]\!] = \mathcal{F}[\![\Gamma]\!]$. If Γ blocks then the result is clear. Assume that Γ is of the form $g; R : F$ and that for some η we have $\Gamma \stackrel{\eta}{\longrightarrow\!\!\!\!\rightarrow} \Gamma'$. The proof proceeds by a case analysis on g.

- If $g \equiv a$ we have by the definition of Ψ if $I(a)$ is true that $\Psi(\mathcal{F})[\![a; R : F]\!] = a \mathbin{\hat{\circ}} \mathcal{F}[\![R; F]\!] =$ (by applying definition 6.3.4) $\mathcal{F}[\![a; R : F]\!]$. If $I(a)$ is not true then $a; R : F \longrightarrow F$ and the result follows from the induction-hypothesis, stating that for Γ' satisfying $c(\Gamma) > c(\Gamma')$ it holds that $\Psi(\mathcal{F})[\![\Gamma']\!] = \mathcal{F}[\![\Gamma']\!]$.
- If $g \equiv p$ then we have that $\Psi(\mathcal{F})[\![p; R : F]\!] = \star \mathbin{\hat{\circ}} \mathcal{F}[\![g; R : F]\!] =$ (by applying the definition of $\mathcal{D}$ and $\mathcal{F}$) $\star \mathbin{\hat{\circ}} \mathcal{D}[\![g]\!]\mathcal{R}[\![R]\!]\mathcal{F}[\![F]\!]$ and the result follows immediately.
- For $g \equiv g_1; g_2$ we have that $\Psi(\mathcal{F})[\![(g_1; g_2); R : F]\!] = \Psi(\mathcal{F})[\![g_1; (g_2; R) : F]\!]$ by the definition of Ψ and by induction this is equal to $\mathcal{F}[\![g_1; (g_2; R) : F]\!]$ which by lemma 6.3.4 equals $\mathcal{F}[\![(g_1; g_2); R : F]\!]$.
- The case $g \equiv g_1 \Box g_2$ is similar.

□

Corollary 6.3.7 $\mathcal{T} = \mathcal{F}$

6.4 Dynamic object creation and synchronous communication with local backtracking

In the sections that follow we extend the language $\mathcal{B}_0$ with primitives for dynamic object creation and communication. An object is a process that is evaluating a goal. A number of objects may be active concurrently. Our first extension $\mathcal{B}_1$ allows communication with local backtracking, local in the sense that the backtracking occurs within the confines of an object without affecting the behavior of other objects. To be able to treat $\mathcal{B}_1$ as a uniform language (cf. section 6.1.2) we have delegated the task of inventing identifiers for newly created objects to the programmer, by providing him with a collection of names for objects.

Syntax As for $\mathcal{B}_0$ we have actions $a \in A$, and procedure variables $p \in Pvar$. Moreover, we assume a set of object names O, for which we use typical elements $\hat{\alpha}$ and $\hat{\beta}$. Further we have a set C of communication intentions, with typical elements c. A communication intention may be either an input statement $\bar{c}$ or an output statement that we also write as c. Note that dependening on the context we may use c for denoting an output statement or for a communication intention in general, including input statements.

We define the extensions $e \in E$ by

$$e ::= new(\hat{\alpha}) \mid c \mid \bar{c}$$

and *goals* $g \in Goal$ by

$$g ::= a \mid p \mid g_1 ; g_2 \mid g_1 \Box g_2 \mid e$$

A declaration D is of the form

$$D = \{p \leftarrow g \mid p \in Pvar, g \in Goal\}$$

and, in order to be able to specify the own activity of an object we associate with each $\hat{\alpha}$ a procedure variable $p \in Pvar$ and assume that we have stated

$$body(\hat{\alpha}) = p$$

relating each $\hat{\alpha}$ to some p.

A *program*, again, is a tuple of the form $< D \mid g >$.

6.4.1 Operational semantics

Our operational semantics is set up in a similar way as for $\mathcal{B}_0$. As the result domain for characterizing the behavior of a program we take

$$\mathbb{R} = \mathcal{P}_{nc}(\Lambda^{\infty})$$

since the concurrent execution of objects gives rise to indeterminate behavior.

We assume a set of objects Obj, with typical elements α and β. These objects correspond in a natural way with the object names from O, in that for each $\alpha \in Obj$ we have $\hat{\alpha} \in O$ and vice versa.

Communication between objects may be either successful or failing. We assume that each output statement c has a number of matching input statements that we write as $\overline{c}$, $\overline{c}_1$, $\overline{c}_2$, ... Moreover we assume to have defined a function $eval : C \times C \rightarrow Goal$, and say that the communication between c and $\overline{c}$ is successful if $eval(c, \overline{c}) = skip$ and failing if $eval(c, \overline{c}) = fail$. We also use a function $\overline{eval} : C \times C \rightarrow Goal$ that depends on *eval* in the following way:

$$\overline{eval}(c, \overline{c}) = \begin{cases} c & \text{if } eval(c, \overline{c}) = fail \\ skip & \text{otherwise} \end{cases}$$

The function *eval* is used at the input side to determine whether backtracking must occur in case the communication fails. If the communication is failing applying $\overline{eval}$ results in repeating the request for communication at the output side. Otherwise, if the communication is successful the output side may proceed, and $\overline{eval}$ results in *skip*. As a comment, the interplay of *eval* and $\overline{eval}$ models the communication over channels in DLP. There we allow the input side to backtrack until a successful communication is possible. The output side, on the other hand, must wait until the input side has found a successful input statement.

We use syntactic success continuations $R \in SuccCo$ and syntactic failure continuations $F \in FailCo$ as introduced for $\mathcal{B}_0$:

$$R ::= \surd \mid g; R$$

$$F ::= \Delta \mid R : F$$

Since each object may be active evaluating a goal, we use a tuple of the form $< \alpha, F >$ which we will also refer to as the object α. A configuration $\Gamma \in Conf = \mathcal{P}(Obj \times FailCo)$ consists of a set of such objects.

The transition rules for $\mathcal{B}_1$ listed below, must be augmented with a general rule

$$\Gamma \xrightarrow{\eta} \Gamma' \Longrightarrow X \cup \Gamma \xrightarrow{\eta} X \cup \Gamma'$$

stating that whenever a transition is possible from Γ to Γ' then any set of objects disjoint with Γ and Γ' may be added without affecting the possibility of a transition.

We have refined the interpretation function I, in order to let the outcome depend on the object by which the evaluation takes place.

$\mathcal{B}_1$

$\{< \alpha, a; R : F >\} \xrightarrow{a} \{< \alpha, R : F >\}$ if $I(a)(\alpha)$ $\longrightarrow \{< \alpha, F >\}$ otherwise	*Action*

$\{< \alpha, p; R : F >\} \xrightarrow{\star} \{< \alpha, g; R : F >\}$ for $p \leftarrow g$ in D	*Rec*

$$\{< \alpha, (g_1; g_2); R : F >\} \longrightarrow \{< \alpha, g_1; (g_2; R) : F >\} \qquad \textit{Seq}$$

$$\{< \alpha, (g_1 \Box g_2); R : F >\} \longrightarrow \{< \alpha, (g_1; R) : (g_2; R) : F >\} \qquad \textit{Alt}$$

$$\{< \alpha, new(\hat{\beta}); R : F >\} \qquad \textit{New}$$

$$\xrightarrow{\star} \{< \alpha, R : F >, < \beta, body(\hat{\beta}); \surd : \Delta >\}$$

$$\{< \alpha.c; R_1 : F_1 >, < \beta, \bar{c}; R_2 : F_2 >\} \qquad \textit{Comm}$$

$$\xrightarrow{\star} \{< \alpha, \overline{eval}(c, \bar{c}); R_1 : F_1 >, < \beta, eval(c, \bar{c}); R_2 : F_2 >\}$$

$$\{< \alpha, \surd : F >\} \longrightarrow \{< \alpha, F >\} \qquad \textit{Tick}$$

Apart from the fact that a configuration is now a collection of processes, the transition system differs from the one for $\mathcal{B}_0$ only by including the axioms *New* and *Comm*. Applying the axiom *New* results in adding an object to the collection of active objects, executing the body of that object. Applying *Comm* has as effect that the output statement c and the input statement $\bar{c}$ are replaced by respectively the outcome of $\overline{eval}(c, \bar{c})$ and $eval(c, \bar{c})$.

As an example of creating a new object, let $body(\hat{\beta}) = p$ and $p \leftarrow a$ in D, then we have the computation

$$\{< \alpha, new(\hat{\beta}); \surd : \Delta >\}$$

$$\xrightarrow{\star} \{< \alpha, \surd : \Delta >, < \beta, p; \surd : \Delta >\} \longrightarrow \{< \alpha, \Delta >, < \beta, p; \surd : \Delta >\}$$

$$\xrightarrow{\star} \{< \alpha, \Delta >, < \beta, a; \surd : \Delta >\}$$

$$\xrightarrow{a} \{< \alpha, \Delta >, < \beta, \surd : \Delta >\} \longrightarrow \{< \alpha, \Delta >, < \beta, \Delta >\}$$

Next we give an example showing the backtracking that may occur in communication.

Let

$$D = \{p_1 = c, p_2 = \bar{c}_1 \Box \bar{c}_2\}.$$

When we moreover define

$$eval(c, \bar{c}_1) = \textit{fail} \text{ and } eval(c, \bar{c}_2) = \textit{skip}$$

then we have the computation

$$\{<\alpha, p_1; \surd : \Delta>, <\beta, p_2; \surd : \Delta>\}$$

$$\xrightarrow{\star} \dots \xrightarrow{\star} \{<\alpha, c; \surd : \Delta>, <\beta, (\bar{c}_1 \,\Box\, \bar{c}_2); \surd : \Delta>\}$$

$$\longrightarrow \{<\alpha, c; \surd : \Delta>, <\beta, (\bar{c}_1; \surd) : (\bar{c}_2; \surd) : \Delta>\}$$

$$\xrightarrow{\star} \{<\alpha, c; \surd : \Delta>, <\beta, (\mathit{fail}; \surd) : (\bar{c}_2; \surd) : \Delta>\}$$

$$\longrightarrow \{<\alpha, c; \surd : \Delta>, <\beta, \bar{c}_2; \surd : \Delta>\}$$

$$\xrightarrow{\star} \{<\alpha, \mathit{skip}; \surd : \Delta>, <\beta, \mathit{skip}; \surd : \Delta>\}$$

$$\xrightarrow{\mathit{skip}} \dots \xrightarrow{\mathit{skip}} \dots \longrightarrow \{<\alpha, \Delta>, <\beta, \Delta>\}$$

Notice that after the first attempt at communication, between c and $\bar{c}_2$ the output side does not change and the input side $\bar{c}_1$ is replaced by *fail.* The second attempt, however, succeeds and results in *skip* on both sides.

We may now define the operational semantics of a program $< D \mid g >$ as a function $\mathcal{O}[\![\cdot]\!] : \mathcal{B}_1 \rightarrow \mathrm{I\!R}$, with $\mathrm{I\!R} = \mathcal{P}_{nc}(\Lambda^{\infty})$.

Definition 6.4.1 $\mathcal{O}[\![< D \mid g >]\!] = \mathcal{T}[\![< \alpha_0, g; \surd : \Delta >]\!]$ *for some initial object* α_0, *where for* $\Psi : (Conf \rightarrow \mathrm{I\!R}) \rightarrow (Conf \rightarrow \mathrm{I\!R})$ *and*

$$\Psi(\phi)[\![\Gamma]\!] = \begin{cases} \{\varepsilon\} & \text{if } \Gamma \text{ blocks} \\ \bigcup\{\eta \,\hat{\circ}\, \phi[\![\Gamma']\!] : \Gamma \xrightarrow{\eta} \Gamma'\} & \text{otherwise} \end{cases}$$

we let $\mathcal{T} = \mathit{fix}\Psi$.

As a difference with the definition given for $\mathcal{B}_0$ it must be noted that now a set of strings over Λ is delivered. The apparent non-determinism of .. program is not due to its backtracking behavior, but comes from the indeterminacy introduced by the concurrent behavior of objects.

6.4.2 Denotational semantics

Since we wish to be able to ignore unresolved attempts at communication, as long as they do not block the computation, taking $\mathrm{I\!R}$ as our domain for giving a denotational semantics no longer suffices.

Therefore we define the process domain $\mathrm{I\!P}$, with typical elements ρ, by the equation

$$\mathrm{I\!P} \cong \{\delta\} \cup \mathcal{P}_{co}(\Lambda \times \mathrm{I\!P} \cup C \times (C \rightarrow \mathrm{I\!P}))$$

For technical convenience, we use a special empty process δ. Non-empty processes in $\mathrm{I\!P}$ are sets containing pairs of the form $\eta \cdot \rho$, with η a non-empty label, and pairs of the form $c \cdot f$, with c a communication intention from C and f an element from $C \rightarrow \mathrm{I\!P}$. Remember that we use the pairing operator $\cdot$ to write pairs $< x, y >$ as $x \cdot y$. We will use syntactic variables ξ to range over elements of a set ρ. Intuitively, a pair $\eta \cdot \rho$ represents a computation step labeled by η and followed by a resumption ρ. A pair $c \cdot f$, on the other hand, represents the intention to communicate, that is to wait for a matching communication intention.

We model the concurrent behavior of a computation by arbitrary interleaving, and define the *merge* operator $\| : \mathbb{P} \times \mathbb{P} \rightarrow \mathbb{P}$ that must satisfy $\delta \parallel \rho = \rho = \rho \parallel \delta$ and for non-empty ρ_1 and ρ_2

$$\rho_1 \parallel \rho_2 = \rho_1 ⫽ \rho_2 \cup \rho_2 ⫽ \rho_1 \cup \rho_1 \mid \rho_2$$

where $⫽$ is the so-called *left-merge* operator defined by

$$\rho_1 ⫽ \rho_2 = \{\eta \cdot (\rho \parallel \rho_2) : \eta \cdot \rho \in \rho_1\} \cup \{c \cdot \lambda c'.(f(c') \parallel \rho_2) : c \cdot f \in \rho_1\}$$

that merges the resumption of the items contained in ρ_1 with ρ_2. Cf. [de Bakker et al, 1984]. By applying the *left-merge* operator twice, we achieve an arbitrary interleaving of the computation steps contained in the respective processes.

We define the communication operator $\mid$ by

$$\rho_1 \mid \rho_2 = \bigcup \{\xi_i \mid \xi_j : \xi_i \in \rho_i, \xi_j \in \rho_j \;\; for \;\; i,j \in \{1,2\} \;\; and \;\; i \neq j\}$$

The definition of communication ensures that all possible communications are taken into account. The result of a communication step is determined by defining the result for two matching communication intentions.

$$\xi_1 \mid \xi_2 = \begin{cases} \{\star \cdot (f_1(\overline{c}) \parallel f_2(c))\} & \text{if } \xi_1 = c \cdot f_1 \text{ and } \xi_2 = \overline{c} \cdot f_2 \\ \emptyset & \text{otherwise} \end{cases}$$

Technically speaking, we must prove the merge operator to exist and be continuous by showing that it is the fixed point of a suitable operator, as has been explained before.

Similarly as for $\mathcal{B}_0$ we use semantic success continuations $R \in Succ = Fail \rightarrow \mathbb{P}$ and semantic failure continuations $F \in Fail = \mathbb{P}$. The function $\mathcal{D}[\![\cdot]\!] : Goal \rightarrow Obj \rightarrow Succ \rightarrow Fail \rightarrow \mathbb{P}$ is defined by the equations below. Let $R_0 = \lambda\rho.\rho$ and $F_0 = \delta$.

$\mathcal{B}_1$

(i) $\mathcal{D}[\![a]\!]\alpha RF = I(a)(\alpha) \rightarrow \{a \cdot RF\}, F$

(ii) $\mathcal{D}[\![p]\!]\alpha RF = \{\star \cdot \mathcal{D}[\![g]\!]\alpha RF\}$ for $p \leftarrow g$ in D_α

(iii) $\mathcal{D}[\![g_1; g_2]\!]\alpha RF = \mathcal{D}[\![g_1]\!]\alpha(\mathcal{D}[\![g_2]\!]\alpha R)F$

(iv) $\mathcal{D}[\![g_1 \square g_2]\!]\alpha RF = \mathcal{D}[\![g_1]\!]\alpha R(\mathcal{D}[\![g_2]\!]\alpha RF)$

(v) $\mathcal{D}[\![new(\hat{\beta})]\!]\alpha RF = \{\star \cdot (RF \parallel \mathcal{D}[\![body(\hat{\beta})]\!]\beta R_0 F_0)\}$

(vi) $\mathcal{D}[\![c]\!]\alpha RF = \{c \cdot f\}$ with $f = \lambda\overline{c} \in C.\mathcal{D}[\![\overline{eval}(c, \overline{c})]\!]\alpha RF)$

(vii) $\mathcal{D}[\![\overline{c}]\!]\alpha RF = \{\overline{c} \cdot f\}$ with $f = \lambda c \in C.\mathcal{D}[\![eval(c, \overline{c})]\!]\alpha RF)$

Recall that the expression RF both in (i) and (v) denotes the application of R to F.

Definition 6.4.2 $\mathcal{M}[\![< D \mid g >]\!] = \mathcal{D}[\![g]\!]\alpha_0 R_0 F_0$ *for some initial object* α_0.

6.4.3 Equivalence between operational and denotational semantics

In contrast to the equivalence results for our previous languages we are not able now to state a direct equivalence between $\mathcal{O}$ and $\mathcal{M}$. We must use a projection π that takes elements from $\mathbb{P}$ to $\mathbb{R}$, yielding sequences of actions. Moreover, our projection eliminates unresolved communication intentions that do not block the computation.

Theorem 6.4.3 $\mathcal{O}[\![< D \mid g >]\!] = \pi \circ \mathcal{M}[\![< D \mid g >]\!]$ *for a suitable projection* π.

Assuming that we have such a projection π we may outline the proof as

$$\begin{aligned} \mathcal{O}[\![< D \mid g >]\!] &= \mathcal{T}[\![\{< \alpha_0, g; \surd : \Delta >\}]\!] \text{ by definition 6.4.1} \\ &= \pi \circ \mathcal{G}[\![\{< \alpha_0, g; \surd : \Delta >\}]\!] \text{ by corollary 6.4.7} \\ &= \pi \circ \mathcal{F}[\![g; \surd : \Delta]\!]\alpha_0 \text{ by definition 6.4.4} \\ &= \pi \circ \mathcal{D}[\![g]\!]\alpha_0 R_0 F_0 \text{ by definition 6.4.4} \\ &= \pi \circ \mathcal{M}[\![< D \mid g >]\!] \text{ by definition 6.4.2} \end{aligned}$$

Apart from the semantic functions $\mathcal{F} : \mathit{FailCo} \rightarrow \mathit{Fail}$ and $\mathcal{R} : \mathit{SuccCo} \rightarrow \mathit{Succ}$, mapping syntactic failure continuations and syntactic success continuations to their semantic counterparts, we also need to have a function $\mathcal{G} : \mathit{Conf} \rightarrow \mathbb{P}$ mapping configurations Γ, which are sets of objects, to an element from $\mathbb{P}$.

Definition 6.4.4

a. $\mathcal{R}[\![\surd]\!]\alpha = \lambda\rho.\rho$

b. $\mathcal{R}[\![g; R]\!]\alpha = \mathcal{D}[\![g]\!]\alpha\mathcal{R}[\![R]\!]\alpha$

c. $\mathcal{F}[\![\Delta]\!]\alpha = \delta$

d. $\mathcal{F}[\![R : F]\!]\alpha = \mathcal{R}[\![R]\!]\alpha\mathcal{F}[\![F]\!]\alpha$

e. $\mathcal{G}[\![\{< \alpha_1, F_1 >, ..., < \alpha_n, F_n >\}]\!] = \mathcal{F}[\![F_1]\!]\alpha_1 \parallel ... \parallel \mathcal{F}[\![F_n]\!]\alpha_n$

As we may see from the definition above, the meaning of a set of objects is simply the merge of the meaning of the individual elements.

Again we have the property that unobservable transitions do not affect the (mathematical) meaning of a configuration.

Lemma 6.4.5 *If* $\Gamma \longrightarrow \Gamma'$ *then* $\mathcal{G}[\![\Gamma]\!] = \mathcal{G}[\![\Gamma']\!]$

Proof: We will treat the case that $\Gamma = \{< \alpha, a; R : F >\}$, assuming that $I(a)(\alpha)$ is *false*.

$$\begin{aligned}\mathcal{G}[\![\Gamma]\!] &= \mathcal{F}[\![a; R : F]\!]\alpha \\ &= \mathcal{D}[\![a]\!]\alpha\mathcal{R}[\![R]\!]\alpha\mathcal{F}[\![F]\!]\alpha \\ &= \mathcal{F}[\![F]\!]\alpha \text{ (since } I(a)(\alpha) \text{ is } \textit{false}) \\ &= \mathcal{G}[\![< \alpha, F >]\!] \text{ as desired.}\end{aligned}$$

□

In order to show that $\pi \circ \mathcal{G}$ is a fixed point of the higher order mapping characterizing $\mathcal{T}$ we will first define the projection operator π that reduces the unresolved communication intentions to $\{\varepsilon\}$, the equivalent of the empty process δ.

First we define a function $rem : \mathbb{P} \rightarrow \mathbb{P}$ by $rem(\delta) = \emptyset$ and

$$rem(\rho) = \rho \backslash \{c \cdot f : c \cdot f \in \rho\}$$

which defines $rem(\rho)$ to be what remains after removing all unresolved communication intentions and occurrences of δ. We then define $\pi : \mathbb{P} \rightarrow \mathbb{R}$ by

$$\pi\,\rho \;=\; \begin{cases} \{\varepsilon\} & \text{if } rem(\rho) = \emptyset \\ \bigcup\{\eta \,\hat{\circ}\, (\pi\,\rho') : \eta \cdot \rho' \in rem(\rho)\} & \text{otherwise} \end{cases}$$

A property of π that we will use below is expressed by $\bigcup\{\eta \,\hat{\circ}\, (\pi\,\rho')\} = \pi\,\{\eta \cdot \rho'\}$ which can easily be verified.

Lemma 6.4.6 $\Psi(\pi \circ \mathcal{G}) = \pi \circ \mathcal{G}$

Proof: We use a complexity measure similar as the one introduced for $\mathcal{B}_0$, but extended in order to cope with configurations containing a collection of objects. What we need is that whenever $\Gamma \longrightarrow \Gamma'$ then $c(\Gamma) > c(\Gamma')$. We define $c(\Gamma) = \Sigma_{x \in \Gamma}\, c(x)$ and let $c(< \alpha, F >) = c(F)$. We further extend the complexity measure for $\mathcal{B}_0$ by taking $c(e) = 1$ for $e \in E$.

We must now prove for all Γ that $\Psi(\pi \circ \mathcal{G})[\![\Gamma]\!] = \pi \circ \mathcal{G}[\![\Gamma]\!]$. It may be observed, since we have defined $\mathcal{G}[\![\{< \alpha_1, F_1 >, \ldots, < \alpha_n, F_n >\}]\!] = \mathcal{F}[\![F_1]\!]\alpha_1 \parallel \ldots \parallel \mathcal{F}[\![F_n]\!]\alpha_n$, that the equality $\mathcal{G}[\![\Gamma \cup \Gamma']\!] = \mathcal{G}[\![\Gamma]\!] \parallel \mathcal{G}[\![\Gamma']\!]$ holds, due to the obvious associativity and commutativity of the parallel merge operator. Hence $\pi \circ \mathcal{G}[\![\Gamma \cup \Gamma']\!] = \pi\,(\mathcal{G}[\![\Gamma]\!] \parallel \mathcal{G}[\![\Gamma']\!])$. This observation allows us, for non-blocking configurations, to restrict our attention to the (syntactic) processes in the configuration Γ that really play a role in the transition taken. If a configuration Γ blocks then, since this is either due to termination or to an unresolved communication intention, the equality $\Psi(\pi \circ \mathcal{G})[\![\Gamma]\!] = \pi \circ \mathcal{G}[\![\Gamma]\!]$ clearly holds. We will treat some selected cases of non-blocking configurations. Let $\overline{R}_i = \mathcal{R}[\![R_i]\!]\alpha_i$ and $\overline{F}_i = \mathcal{F}[\![F_i]\!]\alpha_i$, with subscript i possibly empty.

- If $\Gamma = \{< \alpha, a; R : F >\}$ then in case $I(a)(\alpha)$ we have $\Psi(\pi \circ \mathcal{G})[\![\Gamma]\!] = \bigcup\{a \mathbin{\hat{\circ}} (\pi \circ \mathcal{G})[\![\{< \alpha, R : F >\}]\!]\} = \pi\{a \cdot \mathcal{G}[\![\{< \alpha, R : F >\}]\!]\}$ which, by the definition of $\mathcal{R}$ and $\mathcal{D}$, is equal to $\pi \circ \mathcal{G}[\![\Gamma]\!]$.
  If $I(a)(\alpha)$ is *false* then $\Gamma \rightarrow \Gamma'$ with $\Gamma' = \{< \alpha, F >\}$. Since $c(\Gamma') < c(\Gamma)$ we have by induction $\Psi(\pi \circ \mathcal{G})[\![\Gamma']\!] = \pi \circ \mathcal{G}[\![\Gamma']\!]$ and by lemma 6.4.5 this is equal to $\pi \circ \mathcal{G}[\![\Gamma]\!]$.

- If $\Gamma = \{< \alpha, new(\hat{\beta}); R : F >\}$ then

$$\begin{aligned}
\Psi(\pi \circ \mathcal{G})[\![\Gamma]\!] &= \bigcup\{\star \mathbin{\hat{\circ}} (\pi \circ \mathcal{G})[\![\{< \alpha, R : F >, < \beta, body(\hat{\beta}); \surd : \Delta >\}]\!]\} \\
&= \pi\{\star \cdot \mathcal{G}[\![\{< \alpha, R : F >, < \beta, body(\hat{\beta}); \surd : \Delta >\}]\!]\} \\
&\quad \text{(by the property of } \pi\text{)} \\
&= \pi\{\star \cdot (\overline{RF} \parallel \mathcal{D}[\![body(\hat{\beta})]\!]\beta\mathcal{R}[\![\surd]\!]\beta\mathcal{F}[\![\Delta]\!]\beta)\} = \\
&\quad \text{(by the definition of } \mathcal{G}\text{)} \\
&= \pi\,\mathcal{D}[\![new(\hat{\beta})]\!]\alpha\overline{RF} = \\
&\quad \text{(by the definition of } \mathcal{D}\text{)} \\
&= \pi \circ \mathcal{G}[\![\{< \alpha, new(\hat{\beta}); R : F >\}]\!] \\
&\quad \text{(by applying definition 6.4.4)}
\end{aligned}$$

- Let $\Gamma = \{< \alpha_1, c; R_1 : F_1 >, < \alpha_2, \overline{c}; R_2 : F_2 >\}$. Then

$$\begin{aligned}
\Psi(\pi \circ \mathcal{G})[\![\Gamma]\!] &= \pi\{\star \cdot \mathcal{G}[\![\{< \alpha_1, \overline{eval}(c, \overline{c}); R_1 : F_1 >, < \alpha_2, eval(c, \overline{c}); R_2 : F_2 >\}]\!]\} \\
&\quad \text{(by applying } Comm\text{)} \\
&= \pi\,(\{\star \cdot (\mathcal{D}[\![\overline{eval}(c, \overline{c})]\!]\alpha_1\overline{R}_1\overline{F}_1 \parallel \mathcal{D}[\![eval(c, \overline{c})]\!]\alpha_2\overline{R}_2\overline{F}_2)\}) \\
&\quad \text{(by definition 6.4.4)} \\
&= \pi\,(\{c \cdot \lambda\tau.\mathcal{D}[\![\overline{eval}(c, \tau)]\!]\alpha_1\overline{R}_1\overline{F}_1\} \parallel \{\overline{c} \cdot \lambda\tau.\mathcal{D}[\![eval(\tau, \overline{c})]\!]\alpha_2\overline{R}_2\overline{F}_2\}) \\
&\quad \text{(by the definition of communication)} \\
&= \pi\,(\mathcal{D}[\![c]\!]\alpha_1\overline{R}_1\overline{F}_1 \parallel \mathcal{D}[\![\overline{c}]\!]\alpha_2\overline{R}_2\overline{F}_2) \\
&\quad \text{(by the definition of } \mathcal{D}\text{)} \\
&= \pi \circ \mathcal{G}[\![\{< \alpha_1, c; R_1 : F_1 >, < \alpha_2, \overline{c}; R_2 : F_2 >\}]\!] \\
&\quad \text{(by applying definition 6.4.4 again)}
\end{aligned}$$

□

We may now simply collect our result.

Corollary 6.4.7 $\mathcal{T} = \pi \circ \mathcal{G}$

6.5 Asynchronous rendez-vous with global backtracking

The language $\mathcal{B}_2$, our second extension of $\mathcal{B}_0$, is similar to $\mathcal{B}_1$ in that a number of objects may become concurrently active, but differs from it in the way communication is dealt with. The model of communication employed is that of method call by (asynchronous) rendez-vous. A notable difference with the rendez-vous mechanism as encountered in Ada or POOL is the possible occurrence of backtracking over the resulting answers. In order to maintain this backtrack information a process is created for each rendez-vous. Therefore we no longer identify objects and processes but instead say that multiple processes may refer to a single object. We distinguish between two kinds of processes, namely *constructor* processes that execute the own activity of an object and processes that are created for handling a rendez-vous. As for $\mathcal{B}_1$ we put the burden of creating unique object and process identifiers on the programmers, who may use a collection of object and process names for this purpose.

We regard the rendez-vous as the evaluation of a method call by an object and will therefore speak of methods instead of procedures. For a rendez-vous to take place an object must state its willingness to accept a method call. Acceptance is non-deterministic in that the object may choose to accept one of a number of possible requests.

We speak of an *asynchronous* rendez-vous since the invoking process must explicitly request an answer. The result of a method call is delivered as a *resumption*, which is a goal that performs some action to update the context of the caller according to the outcome of the evaluation of the call.

Syntax We assume a set of actions A, with typical elements a. As primitive actions we assume the actions *fail* and *skip* to be included in A. We have method variables $m \in Mvar$, that act as procedure variables. Further we introduce a set of process names P, with typical elements $\hat{\alpha}$ and $\hat{\beta}$, and assume also a set of object names O, with typical elements $\underline{\hat{\alpha}}$ and $\underline{\hat{\beta}}$, We take O disjoint from P. Since processes refer to an object, for each element $\hat{\alpha}$ in P, we state that there is an object name $\underline{\hat{\alpha}}$ in O.

We assume to have a set of results R, with typical elements r, and moreover assume that with each $m \in Mvar$ is associated an r_m Further we need (asynchronous) method calls of the form $\hat{\alpha}!m$, accept statements of the form $[m_1, ..., m_n]$, resumption requests of the form $\hat{\alpha}?$ and statements to return the answer to a method call that we denote by r.

We define extensions $e \in E$ by

$$e ::= new(\underline{\hat{\alpha}}) \mid \hat{\alpha}!m \mid [m_1, ..., m_n] \mid \hat{\alpha}? \mid r$$

and define *goals* $g \in Goal$ by

$$g ::= a \mid m \mid g_1; g_2 \mid g_1 \square g_2 \mid e$$

A *declaration* D is of the form

$$D = \{m \leftarrow g \mid m \in Mvar, g \in Goal\}$$

and we assume a function *body* defining $body(\underline{\hat{\alpha}}) = m$ for each $\underline{\hat{\alpha}}$.

A *program* is a tuple $< D \mid g >$.

6.5.1 Operational semantics

For characterizing the behavior of a program we use a set of labels $\Lambda = A \cup \{\star\}$ with $\star$ a special symbol to denote visible behavior that cannot further be inspected. The empty label ε will be used to denote invisible behavior and will consequently disappear in the operational semantics.[5]

As the result domain for characterizing the behavior of a program we take

$$\mathbb{R} = \mathcal{P}_{nc}(\Lambda^\infty)$$

the non-empty closed powerset of finite and infinite strings over Λ.

We use a set of processes *Proc*, with typical elements α and β, and further assume a set of objects *Obj*, with typical elements $\underline{\alpha}$ and $\underline{\beta}$. We state that $Obj \subset Proc$, and moreover associate with each element $\alpha \in Proc$ an element $\underline{\alpha} \in Obj$ that we call the object to which α refers. We let *Obj* be contained in *Proc* since we may identify the process executing the constructor for an object with the object itself. For each object name $\hat{\underline{\alpha}}$ we have an object $\underline{\alpha}$ in *Obj*, and for each process name $\hat{a}$ we have a process α in *Proc*. Note that, since O and P are disjoint, the process β derived from the process name $\hat{\beta}$, is distinct from the process $\underline{\beta}$ corresponding to the object name $\hat{\underline{\beta}}$, although the process β does refer to the object $\underline{\beta}$.

Communication by rendez-vous embodies the most important and yet most difficult aspect of our language $\mathcal{B}$. A complication in treating this communication is the possible occurrence of backtracking over the answers produced in a rendez-vous. For this reason we have decomposed a synchronous rendez-vous in a method call of the form $\hat{\beta}!m$ and a request for the answers resulting from evaluating m, of the form $\hat{\beta}?$. A method call $\hat{\beta}!m$ is considered to be addressed to the object $\underline{\beta}$, that is the process $\underline{\beta}$ executing the constructor $body(\hat{\underline{\beta}})$. The caller is assumed to provide the process name $\hat{\beta}$ for the process β that is created to evaluate m.

We have pictured a typical rendez-vous below. A more detailed rendering of the steps is given in figure 6.1.

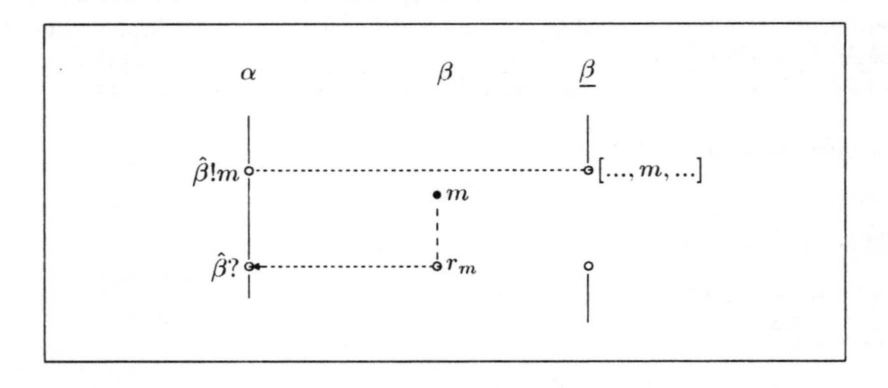

[5]The special label $\star$ is introduced to simplify the equivalence proof.

Figure 6.1: Matching communication pairs in a rendez-vous

Process α is calling a method m, with O bound to $\underline{\beta}$. Process $\underline{\beta}$ is willing to accept a call for method m.

A new process β is created to evaluate the method m. Process α may proceed as soon as the call is accepted.

The evaluation of m continues until β arrives at r. Process α must wait until the request $\hat{\beta}?$ is answered.

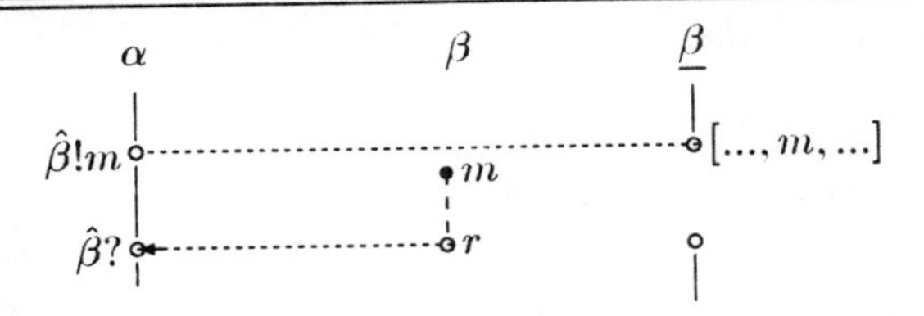

When the first answer has been sent to α, both process α and process $\underline{\beta}$, that has accepted the method call, may continue.

As soon as the call $\hat{\beta}!m$ is accepted, due to the occurrence of $[..., m, ...]$ in $\underline{\beta}$, process α requests for an answer by stating $\hat{\beta}?$. The process β, which refers to the object $\underline{\beta}$, starts evaluating the goal m. Process α must wait until process β has computed an answer. When the first answer is computed it is sent to α. The process $\underline{\beta}$, which is the constructor process for the object $\underline{\beta}$, may then proceed with the evaluation of the constructor $body(\underline{\hat{\beta}})$.

Resumptions To model the communication that takes place in a rendez-vous in a more precise way, we introduce the set *Comm* consisting of elements of the form $\hat{\alpha}!m$, $\overline{m}$, $\hat{\beta}_i?$ and r, respectively denoting a method call, the intention to accept the method call m, the i-th request for a resumption (where we take $\hat{\beta}?$ to stand for $\hat{\beta}_0$) and the readiness to send an answer to the caller of a method.[6]

For the answers r we further differentiate between

- r_m — standing for a normal answer,
- $r_{\delta,\overline{m}}$ — indicating failure, that is the absence of further answers, and
- $r_{\overline{m}}$ — that is used to deliver a record of all the answers.

When we take a closer look at answers r_m, that are associated with a method m, we will see that r_m stands for something of the form $r_{a_1 a_2 ... a_n ...}$, where a_i is the action returned at the i-th request for a resumption.

We may now define the *norm* of r_m, that we write as $\mid r_m \mid$, as the number of possible answers contained in r_m. If $\mid r_m \mid = n$, for some finite n, then evaluating the method m results in finitely many answers, namely the actions $a_1 ... a_n$, that are returned to the invoking process for the first n requests for a resumption. After that the process evaluating the method call must send the record it has of the outcomes all at once.

In order to define the function *res* that delivers the proper actions to the process requesting for the resumption, we have to be able to index r_m as an array of actions. Hence, we define

$$r_m[i] = \begin{cases} a_i & \text{if } 0 < i \leq \mid r_m \mid \\ \mathit{fail} & \text{otherwise} \end{cases}$$

We now define the function *res* by the equations

$$res(r_m[i]) = r_m[i]$$

$$res(r_{\delta,\overline{m}}) = \mathit{fail}$$

$$res(r_{\overline{m}}) = a_1 \,\square\, ... \,\square\, a_n \text{ if } r_m = r_{a_1 ... a_n},\ n \text{ finite}$$

[6] In order to avoid confusion we may write $\hat{\beta}_i?$ as $\hat{\beta}?[i]$, but this will not be necessary.

Intuitively, it will be clear that the recorded answers for a method m are simply the (finite) disjunction of the answers contained in r_m.

To model the actual communication event, we make use of a function $eval : Comm \times Comm \rightarrow Goal$ and its counterpart $\overline{eval} : Comm \times Comm \rightarrow Goal$. This pair of functions allows us to conveniently describe what takes place both at the side of the invoking process and at the side of the process evaluating the method call.

We define *eval*, that takes effect at the process that requests for a resumption, by stating

$$eval(\hat{\beta}_i?, r) = \begin{cases} res(r[i+1]) \,\Box\, \hat{\beta}_{i+1}? & \text{if } r = r_m \\ res(r) & \text{otherwise} \end{cases}$$

and, similarly we define the function $\overline{eval}$, that takes effect at the side of the process sending the answer, by

$$\overline{eval}(\hat{\beta}_i?, r) = \begin{cases} skip & \text{if } r = r_m \\ r_{\overline{m}} & \text{otherwise} \end{cases}$$

Note that $r_{\overline{m}}$ will only be inserted as a goal when $| r_m |$ is finite, since otherwise $r_{\delta,\overline{m}}$ will never be reached.

Summarizing, when the resumption $eval(\hat{\beta}_i?, r) = a_{i+1} \,\Box\, \hat{\beta}_{i+1}?$ then backtracking is allowed due to the (disjunctive) insertion of $\hat{\beta}_{i+1}?$. When the resumption is *fail* then no more answers can be produced and the calling process must backtrack to previous goals. The resumption $a_1 \,\Box \ldots \Box\, a_n$ will then be delivered if such backtracking turns out to be successful.

Our treatment thus far covers both the synchronization and the transfer of results taking place in a rendez-vous. Before we give a more detailed description of the global backtracking as it may occur in a rendez-vous we remind the reader that for DLP we have adopted a protocol of mutual exclusion that guarantees that no other method call becomes active until the first answer is delivered. After having communicated the first result, the process evaluating the method becomes independent, and immediately starts producing an alternative answer concurrently with the own activity of the object to which the method call was addressed.

Backtracking The backtracking that occurs locally in a process is modeled by using syntactic failure continuations, which are stacks of syntactic success continuations, that we have defined as

$$R ::= \surd \mid g; R$$

$$F ::= \Delta \mid R : F$$

A success continuation R represents the part of the program that must be executed to find a solution and corresponds to the sequential evaluation of a goal, without backtracking. As an example in $g; \surd$, for an arbitrary goal g, when g is successfully evaluated then the empty success continuation $\surd$ is reached.

Backtracking requires to keep account of what alternatives remain to be evaluated. For this purpose we use the so-called failure continuations F. The empty failure continuation Δ represents the situation that all possible solutions have been explored. Intuitively, a failure continuation $R : F$ is a stack having a success continuation R on top. If R for some reason fails then the failure continuation F, the remainder of the stack, may be used to find a solution. The evaluation of a goal g is started by the failure continuation $g; \surd : \Delta$. When during the execution an alternative goal, say of the form $g_1 \Box g_2$ is encountered, as represented by $(g_1 \Box g_2); R : F$, then the resulting failure continuation is $(g_1; R) : (g_2; R) : F$, having the success continuation $g_1; R$ on top of the stack and $g_2; R$ as the first alternative to be explored.

Without distributed backtracking we could have processes of the form $< \alpha, F >$, with α a process identifier and F a failure continuation. However, the possible occurrence of distributed backtracking complicates matters, in that we need to introduce yet another kind of syntactic continuations. We define *process continuations* C by

$$C ::= \Xi \mid < \alpha, F >: C$$

The empty process continuation Ξ is simply a process that has nothing left to do. So we may forget about its name. As an example, a process continuation of the form $< \alpha, F >: \Xi$ is simply the process evaluating the failure continuation F. Now suppose that for process $\underline{\beta}$, evaluating the constructor *body*$(\hat{\beta})$, we have a process continuation $< \underline{\beta}, [..., m, ...]; R : F >: \Xi$ then, as we explained previously, a process which for the moment we indicate by $< \beta, m; r_m \Box r_\delta; \surd : \Delta >$, evaluating m, may be started when another process calls for $\hat{\beta}!m$. We cannot, however, have the process $\underline{\beta}$ running concurrently with the process β, since we must block the acceptance of any other method call for $\underline{\beta}$ until β has delivered its first answer. Our solution to modeling this protocol of mutual exclusion is simply to put $< \beta, (m; r_m \Box r_\delta); \surd : \Delta >$ in front of the process continuation $< \underline{\beta}, R : F >: \Xi$, thus blocking the execution of $\underline{\beta}$. In other words a process continuation may be regarded as a process stack, of which the top is the active process. Then, as soon as a solution has been computed, which is represented by the process continuation $< \beta, r_m; R' : F' >:< \beta, R : F >: \Xi$, we may communicate the answer to the process asking for it. From then on, we have two processes running concurrently, namely $< \beta, R' : F' >: \Xi$ to explore any alternative solutions contained in the failure continuation $R' : F'$. The process $< \underline{\beta}, R : F >: \Xi$, which is the process evaluating the constructor for $\hat{\beta}$, may now accept new method calls.

As indicated, configurations $\Gamma \in Conf = \mathcal{P}(ProcCo)$ are sets of syntactic process continuations.

The transition rules are listed below. We assume a general rule of the form

$$\Gamma \xrightarrow{\eta} \Gamma' \Longrightarrow X \cup \Gamma \xrightarrow{\eta} X \cup \Gamma'$$

for $X \in Conf$ disjoint from Γ and Γ'.

To give meaning to the actions we assume an abstract interpretation function $I : A \rightarrow Proc \rightarrow \{true, false\}$ defining for each action whether it is successful or fails. The function I must satisfy $I(skip)(\alpha) = true$ and $I(fail)(\alpha) = false$, for any process α.

$\mathcal{B}_2$

$$\{<\alpha, a; R : F >: C\} \xrightarrow{a} \{<\alpha, R : F >: C\} \text{ if } I(a)(\alpha) \qquad \textit{Action}$$
$$\longrightarrow \{<\alpha, F >: C\} \text{ otherwise}$$

$$\{<\alpha, m; R : F >: C\} \xrightarrow{\star} \{<\alpha, g; R : F >: C\} \text{ for } m \leftarrow g \text{ in } D \qquad \textit{Rec}$$

$$\{<\alpha, (g_1; g_2); R : F >: C\} \longrightarrow \{<\alpha, g_1; (g_2; R) : F >: C\} \qquad \textit{Seq}$$

$$\{<\alpha, (g_1 \Box g_2); R : F >: C\} \qquad \textit{Alt}$$
$$\longrightarrow \{<\alpha, (g_1; R) : (g_2; R) : F >: C\}$$

$$\{<\alpha, new(\hat{\beta}); R : F >: C\} \qquad \textit{New}$$
$$\xrightarrow{\star} \{<\alpha, R : F >: C, <\underline{\beta}, body(\hat{\beta}); \surd : \Delta >: \Xi\}$$

$$\{<\alpha, \hat{\beta}!m; R_1 : F_1 >: C_1, <\underline{\beta}, [..., m, ...]; R_2 : F_2 >: C_2\} \qquad \textit{Method}$$
$$\xrightarrow{\star} \{<\alpha, \hat{\beta}?; R_1 : F_1 >: C_1,$$
$$<\beta, (m; r_m \Box r_{\delta,\overline{m}}); \surd : \Delta >:<\underline{\beta}, R_2 : F_2 >: C_2\}$$

$$\{<\alpha, \hat{\beta}?; R_1 : F_1 >: C_1, <\beta, r; R_2 : F_2 >: C_2\} \qquad \textit{Result}$$
$$\xrightarrow{\star} \{<\alpha, eval(\hat{\beta}?, r); R_1 : F_1 >: C_1,$$
$$<\beta, \overline{eval}(\hat{\beta}?, r); R_2 : F_2 >: \Xi, C_2\}$$

$$\{<\alpha, \surd : F >: C\} \longrightarrow \{<\alpha, F >: C\} \qquad \textit{Tick}$$

The *operational semantics* of a program $< D \mid g >$ is defined in the usual way.

Definition 6.5.1 $\mathcal{O}[\![< D \mid g >]\!] = \mathcal{T}[\![<\alpha_0, g; \surd : \Delta >: \Xi]\!]$ *for an initial process* α_0, *where for*

$$\Psi(\phi)[\![\Gamma]\!] = \begin{cases} \{\varepsilon\} & \textit{if } \Gamma \textit{ blocks} \\ \bigcup\{\eta \mathbin{\hat{\circ}} \phi[\![\Gamma']\!] : \Gamma \xrightarrow{\eta} \Gamma'\} & \textit{otherwise} \end{cases}$$

we let $\mathcal{T} = \mathit{fix}\Psi$.

6.5.2 Examples

We will illustrate the use of the axioms *Method* and *Result* with some examples.

Synchronous rendez-vous Let $D = \{m \leftarrow a_1 \Box a_2\}$ and $r_m = r_{a_1' \, a_2'}$. Then

$$\{< \alpha, \hat{\beta}!m; \hat{\beta}?; \surd : \Delta >: \Xi, < \underline{\beta}, [..., m, ...]; \surd : \Delta >: \Xi\}$$

$$\xrightarrow{\star} \{< \alpha, \hat{\beta}?; \surd : \Delta >: \Xi, < \beta, ((m; r_m) \Box r_{\delta,\overline{m}}); \surd : \Delta >:< \underline{\beta}, \surd : \Delta >: \Xi\}$$

by applying the axiom *Method*. The call $\hat{\beta}!m$ is directly followed by the request for an answer $\hat{\beta}?$, where $\hat{\beta}$ is the name for the process evaluating the method m. The process β itself is pushed on the stack for the object $\underline{\beta}$, thus blocking any further activity of $\underline{\beta}$. The next transitions come from the evaluation of m, after putting $r_{\delta,\overline{m}}$, the reply in case of failure, as the last alternative on the failure stack of β.

$$\longrightarrow \{< \alpha, \hat{\beta}?; \surd : \Delta >: \Xi,$$
$$< \beta, ((m; r_m); \surd) : (r_{\delta,\overline{m}}; \surd) : \Delta >:< \underline{\beta}, \surd : \Delta >: \Xi\}$$

$$\longrightarrow \{< \alpha, \hat{\beta}?; \surd : \Delta >: \Xi,$$
$$< \beta, m; (r_m; \surd) : (r_{\delta,\overline{m}}; \surd) : \Delta >:< \underline{\beta}, \surd : \Delta >: \Xi\}$$

$$\xrightarrow{\star} \{< \alpha, \hat{\beta}?; \surd : \Delta >: \Xi,$$
$$< \beta, (a_1 \Box a_2); (r_m; \surd) : (r_{\delta,\overline{m}}; \surd) : \Delta >:< \underline{\beta}, \surd : \Delta >: \Xi\}$$

Process β starts the evaluation of the body of m.

$$\longrightarrow \{< \alpha, \hat{\beta}?; \surd : \Delta >: \Xi,$$
$$< \beta, a_1; (r_m; \surd) : a_2; (r_m; \surd) : (r_{\delta,\overline{m}}; \surd) : \Delta >:< \underline{\beta}, \surd : \Delta >: \Xi\}$$

$$\xrightarrow{a_1} \{< \alpha, \hat{\beta}?; \surd : \Delta >: \Xi,$$
$$< \beta, (r_m; \surd) : a_2; (r_m; \surd) : (r_{\delta,\overline{m}}; \surd) : \Delta >:< \underline{\beta}, \surd : \Delta >: \Xi\}$$

The process β is ready to communicate its first result, which is a_1' since $r_m = r_{a_1' \, a_2'}$.

$$\xrightarrow{\star} \{< \alpha, (\, a_1' \Box \hat{\beta}_1?); \surd : \Delta >: \Xi,$$
$$< \beta, \mathbf{skip}; \surd : a_2; (r_m; \surd) : (r_{\delta,\overline{m}}; \surd) : \Delta >: \Xi, < \underline{\beta}, \surd : \Delta >: \Xi\}$$

The object $\underline{\beta}$ may now continue its own activity and β may concurrently search for alternative answers. We will omit the evaluation of *skips*.

$$\xrightarrow{a'_1} \ldots \longrightarrow \{< \alpha, \hat{\beta}?; \surd : \Delta >: \Xi, \\ < \beta, a_2; (r_m; \surd) : (r_{\delta,\overline{m}}; \surd) : \Delta >: \Xi, < \underline{\beta}, \Delta >: \Xi\}$$

$$\xrightarrow{a_2} \{< \alpha, \hat{\beta}?; \surd : \Delta >: \Xi, < \beta, (r_m; \surd) : (r_{\delta,\overline{m}}; \surd) : \Delta >: \Xi, < \underline{\beta}, \Delta >: \Xi\}$$

Now β is ready to communicate its second answer.

$$\xrightarrow{\star} \{< \alpha, (a'_2 \,\Box\, \hat{\beta}_2?); \surd : \Delta >: \Xi, \\ < \beta, skip; \surd : (r_{\delta,\overline{m}}; \surd) : \Delta >: \Xi, \Xi, < \underline{\beta}, \Delta >: \Xi\}$$

$$\xrightarrow{a'_2} \ldots \longrightarrow \{< \alpha, \hat{\beta}_2?; \surd : \Delta >: \Xi, < \beta, r_{\delta,\overline{m}}; \surd : \Delta >: \Xi, \Xi, < \underline{\beta}, \Delta >: \Xi\}$$

Finally β communicates failure issued by $r_{\delta,\overline{m}}$, since no more answers are available.

$$\xrightarrow{\star} \{< \alpha, fail; \surd : \Delta >: \Xi, < \beta, r_{\overline{m}}; \surd : \Delta >: \Xi, \Xi, < \underline{\beta}, \Delta >: \Xi\}$$

$$\longrightarrow \ldots \longrightarrow \{< \alpha, \Delta >: \Xi, < \beta, r_{\overline{m}}; \surd : \Delta >: \Xi, \Xi, < \underline{\beta}, \Delta >: \Xi\}$$

The process β will now remain forever ready to produce a record of the answers computed for m.

When an answer is communicated the process that has produced the answer is popped from the process stack in order to enable both the process and the remainder of the stack to run concurrently. In practice the stack contains never more than two non-empty processes. In the case that it contains only one non-empty process, the empty process is added to the collection of processes.

Asynchronous rendez-vous Let $D = \{m \leftarrow a'_1 \,\Box\, a'_2\}$ and $r_m = r_{a''_1 a''_2}$. Then starting our computation with the configuration

$$\{< \alpha, \hat{\beta}!m; (a_1 \,\Box\, a_2); \hat{\beta}?; \surd : \Delta >: \Xi, < \underline{\beta}, [\ldots, m, \ldots]; \surd : \Delta >: \Xi\}$$

will by applying *Method* lead to

$$\xrightarrow{\star} \{< \alpha, (a_1 \,\Box\, a_2); \hat{\beta}?; \surd : \Delta >: \Xi, \\ < \beta, ((m; r_m) \,\Box\, r_{\delta,\overline{m}}); \surd : \Delta >:< \underline{\beta}, \surd : \Delta >: \Xi\}$$

which will result in

$$\longrightarrow \ldots \xrightarrow{a_1} \{< \alpha, \hat{\beta}?; \surd : a_2; \hat{\beta}?; \surd : \Delta >: \Xi, \\ < \beta, a'_1; r_m; \surd : a'_2; r_m; \surd : r_{\delta,\overline{m}}); \surd : \Delta >:< \underline{\beta}, \surd : \Delta >: \Xi\}$$

which leads, after sending an answer, to

$$\xrightarrow{a_1'} \dots \xrightarrow{\star} \{< \alpha, (a_1'' \,\Box\, \hat{\beta}_1?); \surd : a_2; \hat{\beta}?; \surd : \Delta >: \Xi,$$
$$< \beta, skip; \surd : a_2'; r_m; \surd : r_{\delta,\overline{m}}); \surd : \Delta >: \Xi, < \underline{\beta}, \surd : \Delta >: \Xi\}$$

The resumption a_1'' will be executed in process α, and then the second result will be sent.

$$\xrightarrow{a_1''} \dots \xrightarrow{a_2'} \dots \xrightarrow{\star} \{< \alpha, (a_2'' \,\Box\, \hat{\beta}_2?); \surd : a_2; \hat{\beta}?; \surd : \Delta >: \Xi,$$
$$< \beta, skip; \surd : r_{\delta,\overline{m}}); \surd : \Delta >: \Xi, < \underline{\beta}, \surd : \Delta >: \Xi\}$$

This will then, due to the failure of the request $\hat{\beta}_2?$, result in the configuration

$$\xrightarrow{a_2''} \dots \longrightarrow \{< \alpha, a_2; \hat{\beta}?; \surd : \Delta >: \Xi,$$
$$< \beta, r_{\delta,\overline{m}}); \surd : \Delta >: \Xi, < \underline{\beta}, \surd : \Delta >: \Xi\}$$

and hence, after evaluating a_2 in

$$\xrightarrow{a_2} \dots \xrightarrow{\star} \{< \alpha, (a_1'' \,\Box\, a_2''); \surd : \Delta >: \Xi,$$
$$< \beta, r_{\delta,\overline{m}}); \surd : \Delta >: \Xi, < \underline{\beta}, \surd : \Delta >: \Xi\}$$

6.5.3 Denotational semantics

We construct our domain in a similar way as for $\mathcal{B}_1$ but, since communication in $\mathcal{B}_2$ is more complex the part taking care of the communication intentions is correspondingly more involved.

We first define a set $C = Proc \times Comm$, with typical elements c. In other words C has elements of the form $[\alpha, \hat{\beta}!m]$, $[\alpha, \overline{m}]$, $[\alpha, \hat{\beta}?]$ and $[\alpha, r]$. We further assume to have a set $T = Proc \cup Comm$ and define the domain $\mathbb{P}$, with typical elements ρ and q by

$$\mathbb{P} \cong \{\delta\} \cup \mathcal{P}_{co}(\Lambda \times \mathbb{P} \cup C \times \mathbb{P} \cup C \times (T \to \mathbb{P}))$$

We let ξ range over elements of a set ρ, and f over functions from $T \to \mathbb{P}$.

As an example of a process in $\mathbb{P}$ consider the set $\{a \cdot \rho, c_1 \cdot \rho', c_2 \cdot f\}$, containing one action a with resumption ρ and two communication intentions, one with resumption from $\mathbb{P}$ and one with a resumption from $T \to \mathbb{P}$.

We have to adapt the *parallel merge* operator given for $\mathcal{B}_1$ to the present situation. The operator $\| : \mathbb{P} \times \mathbb{P} \to \mathbb{P}$ must satisfy $\delta \parallel \rho = \rho = \rho \parallel \delta$ and for non-empty ρ_1 and ρ_2

$$\rho_1 \parallel \rho_2 = \rho_1 ⫝̸ \rho_2 \cup \rho_2 ⫝̸ \rho_1 \cup \rho_1 \mid \rho_2$$

with the *left merge* operator ⫝̸ defined by

$$\rho_1 ⫝̸ \rho_2 = \{\eta \cdot (\rho \parallel \rho_2) : \eta \cdot \rho \in \rho_1\} \cup \{c \cdot (\rho \parallel \rho_2) : c \cdot \rho \in \rho_1\} \cup$$
$$\{c \cdot \lambda\tau.(f(\tau) \parallel \rho_2) : c \cdot f \in \rho_1\}$$

and the communication operator $\mid$ by

$$\rho_1 \mid \rho_2 = \bigcup\{\xi_i \mid \xi_j : \xi_i \in \rho_i, \xi_j \in \rho_j \;\; for \;\; i,j \in \{1,2\} \;\; and \;\; i \neq j\}$$

As for $\mathcal{B}_0$, the definition of communication ensures that all possible communications are taken into account. The result of a communication step is now determined by defining the result for all possible pairs of matching communication intentions.

$$\xi_1 \mid \xi_2 = \begin{cases} \{\star \cdot (\rho \parallel f(\beta))\} & \text{if } \xi_1 = [\alpha.\hat{\beta}!m] \cdot \rho \text{ and } \xi_2 = [\underline{\beta}, \overline{m}] \cdot f \\ \{\star \cdot (f(r) \parallel \rho)\} & \text{if } \xi_1 = [\alpha, \hat{\beta}?] \cdot f \text{ and } \xi_2 = [\beta, r] \cdot \rho \\ \emptyset & \text{otherwise} \end{cases}$$

Process insertion When a request for a method call is granted, the process evaluating the call has exclusive access to the object to which the method call was directed, exclusive in the sense that no other process referring to that object will be active until the first answer or failure is returned to the invoking process. However, when this happens, that is when the invoking process receives the first answer, the (constructor) process that accepted the request for a rendez-vous may continue its computation, in parallel with everything else that is going on. In order to let the accepting process be active immediately after the first result has been returned we need an *insertion operator* that grafts the resumption of this process at the right place in the (semantic) process due to evaluating the method call.

We define the insertion operator $\rhd_\alpha : \mathbb{P} \times \mathbb{P} \to \mathbb{P}$ by $\delta \rhd_\alpha \delta = \delta$. $\delta \rhd_\alpha \rho = \rho$, $\rho \rhd_\alpha \delta = \delta$ and for non-empty ρ and q

$$\begin{aligned} \rho \rhd_\alpha q = \{\eta \cdot \rho \rhd_\alpha q' : \eta \cdot q' \in q\} \;\; &\cup \;\; \{[\alpha, r] \cdot (\rho \parallel q') : [\alpha, r] \cdot q' \in q\} \;\; \cup \\ &\{c \cdot \rho \rhd_\alpha q' : c \cdot q' \in q \;\; for \;\; c \neq [\alpha, r]\} \;\; \cup \\ &\{c \cdot \lambda\tau.\rho \rhd_\alpha f(\tau) : c \cdot f \in q\} \end{aligned}$$

In other words the first time that the intention for communicating an answer substitution of the form $[\alpha, r] \cdot q'$ is encountered, the inserted process ρ is put in parallel with the resumption awaiting a successful communication. We may then not put $[\alpha, r] \cdot \rho \rhd_\alpha q'$ in also. In definition 6.5.4 we will encounter the equivalence $\mathcal{C}[\![< \alpha, F >: C]\!] = \mathcal{C}[\![C]\!] \rhd_\alpha \mathcal{F}[\![F]\!]\alpha$, where $\mathcal{C}[\![C]\!]$ is the meaning of the (syntactic) process continuation C and $\mathcal{F}[\![F]\!]\alpha$ the meaning of the (syntactic) failure continuation F. We regard this equation to embody the intuition behind the insertion operator.

Again, we remark that in order to prove the operators $\parallel$ and $\rhd_\alpha$ do exist and behave properly by being continuous, we may define them using contracting higher order mappings.

The semantic function $\mathcal{D}[\![\cdot]\!] : Goal \to Proc \to Succ \to Fail \to \mathbb{P}$ is given by the equations below. Let $R_0 = \lambda\rho.\rho$ and $F_0 = \delta$.

$\mathcal{B}_2$

(i) $\mathcal{D}[\![a]\!]\alpha RF = I(a)(\alpha) \to \{a \cdot RF\}, F$

(ii) $\mathcal{D}[\![m]\!]\alpha RF = \{\star \cdot \mathcal{D}[\![g]\!]\alpha RF\}$ for $m \leftarrow g$ in D

(iii) $\mathcal{D}[\![g_1; g_2]\!]\alpha RF = \mathcal{D}[\![g_1]\!]\alpha(\mathcal{D}[\![g_2]\!]\alpha R)F$

(iv) $\mathcal{D}[\![g_1 \Box g_2]\!]\alpha RF = \mathcal{D}[\![g_1]\!]\alpha R(\mathcal{D}[\![g_2]\!]\alpha RF)$

(v) $\mathcal{D}[\![new(\underline{\hat{\beta}})]\!]\alpha RF = \{\star \cdot (RF \,\|\, \mathcal{D}[\![body(\underline{\hat{\beta}})]\!]\underline{\beta} R_0 F_0)\}$

(vi) $\mathcal{D}[\![\hat{\beta}!m]\!]\alpha RF = \{[\alpha, \hat{\beta}!m] \cdot RF\}$

(vii) $\mathcal{D}[\![[m_1, ..., m_n]]\!]\alpha RF = \{[\alpha, \overline{m_i}] \cdot f_i : i = 1, ..., n\}$
with $f_i = \lambda\beta \in Proc.RF \rhd_\beta \mathcal{D}[\![m_i; r_{m_i} \Box r_{\delta,\overline{m}}]\!]\beta R_0 F_0$

(viii) $\mathcal{D}[\![\hat{\beta}?]\!]\alpha RF = \{[\alpha, \beta?] \cdot f\}$
with $f = \lambda c \in Comm.\mathcal{D}[\![eval(\hat{\beta}?, c)]\!]\alpha RF$

(ix) $\mathcal{D}[\![r]\!]\alpha RF = \{[\alpha, r] \cdot \rho\}$
with $\rho = \mathcal{D}[\![\overline{eval}(\hat{\alpha}?, r)]\!]\alpha RF$

Remark: The denotational function $\mathcal{D}[\![\cdot]\!]$ is itself a fixed point of a higher order (contracting) mapping, so there is no need to introduce an extra environment-parameter for modeling recursive procedure calls.

We leave the examples $\mathcal{D}[\![\hat{\beta}!m; \hat{\beta}?]\!]\alpha R_0 F_0 \,\|\, \mathcal{D}[\![[.., m, ..]]\!]\underline{\beta} R_0 F_0$ with $m \leftarrow a_1 \Box a_2$ (synchronous rendez-vous) and $\mathcal{D}[\![\hat{\beta}!m; a_1 \Box a_2; \hat{\beta}?]\!]\alpha R_0 F_0 \,\|\, \mathcal{D}[\![[.., m, ..]]\!]\underline{\beta} R_0 F_0$ with $m \leftarrow a_1' \Box a_2'$ (asynchronous rendez-vous) as an exercise to the reader.

Definition 6.5.2 $\mathcal{M}[\![< D \mid g >]\!] = \mathcal{D}[\![g]\!]\alpha_0 R_0 F_0$ *for some initial process* α_0.

6.5.4 Equivalence between operational and denotational semantics

We augment π (see section 6.4.3) by redefining, for non-empty ρ

$$rem(\rho) = \rho \backslash (\{c \cdot \rho' : c \cdot \rho' \in \rho\} \cup \{c \cdot f : c \cdot f \in \rho\})$$

and we state, in a by now familiar fashion:

Theorem 6.5.3 $\mathcal{O}[\![< D \mid g >]\!] = \pi \circ \mathcal{M}[\![< D \mid g >]\!]$

the proof of which is summarized by

$$\begin{aligned}\mathcal{O}[\![< D \mid g >]\!] &= \mathcal{T}[\![\{< \alpha_0, g; \surd : \Delta >: \Xi\}]\!] \text{ by definition 6.5.1}\\ &= \pi \circ \mathcal{G}[\![\{< \alpha_0, g; \surd; \Delta >: \Xi\}]\!] \text{ by corollary 6.5.7}\\ &= \pi \circ \mathcal{F}[\![g; \surd : \Delta]\!]\alpha_0 \text{ by definition 6.5.4}\\ &= \pi \circ \mathcal{D}[\![g]\!]\alpha_0 R_0 F_0 \text{ by definition 6.5.4}\\ &= \pi \circ \mathcal{M}[\![< D \mid g >]\!] \text{ by definition 6.5.2}\end{aligned}$$

In addition to the functions $\mathcal{R} : SuccCo \rightarrow Succ$ and $\mathcal{F} : FailCo \rightarrow Fail$ we need a function

$$\mathcal{C} : ProcCo \rightarrow \mathbb{P}$$

to give meaning to syntactic process continuations. As for $\mathcal{B}_1$ we also have a function $\mathcal{G} : Conf \rightarrow \mathbb{P}$, mapping configurations to processes in $\mathbb{P}$.

Definition 6.5.4

a. $\mathcal{R}[\![\surd]\!]\alpha = \lambda\rho.\rho$

b. $\mathcal{R}[\![g; R]\!]\alpha = \mathcal{D}[\![g]\!]\alpha\mathcal{R}[\![R]\!]\alpha$

c. $\mathcal{F}[\![\Delta]\!]\alpha = \delta$

d. $\mathcal{F}[\![R : F]\!]\alpha = \mathcal{R}[\![R]\!]\alpha\mathcal{F}[\![F]\!]\alpha$

e. $\mathcal{C}[\![\Xi]\!] = \delta$

f. $\mathcal{C}[\![< \alpha, F >: C]\!] = \mathcal{C}[\![C]\!] \rhd_\alpha \mathcal{F}[\![F]\!]\alpha$

g. $\mathcal{G}[\![\{C_1, ..., C_n\}]\!] = \mathcal{C}[\![C_1]\!] \parallel ... \parallel \mathcal{C}[\![C_n]\!]$

We can state the following property.

Lemma 6.5.5 *If* $\Gamma \longrightarrow \Gamma'$ *then* $\mathcal{G}[\![\Gamma]\!] = \mathcal{G}[\![\Gamma']\!]$

Proof: As an example, let $\Gamma = \{< \alpha, (g_1; g_2); R : F >: C\}$. We have that

$$\begin{aligned}\mathcal{G}[\![\Gamma]\!] &= \mathcal{C}[\![C]\!] \rhd_\alpha \mathcal{F}[\![(g_1; g_2); R : F]\!]\alpha\\ &= \mathcal{C}[\![C]\!] \rhd_\alpha \mathcal{F}[\![g_1; (g_2; R) : F]\!]\alpha \text{ (similar as for } \mathcal{B}_1)\\ &= \mathcal{G}[\![\{< \alpha, g_1; (g_2; R) : F >: C\}]\!] \text{ (according to definition 6.5.4).}\end{aligned}$$

□

In order to show that $\pi \circ \mathcal{G}$ is a fixed point of the higher order mapping characterizing $\mathcal{T}$ we will first define the projection operator π that reduces the unresolved communication intentions to $\{\varepsilon\}$, the equivalent of the empty process δ.

First we define a function $rem : \mathbb{P} \rightarrow \mathbb{P}$ by $rem(\delta) = \emptyset$ and

$$rem(\rho) = \rho \backslash (\{c \cdot \rho' : c \cdot \rho' \in \rho\} \cup \{c \cdot f : c \cdot f \in \rho\})$$

which defines $rem(\rho)$ to be what remains after removing all unresolved communication intentions and occurrences of δ. We then define $\pi : \mathbb{P} \rightarrow \mathbb{R}$ by

$$\pi\, \rho \;=\; \begin{cases} \{\varepsilon\} & \text{if } rem(\rho) = \emptyset \\ \bigcup\{\eta \;\hat{\circ}\; (\pi\, \rho') : \eta \cdot \rho' \in rem(\rho)\} & \text{otherwise} \end{cases}$$

A property of π that we will use below is expressed by $\bigcup\{\eta \;\hat{\circ}\; (\pi\, \rho')\} = \pi\, \{\eta \cdot \rho'\}$, which can easily be verified.

Lemma 6.5.6 $\Psi(\pi \circ \mathcal{G}) = \pi \circ \mathcal{G}$

Proof: We introduce a complexity measure c on $\Gamma \in ProcCo$ such that whenever $\Gamma \longrightarrow \Gamma'$ we have that $c(\Gamma) > c(\Gamma')$. We start by defining

$$c(\Delta) = 0 \text{ and } c(g; R : F) = c(g) + c(F)$$

$$c(a) = c(p) = c(e) = c(\surd) = 1$$

$$c(g_1; g_2) = c(g_1 \,\square\, g_2) = c(g_1) + c(g_2) + 1$$

and we extend this measure in order to cope with configurations containing a collection of objects. We define $c(\Gamma) = \Sigma_{x \in \Gamma}\, c(x)$ and let $c(<\alpha, F>: C) = c(F) + c(C)$, with $c(\Xi) = 0$. It is easy to establish the required property of c, stating that if $\Gamma \rightarrow \Gamma'$ then $c(\Gamma) > c(\Gamma')$ holds.

As an example,

$$\begin{aligned} c(<\alpha, (g_1; g_2); R : F>: C) &= c((g_1; g_2); R : F) + c(C) \\ &> c(g_1; (g_2; R) : F) + c(C) \\ &= c(<\alpha, g_1; (g_2; R) : F>: C) \end{aligned}$$

Now we must prove for all Γ that $\Psi(\pi \circ \mathcal{G})[\![\Gamma]\!] = \pi \circ \mathcal{G}[\![\Gamma]\!]$. For blocking configurations the result is immediate. For non-blocking configurations we treat the cases corresponding to *Action* and *Result*. Let $\overline{R}_i = \mathcal{R}[\![R_i]\!]\alpha_i$, $\overline{F}_i = \mathcal{F}[\![F_i]\!]\alpha_i$ and $\overline{C}_i = \mathcal{C}[\![C_i]\!]$. Below we will use the fact that $\bigcup\{\eta \;\hat{\circ}\; (\pi\, \rho)\} = \pi\, \{\eta \cdot \rho\}$.

- If $\Gamma = \{<\alpha, a; R : F>: C\}$ then if $I(a)(\alpha)$ is *true* we have

$$\begin{aligned} \Psi(\pi \circ \mathcal{G})[\![\Gamma]\!] &= \bigcup\{a \;\hat{\circ}\; (\pi \circ \mathcal{G})[\![\{<\alpha, R : F>: C\}]\!]\} \\ &\qquad \text{(by the definition of } \Psi) \\ &= \pi\, \{a \cdot \mathcal{G}[\![\{<\alpha, R : F>: C\}]\!]\} \\ &\qquad \text{(by the property of } \pi) \end{aligned}$$

$$= \pi\,\{a \cdot (\mathcal{C}[\![C]\!] \rhd_\alpha \mathcal{F}[\![R : F]\!]\alpha)\}$$
(by definition 6.5.4
$$= \pi\,(\mathcal{C}[\![C]\!] \rhd_\alpha \{a \cdot \mathcal{F}[\![R : F]\!]\alpha\})$$
(by the definition of $\rhd_\alpha$)
$$= \pi\,(\mathcal{C}[\![C]\!] \rhd_\alpha \mathcal{F}[\![a; R : F]\!])$$
(by applying the definition of $\mathcal{D}$ and $\mathcal{F}$)
$$= \pi\,\mathcal{C}[\![< \alpha, a; R : F >: C]\!]$$
$$= \pi \circ \mathcal{G}[\![\{< \alpha, a; R : F >: C\}]\!]$$

If $I(a)(\alpha)$ is not *true* we use the induction hypothesis as in the proof for $\mathcal{B}_1$.

- If $\Gamma = \{< \alpha_1, \hat{\alpha}_2?; R_1 : F_1 >: C, < \alpha_2, r; R_2; F_2 >: C_2\}$ then

$$\Psi(\pi \circ \mathcal{G})[\![\Gamma]\!] = \pi\,\{\star \cdot \mathcal{G}[\![\{< \alpha_1, eval(\hat{\alpha}_2?, r); R_1 : F_1 >: C_1,$$
$$< \alpha_2, \overline{eval}(\hat{\alpha}_2?, r); R_2 : F_2 >: \Xi, C_2\}]\!]\})$$
(by definition 6.5.4)
$$= \pi\,\{\star \cdot (\mathcal{C}[\![< \alpha_1, eval(\hat{\alpha}_2?, r); R_1 : F_1 >: C_1]\!]$$
$$\parallel \mathcal{C}[\![< \alpha_2, \overline{eval}(\hat{\alpha}_2?, r); R_2 : F_2 >: \Xi]\!] \parallel \overline{C}_2)\})$$
(taking $f = \lambda\tau.\overline{C}_1 \rhd_{\alpha_1} \mathcal{F}[\![eval(\hat{\alpha}_2?, \tau); R_1 : F_1]\!]\alpha_1$
and $\rho = \mathcal{D}[\![\overline{eval}(\hat{\alpha}_2?, r)]\!]\alpha_2\overline{R}_2\overline{F}_2$)
$$= \pi\,\{\star \cdot (f(r) \parallel \rho \parallel \overline{C}_2)\}$$
(by the definition of communication)
$$= \pi\,(\{[\alpha_1, \hat{\alpha}_2?] \cdot f\} \parallel \{[\alpha_2, r] \cdot (\rho \parallel \overline{C}_2)\})$$
(by the definition of $\rhd_{\alpha_1}$ and $\rhd_{\alpha_2}$
with $f' = \lambda\tau.\mathcal{F}[\![eval(\hat{\alpha}_2?, \tau); R_1 : F_1]\!]\alpha_1$)
$$= \pi\,((\overline{C}_1 \rhd_{\alpha_1} \{[\alpha_1, \hat{\alpha}_2?] \cdot f'\}) \parallel (\overline{C}_2 \rhd_{\alpha_2} \{[\alpha_2, r] \cdot \rho\}))$$
$$= \pi\,((\overline{C}_1 \rhd_{\alpha_1} \mathcal{D}[\![\hat{\alpha}_2?]\!]\alpha_1\overline{R}_1\overline{F}_1) \parallel (\overline{C}_2 \rhd_{\alpha_2} \mathcal{D}[\![r]\!]\alpha_2\overline{R}_2\overline{F}_2))$$
$$= \pi\,(\mathcal{C}[\![< \alpha_1, \hat{\alpha}_2?; R_1 : F_1 >: C_1]\!] \parallel \mathcal{C}[\![< \alpha_2, r; R_2 : F_2 >: C_2]\!])$$
$$= \pi \circ \mathcal{G}[\![\Gamma]\!] \text{ as desired.}$$

□

Corollary 6.5.7 $\mathcal{T} = \pi \circ \mathcal{G}$

7

An abstract version of DLP and its operational semantics

- The slow return from the fire...
the pause when the bell strikes suddenly again,
the listener on the alert -
Walt Whitman, *Leaves of Grass*

Now we wish to put some flesh on the skeleton provided in the previous chapter, where we gave the semantics of process creation, communication and backtracking in an abstract, uninterpreted, setting.

As a first step, we will give an operational characterization of an abstract language $\mathcal{L}$ which represents what we consider to be the core of DLP, and that is referred to as DLP_2 in section 3.9. In the next chapter, we will extend the comparative semantics given for the uniform languages $\mathcal{B}_0$, $\mathcal{B}_1$ and $\mathcal{B}_2$ to the comparative semantics for the languages $\mathcal{L}_0$, $\mathcal{L}_1$ and $\mathcal{L}_2$ that represent various subsets of DLP. The operational semantics for the language $\mathcal{L}$ is identical to the operational semantics for $\mathcal{L}_2$ given there. The reader, not interested in a more intuitive account of the operational semantics of DLP_2 is invited to skip this chapter and to continue with the comparative semantics for DLP, in chapter 8.

The DLP language is an extension of Prolog with *objects* and *special forms* for dealing with non-logical variables, object creation, and engaging in a rendez-vous. Objects in DLP are module-like entities with private non-logical (instance) variables and methods that have access to these variables in a protected way. Methods are defined by clauses that are written as Prolog clauses; these clauses may however contain as goals the special forms mentioned. We will treat here the subset DLP_2, covering the special forms listed below. An important restriction of *DLP_2* is that *accept* goals may occur only in the constructor process.

For reasons of syntactic clarity we no longer overload the equality symbol but introduce separate symbols for goals having side-effects, the assignment to non-logical variables and the creation of objects and processes. The special forms include:

- $v := t$ - to assign (the value of) the term t to the non-logical variable v
- $O::new(c(t))$ - to create a new instance of the object c and start the constructor process evaluating the goal $c(t)$, O thereafter refers to the newly created object
- $Q :: O!m(t)$ - to request a rendez-vous with the object to which O refers, Q will thereafter refer to the process created for evaluating the method call $m(t)$
- $Q?$ - to collect the answers resulting from the goal evaluated by the process to which Q refers,
- *accept*$(m_1, ..., m_n)$ - to state the willingness to accept methods $m_1, ..., m_n$

When assigning a term t to a non-logical variable, all non-logical variables in the term are first replaced by their values. The same applies when unifying two terms.

In particular we will concentrate on the issues of object creation and the communication occurring in a rendez-vous. Instances of objects are created by using the special form $O :: new(c(t))$ that results in binding O to the newly created instance of object c. When creating the object the constructor process evaluating the goal $c(t)$ is started for it. An asynchronous rendez-vous is initiated by a request of the form $Q :: O!m(t)$, with O bound to an object. When the request is accepted the logical variable Q will become bound to a pointer to the process created to evaluate the goal $m(t)$. A resumption request of the form $Q?$, where Q must be bound to a process, is used to collect the results of a rendez-vous. Recall that the synchronous rendez-vous, initiated by a method call of the form $O!m(t)$, is defined by a clause of the form

```
O!G :-  Q::O!G, Q?.
```

For a rendez-vous to take place the object must state its willingness to answer a method call by an accept statement of the form *accept*$(m_1, ..., m_n)$.

The distinguishing feature of DLP, compared with other approaches, is the possible occurrence of distributed backtracking in a rendez-vous. In the absence of distributed backtracking we may identify an object with a process, since an object then is either executing its own activity or evaluating a method call. Backtracking, however, requires to keep administration of what part of the search space has been explored. A notion of processes, separate from objects, is thus motivated by the need to keep a record of this information. Processes are created for each method call to enable backtracking over the answers.

The intent of this chapter is to provide a more precise definition of objects and processes, and to give a description of their behavior during a rendez-vous. Before going into any details, however, we will briefly repeat the informal account given of objects, processes and how backtracking may interact with the use of non-logical variables.

7.1 Objects, processes and backtracking

Objects serve as a means for modularization and provide protection for (local) data. Non-logical variables may be used to store the data encapsulated by an object. The clauses defined for an object act as methods, in that they have exclusive access to these data.

An object declaration in DLP contains the names of the non-logical variables of (instances of) the object and a definition of both the constructor clauses and method clauses. The clauses are written in standard Prolog format, but may contain as goals the special forms listed previously. A clause is considered a constructor clause when the predicate name of the head of the clause is identical to the name of the declared object. A method for an object is defined by all clauses having that method name as the predicate name of their head.

When a new object is created, by a goal of the form $O :: new(c(t))$, then this newly created object contains a copy of the non-logical variables of the declared object and also (conceptually) a copy of all its clauses. We will consider only active objects, that is objects with own activity arising from evaluating the constructor for that object. Since inheritance is effected by copying the non-logical variables and clauses from the inherited objects, then for giving a semantic characterization of the interpretation of DLP programs it suffices to look at DLP without inheritance.

Processes are created on the occasion of creating a new object, and when requesting a rendez-vous. When a new object is created, the constructor process, defined by clauses for the predicate with the name of the object, is started. When a rendez-vous is requested by a method call, a process is started for evaluating the method call. Creating a new process for evaluating such a goal is necessitated by our approach to distributed backtracking. Both the constructor process and the processes started for evaluating a goal by an object are said to refer to that object.

Backtracking may occur when multiple answer substitutions result from evaluating a method call. As an example, a method call to the object declared below may generate an indefinite number of solutions.

nat

```
object nat {
nat() :-   accept(num), nat().
num(0).
num(s(X)) :-   num(X).
}
```

The constructor clause for the object states that any call to *num* will be accepted.

Evaluating the goal

```
:-  O::new(nat()), Q::O!num(X), Q?, write(X), fail.
```

results in printing all natural numbers, eventually. The process created for evaluating num(X) backtracks each time that backtracking over Q? is tried due to the occurrence of fail in the goal.

In the example above, multiple processes could safely be active for the object simultaneously. Obviously, in the presence of non-logical variables, protection is needed from concurrently changing the value of a such a variable, by disallowing method calls to be simultaneously active. To what extent, however, do we wish to guarantee such mutual exclusion? In dealing with the semantics of our language we proceed from the assumption that any state change due to an assignment to a non-logical variable may safely occur before the first answer. For backtracking over the remaining answers, the state may be fixed in a non-logical variable in order to avoid interference from other method calls. We thus allow multiple processes referring to a single object to backtrack concurrently over answer substitutions generated in a rendez-vous, since by a decision of design, we do not wish to exclude other processes from having a method call evaluated by that object, any longer than until the first answer substitution or failure has been delivered.

Related to the issue of mutual exclusion is the question whether in backtracking any assignment made to non-logical variables must be undone. Again, as a matter of design, we have decided that assignments to non-logical variables are permanent. Non-logical variables were introduced for storing persistent data, shared by all processes referring to an object. We observe moreover that restoring a state may be programmed, using additional non-logical variables. From the point of view of a semantic description, neither choice seems to present any serious difficulties.

7.2 The language $\mathcal{L}$

The language $\mathcal{L}$ that we will define here extends the language $\mathcal{B}_2$ to allow an interpretation of the actions and the primitives for process creation and communication.

A special feature of our abstract language is, apart from the special forms for object creation and communication, the occurrence of a goal for unbinding variables, that may have become bound previously. Goals to unbind variables occur in what we have called method declarations and are also inserted to allow backtracking over alternative solutions in a rendez-vous. We have chosen for introducing *undo* actions to avoid the use of stacks of substitutions recording the bindings on backtrack points, that, although it is perhaps conceptually more elegant, burdens the notation considerably.

Terms are either empty, variables (logical and non-logical) or function terms built from a function symbol and zero or more terms. Constants are considered zero-ary function terms. As special constants we introduce a set of object names *Objname*, with typical elements c, and a set of method names *Method*, with typical elements m. We let *Objname* $\subset$ *Method*. Furthermore, we assume to have a set *Var* of logical variables, with typical elements denoted by capitals X, O and Q; a set *Nlvar* of non-logical variables, with typical elements v; and a set *Term* of terms, with typical elements t, constructed according to

$$t ::= \varepsilon \mid X \mid v \mid f(t_1, ..., t_n) : f \text{ a function symbol, } n \geq 0$$

The set of function symbols include the set of object names and method names. Constants are zero-ary functions. When $t = \varepsilon$ we write $f()$ instead of $f(\varepsilon)$.[1]

Actions $a \in Action$ may take one of the following forms.

$$a ::= u(t) \mid v := t \mid t_1 = t_2$$

Elementary actions a can be goals of the form $u(t)$, for undoing the bindings of the logical variables in a term t, non-logical variable assignments of the form $v := t$, or unification goals of the form $t_1 = t_2$. Occasionally, we will use an action *fail*, that always fails.

Primitives $e \in Prim$ are needed for object creation and engaging in a rendez-vous. These primitives, by which $\mathcal{L}$ extends Prolog, are defined as

$$e ::= O :: new(c(t)) \mid Q :: O!m(t) \mid Q? \mid accept(m_1, ..., m_n) \mid !t$$

where m ranges over the set of method names, and c over the set of object names. Goals of the form $O :: new(c(t))$ are used for creating a new object. A goal of the form $Q :: O!m(t)$ is used to initiate a rendez-vous to call the method $m(t)$ for the object denoted by O. Goals of the form $Q?$ are used to request the answers resulting from the evaluation of a goal. The accept goal $accept(m_1, ..., m_n)$ indicates the willingness to accept a method call for m_i, $i = 1, ..., n$. As a restriction to the use of accept goals we require that accept goals may occur in the constructor process only. Finally, a goal of the form $!t$ is used to send the result of evaluating a method call to the invoking process. In contrast to the other extensions, goals of the form $!t$ may not be used by the programmer since these goals will be inserted dynamically.

Goals $g \in Goal$ are given by

$$g ::= a \mid m(t) \mid g_1 ; g_2 \mid g_1 \Box g_2 \mid e$$

Goals of the form $m(t)$ are used for a kind of (recursive) procedure call. These goals correspond to both local method goals and constructor goals in DLP_2. For convenience we assume that calls $m(t)$ have a single argument t, with t possibly equal to ε. The goals $g_1 ; g_2$ and $g_1 \Box g_2$ stand for, respectively, sequential composition and alternative composition of goals g_1 and g_2. Dynamically, alternative composition amounts to backtracking, in a sequential fashion.

Method declarations take the form $m \leftarrow b$ where $b \equiv \lambda\tau.g$ for some goal g is called the body of m. As has been explained in our description of DLP, a method definition for an object consists of a number of clauses, that differ from common Prolog clauses only by the possible occurrence of the special forms by which DLP extends Prolog. We show how such clauses correspond to a method declaration in our language $\mathcal{L}$. A predicate definition of the form

[1] The term ε represents the empty term, that is also called the *unit*. We assume that $f(\varepsilon, \varepsilon, ..., \varepsilon) = f()$ and that $f(\varepsilon, t) = f(t, \varepsilon) = f(t)$.

$$m(t_1) :\!- A_{11}, ..., A_{1m_1}.$$
$$m(t_2) :\!- A_{21}, ..., A_{2m_2}.$$
$$...$$
$$m(t_n) :\!- A_{n1}, ..., A_{nm_n}.$$

may be represented as

$$\begin{aligned} m \leftarrow \lambda\tau.(\ &(\tau = t_1; A_{11}; ...; A_{1m_1}) \Box \\ &(u(\tau); \tau = t_2; A_{21}; ...; A_{2m_2}) \Box \\ &... \\ &(u(\tau); \tau = t_n; A_{n1}; ...; A_{nm_n})) \end{aligned}$$

The clauses for a predicate appear as components of an alternative composition, that we will also call disjuncts.[2] The goals $\tau = t_i$ take care of unifying the parameters of the clause with the arguments of the call. We note that in a DLP clause only the actions $v := t$, and $t_1 = t_2$ may occur. Moreover only the primitives $O :: new(c(t))$, $Q :: O!m(t)$, $Q?$ and $accept(m_1, ..., m_n)$ are allowed. The communication of answers resulting in a rendez-vous is modeled by the dynamic insertion of goals of the form $!t$ for sending a result. These goals are hidden from the user of the language.

We assume that the components of the alternative composition share no logical variables. However, since these alternatives will be executed sequentially, the unbinding of the logical variables of the goal must be taken care of. For this purpose we insert the action $u(\tau)$ in each disjunct, starting with the second, in order to undo any binding resulting from the evaluation of a previous disjunct.

Object declarations are 3-tuples of the form

$$(c \leftarrow b_c, < v_i >_{i=1,...,r}, < m_i \leftarrow b_i >_{i=1,...,k})$$

containing the *name* c of an object, its *constructor* $c \leftarrow b_c$, a possibly empty sequence of r *non-logical variables* and a possibly empty sequence of k *methods*, that is groups of clauses that define a predicate. The constructor $c \leftarrow b_c$ may be called in the same way as a method.

Programs are tuples of the form $< D \mid g >$, where D is a collection of object declarations and g a goal statement.

---

[2]The translation given here applies also to the languages $\mathcal{L}_0$, $\mathcal{L}_1$ and $\mathcal{L}_2$ treated in the next chapter. The only significant difference with the Prolog clause format is the explicit use of an alternative construct of the form $g_1 \Box g_2$ to model the behavior of alternative clauses for a predicate, and the insertion of undo actions for unbinding variables.

7.3 Configurations

Evaluating a program $< D \mid g >$ may result in a collection of processes concurrently active in evaluating their goal, and occasionally entering in communication with other processes. In defining the possible computation steps that such a collection of processes may take, we use a syntactic representation of this collection together with a state on which these processes operate, for instance by changing the value of a variable.

Representing objects and processes An *object* is a tuple (c, n) containing the *name* c of a declared object and its *instance number* n, indicating that it is the n-th instance of c. Hence we define the set of objects as

$$Obj = \{(c, n) : c \text{ an object name}, n \in \mathbb{N}\}$$

A *process* is a tuple (c, n, k) containing the *name* and *instance number* of the object it refers to, and a counter k that uniquely identifies the k-th process referring to the object (c, n). We define the set of processes, with typical elements α and β, by

$$Proc = \{(c, n, k) : (c, n) \in Obj, k \in \mathbb{N}\}$$

With each object (c, n) is associated a process $(c, n, 0)$ executing the constructor $b_c(t)$ for some t. The other processes referring to the object (c, n), created for answering a method call, are represented by (c, n, k), with $k \geq 1$.

In the following we will identify the constructor process $(c, n, 0)$ with the object (c, n) to which it refers. In particular, the request for a rendez-vous addressed at the process $(c, n, 0)$ will be interpreted as a method call for the object (c, n). To access the object to which a process refers we define a function *obj* by $obj(c, n, k) = (c, n)$.

We have introduced α, β as typical elements of the set *Proc* of process identifiers. We introduce no syntactic variables for objects, but will use the function *obj* for which it holds that $obj(\alpha) \in Obj$ when $\alpha \in Proc$.

Further we extend the set of terms by redefining t as

$$t ::= \varepsilon \mid \delta \mid [t_1, ..., t_n] \mid (t_1, t_2) \mid X \mid v \mid \alpha \mid f(t_1, ..., t_n) : f \text{ a function symbol}$$

where δ, $[t_1, ..., t_n]$ and (t_1, t_2) are special terms that are used for communicating the results of a method call. The extension also allows process identifiers to occur as terms.

Logical variables may become bound to terms. The binding of logical variables is recorded in a substitution of type $Subst = Var \rightarrow Term$. We will write $t\theta$ to denote the term t modified by applying the substitution θ, where we assume that θ is extended to terms in a standard fashion. We say that a substitution is a unifier of two terms if the two terms become syntactically equal after applying the substitution. When the terms involved are process identifiers this means that they must be pointing to the same process. A unifier θ is more general than a unifier θ' if there is a substitution ξ such that $\xi \circ \theta = \theta'$. It is a well-known fact that if a unifier exists for two terms, then there exists also a most general unifier. Most general unifiers are unique, up to renaming variables. We assume a function $mgu : Term \times Term \rightarrow Subst$ that computes an idempotent most general unifier of two terms, if it exists. Composition of unifiers $\xi \circ \theta$ is defined by $t(\xi \circ \theta) = (t\theta)\xi$.

States The actions of our language operate on states. States contain the dynamic information that must be kept during the execution of a program, such as the bindings of logical variables due to the evaluation of a goal by a process, the values of the non-logical variables of each object and global information concerning the objects and processes that are in use.

We define states $\sigma \in \Sigma$ as triples (θ, s, i) containing respectively a *substitution* for each process, a *store* for the values of the non-logical variables for each object, and a *count* function for keeping record of the number of instances of an object and the like.

The **substitution** function θ has type $Proc \rightarrow Subst$; by θ_α we denote the substitution that delivers the bindings of the variables for process α.

In order to deal with recorded solutions, necessitated by our wish to preserve completeness when combining the results of an asynchronous rendez-vous with the results of an intermittent goal, we will store both the call and the outcome of the evaluation of a method call by a process in the substitution of that process. For a call $m(t)$ that is evaluated by process α we may then have that $\theta_\alpha(goal) = t$ and $\theta_\alpha(sols) = [t_1, ..., t_n]$, where $[t_1, ..., t_n]$ is the list of terms that represents the alternative solutions. We define

$$[t_1, ..., t_n] \cdot t = [t_1, ..., t_n, t]$$

in order to add a term t to the list of solutions $[t_1, ..., t_n]$.

The **store** function s has type $Obj \rightarrow Store$, with $Store = Nlvar \rightarrow Term$. Similarly $s_{obj(\alpha)}$ is the function that delivers the values of the non-logical variables of the object to which α refers. The non-logical variables of an object (c, n) are thus shared by all processes (c, n, k) referring to that object.

In order to be able to replace the occurrence of a non-logical variable in a term by its value we interprete $s_{obj(\alpha)}$ as to be extended to terms.

The **count** function i is used to take care of a number of administrative details. It consists of a function of type $Objname \rightarrow \mathbb{N}$, that is used to store for each declared object c its current instance number n. It contains moreover a function of type $Obj \rightarrow \mathbb{N}$ that gives for each object $(c.n)$ the number of processes created for answering a method call. Also i contains a function of type $Proc \times Method \rightarrow \mathbb{N}$, that is needed for renaming logical variables. It keeps count of the number of times a method m is called (locally) for process α. This number, called the invocation depth of m in α, is represented by $i(\alpha, m)$ and is updated with each call of the form $m(t)$. More precisely, i is the union of these functions, and is of type

$$Objname \rightarrow \mathbb{N} \quad \cup \quad Obj \rightarrow \mathbb{N} \quad \cup \quad Proc \times Method \rightarrow \mathbb{N}$$

A renaming function is a function of type $Var \rightarrow Var$ that substitutes (possibly renamed) variables for variables, when applied to a term or a goal. We assume a function $\nu \in Proc \times Method \times \mathbb{N} \rightarrow Var \rightarrow Var$ that given a process name, a method name and a natural number indicating the invocation depth, delivers a renaming function working on variables. Such renaming functions are extended to terms in a natural way. Applying a renaming function $\nu_{\alpha m i(\alpha,m)}$ results in renaming the variables of a term as shown in the example $f(a, X)\nu_{\alpha m i(\alpha,m)}$ that gives $f(a, X_{(\alpha,m,n)})$, when $i(\alpha, m) = n$. On the level of the implementation we assume an injective mapping from indexes of the form (α, m, n) to storage locations for logical variables. Since renaming is typically applied to the body of a method we define $b\nu_{ami(\alpha,m)} = \lambda\tau.g\nu_{ami(\alpha,m)}$ for $b = \lambda\tau.g$. Obviously, the renaming does not affect the parameter τ.

Interpretation The effect of actions on states can be described by defining a function *effect* : $Proc \rightarrow Goal \rightarrow \Sigma \rightarrow \Sigma$. As an abbreviation we write $\sigma(a)(\alpha)$ for $effect(\alpha)(a)(\sigma)$, which denotes the state resulting from executing a for α in state σ. The *effect* function is partial.

To model the state changes we define function variants of a function f by

$$f\{x/v\}(y) = \begin{cases} v & \text{if } x \equiv y \\ f(y) & \text{otherwise} \end{cases}$$

As abbreviations we define

$$\theta\{\alpha/X \leftarrow t\} = \theta\{\alpha/\theta_\alpha\{X/t\}\}$$

$$s\{obj(\alpha)/v \leftarrow t\} = s\{obj(\alpha)/s_{obj(\alpha)}\{v/t\}\}$$

denoting, respectively, the modification of the substitution θ_α by binding X to t, and the modification of the store for the object to which α refers by setting the value of the non-logical variable v to t.

An example of the function *effect* is given by the interpretation of the goal $u(t)$ that is introduced to undo the bindings of variables

- $\sigma(u(t))(\alpha) = (\theta', s, i)$ for $\sigma = (\theta, s, i)$ with $\theta' = \theta\{\alpha/X \leftarrow X\}_{X \in varsof(t)}$

thereby defining the effect of evaluating the goal as undoing the possible bindings of the variables occurring in the term t, by changing θ_α to behave as the identity for these variables.

Communication by rendez-vous We have introduced the major ingredients of our operational semantics. Executing a program will be modeled by a collection of processes, each evaluating a goal, and possibly modifying the state when executing an action.

Communication between processes is by asynchronous rendez-vous, initiated by calling a method. Backtracking over the resulting answers may occur. A (synchronous) method call consists of a request of the form $Q{::}O!m(t)$, with O assumed to be bound to the identifier for the constructor process of an object, followed by a request for the answer substitutions resulting from evaluating $m(t)$, of the form $Q?$, with Q bound to (a pointer to) the process that evaluates $m(t)$. By an answer substitution we mean the substitution computed in finding a solution for the goal $m(t)$ restricted to the unbound variables occurring in t.

In the figure below we picture the communication occurring in a rendez-vous.

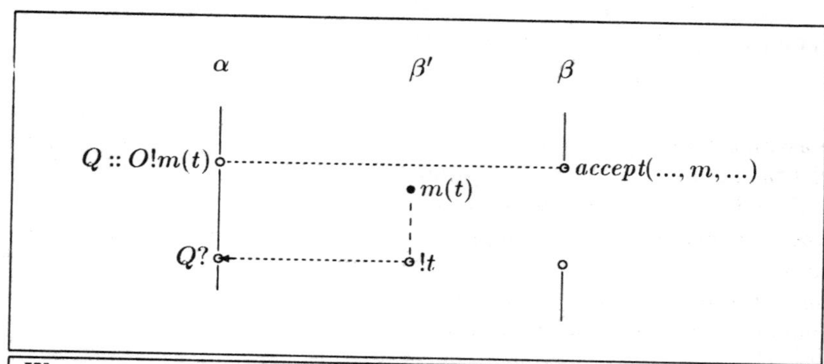

We assume that O is bound to $\beta = (c, n, 0)$, the constructor process for the object (c, n). Process $\beta' = (c, n, k)$, for some k, is a variant of β in that $obj(\beta) = obj(\beta')$. In accepting the call Q becomes bound to β'.

As soon as the request $Q :: O!m(t)$, with O bound to β, is accepted, α proceeds to its next goal $Q?$, that is a request for the answer substitutions resulting from the evaluation of $m(t)$. The process β', which is a variant of the process β in that they refer to the same object, starts evaluating $m(t)$. Process α must wait until the process β' has computed an answer substitution. When the first answer substitution is computed, it is sent to α; and the goal $Q?$ succeeds. The process β, which is the constructor process $(c, n, 0)$ for the object $obj(\beta) = (c, n)$, may then proceed with the evaluation of the constructor goal. When backtracking occurs in α, the goal $Q?$ succeeds as many times as there are alternative answer substitutions produced by β'. Backtracking in β' runs concurrently with the activity of process β.

A successful rendez-vous consists of two communication steps. The step that initiates the rendez-vous is represented by the pair

$$(Q :: O!m(t), accept(..., m, ...))$$

containing both the request $Q :: O!m(t)$ and the accept goal $accept(..., m, ...)$, stating the willingness to accept the method m.

For returning the results we will use the pair

$$(Q?, !t)$$

composed of the request for an answer $Q?$, and the goal $!t$, that indicates that a solution has been found.

Resumptions To model the communication that takes place in a rendez-vous we differentiate between answers $!t$ to stand for respectively

- $!\delta$ — indicating failure, that is the absence of further answers, and
- $!(t', [t_1, ..., t_n])$ — which is used to deliver a record of all the answers

otherwise $!t$ stands for a normal answer.

Resumptions can now be defined by the function *res*, as follows

$$
res(t)(\sigma)(\alpha,\beta) = \begin{cases} fail & \text{if } t = \delta \\ t'\theta_\alpha = t_1 \Box \ldots \Box u(t'\theta_\alpha); t'\theta_\alpha = t_n & \text{if } t = (t', [t_1, .., t_n]) \\ t\theta_\alpha = t\theta_\beta & \text{otherwise} \end{cases}
$$

where we assume that $\sigma = (\theta, s, i)$.

To model the actual communication event, we make use of a function $eval : Comm \times Comm \to \Sigma \to Proc \times Proc \to Goal$ and its counterpart $\overline{eval} : Comm \times Comm \to \Sigma \to Proc \times Proc \to Goal$. As explained in section 6.5.1, this pair of functions allows us to conveniently describe what takes place both at the side of the invoking process and at the side of the process evaluating the method call.

We define *eval*, which takes effect in the process requesting a resumption, by stating

$$
eval(Q?, !t)(\sigma)(\alpha,\beta) = \begin{cases} res(t)(\sigma)(\alpha,\beta) & \text{if } t = \delta \text{ or} \\ & t = (t', [t_1, .., t_n]) \\ res(t)(\sigma)(\alpha,\beta) \Box u(t\theta_\alpha); Q? & \text{otherwise} \end{cases}
$$

and, similarly we define the function $\overline{eval}$, which takes effect in the process sending the answer, by

$$
\overline{eval}(Q?, !t)(\sigma)(\alpha,\beta) = \begin{cases} !(\theta_\beta(goal), \theta_\beta(sols)) & \text{if } t = \delta \\ !t & \text{if } t = (t', [t_1, \ldots, t_n]) \\ skip & \text{otherwise} \end{cases}
$$

Note that $!(t', [t_1, \ldots, t_n])$ will only be inserted as a goal when the number of solutions n is finite, since otherwise $!\delta$ will never be reached.

To model the effect of a communication on a particular state we extend the effect function by a function of type $Prim \times Prim \to Proc \times Proc \to \Sigma \to \Sigma$, for which we use the obvious abbreviation $\sigma(e_1, e_2)(\alpha, \beta)$ for $e_1, e_2 \in Prim$.

Syntactic continuations are used to model the backtracking behavior of a program. We introduce three types of syntactic continuations.

The first type of continuations are called *success continuations* $R \in SuccCo$, defined by

$$R ::= \surd \mid g; R$$

which correspond to the sequential evaluation of a goal, without backtracking.

We use *failure continuations* $F \in FailCo$, defined by

$$F ::= \Delta \mid R : F$$

to model the backtracking local to a process. Intuitively, a failure continuation may be regarded as a stack of success continuations, with Δ the empty stack.

To model distributed backtracking we define *process continuations* $C \in ProcCo$ by

$$C ::= \Xi \mid \ < \alpha, F >: C$$

which allows to create a stack of processes of which the process on top is considered to be active. The empty process continuation Ξ may be regarded as the empty stack.

Finally, we may define configurations (Γ, σ), as consisting of a set $\Gamma \in \mathcal{P}(ProcCo)$ of process continuations and a state $\sigma \in \Sigma$.

7.4 Transition rules

The transition system below, describing the computation rules for evaluating a goal g given a declaration D, consists of axioms of the form $(\Gamma,\sigma) \xrightarrow{\eta} (\Gamma',\sigma')$ meaning that the configuration (Γ,σ) may be taken to (Γ',σ'), while displaying label η. The label η may be empty or an element of the set $\Lambda = Action \cup \{\star\}$. When the label is empty we also speak of unlabeled transitions. Although we make no further use of these labels here, we may comment that the empty label represents invisible behavior. The special label $\star$ represents visible but in a sense silent behavior, that cannot further be inspected. Labels from *Action* merely represent the action being executed.

An axiom may be applied only if the *effect* function used is defined for its arguments. We indicate the state modified by the *effect* function by $\sigma^\star$. In other words $\sigma^\star$ abbreviates $\sigma(g)(\alpha)$ or $\sigma(e_1,e_2)(\alpha,\beta)$. The axiom for Action is conditional, in that whenever $\sigma^\star$ is defined the first transition must be applied, and if $\sigma^\star$ is not defined then the alternative transition must be applied.

We assume a general rule of the form

$$(\Gamma,\sigma) \xrightarrow{\eta} (\Gamma',\sigma') \Longrightarrow (X \cup \Gamma,\sigma) \xrightarrow{\eta} (X \cup \Gamma',\sigma')$$

for $X \in \mathcal{P}(ProcCo)$ disjoint from Γ and Γ'.

In the following we assume that $\sigma = (\theta, s, i)$.

Actions can be either goals of the form $u(t)$ to undo the bindings of logical variables, non-logical variable assignments of the form $v := t$, or unification goals of the form $t_1 = t_2$. In both the latter goals the terms t, t_1, t_2 are simplified using $s_{obj(\alpha)}$ in order to replace non-logical variables by their values.

$\mathcal{L}$

$$(\{<\alpha, a; R : F >: C\},\sigma) \xrightarrow{a} (\{<\alpha, R : F >: C\},\sigma^\star) \qquad Action$$

$$\longrightarrow (\{<\alpha, F >: C\},\sigma)$$

with for $a \in \{u(t), v := t, t_1 = t_2\}$ the interpretation

- $\sigma(u(t))(\alpha) = (\theta', s, i)$ where
  $\theta' = \theta\{\alpha/X \leftarrow X\}_{X \in varsof(t)}$
- $\sigma(v := t)(\alpha) = (\theta, s', i)$ where
  $s' = s\{obj(\alpha)/v \leftarrow s_{obj(\alpha)}(t)\theta_\alpha\}$
- $\sigma(t_1 = t_2)(\alpha) = (\theta', s, i)$ where
  $\theta' = \theta\{\alpha/mgu(s_{obj(\alpha)}(t_1)\theta_\alpha, s_{obj(\alpha)}(t_2)\theta_\alpha) \mathbin{\hat{\circ}} \theta_\alpha\}$

Local method calls amount to replacing calls of the form $m(t)$ by the goal $b(t)$ when $m \leftarrow b$ occurs as a method for c in D, assuming that $\alpha \equiv (c,n,k)$. Before inserting the body as a goal, the renaming function $\nu_{ami(\alpha,m)}$ must be applied.

When a local method call is executed the argument is instantiated with the current substitution. Any variable that is then unbound may receive a binding due to evaluating the body of the method. Hence when disjuncts of a body are executed sequentially, any binding resulting from the evaluation of a previous disjunct must be undone. Recall that in our representation of method declarations we have inserted undo statements for unbinding these variables. Since the argument is instantiated, only the variables that were unbound are visible as variables. All other variables are replaced by their instantiation and hence not affected by the undo statements.

$$(\{< \alpha, m(t); R : F >: C\}, \sigma) \qquad \textit{Rec}$$

$$\xrightarrow{\star} (\{< \alpha, b\nu_{\alpha m i(\alpha,m)}(t\theta_\alpha); R : F >: C\}, \sigma^\star)$$

for $m \leftarrow b$ in D for the object of α, with the interpretation

- $\sigma(m(t))(\alpha) = (\theta, s, i\{(\alpha, m)/i(\alpha, m) + 1\})$

Sequential composition and backtracking are defined as in [de Bakker, 1991]. A sequential statement is decomposed to enable the inspection of the first component.

When an alternative statement is encountered, a new success continuation containing the first alternative is put on top of the failure stack. The part that has to follow after a successful execution of either statement remains the same for both statements.

$$(\{< \alpha, (g_1; g_2); R : F >: C\}, \sigma) \qquad \textit{Seq}$$

$$\longrightarrow (\{< \alpha, g_1; (g_2; R) : F >: C\}, \sigma)$$

$$(\{< \alpha, (g_1 \Box g_2); R : F >: C\}, \sigma) \qquad \textit{Alt}$$

$$\longrightarrow (\{< \alpha, (g_1; R) : (g_2; R) : F >: C\}, \sigma)$$

New statements give rise to the execution of a new process executing the constructor for the newly created object. As an effect of executing a new statement the state is modified with respect to the counter for the number of copies of a named object. In the interpretation given below we have omitted the initialization of non-logical variables, since we assume that the constructor process takes care of this.

$$(\{< \alpha, O :: new(c(t)); R : F >: C\}, \sigma) \qquad \textit{New}$$

$$\xrightarrow{\star} (< \alpha, R : F >: C, < \beta, F_\beta >: \Xi, \sigma^\star)$$

where $F_\beta \equiv c(s_{obj(\alpha)}(t)\theta_\alpha); \surd : \Delta$ with the interpretation

- $\sigma(O :: new(c(t)))(\alpha) = (\theta', s, i')$ where
  $\theta' = \theta\{\alpha/O \leftarrow \beta\}$ with $\beta = (c, i'(c), 0)$
  and $i' = i\{c/i(c) + 1\}$

Method calls result in creating a new item on top of the process stack of the object that receives the request. Accordingly the state is changed by raising the process counter for the object. The newly created process β' evaluates the goal $m(t'); !t' \Box !\delta$. The sequence $m(t'); !t'$ represents the evaluation of the method call $m(t')$ followed by the goal $!t'$ to communicate the results to the invoking process. The alternative $!\delta$ will be evaluated when there are no more solutions for $m(t')$. The system will block when the method is not defined for that object.

$$(\{< \alpha, Q :: O!m(t); R_1 : F_1 >: C_1, \qquad \textit{Method}$$

$$< \beta, \textit{accept}(..., m, ...); R_2 : F_2 >: C_2\}, \sigma)$$

$$\xrightarrow{\star} (\{< \alpha, Q?; R_1 : F_1 >: C_1,$$

$$< \beta', F_{\beta'} >:< \beta, R_2 : F_2 >: C_2\}, \sigma^\star)$$

if $\beta = O\theta_\alpha$, where $F_{\beta'} \equiv (m(t'); !t' \Box !\delta); \surd : \Delta$

for $t' = s_{obj(\alpha)}(t)\theta_\alpha$ with the interpretation

- $\sigma(Q :: O!m(t), \textit{accept}(..., m, ...))(\alpha, \beta) = (\theta', s, i')$ where for $\beta = (c, n, 0)$ and Q a fresh variable it holds that $\beta' = (c, n, i'(c, n))$, $i' = i\{(c, n)/i(c, n) + 1\}$, $\theta' = \theta\{\alpha/Q \leftarrow \beta'\}$ and $\theta'_\beta(\textit{goal}) = t$

Results are communicated back to the process that requested the rendez-vous, by stating the goal $Q?$, on occurrence of the goal $!t$ in the process evaluating the call. A failure arises in the process that requested the result when no more answers can be generated, that is when $t = \delta$. Otherwise, by the definition of *eval*, the request is replaced by the goal $t\theta_\alpha = t\theta_\beta \Box u(t\theta_\alpha); Q?$. The first component $t\theta_\alpha = t\theta_\beta$ effects the resulting answer substitution in the context of the process that requested the answer. To allow backtracking over multiple answers the second component contains a repeated request for an answer. The variable bindings of t that result from a previous answer must, however, first be undone, as expressed by the inclusion of the statement $u(t\theta_\alpha)$. See section 7.3.

$$(\{< \alpha, Q?; R_1 : F_1 >: C_1, < \beta, !t; R_2 : F_2 >: C_2\}, \sigma) \qquad \textit{Result}$$

$$\xrightarrow{\star} (\{< \alpha, \textit{eval}(Q?, !t)(\sigma)(\alpha, \beta); R_1 : F_1 >: C_1,$$

$$< \beta, \overline{\textit{eval}}(Q?, !t)(\sigma)(\alpha, \beta); R_2 : F_2 >: \Xi, C_2\}, \sigma^\star)$$

provided that $Q\theta_\alpha = \beta$

with the interpretation

- $\sigma(Q?, !t)(\alpha, \beta) = (\theta', s, i)$ where $\theta'_\beta(\textit{sols}) = \theta_\beta(\textit{sols}) \cdot t\theta_\beta$ if t is not equal to δ or $(t', [t_1, ..., t_n])$, and $\theta' = \theta$ otherwise

A similar argument as given for *Rec* holds for the occurrence of the undo action in the axiom *Result*. Only the variables that are unbound at the moment of requesting the rendez-vous are affected by the undo action inserted before the repeated request for an answer substitution. These variables may receive a binding due to evaluating the method call, and hence must be freed from this binding when looking for alternative solutions.

An operational semantics, in terms of the observable behavior of a program, may now readily be defined as the set of possible transition sequences. We will pursue this issue in the following chapter, where we give both an operational and denotational semantics for various subsets of DLP.

7.5 An example

To give some feeling for what occurs in the execution of a program we present (a part of) the steps taken by the program computing all natural numbers.

```
object nat {
nat() :-   accept(num), nat().
num(0).
num(s(X))  :-   num(X).
}
```

As a goal we state

```
:-  O::new(nat()), Q::O!num(Y), fail.
```

Translating this program into the language $\mathcal{L}$ gives the declaration

$$D = \{< nat \leftarrow \lambda t.(accept(num); nat()),$$
$$< \varepsilon >,$$
$$< num \leftarrow \lambda t.(t = 0 \;\Box\; (u(t); t = s(X); num(X))) >$$
$$>\}$$

where the component $< \varepsilon >$ indicates the absence of non-logical variables.

Our goal translates to

$$O :: new(nat()); Q :: O!num(Y); Q?; fail$$

and we may make the derivation below, assuming that *fail* always fails. We will omit applications of the axiom *Seq*, since this merely amounts to reshuffling the brackets.

Let $\sigma = (\theta, s, i)$ and $\sigma_k = (\theta_k, s_k, i_k)$ for $k = 1, 2, \ldots$ Starting in an initial state σ, with α the process evaluating the goal, we have

$$(\;\{\; < \alpha, O :: new(nat()); Q :: O!num(Y); Q?; fail; \surd : \Delta >: \Xi \;\}, \sigma)$$

Applying *New* leads to

$$\xrightarrow{\star} (\ \{\ < \alpha, Q :: O!num(Y); Q?; fail; \surd : \Delta >: \Xi,$$
$$< \beta, nat(); \surd : \Delta >: \Xi$$
$$\}, \sigma_1)$$

with $\sigma_1 = (\theta\{\alpha/O \leftarrow \beta\}, s, i\{nat/i(nat) + 1\})$. Here $\beta = (nat, 1, 0)$, and the instance counter for *nat* is increased by one. By expanding *nat*(), using the axiom *Rec*, we arrive at

$$\xrightarrow{\star} (\ \{\ < \alpha, Q :: O!num(Y); Q?; fail; \surd : \Delta >: \Xi,$$
$$< \beta, accept(num); nat(); \surd : \Delta >: \Xi$$
$$\}, \sigma_2)$$

with $\sigma_2 = (\theta_1, s_1, i_1\{(\beta, nat)/i(\beta, nat) + 1\})$. The increase of the count for (β, nat) is due to the renumbering of variables, which is irrelevant in this case.

Now we may apply *Method*, which results in

$$\xrightarrow{\star} (\ \{\ < \alpha, Q?; fail; \surd : \Delta >: \Xi,$$
$$< \beta', (num(Y); !Y \,\Box\, !\delta); \surd : \Delta >:$$
$$< \beta, nat(); \surd : \Delta >: \Xi$$
$$\}, \sigma_3)$$

with $\sigma_3 = (\theta_2\{\alpha/Q \leftarrow \beta'\}, s_2, i_2\{(nat, n)/i_2(nat, n)+1)\})$, where $\theta_3 = \theta_2\{\alpha/Q \leftarrow \beta'\}$, for $\beta = (nat, n, 0)$, thus binding Q to $\beta' = (nat, n, 1)$. We also have that $\theta_{3_\beta}(goal) = Y$. Notice that the process $< \beta', ... >$ is put on the process stack containing $< \beta, ... >$ and Ξ. Applying *Alt* for β' gives

$$\longrightarrow (\ \{\ < \alpha, Q?; fail; \surd : \Delta >: \Xi,$$
$$< \beta', num(Y); !Y; \surd : (!\delta; \surd) : \Delta >:$$
$$< \beta, nat(); \surd : \Delta >: \Xi$$
$$\}, \sigma_3)$$

Applying the axiom *Rec* for β', to call $num(Y)$, gives

$$\xrightarrow{\star} (\ \{\ < \alpha, Q?; fail; \surd : \Delta >: \Xi,$$
$$< \beta', (Y = 0 \,\Box\, (u(Y); Y = s(X'); num(X'))); !Y; \surd : (!\delta; \surd) : \Delta >:$$
$$< \beta, nat(); \surd : \Delta >: \Xi$$
$$\}, \sigma_4)$$

with $\sigma_4 = (\theta_3, s_3, i_3\{(\beta', num)/i_3(\beta', num) + 1\})$. We use X' to denote the renamed variable X. The variable, X' is the variable X indexed by $(\beta', num, i_3(\beta', num))$.

By applying *Alt* for β' we get

$$\longrightarrow (\ \{\ < \alpha, Q?; fail; \surd : \Delta >: \Xi,$$

$$< \beta', (Y = 0; !Y; \surd) : (u(Y); Y = s(X'); num(X'); !Y; \surd) : (!\delta; \surd) : \Delta >:$$
$$< \beta, nat(); \surd : \Delta >: \Xi$$
$$\}, \sigma_4)$$

which allows us to apply *Action* for β', giving

$$\xrightarrow{Y=0} (\{ < \alpha, Q?; fail; \surd : \Delta >: \Xi,$$
$$< \beta', !Y; \surd : (u(Y); Y = s(X'); num(X'); !Y; \surd) : (!\delta; \surd) : \Delta >:$$
$$< \beta, nat(); \surd : \Delta >: \Xi$$
$$\}, \sigma_5)$$

with $\sigma_5 = (\theta_4\{\beta'/Y \leftarrow 0\}, s_4, i_4)$. Now β' is ready to send its first answer substitution.
Applying *Result* gives, since $eval(Q?, !Y)(\alpha, \beta') \equiv Y = 0 \,\square\, u(Y); Q?$,

$$\xrightarrow{\star} (\{ < \alpha, (Y = 0 \,\square\, u(Y); Q?); fail; \surd) : \Delta >: \Xi,$$
$$< \beta', (skip; \surd : u(Y); Y = s(X'); num(X'); !Y; \surd) : (!\delta; \surd) : \Delta >: \Xi,$$
$$< \beta, nat(); \surd : \Delta >: \Xi$$
$$\}, \sigma_5)$$

From now on β is free to accept requests for a rendez-vous again and β' may continue to generate further answer substitutions, indefinitely.
Applying *Alt* for α and *Action* for β' leads to

$$\longrightarrow \ldots \xrightarrow{u(Y)} (\{ < \alpha, (Y = 0; fail; \surd) : (u(Y); Q?; fail; \surd) : \Delta >: \Xi,$$
$$< \beta', (u(Y); Y = s(X'); num(X'); !Y; \surd) : (!\delta; \surd) : \Delta >: \Xi,$$
$$< \beta, nat(); \surd : \Delta >: \Xi$$
$$\}, \sigma_6)$$

with $\sigma_6 = (\theta_5\{\beta/Y \leftarrow Y\}, s_5, i_5)$.
Note that the substitution value of Y in β has already been substituted. Applying *Action* for α gives

$$\xrightarrow{Y=0} (\{ < \alpha, fail; \surd : (u(Y); Q?; fail; \surd) : \Delta >: \Xi,$$
$$< \beta', (Y = s(X'); num(X'); !Y; \surd) : (!\delta; \surd) : \Delta >: \Xi,$$
$$< \beta, nat(); \surd : \Delta >: \Xi$$
$$\}, \sigma_7)$$

with $\sigma_7 = (\theta_6\{\alpha/Y \leftarrow 0\}, s_6, i_6)$.
Since *fail* is assumed to fail, applying *Action* results in popping the failure stack for α. Then the variable Y must be unbound for process α. When we moreover evaluate $Y = s(X')$ for β' we arrive at the configuration

$$
\begin{aligned}
\longrightarrow (\{ & < \alpha, Q?\text{: } \mathit{fail}; \surd : \Delta >: \Xi, \\
& < \beta', \mathit{num}(X'); !Y; \surd : (!\delta; \surd) : \Delta >: \Xi, \\
& < \beta, \mathit{nat}(); \surd : \Delta >: \Xi \\
\}, & \sigma_8)
\end{aligned}
$$

with $\sigma_8 = (\theta_7\{\alpha/Y \leftarrow s(X')\}, s_7.i_7)$, which resembles the configuration having state σ_3 except for the binding of Y to $s(X')$.

8

Comparative semantics for DLP

- *We see therefore at first the picture as a whole with its individual parts still more or less kept in the background; we observe the movements, transitions, connections, rather than the things that move, combine and are connected.* -
Friedrich Engels

In chapter 6 we have given the comparative semantics for the languages $\mathcal{B}_0$, $\mathcal{B}_1$ and $\mathcal{B}_2$, three uniform abstract languages with backtracking, with special attention to process creation and communication. We now introduce the languages $\mathcal{L}_0$, $\mathcal{L}_1$ and $\mathcal{L}_2$, that may be regarded as augmenting $\mathcal{B}_0$, $\mathcal{B}_1$ and $\mathcal{B}_2$ with the details necessary to model the actual (logic) programming aspects of DLP, such as the assignment to non-logical variables, parameter passing and unification. The languages $\mathcal{L}_0$, $\mathcal{L}_1$ and $\mathcal{L}_2$ correspond in an obvious way to the subsets of DLP distinguished in chapter 3.9, that are listed below.

The most simple language DLP_0 is a sequential language with backtracking, modeling the Prolog base component.

A first extension of DLP_0 is DLP_1, that adds *dynamic object creation* and *synchronous communication over channels.*

A second extension is given by the language DLP_2, that supports *dynamic object creation* and *asynchronous method call by rendez-vous.*

DLP_0 = *Prolog + non-logical variables*		
non-logical variables	$v := t$	assigns t to v
$DLP_1 = DLP_0$ + *object creation + communication over channels*		
object creation	$new(c(t))$	creates active instance c
channels	$C :: new(channel)$	creates a new channel
	$C!t$	output statement
	$C?t$	input statement
$DLP_2 = DLP_0$ + *object creation + method call by rendez-vous*		
object creation	$O :: new(c(t))$	creates active instance c
rendez-vous	$Q :: O!m(t)$	calls the method $m(t)$ for O
	$Q?$	requests resumption from Q
	$accept(m_1, ..., m_n)$	accept methods $m_1, ..., m_n$

Correspondingly, the language $\mathcal{L}_0$ covers an abstraction of the base language Prolog, and represents a simple logic programming language with backtracking but without cut. $\mathcal{L}_0$ extends a Prolog-like language by non-logical variables that may be assigned terms as values, in an imperative way. Our treatment may be regarded as a warming-up, preparing the way for a semantic treatment of the remaining subsets.

The language $\mathcal{L}_1$ covers dynamic object creation and communication over channels. For $\mathcal{L}_1$ objects are identical to processes, since each object is active only with executing its so-called constructor process. The semantics given for this sublanguage extends the semantics for $\mathcal{L}_0$ with features for dealing with process creation and communication. A provision has to be made for the backtracking that may occur in an attempt at communication, when selecting an appropriate input statement. As for $\mathcal{L}_0$, we give both an operational semantics and a denotational semantics. The equivalence proof relating them extends the proof given for $\mathcal{L}_0$ in a rather straightforward way.

Lastly, the language $\mathcal{L}_2$ covers, apart from dynamic object creation, also method call by (asynchronous) rendez-vous. In order to deal with the distributed backtracking that may occur when a method call gives rise to multiple answer substitutions we had to make an explicit distinction between objects and processes, and as a consequence we had to invent an appropriate semantic operator that relates the meaning of processes created for handling a rendez-vous to the meaning of the process executing the own activity of the object.

8.1 Backtracking

The first language $\mathcal{L}_0$ that we deal with is a simple sequential logic programming language, without cut. Modeling the base language of DLP, it provides a starting point for the treatment of backtracking, access to non-logical variables and unification.

The language $\mathcal{L}_0$ extends the language $\mathcal{B}_0$ by introducing terms. Actions, involving terms, may be interpreted as undoing variable bindings, assigning a term t to a non-logical variable, or the unification of two terms. Another difference with $\mathcal{B}_0$ is that recursive procedure calls now take a term as a parameter. Correspondingly we now use procedure declarations of the form $p \leftarrow \lambda\tau.g$ to represent the clauses for a predicate p. The only significant difference with the Prolog clause format is the explicit use of an alternative construct and the insertion of undo actions for unbinding variables. We have chosen to employ undo actions for undoing bindings on backtracking for reasons of notational convenience. See also section 7.2.

Syntax As *constants* we assume a set *Procname* of procedure names, with typical elements p. For *variables* we will distinguish between logical variables $X \in Var$ and non-logical variables $v \in Nlvar$. Now we can define terms comprising the set *Term*, with typical elements t, by

$$t ::= \varepsilon \mid X \mid v \mid f(t_1, ..., t_n) \; : \; f \text{ a function symbol, } n \geq 0$$

We will write $f()$ for terms of the form $f(\varepsilon)$.[1]

As *actions* we define elements $a \in Action$ by

$$a ::= u(t) \mid v := t \mid t_1 = t_2$$

representing, respectively, undoing variable bindings, the assignment of a term t to the non-logical variable v, and the unification of terms t_1 and t_2. In the following we also assume an action *fail*.

Now *goals* $g \in Goal$ are given by

$$g ::= a \mid p(t) \mid g_1; g_2 \mid g_1 \,\Box\, g_2$$

where a is an action, $p(t)$ a procedure call to p with argument t, and $g_1; g_2$ the sequential composition of goals g_1 and g_2. and $g_1 \,\Box\, g_2$ the alternative composition of these goals.

The clauses defining a predicate are given as *procedure declarations* of the form $p \leftarrow b$, where p is a predicate name and b of the form $\lambda\tau.g$, for g a goal. We call b the body of a procedure declaration.

A *program* is a tuple $< D \mid g >$, with D a collection of procedure declarations and g a goal statement

8.1.1 Operational semantics

We will describe the computation steps taken by the system when evaluating a program in $\mathcal{L}_0$ by means of a *transition system*, that specifies for each kind of *configuration* (which is more or less the state of a system in execution) the steps, if any, by which to reach a subsequent configuration.

A *substitution* $\theta \in Subst = Var \rightarrow Term$ is given as a function from (logical) variables to terms. Applying a substitution to a term amounts to replacing all logical variables by their substitution values. In the following we assume a function *mgu* :

[1] As in section 7.2 the term ε represents the empty term, that is also called the *unit*. We also assume that $f(\varepsilon, \varepsilon, ..., \varepsilon) = f()$ and that $f(\varepsilon, t) = f(t, \varepsilon) = f(t)$.

$Term \times Term \to Subst$ that computes an idempotent most general unifier of two terms, if it exists.

We also employ a *store* $s \in Store = Nlvar \to Term$, which is a function assigning terms to non-logical variables. Applying a store to a term results in replacing all non-logical variables by their values.

For renaming logical variables we need a *count* $i \in Count = Procname \to \mathbb{N}$, that assigns a natural number to a procedure name.

As part of a configuration we use *states* Σ, with typical elements σ, defined by

$$\Sigma = \{(\theta, s, i) \mid \theta \in Subst, s \in Store, i \in Count\}$$

to record the substitution, store and count at a certain point in the computation. We will apply the function variant notation for changing states, as in $f\{x/v\}$ which for an argument y has as value v if $x = y$ and $f(y)$ otherwise.

Variable renaming is effected by a function $\nu \in Procname \times \mathbb{N} \to Var \to Var$, that takes a procedure name, a natural number (given by the count for this procedure name) and a variable for which it delivers a fresh variable. See section 7.3. Applying a renaming $\nu_{pi(p)}$ is illustrated, for example, by $f(a, X)\nu_{pi(p)} = f(a, X_{(p,i(p))})$, where a new variable X with index $(p, i(p))$ is created. Renaming the body of a procedure declaration is defined by $b\nu_{pi(p)} = \lambda\tau.g\nu_{pi(p)}$, for $b = \lambda\tau.g$.

To model how a state is modified due to the evaluation of a goal we define an *effect function effect* : $Goal \times \Sigma \to \Sigma$, by equations of the form $\sigma(a) = \sigma'$, where $\sigma(a)$ abbreviates *effect*$(a)(\sigma)$. The function *effect* is partial.

The operational semantics of a program is given in terms of the observable behavior displayed when executing a program. For this reason we have labeled the transition rules with *labels* from a set

$$\Lambda = Action \cup \{\star\}.$$

The label $\star$ is used to indicate that on expanding a procedure call with its body, a computation step is made that we cannot further inspect. We consider all actions a visible in the sense that they may be observed by an external observer. The empty label, denoted by the empty word ε, is used to indicate invisible behavior and is usually omitted. We take

$$\Lambda^\infty = \Lambda^\star \cup \Lambda^\omega$$

as the set of strings over Λ and use a concatenation operator $\hat{\circ} : \Lambda^\infty \times \Lambda^\infty \to \Lambda^\infty$ defined by $w_1 \hat{\circ} w_2 = w_1 w_2$ if w_1 is of finite length and w_1 otherwise. We extend this operator to sets of strings over Λ by defining

$$w \hat{\circ} X = \{w \hat{\circ} x : x \in X\}$$

We moreover require that $\varepsilon \hat{\circ} w = w = w \hat{\circ} \varepsilon$.

Syntactic continuations are used in order to specify the backtracking behavior of a program.

We distinguish between *success continuations* $R \in SuccCo$ defined by

$$R ::= \surd \mid g; R$$

with $\surd$ the empty success continuation, denoting success, and $g; R$ the sequential composition of a goal and a success continuation; and *failure continuations* $F \in FailCo$ given by

$$F ::= \Delta \mid R : F$$

with Δ the empty failure continuation, denoting failure and $R : F$ representing a stack with a success continuation on top, modeling in a sense the alternative composition of goals.

Syntactic continuations of this kind are also used in [de Vink, 1989], although there the substitution resulting from the computation thus far is part of the success continuation. Since later on we have to deal with dynamic object and process creation, we have a (global) state parameter in our configurations to represent the substitution and have introduced an auxiliary action for undoing the bindings of logical variables.

Transition rules specifying the behavior of the system, are given as axioms of the form $(\Gamma, \sigma) \xrightarrow{\eta} (\Gamma', \sigma')$, meaning that the configuration (Γ, σ) may be taken to the configuration (Γ', σ') while the label η is displayed. The label η may be empty. Transitions with the empty label ε will also be called unlabeled transitions. A configuration $(\Gamma, \sigma) \in Conf$ consists of a (syntactic) failure continuation Γ and a state σ. The axioms specifying the possible computation steps, for a particular declaration D define the relation $\longrightarrow \subset Conf \times \Lambda \times Conf$. A *transition system* for D then is a triple $(Conf, \Lambda, \longrightarrow)$.

In the rules below, we have used the notation $\sigma^\star$ to indicate the state σ modified by the effect function, in other words $\sigma^\star$ abbreviates $\sigma(g)$ for a goal g. We allow for a branching behavior of the computation to the extent that whenever the function *effect* is defined then the step in which the effect function occurs must be taken. Only if the function *effect* is undefined may the alternative step be taken. Such a branching behavior is exemplified in the rule *Action*.

Let $\sigma = (\theta, s, i)$.

$\mathcal{L}_0$

Action

$$(a; R : F, \sigma) \xrightarrow{a} (R : F, \sigma^\star)$$

$$\longrightarrow (F, \sigma)$$

with for $a \in \{u(t), v := t, t_1 = t_2\}$ the interpretation

- $\sigma(u(t)) = (\theta', s, i)$ where $\theta' = \theta\{X/X\}_{X \in varsof(t)}$
- $\sigma(v := t) = (\theta, s', i)$ where $s' = s\{v/s(t)\theta\}$
- $\sigma(t_1 = t_2) = (\theta', s, i)$ if $\theta' = mgu(s(t_1)\theta, s(t_2)\theta) \hat{\circ}\ \theta$

$(p(t); R : F, \sigma) \xrightarrow{\star} (b\nu_{pi(p)}(t\theta); R : F, \sigma^\star)$ for $p \leftarrow b$ in D *Rec*

with the interpretation

- $\sigma(p(t)) = (\theta, s, i\{p/i(p)+1\})$

$((g_1; g_2); R : F, \sigma) \longrightarrow (g_1; (g_2; R) : F, \sigma)$ *Seq*

$((g_1 \Box g_2); R : F, \sigma) \longrightarrow ((g_1; R) : (g_2; R) : F, \sigma)$ *Alt*

$(\surd : F, \sigma) \longrightarrow (F, \sigma)$ *Tick*

The axioms for this simple language are quite obvious. A brief comment must suffice. Actions may be executed when the effect function $\sigma(a)$ is defined, otherwise failure arises and the success continuation R on top of the stack is popped to enable the execution of the remaining failure continuation F. The interpretation of the various actions is straightforward. For instance $\sigma(u(t))$ delivers the state σ where all (logical) variables occurring in t have become unbound. A variable X becomes unbound by making θ' the identity substitution for X. The effect of a unification statement $t_1 = t_2$ consists of modifying the substitution component of the state by the most general unifier of (the instantiated versions of) t_1 and t_2. Expanding a procedure call requires renaming of the variables occurring in the body of the procedure by a renaming function set by the procedure name and its current invocation depth as stored in the *count* parameter of the state. The count for p must accordingly be increased by one. The axioms for *Action* and *Rec* are the only axioms with a non-empty label. Having a non-empty label intuitively denotes a non-trivial computation step, that takes some time to perform. The axiom for sequential composition simply states that the compound goal $g_1; g_2$ is decomposed so that the goal g_1 may be executed with g_2 part of the success continuation. The axiom for alternative composition specifies that to execute $g_1 \Box g_2$, the goal g_1 must be executed while storing g_2 as an alternative. A new success continuation is created for this purpose and inserted in the failure stack. On failure, backtracking over g_2 may occur.

Computation sequences consist of the steps that represent observable behavior. We define a relation $\xrightarrow{\eta}\!\!\!\rightarrow$, for η non-empty, by stating that $(\Gamma, \sigma) \xrightarrow{\eta}\!\!\!\rightarrow (\Gamma', \sigma')$ whenever there is a transition with label η preceded by zero or more unlabeled transitions. We will say that (Γ, σ) *blocks* if there is no label η and configuration (Γ', σ') for which $(\Gamma, \sigma) \xrightarrow{\eta}\!\!\!\rightarrow (\Gamma', \sigma')$.

As our result domain, for characterizing the behavior of a program in $\mathcal{L}_0$, we take

$$\mathbb{R} = \Sigma \rightarrow \Lambda^\infty$$

and define the *operational semantics* of a program $< D \mid g >$ by the function $\mathcal{O} : \mathcal{L}_0 \to \mathbb{R}$ as below.

Definition 8.1.1 $\mathcal{O}[\![< D \mid g >]\!] = \mathcal{T}[\![g; \surd : \Delta]\!]$ *where for*

$$\Psi : (FailCo \to \mathbb{R}) \to (FailCo \to \mathbb{R})$$

and

$$\Psi(\phi)[\![\Gamma]\!](\sigma) = \begin{cases} \varepsilon & \text{if } (\Gamma, \sigma) \text{ blocks} \\ \eta \,\hat{\circ}\, \phi[\![\Gamma']\!](\sigma') \text{ if } (\Gamma, \sigma) \xrightarrow{\eta} (\Gamma', \sigma') & \text{otherwise} \end{cases}$$

we let $\mathcal{T} = fix\Psi$.

8.1.2 Denotational semantics

For $\mathcal{L}_0$ we may take $\mathbb{R}$, with typical elements ρ, as a domain. To model the backtracking behavior we will employ semantic continuations. We use failure continuations $F \in Fail$, with $Fail = \mathbb{R}$. Semantic success continuations $R \in Succ = Fail \to \mathbb{R}$ take a failure continuation as an argument to compute the resulting behavior. We define the semantic function $\mathcal{D}[\![\cdot]\!] : Goal \to Succ \to Fail \to \mathbb{R}$ by the equations below. In the equations for $\mathcal{D}[\![\cdot]\!]$ we use the interpretation function as defined for the transition system. We again assume that $\sigma = (\theta, s, i)$.

$\mathcal{L}_0$

(i) $\mathcal{D}[\![a]\!]RF = \lambda\sigma.\sigma(a) defined \to a \,\hat{\circ}\, RF\sigma(a), F\sigma$

(ii) $\mathcal{D}[\![p(t)]\!]RF = \lambda\sigma. \star \,\hat{\circ}\, \mathcal{D}[\![b\nu_{pi(p)}(t\theta)]\!]RF\sigma(p(t))$ for $p \leftarrow b$ in D

(iii) $\mathcal{D}[\![g_1; g_2]\!]RF = \mathcal{D}[\![g_1]\!](D[\![g_2]\!]R)F$

(iv) $\mathcal{D}[\![g_1 \,\square\, g_2]\!]RF = \mathcal{D}[\![g_1]\!]R(D[\![g_2]\!]RF)$

The conditional form of the axiom *Action* is reflected in the conditional expression on the right-hand side of the equation for actions a, abbreviating *if* $\sigma(a)$ *is defined then* $a \,\hat{\circ}\, R(F)(\sigma(a))$ *else* $F\sigma$. Note the similarity with the definition in section 6.3.2.

Remark: As we have explained in the chapter introducing metric semantics (section 6.2.2), we may define a higher order mapping

$$\Phi : (Goal \to Succ \to Fail \to \mathbb{R}) \to (Goal \to Succ \to Fail \to \mathbb{R})$$

and state that $\mathcal{D} = fix\Phi$, in order to establish that $\mathcal{D}[\![\cdot]\!]$ is well-defined.

We may now define the meaning of a program $< D \mid g >$.

Definition 8.1.2 $\mathcal{M}[\![< D \mid g >]\!] = \mathcal{D}[\![g]\!] R_0 F_0$ *with* $R_0 = \lambda\rho.\rho$ *and* $F_0 = \lambda\sigma.\varepsilon$

8.1.3 Equivalence between operational and denotational semantics

For a program $< D \mid g >$ the operational semantics characterizes the observable behavior of a program. A denotational semantics gives, in a compositional way, mathematical meaning to the constructs of the language. We wish both characterizations to be equivalent.

Theorem 8.1.3 $\mathcal{O}[\![< D \mid g >]\!] = \mathcal{M}[\![< D \mid g >]\!]$

We will present an outline of the proof and fill in the details later.

$$\begin{aligned} \mathcal{O}[\![< D \mid g >]\!] &= \mathcal{T}[\![g; \surd : \Delta]\!] \quad \text{by definition 8.1.1} \\ &= \mathcal{F}[\![g; \surd : \Delta]\!] \quad \text{by corollary 8.1.7} \\ &= \mathcal{D}[\![g]\!] R_0 F_0 \quad \text{by definition 8.1.4} \\ &= \mathcal{M}[\![< D \mid g >]\!] \quad \text{by definition 8.1.2} \end{aligned}$$

In the proof we make use of an auxiliary function $\mathcal{F} : \mathit{FailCo} \rightarrow \mathit{Fail}$ that maps syntactic failure continuations to semantic failure continuations. Also we will make use of a function $\mathcal{R} : \mathit{SuccCo} \rightarrow \mathit{Succ}$ for mapping syntactic success continuations to semantic success continuations.

Definition 8.1.4

a. $\mathcal{R}[\![\surd]\!] = \lambda\rho.\rho$

b. $\mathcal{R}[\![g; R]\!] = \mathcal{D}[\![g]\!]\mathcal{R}[\![R]\!]$

c. $\mathcal{F}[\![\Delta]\!] = \lambda\sigma.\varepsilon$

d. $\mathcal{F}[\![R : F]\!] = \mathcal{R}[\![R]\!]\mathcal{F}[\![F]\!]$

Now we can state the following property.

Lemma 8.1.5 *If* $(F, \sigma) \longrightarrow (F', \sigma)$ *then* $\mathcal{F}[\![F]\!]\sigma = \mathcal{F}[\![F']\!]\sigma$

The key step in the proof that $\mathcal{O} = \mathcal{M}$ consists of showing that the function $\mathcal{F}$ is a fixed point of the operator that characterizes the operational meaning of a program.

Lemma 8.1.6 $\Psi(\mathcal{F}) = \mathcal{F}$

Proof: We introduce a complexity measure c on $\Gamma \in \mathit{FailCo}$ such that whenever $(\Gamma, \sigma) \longrightarrow (\Gamma', \sigma)$ we have that $c(\Gamma) > c(\Gamma')$, by defining

$$c(a) = c(p(t)) = c(\surd) = 1$$

$$c(g_1; g_2) = c(g_1 \,\Box\, g_2) = c(g_1) + c(g_2) + 1$$

$$c(\Delta) = 0 \quad \text{and} \quad c(g; R : F) = c(g) + c(F)$$

We must prove for each Γ and σ that $\Psi(\mathcal{F})[\![\Gamma]\!]\sigma = \mathcal{F}[\![\Gamma]\!]\sigma$. If (Γ, σ) blocks then the result is clear. Assume that Γ is of the form $g; R : F$ and that for some η we have $(\Gamma, \sigma) \xrightarrow{\eta} (\Gamma', \sigma')$. The proof proceeds by a case analysis on g. We will treat the case that $g \equiv a$.

- If $g \equiv a$ we have by the definition of Ψ if $\sigma(a)$ is defined that

$$\begin{aligned}\Psi(\mathcal{F})[\![a; R : F]\!]\sigma &= a \;\hat{\circ}\; \mathcal{F}[\![R; F]\!]\sigma(a)\\ &= \mathcal{F}[\![a; R : F]\!]\sigma \text{ (by applying definition 8.1.4).}\end{aligned}$$

  If $\sigma(a)$ is not defined then $(a; R : F, \sigma) \longrightarrow (F, \sigma)$ and the result follows from the induction hypothesis, stating that for Γ' satisfying $c(\Gamma) > c(\Gamma')$ it holds that $\Psi(\mathcal{F})[\![\Gamma']\!]\sigma = \mathcal{F}[\![\Gamma']\!]\sigma$. □

Corollary 8.1.7 $\mathcal{T} = \mathcal{F}$

8.2 Dynamic object creation and communication over channels

The language $\mathcal{L}_1$ extends $\mathcal{L}_0$ by providing constructs for dynamic object creation and communication over channels. It extends $\mathcal{B}_1$, apart from the introduction of terms, by the occurrence of primitives for the creation of channels and the explicit use of channel names.

A program is organized as a collection of object declarations. For the language $\mathcal{L}_1$, creating an instance of an object means creating a process (which executes the *constructor* for that object). Hence, we may identify objects and processes. Apart from objects, an indefinite number of channels may be created. Point-to-point connections exist when two processes have access to the same channel. Communication over channels allows a limited form of backtracking, namely the input side is allowed to backtrack until an input term is found that is unifiable with the output term.

Syntax As *constants* we need a set of object names *Objname*, with typical elements c, and a set of procedure names $p \in$ *Procname*. We assume that each object has a constructor, and hence that *Objname* $\subset$ *Procname*.

Terms and actions are as for $\mathcal{L}_0$. For logical variables that will become bound to a channel we will use by convention a capital C.

The *primitives* $e \in$ *Prim* by which $\mathcal{L}_1$ extends $\mathcal{L}_0$, are defined by

$$e ::= C :: new(channel) \mid new(c(t)) \mid C!t \mid C?t$$

In addition to $\mathcal{L}_0$ we thus have a statement to create a new channel, a statement to create a new (active) object, and the communication statements $C!t$ for output and $C?t$ for input.

The set of *goals* $g \in Goal$ is given by

$$g ::= a \mid p(t) \mid g_1; g_2 \mid g_1 \square g_2 \mid e$$

which differs from that given for $\mathcal{L}_0$ only by the extensions.

The clauses for a predicate p are, as for $\mathcal{L}_0$, collected in *procedure declarations* of the form $p \leftarrow b$, with b of the form $\lambda\tau.g$.

We assume *object declarations* of the form

$$(c \leftarrow b_c, < v_i >_{i=1,\ldots,r}, < p_i \leftarrow b_i >_{i=1,\ldots,k})$$

for named objects c, with b_c defining the constructor for c, v_i the non-logical variables of c, and $p_i \leftarrow b_i$ the procedure declarations corresponding to the clauses of the object c.

A *program* $< D \mid g >$ consists of a collection of object declarations D and a goal g.

8.2.1 Operational semantics

Since the language $\mathcal{L}_1$ allows for dynamic object creation the transition system that specifies how to execute a program must deal with sets of objects, rather than a single object as for $\mathcal{L}_0$. Moreover, we need to distinguish between two distinct objects even if they show the same behavior.

To identify *objects* it suffices to have an object name and its instance number. We define the set Obj, with typical elements α and β by

$$Obj = \{(c, n) \mid c \text{ an object name, } n \in \mathbb{N}\}$$

For an object $\alpha = (c, n)$ we will write D_α to denote the object declaration for c. We will use $\gamma \in Channel = \mathbb{N}$ for referring to channels.

Similarly as for $\mathcal{L}_0$ we extend the set of terms by redefining

$$t ::= \varepsilon \mid X \mid v \mid \gamma \mid f(t_1, \ldots, t_n) \;:\; f \text{ a function symbol, } n \geq 0$$

where we introduce terms γ to be able to bind variables to channels.

Since the state of a configuration no longer concerns a single (sequential) process but a collection of processes executing in parallel, we use generalized *substitutions* $\theta \in Subst^+ = Obj \rightarrow Subst$ that depend on an object $\alpha \in Obj$, and we let $\theta_\alpha \in Subst$ denote a substitution that belongs to a particular object α. In other words, $\theta_\alpha = \theta(\alpha)$ which is the (local) substitution of the object α.

Similarly, we generalize the notion of a *store* $s \in Store^+ = Obj \rightarrow Store$, and let $s_\alpha \in Store$ denote the store belonging to the object α.

We must keep a *count* $i \in Count^+ = (Objname \cup \{ch\} \cup Obj \times Procname) \rightarrow \mathbb{N}$, for administrative reasons. The count function may be split into a function from $Objname \rightarrow \mathbb{N}$, to keep track of the number of instances of a particular object, a function from $\{ch\} \rightarrow \mathbb{N}$, to generate new channels (where ch is a special constant introduced for technical reasons), and a function from $Obj \times Procname \rightarrow \mathbb{N}$ to be used in renaming variables.

The states σ that we use in the configurations come from the set

$$\Sigma = \{(\theta, s, i) \mid \theta \in Subst^+, s \in Store^+, i \in Count^+\}$$

For modifying states we use function variants (again) and introduce the abbreviations

$$\theta\{\alpha/X \leftarrow t\} = \theta\{\alpha/\theta_\alpha\{X/t\}\}$$

$$s\{\alpha/v \leftarrow t\} = s\{\alpha/s_\alpha\{v/t\}\}$$

For *renaming* variables a function $\nu \in Obj \times Procname \times \mathbb{N} \rightarrow Var \rightarrow Var$ is used, which generalizes the renaming function introduced in the previous section 8.1, by the *Obj* parameter. A typical use of this function is illustrated by $b\nu_{\alpha p i(\alpha,p)}$ which renames the variables in b according to the triple $(\alpha, p, i(\alpha, p))$.

To describe the effect of evaluating goals on states we generalize the *effect function* given previously to $effect : Obj \rightarrow Goal \rightarrow \Sigma \rightarrow \Sigma$ and we abbreviate $effect(\alpha)(g)(\sigma)$ as $\sigma(g)(\alpha)$. We must however also extend the effect function to (matching) pairs of communication intentions, by a function of type $Obj \times Obj \rightarrow \mathsf{C} \times \mathsf{C} \rightarrow \Sigma \rightarrow \Sigma$, with $\mathsf{C} = \{\gamma!t, \gamma?t : \gamma \in Channel, t \in Term\}$, and write for this $\sigma(c, \overline{c})(\alpha, \beta)$, for $c, \overline{c} \in \mathsf{C}$. However, we are only interested in the special cases having the form $\sigma(\gamma!t_1, \gamma?t_2)(\alpha, \beta)$. As before the effect function is partial, and thereby influences the decision which axiom must be applied.

We use, just as before, success continuations from *SuccCo* given by $R ::= \surd \mid g; R$ and failure continuations from *FailCo* given by $F ::= \Delta \mid R : F$.

The transition rules below specify labeled transitions of the form $(\Gamma, \sigma) \xrightarrow{\eta} (\Gamma', \sigma')$, with η empty or an element of $\Lambda = Action \cup \{\star\}$. In contrast to the previous section, Γ represents a collection of objects, so $\Gamma \in \mathcal{P}(Obj \times FailCo)$, the set consisting of all subsets of pairs of object identifiers and failure continuations.

We assume to have a general rule of the form

$$(\Gamma, \sigma) \xrightarrow{\eta} (\Gamma', \sigma') \Longrightarrow (X \cup \Gamma, \sigma) \xrightarrow{\eta} (X \cup \Gamma', \sigma')$$

for $X \in \mathcal{P}(Obj \times FailCo)$ disjoint from Γ and Γ'. Let $\sigma = (\theta, s, i)$.

$\mathcal{L}_1$

$$(\{< \alpha, a; R : F >\}, \sigma) \xrightarrow{a} (\{< \alpha, R : F >\}, \sigma^\star) \qquad \textit{Action}$$

$$\longrightarrow (\{< \alpha, F >\}, \sigma)$$

with for $a \in \{u(t), v := t, t_1 = t_2\}$ the interpretation

- $\sigma(u(t))(\alpha) = (\theta', s, i)$
  where $\theta' = \theta\{\alpha/X \leftarrow X\}_{X \in varsof(t)}$
- $\sigma(v := t)(\alpha) = (\theta, s', i)$
  where $s' = s\{\alpha/v \leftarrow s_\alpha(t)\theta_\alpha\}$
- $\sigma(t_1 = t_2)(\alpha) = (\theta', s, i)$
  where $\theta' = \theta\{\alpha/mgu(s_\alpha(t_1)\theta_\alpha, s_\alpha(t_2)\theta_\alpha) \circ \theta_\alpha\}$

$(\{< \alpha, p(t); R : F >\}, \sigma)$ *Rec*

$$\xrightarrow{\star} (\{< \alpha, b\nu_{\alpha p i(\alpha,p)}(t\theta_\alpha); R : F >\}, \sigma^\star)$$

for $p \leftarrow b$ in D_α, with the interpretation

- $\sigma(p(t))(\alpha) = (\theta, s, i\{(\alpha, p)/i(\alpha, p) + 1\})$

$(\{< \alpha, (g_1; g_2); R : F >\}, \sigma) \longrightarrow (\{< \alpha, g_1; (g_2; R) : F >\}, \sigma)$ *Seq*

$(\{< \alpha, (g_1 \Box g_2); R : F >\}, \sigma)$ *Alt*

$$\longrightarrow (\{< \alpha, (g_1; R) : (g_2; R) : F >\}, \sigma)$$

$(\{< \alpha, C :: new(channel); R : F >\}, \sigma)$ *Chann*

$$\xrightarrow{\star} (\{< \alpha, R : F >\}, \sigma^\star)$$

with the interpretation

- $\sigma(C :: new(channel))(\alpha) = (\theta', s, i')$
  where $\theta' = \theta\{\alpha/C \leftarrow \gamma\}$, $\gamma = i'(ch)$
  and $i' = i\{ch/i(ch) + 1\}$

$(\{< \alpha, new(c(t)); R : F >\}, \sigma)$ *New*

$$\xrightarrow{\star} (\{< \alpha, R : F >, < \beta, F_\beta >\}, \sigma^\star)$$

where $F_\beta \equiv c(s_\alpha(t)\theta_\alpha); \surd : \Delta$, with the interpretation

- $\sigma(new(c(t)))(\alpha) = (\theta, s, i')$
  where $\beta = (c, i'(c), 0)$ and $i' = i\{c/i(c) + 1\}$

$(\{< \alpha, C_1!t_1; R_1 : F_1 >, < \beta, C_2?t_2; R_2 : F_2 >\}, \sigma)$ *Comm*

$$\xrightarrow{\star} (\{< \alpha, R_1 : F_1 >, < \beta, R_2 : F_2 >\}, \sigma^\star)$$

$$\xrightarrow{\star} (\{< \alpha, C_1!t_1; R_1 : F_1 >, < \beta, F_2 >\}, \sigma)$$

if $C_1\theta_\alpha = \gamma = C_2\theta_\beta$, with the interpretation

- $\sigma(\gamma!t_1, \gamma?t_2)(\alpha, \beta) = (\theta', s, i)$
  where $\theta' = \theta\{\alpha/\zeta \circ \theta_\alpha, \beta/\zeta \circ \theta_\beta\}$
  for $\zeta = mgu(t_1\theta_\alpha, t_2\theta_\beta)$

$$(\{<\alpha, \surd : F>\}, \sigma) \longrightarrow (\{<\alpha, F>\}, \sigma) \qquad \textit{Tick}$$

The transition rules for actions, recursive procedure call, sequential composition and alternative composition are to a large extent similar to the corresponding rules for $\mathcal{L}_0$, but for the generalization to collections of objects. New are the axioms for the creation of channels and objects, and the axioms for communication. Only the axioms for action and communication are conditional. Which alternative to choose depends on whether $\sigma^\star$ (which is the state that results from applying the effect function) is defined. Communication succeeds if the input term is unifiable with the output term, in which case both processes proceed; otherwise the input side fails and starts backtracking. The condition that both processes refer to the same channel is necessary, since if this condition is not satisfied neither transition may be taken.

Since the behavior of programs in $\mathcal{L}_1$ is indeterminate, because objects may be active concurrently, we take

$$\mathbb{R} = \Sigma \rightarrow \mathcal{P}_{nc}(\Lambda^\infty)$$

and define $\mathcal{O} : \mathcal{L}_1 \rightarrow \mathbb{R}$, giving the operational semantics of a program $< D \mid g >$.

Definition 8.2.1 *$\mathcal{O}[\![< D \mid g >]\!] = \mathcal{T}[\![\{< \alpha_0, g; \surd : \Delta >\}]\!]$ for an initial object α_0, where for*

$$\Psi : (\mathcal{P}(Obj \times FailCo) \rightarrow \mathbb{R}) \rightarrow (\mathcal{P}(Obj \times FailCo) \rightarrow \mathbb{R})$$

and

$$\Psi(\phi)[\![\Gamma]\!](\sigma) = \begin{cases} \{\varepsilon\} & \textit{if } (\Gamma, \sigma) \textit{ blocks} \\ \bigcup\{\eta \,\hat{\circ}\, \phi[\![\Gamma']\!](\sigma') : (\Gamma, \sigma) \xrightarrow{\eta} (\Gamma', \sigma')\} & \textit{otherwise} \end{cases}$$

we define $\mathcal{T} = fix\Psi$.

8.2.2 Denotational semantics

As a domain, reflecting the additional constructs for communication, we take a branching structure $\mathbb{P}$, with typical elements ρ, given by

$$\mathbb{P} \cong \{\delta\} \cup \Sigma \rightarrow \mathcal{P}_{co}(\Sigma \times \mathbb{P} \;\cup\; \mathsf{C} \times (T \rightarrow \mathbb{P}))$$

where $T = \{true, false\}$ and $\mathsf{C} = \{\gamma!t, \gamma?t : \gamma \in Channel, t \in Term\}$. The set $\rho(\sigma)$ for some σ, may contain apart from computation steps of the form $\sigma' \cdot \rho'$ also communication intentions of the form $c \cdot f$, with $c \in \mathsf{C}$. Communication intentions are used to indicate that a process is willing to communicate with other processes. The part c of a communication intention $c \cdot f$. consists of a channel and a term that is unified across the channel. Functions $f \in T \rightarrow \mathbb{P}$ are of the form $\lambda\tau.\rho$. They represent the remainder of the computation after communication has taken place. Such a function takes a truth value to deliver a resumption from $\mathbb{P}$. The truth value indicates whether a communication succeeds or fails, which depends on the effect function as described in section 8.2.1.

Our domain equation differs from the one given in section 6.4.2 in the component representing the communication intentions. Since we are now dealing with the non-uniform case, we are not able to use the more elegant syntactic solution provided there. We will denote typical elements of a set $\rho(\sigma)$ by ξ.

Semantically, we will model dynamic object creation and communication by means of a *parallel merge* operator and a communication operator.

The merge operator $\| : \mathbb{P} \times \mathbb{P} \rightarrow \mathbb{P}$ must satisfy $\delta \parallel \rho = \rho = \rho \parallel \delta$ and

$$\begin{aligned} \rho_1 \parallel \rho_2 = \lambda\sigma.(\; & \{\sigma' \cdot (\rho_i' \parallel \rho_j) : \sigma' \cdot \rho_i' \in \rho_i(\sigma) \;\; \textit{for} \;\; i,j \in \{1,2\} \;\; \textit{and} \;\; i \neq j\} \cup \\ & \{c \cdot \lambda\tau.(f(\tau) \parallel \rho_j) : c \cdot f \in \rho_i(\sigma) \;\; \textit{for} \;\; i,j \in \{1,2\} \;\; \textit{and} \;\; i \neq j\} \cup \\ & (\rho_1 \;|_\sigma\; \rho_2) \;) \end{aligned}$$

with the communication operator $|_\sigma$ defined by

$$\rho_1 \;|_\sigma\; \rho_2 = \bigcup\{\xi_i \,|_\sigma \xi_j : \xi_i \in \rho_i(\sigma), \xi_j \in \rho_j(\sigma) \;\; \textit{for} \;\; i,j \in \{1.2\} \;\; \textit{and} \;\; i \neq j\}$$

and

$$\xi_1 \,|_\sigma\, \xi_2 = \begin{cases} \{\sigma^\star \cdot (f_1(\textit{true}) \parallel f_2(\textit{true}))\} & \text{if } \xi_1 = \gamma!t_1 \cdot f_1 \text{ and } \xi_2 = \gamma?t_2 \cdot f_2 \\ & \text{and } \sigma^\star = \sigma(\gamma!t_1, \gamma?t_2)(\alpha,\beta) \text{ defined} \\ \{\sigma \cdot (f_1(\textit{false}) \parallel f_2(\textit{false}))\} & \text{if } \xi_1 = \gamma!t_1 \cdot f_1 \text{ and } \xi_2 = \gamma?t_2 \cdot f_2 \\ & \text{and } \sigma(\gamma!t_1, \gamma?t_2)(\alpha,\beta) \text{ not defined} \\ \emptyset & \text{otherwise} \end{cases}$$

Intuitively, by merging two processes all possible computation sequences are obtained, by interleaving. Moreover, an attempt is made to communicate when possible. When the effect function finds two communication intentions compatible, which is the case if they address the same channel, then the state σ is accordingly modified. Otherwise, the state remains the same and the computation proceeds by merging the respective resumptions.

The function $\mathcal{D}[\![\cdot]\!] : \textit{Goal} \rightarrow \textit{Obj} \rightarrow \textit{Succ} \rightarrow \textit{Fail} \rightarrow \mathbb{P}$ that defines the meaning of constructs from $\mathcal{L}_1$ extends the function $\mathcal{D}[\![\cdot]\!]$ given for $\mathcal{L}_0$ by taking an extra parameter from *Obj*, and also by having the more complex result domain $\mathbb{P}$. We take $\textit{Succ} = \textit{Fail} \rightarrow \mathbb{P}$ and $\textit{Fail} = \mathbb{P}$. Again we use the effect function as defined in the transition system for $\mathcal{L}_1$. Notice that in equation (vi), when creating a new object, applying the effect function results in a new process identifier β that is given as an argument to the meaning representing the evaluation of the constructor.

Let $\sigma = (\theta, s, i)$, $R_0 = \lambda\rho.\rho$ and $F_0 = \delta$.

$\mathcal{L}_1$

(i) $\mathcal{D}[\![a]\!]\alpha RF = \lambda\sigma.\sigma(a)(\alpha) defined \rightarrow \{\sigma(a)(\alpha)\cdot RF\}, F\sigma$

(ii) $\mathcal{D}[\![p(t)]\!]\alpha RF = \lambda\sigma.\{\sigma(p(t))(\alpha)\cdot \mathcal{D}[\![b\nu_{\alpha pi(\alpha,p)}(t\theta_\alpha)]\!]\alpha RF\}$
for $p \leftarrow b$ in D_α

(iii) $\mathcal{D}[\![g_1; g_2]\!]\alpha RF = \mathcal{D}[\![g_1]\!]\alpha(\mathcal{D}[\![g_2]\!]\alpha R)F$

(iv) $\mathcal{D}[\![g_1 \,\Box\, g_2]\!]\alpha RF = \mathcal{D}[\![g_1]\!]\alpha R(\mathcal{D}[\![g_2]\!]\alpha RF)$

(v) $\mathcal{D}[\![C :: new(channel)]\!]\alpha RF = \lambda\sigma.\{\sigma^\star \cdot RF\}$
with $\sigma^\star = \sigma(C :: new(channel))(\alpha)$

(vi) $\mathcal{D}[\![new(c(t))]\!]\alpha RF = \lambda\sigma.\{\sigma^\star \cdot (RF \,\|\, \mathcal{D}[\![c(s_\alpha(t)\theta_\alpha)]\!]\beta R_0 F_0)\}$
with $\sigma^\star = \sigma(new(c(t)))(\alpha)$

(vii) $\mathcal{D}[\![C!t]\!]\alpha RF = \lambda\sigma.\{C\theta_\alpha!t \cdot f\}$
with $f = \lambda\tau \in T.\tau \rightarrow RF, \mathcal{D}[\![C!t]\!]\alpha RF$

(viii) $\mathcal{D}[\![C?t]\!]\alpha RF = \lambda\sigma.\{C\theta_\alpha?t \cdot f\}$
with $f = \lambda\tau \in T.\tau \rightarrow RF, F$

The first four equations are straightforward extensions of the equations given for $\mathcal{L}_0$. In the equation for $new(c(t))$ the meaning of the newly created object is merged with the meaning stored in the continuations. Communication statements result in a communication intention containing a function that decides what must be done when the communication succeeds and what must be done on failure. For the output intention the resumption that must be taken when communication fails, simply repeats the meaning of the output statement.

We remark that the technique used in section 6.2.2 also applies to the equations presented above.

Definition 8.2.2 $\mathcal{M}[\![< D \mid g >]\!] = \mathcal{D}[\![g]\!]\alpha_0 R_0 F_0$ *for some initial object* α_0.

8.2.3 Equivalence between operational and denotational semantics

Since, operationally, unresolved communication intentions result in blocking the computation, we need a projection π, mapping elements from $\mathbb{P}$ to elements of $\mathbb{R}$, that removes communication intentions for which an alternative is available; and moreover yields all computation sequences that may arise from a certain state. In other words, the projection operator eliminates the branching inherent in the process structure by computing all possible sequences.

Our equivalence result for $\mathcal{L}_1$ may be stated as

Theorem 8.2.3 $\mathcal{O}[\![< D \mid g >]\!] = \pi \circ \mathcal{M}[\![< D \mid g >]\!]$ *for a suitable projection* π

The proof looks as follows.

$$\begin{aligned}\mathcal{O}[\![< D \mid g >]\!] &= \mathcal{T}[\![\{< \alpha_0, g; \surd : \Delta >\}]\!] \text{ by definition 8.2.1} \\ &= \pi \circ \mathcal{G}[\![\{< \alpha_0, g; \surd ; \Delta >\}]\!] \text{ by corollary 8.2.7} \\ &= \pi \circ \mathcal{F}[\![g; \surd : \Delta]\!]\alpha_0 \text{ by definition 8.2.4} \\ &= \pi \circ \mathcal{D}[\![g]\!]\alpha_0 R_0 F_0 \text{ by definition 8.2.4} \\ &= \pi \circ \mathcal{M}[\![< D \mid g >]\!] \text{ by definition 8.2.2}\end{aligned}$$

As before we need an intermediary function $\mathcal{F} : Obj \rightarrow FailCo \rightarrow Fail$ to take syntactic failure continuations to semantic failure continuations, and a function $\mathcal{R} : Obj \rightarrow SuccCo \rightarrow Succ$, to take syntactic success continuations to semantic success continuations. Moreover, we need a function $\mathcal{G} : \mathcal{P}(Obj \times FailCo) \rightarrow \mathbb{P}$ that maps collections of objects to their semantic counterparts in $\mathbb{P}$.

Definition 8.2.4

a. $\mathcal{R}[\![\surd]\!]\alpha = \lambda\rho.\rho$

b. $\mathcal{R}[\![g; R]\!]\alpha = \mathcal{D}[\![g]\!]\alpha\mathcal{R}[\![R]\!]\alpha$

c. $\mathcal{F}[\![\Delta]\!]\alpha = \delta$

d. $\mathcal{F}[\![R : F]\!]\alpha = \mathcal{R}[\![R]\!]\alpha\mathcal{F}[\![F]\!]\alpha$

e. $\mathcal{G}[\![\{< \alpha_1, F_1 >, ..., < \alpha_n, F_n >\}]\!] = \mathcal{F}[\![F_1]\!]\alpha_1 \parallel ... \parallel \mathcal{F}[\![F_n]\!]\alpha_n$

Again we have the property that unlabeled transitions do not affect the meaning.

Lemma 8.2.5 *If* $(\Gamma, \sigma) \longrightarrow (\Gamma', \sigma)$ *then* $\mathcal{G}[\![\Gamma]\!]\sigma = \mathcal{G}[\![\Gamma']\!]\sigma$

The key step in the proof that $\mathcal{O} = \pi \circ \mathcal{M}$ consists of showing that $\pi \circ \mathcal{G}$ is a fixed point of the operator that characterizes the operational meaning of a program (see definition 8.2.1).

We define a projection operator that reduces the unresolved communication intentions to $\lambda\sigma.\{\varepsilon\}$, the equivalent of the empty process δ.

We first define a function $rem : \mathbb{P} \rightarrow \mathbb{P}$ by

$$rem(\rho)(\sigma) = \rho(\sigma)\backslash\{c \cdot f : c \cdot f \in \rho(\sigma)\}$$

In other words $rem(\rho)(\sigma)$ is what remains after removing all unresolved communication intentions.

In order to lay hands on the behavior that gives rise to a state we define a labeling function $\dot{}: \Sigma \to \Lambda$ by $\dot{\sigma}(a)(\alpha) = a$ and $\dot{\sigma} = \star$ otherwise, as an inverse to the effect function.

We then define $\pi : \mathbb{P} \to \mathbb{R}$ by

$$\pi\,\rho = \begin{cases} \lambda\sigma.\{\varepsilon\} & \text{if } \rho = \delta \text{ or } rem(\rho)(\sigma) = \emptyset \\ \lambda\sigma.\bigcup\{\dot{\sigma}' \,\hat{\circ}\, (\pi\,\rho')(\sigma') : \sigma' \cdot \rho' \in rem(\rho)(\sigma)\} & \text{otherwise} \end{cases}$$

Below we will use the property $\lambda\sigma.\bigcup\{\dot{\sigma}' \,\hat{\circ}\, (\pi\,\rho')(\sigma')\} = \pi\,\lambda\sigma.\{\sigma' \cdot \rho'\}$, which can easily be verified.

Lemma 8.2.6 $\Psi(\pi \circ \mathcal{G}) = \pi \circ \mathcal{G}$

Proof: We use a complexity measure similar as the one introduced for $\mathcal{L}_0$, but extended in order to cope with configurations containing a collection of processes. We define

$$c(\Gamma) = \Sigma_{x \in \Gamma} c(x) \quad \text{and} \quad c(< \alpha, F >) = c(F)$$

We also let

$$c(C :: new(channel)) = c(new(c(t))) = c(C!t) = c(C?t) = 1$$

We must now prove that for all Γ and all σ we have $\Psi(\pi \circ \mathcal{G})[\![\Gamma]\!]\sigma = \pi \circ \mathcal{G}[\![\Gamma]\!]\sigma$. We will treat some selected cases. Let $\overline{R}_i = \mathcal{R}[\![R_i]\!]\alpha_i$ and $\overline{F}_i = \mathcal{F}[\![F_i]\!]\alpha_i$, with subscript i possibly empty.

- If $\Gamma = \{< \alpha, new(c(t)); R : F >\}$ then for $\sigma^\star = \sigma(new(c(t)))(\alpha)$ with $\sigma = (\theta, s, i)$

$$\begin{aligned}
\Psi(\pi \circ \mathcal{G})[\![\Gamma]\!] &= \lambda\sigma.\bigcup\{\dot{\sigma}^\star \,\hat{\circ}\, (\pi \circ \mathcal{G})[\![\{< \alpha, R : F >, < \beta, c(s_\alpha(t)\theta_\alpha); \surd : \Delta >\}]\!](\sigma^\star)\} \\
&= \pi\,\lambda\sigma.\{\sigma^\star \cdot \mathcal{G}[\![\{< \alpha, R : F >, < \beta, c(s_\alpha(t)\theta_\alpha); \surd : \Delta >\}]\!]\} \\
&\quad \text{(by the property of } \pi \text{)} \\
&= \pi\,\lambda\sigma.\{\sigma^\star \cdot (\overline{RF} \parallel \mathcal{D}[\![c(s_\alpha(t)\theta_\alpha)]\!]\beta\mathcal{R}[\![\surd]\!]\alpha\mathcal{F}[\![\Delta]\!]\alpha)\} \\
&\quad \text{(by the definition of } \mathcal{G} \text{)} \\
&= \pi\,\mathcal{D}[\![new(c(t))]\!]\alpha\overline{RF} \\
&\quad \text{(by the definition of } \mathcal{D}\text{)} \\
&= \pi \circ \mathcal{G}[\![\{< \alpha, new(c(t)); R : F >\}]\!] \\
&\quad \text{(by applying definition 8.2.4).}
\end{aligned}$$

- Let $\Gamma = \{< \alpha_1, C_1!t_1; R_1 : F_1 >, < \alpha_2, C_2?t_2; R_2 : F_2 >\}$ and $\sigma^\star = \sigma(\gamma!t_1, \gamma?t_2)(\alpha_1, \alpha_2)$ for $\sigma = (\theta, s, i)$ and $C_1\theta_{\alpha_1} = \gamma = C_2\theta_{\alpha_2}$.

If $\sigma^\star$ is defined then

$$\begin{aligned}
\Psi(\pi \circ \mathcal{G})[\![\Gamma]\!]\sigma &= (\pi\ \lambda\sigma.\{\sigma^\star \cdot \mathcal{G}[\![\{<\alpha_1, R_1 : F_1>, <\alpha_2, R_2 : F_2>\}]\!]\ \})(\sigma) \\
&\quad \text{(by applying } Comm\text{)} \\
&= (\pi\ \lambda\sigma.\{\sigma^\star \cdot (\overline{R}_1\overline{F}_1 \parallel \overline{R}_2\overline{F}_2)\})(\sigma) \\
&\quad \text{(by definition 8.2.4)} \\
&= (\pi\ (\mathcal{D}[\![C_1!t_1]\!]\alpha_1\overline{R}_1\overline{F}_1 \parallel \mathcal{D}[\![C_2?t_2]\!]\alpha_2\overline{R}_2\overline{F}_2)\ )(\sigma) \\
&\quad \text{(by the definition of merging)} \\
&= \pi \circ \mathcal{G}[\![\{<\alpha_1, C_1!t_1; R_1 : F_1>, <\alpha_2, C_2?t_2; R_2 : F_2>\}]\!]\sigma \\
&\quad \text{(by applying definition 8.2.4 again).}
\end{aligned}$$

When $\sigma^\star$ is not defined then

$$\begin{aligned}
\Psi(\pi \circ \mathcal{G})[\![\Gamma]\!]\sigma &= (\pi\ \lambda\sigma.\{\sigma \cdot \mathcal{G}[\![\{<\alpha_1, C_1!t_1; R_1 : F_1>, <\alpha_2, F_2>\}]\!]\ \}\ )(\sigma) \\
&\quad \text{(by applying } Comm\text{)} \\
&= (\pi\ \lambda\sigma.\{\sigma \cdot (\mathcal{D}[\![C_1!t_1]\!]\alpha_1\overline{R}_1\overline{F}_1 \parallel \overline{F}_2)\})(\sigma) \\
&\quad \text{(by definition 8.2.4)} \\
&= (\pi\ (\mathcal{D}[\![C_1!t_1]\!]\alpha_1\overline{R}_1\overline{F}_1 \parallel \mathcal{D}[\![C_2?t_2]\!]\alpha_2\overline{R}_2\overline{F}_2))(\sigma) \\
&\quad \text{(by the definition of merging)} \\
&= \pi \circ \mathcal{G}[\![\Gamma]\!]\sigma \text{ as desired.}
\end{aligned}$$

□

As a consequence of the previous lemma we may state

Corollary 8.2.7 $\mathcal{T} = \pi \circ \mathcal{G}$

8.3 Dynamic object creation and method calls by rendez-vous

The language $\mathcal{L}_2$ extends $\mathcal{B}_2$ by providing the primitives for communication as actually used in DLP. $\mathcal{L}_2$ is to a certain extent similar to $\mathcal{L}_1$. Instead of communication over channels, however, it provides the possibility for processes to communicate in a kind of rendez-vous. An object, or rather a process associated to an object, may call for a method to be evaluated by another object. Since backtracking may occur over the answers produced in evaluating the method, for each such rendez-vous a process is created. Instead of a single process, as for $\mathcal{L}_1$, multiple processes may now refer to a single object. We distinguish between the constructor process, executing the own activity of an object, and the processes created for evaluating a method. The process that called for the method is given a pointer to the process evaluating the call, and may through this pointer ask for all the answers that result from the evaluation. Backtracking over these answers is initiated by the invoking process. Since multiple processes are involved, we speak of distributed (or global) backtracking, as opposed to the backtracking occurring locally in a process.

Syntax Terms and actions are as for $\mathcal{L}_0$; however, as additional *constants* we need object names $c \in Objname$, and method names $m \in Method$. We assume that $Objname \subset Method$. We adopt the convention to use capital O for logical variables that may refer to an object and Q for variables that may become bound to pointers to evaluation processes.

As *primitives* $e \in Prim$, by which $\mathcal{L}_2$ extends $\mathcal{L}_0$, we now have

$$e ::= O :: new(c(t)) \mid Q :: O!m(t) \mid Q? \mid accept(m_1, ..., m_n) \mid !t$$

And, we define the set goals $g \in Goal$ by

$$g ::= a \mid m(t) \mid g_1; g_2 \mid g_1 \Box g_2 \mid e$$

The goal $O :: new(c(t))$ can be used to create a new instance of the object c, for which the constructor $c(t)$ is evaluated. The variable O will become bound to this newly created object. The goal $Q :: O!m(t)$ initiates a rendez-vous, in that the object denoted by O is asked to evaluate the goal $m(t)$. As a result the variable Q will be bound to a pointer to the process evaluating this goal. The request $Q?$ is used to ask for the answer substitutions resulting from the evaluation performed by the process that will become bound to Q. The goal $accept(m_1, ..., m_n)$ may be used to state the willingness to wait for and accept any of the methods $m_1, ..., m_n$. As a restriction we require that accept goals may occur only in constructor processes. The goal $!t$ is an auxiliary goal used for sending back the answer substitutions. These auxiliary goals do not correspond to any goal in a method declaration resulting from the translation of clauses.

The clauses for a method m, are collected in a *method declaration* of the form $m \leftarrow b$ with $b \equiv \lambda\tau.g$, which corresponds to a procedure declaration in $\mathcal{L}_0$ and $\mathcal{L}_1$.

As for $\mathcal{L}_1$ we assume *object declarations* of the form

$$(c \leftarrow b_c, < v_i >_{i=1,...,r}, < m_i \leftarrow b_i >_{i=1,...,k}>)$$

A *program* $< D \mid g >$ consists of a collection of object declarations D and a goal g.

8.3.1 Operational semantics

Our solution to the distributed backtracking that may arise in answering a method call forces us to distinguish between objects and processes.

The set of *objects*

$$Obj = \{(c, n) : c \text{ an object name}, n \in \mathbb{N}\}$$

consists of all pairs containing an object name and an instance number. We need process identifiers $\alpha, \beta \in Proc$, with $Proc$ defined by

$$Proc = \{(c, n, k) : (c, n) \in Obj, k \in \mathbb{N}\}$$

to be able to refer to particular processes. The elements in the set *Proc* differ from those in *Obj* only in having a process number, indicating how many processes referring to the object (c, n) have been created. We have adopted the convention to identify the process $(c, n, 0)$, evaluating the constructor of c. with the object (c, n). We use a function *obj*, defined by $obj(c, n, k) = (c, n)$ to denote the object to which a process refers. For $\alpha = (c, n, k)$ we write D_α for the object declaration for c.

We extend the set of terms by redefining

$$t ::= \varepsilon \mid \delta \mid [t_1, ..., t_n] \mid (t_1, t_2) \mid X \mid v \mid \alpha \mid f(t_1, ..., t_n)\text{: } f \text{ a function symbol, } n \geq 0$$

We have introduced the terms δ, $[t_1, ..., t_n]$ and (t_1, t_2) for communicating the results of a method call.

We now use generalized substitutions *substitutions* $\theta \in Subst^\star = Proc \rightarrow Subst$ with $\theta_\alpha \in Subst$ the substitution belonging to some process α.

Further, we extend substitutions so that they may contain information on what goal is evaluated by a process and what solutions have resulted thus far. For a call $m(t)$ that is evaluated by process α we may have that $\theta_\alpha(goal) = t$ and $\theta_\alpha(sols) = [t_1, ..., t_n]$, where $[t_1, ..., t_n]$ is the list of terms that represents the alternative solutions. In addition, we define

$$[t_1, ..., t_n] \cdot t = [t_1, ..., t_n, t]$$

in order to add a term t to the list of solutions $[t_1, ..., t_n]$.

We also need a *store* $s \in Store^+ = Obj \rightarrow Store$, and write $s_{obj(\alpha)} \in Store$ for the store for object $obj(\alpha)$.

A *count* $i \in Count^\star = (Objname \cup Obj \cup Proc \times Method) \rightarrow \mathbb{N}$ is used to administrate, respectively, the current instance number of a named object, the number of processes active for an object and the number of times a method has been called (locally) from within a process.

Our *states* σ come from the set

$$\Sigma = \{(\theta, s, i) : \theta \in Subst^\star, s \in Store^+, i \in Count^\star\}$$

and we will use the abbreviations, as introduced for $\mathcal{L}_1$,

$$\theta\{\alpha/X \leftarrow t\} = \theta\{\alpha/\theta_\alpha\{X/t\}\}$$

$$s\{obj(\alpha)/v \leftarrow t\} = s\{obj(\alpha)/s_{obj(\alpha)}\{v/t\}\}$$

For *renaming* we use a function $\nu \in Proc \times Method \times \mathbb{N} \rightarrow Var \rightarrow Var$.

For dealing with *communication* we need a set *Comm* of communication intentions, having elements of the form

$$Q :: \alpha!m(t),\ \overline{m},\ \alpha? \text{ and } !t$$

We speak of (syntactically) matching communication intentions whenever we encounter one of the pairs $(Q :: \alpha!m(t), \overline{m})$ or $(\alpha?, !t)$.

Resumptions To model the communication that takes place in a rendez-vous in we differentiate between answers $!t$ to stand for respectively

- $!\delta$ — indicating failure, that is the absence of further answers, and
- $!(t', [t_1, \ldots, t_n])$ — that is used to deliver a record of all the answers

In all other cases $!t$ stands for a normal answer.

Resumptions can now be defined by the function *res*, as follows

$$res(t)(\sigma)(\alpha,\beta) \;=\; \begin{cases} fail & \text{if } t = \delta \\ t'\theta_\alpha = t_1 \,\square \ldots \square\, u(t'\theta_\alpha); t'\theta_\alpha = t_n & \text{if } t = (t', [t_1, .., t_n]) \\ t\theta_\alpha = t\theta_\beta & \text{otherwise} \end{cases}$$

where we assume that $\sigma = (\theta, s, i)$.

To model the actual communication event, we make use of a function $eval : Comm \times Comm \rightarrow \Sigma \rightarrow Proc \times Proc \rightarrow Goal$ and its counterpart $\overline{eval} : Comm \times Comm \rightarrow \Sigma \rightarrow Proc \times Proc \rightarrow Goal$. As explained in section 6.5.1, this pair of functions allows us to conveniently describe what takes place both at the side of the invoking process and at the side of the process evaluating the method call.

We define *eval*, which takes effect at the process requesting a resumption, by stating

$$eval(Q?, !t)(\sigma)(\alpha,\beta) \;=\; \begin{cases} res(t)(\sigma)(\alpha,\beta) & \text{if } t = \delta \\ & \text{or } t = (t', [t_1, .., t_n]) \\ res(t)(\sigma)(\alpha,\beta) \,\square\, u(t\theta_\alpha); Q? & \text{otherwise} \end{cases}$$

and, similarly we define the function $\overline{eval}$, which takes effect at the side of the process sending the answer, by

$$\overline{eval}(Q?, !t)(\sigma)(\alpha,\beta) \;=\; \begin{cases} !(\theta_\beta(goal), \theta_\beta(sols)) & \text{if } t = \delta \\ !t & \text{if } t = (t', [t_1, \ldots, t_n]) \\ skip & \text{otherwise} \end{cases}$$

Note that $!(t', [t_1, \ldots, t_n])$ will only be inserted as a goal if the number of solutions n is finite, since otherwise $!\delta$ will never be reached.

We write $\sigma(c, \overline{c})(\alpha,\beta)$ to denote the application of the *effect* function to a pair of matching communication intentions $c, \overline{c} \in Comm$.

As for $\mathcal{L}_0$ and $\mathcal{L}_1$ we use syntactic success continuations from *SuccCo* defined by $R ::= \surd \,|\, g; R$, and syntactic failure continuations from *FailCo*, defined by $F ::= \Delta \,|\, R : F$, to model the (local) backtracking behavior. In order to model the distributed backtracking (possibly) occurring in a rendez-vous we need syntactic process continuations from *ProcCo* defined by

$$C ::= \Xi \mid \; < \alpha, F >: C$$

The empty process continuation Ξ is the process that has nothing left to do. Intuitively, a non-empty process continuation of the form $< \alpha, F >: C$ represents a stack of processes from which the top must be popped if it communicates successfully with another process. When this happens the process continuation C starts to be executed in parallel with the left-overs from $<\alpha, F>$. We use configurations (Γ,σ) with $\Gamma \in \mathcal{P}(ProcCo)$.

Again, we assume a general rule of the form

$$(\Gamma,\sigma) \xrightarrow{\eta} (\Gamma',\sigma') \Longrightarrow (X \cup \Gamma,\sigma) \xrightarrow{\eta} (X \cup \Gamma',\sigma')$$

for $X \in \mathcal{P}(ProcCo)$ disjoint from Γ and Γ'. Let $\sigma = (\theta, s, i)$.[2]

$\mathcal{L}_2$

$(\{<\alpha, a; R : F>: C\},\sigma) \xrightarrow{a} (\{<\alpha, R : F>: C\},\sigma^\star)$ *Action*

$\longrightarrow (\{<\alpha, F>: C\},\sigma)$

with for $a \in \{u(t), v := t, t_1 = t_2\}$ the interpretation

- $\sigma(u(t))(\alpha) = (\theta', s, i)$
  where $\theta' = \theta\{\alpha/X \leftarrow X\}_{X \in varsof(t)}$
- $\sigma(v := t)(\alpha) = (\theta, s', i)$
  where $s' = s\{\alpha/v \leftarrow s_{obj(\alpha)}(t)\theta_\alpha\}$
- $\sigma(t_1 = t_2)(\alpha) = (\theta', s, i)$
  where $\theta' = \theta\{\alpha/mgu(t_1', t_2') \circ \theta_\alpha\}$
  for $t_i' = s_{obj(\alpha)}(t_i)\theta_\alpha$

$(\{<\alpha, m(t); R : F>: C\},\sigma)$ *Rec*

$\xrightarrow{\star} (\{<\alpha, b\nu_{\alpha mi(\alpha,m)}(t\theta_\alpha); R : F>: C\},\sigma^\star)$

for $m \leftarrow b$ in D_α, with the interpretation

- $\sigma(m(t))(\alpha) = (\theta, s, i\{(\alpha,m)/i(\alpha,m)+1\})$

$(\{<\alpha, (g_1; g_2); R : F>: C\},\sigma)$ *Seq*

$\longrightarrow (\{<\alpha, g_1; (g_2; R) : F>: C\},\sigma)$

$(\{<\alpha, (g_1 \,\Box\, g_2); R : F>: C\},\sigma)$ *Alt*

$\longrightarrow (\{<\alpha, (g_1; R) : (g_2; R) : F>: C\},\sigma)$

---

[2]The axioms given here are identical to the axioms given for $\mathcal{L}$ in the previous chapter (section 7.4), except for the application of the effect function in *Method* that is slightly more complicated since it must be used in the denotational semantics as well.

New

$$(\{<\alpha, O :: new(c(t)); R : F >: C\}, \sigma)$$

$$\xrightarrow{\star} (\{<\alpha, R : F >: C, <\beta, F_\beta >: \Xi\}, \sigma^\star)$$

where $F_\beta \equiv c(s_{obj(\alpha)}(t)\theta_\alpha; \surd : \Delta$, with the interpretation

- $\sigma(O :: new(c(t)))(\alpha) = (\theta', s, i')$
  where $\theta' = \theta\{\alpha/O \leftarrow \beta\}$ with $\beta = (c, i'(c), 0)$
  and $i' = i\{c/i(c) + 1\}$

Method

$$(\{<\alpha, Q :: O!m(t); R_1 : F_1 >: C_1,$$

$$<\beta, accept(..., m, ...); R_2 : F_2 >: C_2\}, \sigma)$$

$$\xrightarrow{\star} (\{<\alpha, Q?; R_1 : F_1 >: C_1,$$

$$<\beta', F_{\beta'} >:<\beta, R_2 : F_2 >: C_2\}, \sigma^\star)$$

if $O\theta_\alpha = \beta$,

where $F_{\beta'} \equiv (m(t'); !t' \,\square\, !\delta) : \surd : \Delta$, for $t' = s_{obj(\alpha)}(t)\theta_\alpha$

with the interpretation

- $\sigma(Q :: \beta!m(t), \overline{m})(\alpha, \beta) = (\theta', s, i')$
  where for $\beta = (c, n, 0)$ and a fresh variable Q it holds
  that $\beta' = (c, n, i'(c, n))$, $i' = i\{(c, n)/i(c, n) + 1\}$
  and $\theta' = \theta\{\alpha/Q \leftarrow \beta'\}$ and $\theta'_\beta(goal) = t$

Result

$$(\{<\alpha, Q?; R_1 : F_1 >: C_1, <\beta, !t; R_2 : F_2 >: C_2\}, \sigma)$$

$$\xrightarrow{\star} (\{<\alpha, eval(Q?, !t)(\sigma)(\alpha, \beta); R_1 : F_1 >: C_1,$$

$$<\beta, \overline{eval}(Q?, !t)(\sigma)(\alpha, \beta); R_2 : F_2 >: \Xi, C_2\}, \sigma^\star)$$

provided that $Q\theta_\alpha = \beta$

with the interpretation

- $\sigma(Q?, !t)(\alpha, \beta) = (\theta', s, i)$
  where $\theta'_\beta(sols) = \theta_\beta(sols) \cdot t\theta_\beta$ if t is not equal to δ
  or $(t', [t_1, ..., t_n])$, and $\theta' = \theta$ otherwise

Tick

$$(\{<\alpha, \surd : F >: C\}, \sigma) \longrightarrow (\{<\alpha, F >: C\}, \sigma)$$

The axioms given above are, apart from *Method* and *Result*, straightforwardly adapted from the ones given for $\mathcal{L}_1$.

To be able to apply *Method*, the condition $O\theta_\alpha = \beta$ must be fulfilled, otherwise no transition is possible. The rule operates on a pair $O!m(t)$ and $accept(..., m, ...)$ indicating both the call for a method m and the willingness to accept the call. As a result, a process β' is created and put on top of the process stack for β. The variable Q is introduced to be able to refer to β'. The process β' executes the goal $m(t'); !t' \,\square\, !\delta$, of which the first part represents the sequential composition of evaluating the call and sending the results. The second alternative states that no more answers are available.

These two parts correspond to the two possible ways in which the axiom *Result* may be applied. If the answered term is δ then the requesting process pops its failure stack, otherwise the answer substitution will be computed by unifying $t\theta_\alpha$ with $t\theta_\beta$. Since other answers may be produced an alternative request is made, preceded by the action $u(t\theta_\alpha)$ in order to undo the previous bindings of the argument t.

We take $\mathbb{R} = \Sigma \to \mathcal{P}_{nc}(\Lambda^\infty)$.

Definition 8.3.1 $\mathcal{O}[\![< D \mid g >]\!] = \mathcal{T}[\![\{< \alpha_0, g; \surd : \Delta >: \Xi\}]\!]$ *for some initial process* α_0, *where for*

$$\Psi : (\mathcal{P}(ProcCo) \to \mathbb{R}) \to (\mathcal{P}(ProcCo) \to \mathbb{R})$$

and

$$\Psi(\phi)[\![\Gamma]\!](\sigma) = \begin{cases} \{\varepsilon\} & \textit{if } (\Gamma, \sigma) \textit{ blocks} \\ \bigcup\{\eta \,\hat{\circ}\, \phi[\![\Gamma']\!](\sigma') \mid (\Gamma, \sigma) \xrightarrow{\eta} (\Gamma', \sigma')\} & \textit{otherwise} \end{cases}$$

we define $\mathcal{T} = fix\Psi$.

8.3.2 Denotational semantics

As a domain we take $\mathbb{P}$, with typical elements ρ and q, given by

$$\mathbb{P} \cong \{\delta\} \cup \Sigma \to \mathcal{P}_{co}(\Sigma \times \mathbb{P} \cup \mathsf{C} \times \mathbb{P} \cup \mathsf{C} \times (Proc \to Term \to \mathbb{P}))$$

where $\mathsf{C} = Proc \times Comm$, with $Comm$ the set of communication intentions as defined in section 8.3.1. We will denote elements of C by c and elements of $Proc \to Term \to \mathbb{P}$ by f. Take note that δ here denotes the empty process and not the special term. For non-empty $\rho \in \mathbb{P}$, the set $\rho(\sigma)$, for some σ, may contain ordinary computation steps of the form $\sigma' \cdot \rho'$, or communication intentions of the form $[\alpha, Q{::}\beta!m(t)] \cdot \rho'$, $[\alpha, \overline{m}] \cdot f$, $[\alpha, \beta?] \cdot f$ or $[\alpha, !t] \cdot \rho'$. Other communication intentions will simply not arise. We use ξ to denote the elements of such a set $\rho(\sigma)$.

We have to adapt the *parallel merge* operator given for $\mathcal{L}_1$ to the present situation. The operator $\| : \mathbb{P} \times \mathbb{P} \to \mathbb{P}$ must satisfy $\delta \| \rho = \rho = \rho \| \delta$ and

$$\begin{aligned} \rho_1 \| \rho_2 = \lambda\sigma.(\ & \{\sigma' \cdot (\rho_i' \| \rho_j) : \sigma' \cdot \rho_i' \in \rho_i(\sigma) \ \textit{ for } i, j \in \{1,2\} \ \textit{ and } i \neq j\} \cup \\ & \{c \cdot (\rho_i' \| \rho_j) : c \cdot \rho_i' \in \rho_i(\sigma) \ \textit{ for } i, j \in \{1,2\} \ \textit{ and } i \neq j\} \cup \end{aligned}$$

$$\{c \cdot \lambda\beta t.(f(\beta)(t) \parallel \rho_j) : c \cdot f \in \rho_i(\sigma) \ \ for \ \ i, j \in \{1, 2\}, i \neq j\} \cup$$
$$(\rho_1 \ |_\sigma \ \rho_2))$$

The communication operator $|_\sigma$, that is dependent on the state σ, is characterized by

$$\rho_1 \ |_\sigma \ \rho_2 = \bigcup\{\xi_i \,|_\sigma\, \xi_j : \xi_i \in \rho_i(\sigma), \ \xi_j \in \rho_j(\sigma) \ \ for \ \ i, j \in \{1, 2\} \ \ and \ \ i \neq j\}$$

and

$$\xi_1 \,|_\sigma\, \xi_2 = \begin{cases} \{\sigma^\star \cdot (\rho \parallel f(\beta')(t))\} & \text{if } \xi_1 = [\alpha, Q :: \beta!m(t)] \cdot \rho \\ & \text{and } \xi_2 = [\beta, \overline{m}] \cdot f \\ & \text{where } \sigma^\star = \sigma(Q :: \beta!m(t).\overline{m})(\alpha, \beta) \\ & \text{and } \beta' = (c, n, i(c, n) + 1) \\ & \text{for } \beta = (c, n, 0) \\ \{\sigma \cdot (f_1(\beta)(t) \parallel f_2(\alpha)(\beta))\} & \text{if } \xi_1 = [\alpha, \beta?] \cdot f_1 \\ & \text{and } \xi_2 = [\beta, !t] \cdot f_2 \\ \emptyset & \text{otherwise} \end{cases}$$

When a method call takes place, the state is modified to account for the process that is created to evaluate the call. Also, the substution function will be affected due to applying the effect function. Notice that, when communicating an answer substitution the state σ is not changed, since the actual state change will be effected afterwards by the process asking for the solution.

In order to model our protocol of mutual exclusion (cf. section 6.5.3) we define the *insertion* operator $\triangleright_\alpha : \mathbb{P} \times \mathbb{P} \to \mathbb{P}$ by $\delta \triangleright_\alpha \delta = \delta, \delta \triangleright_\alpha \rho = \rho, \rho \triangleright_\alpha \delta = \delta$ and

$$\begin{aligned} \rho \triangleright_\alpha q = \lambda\sigma.(\ & \{\sigma' \cdot \rho \triangleright_\alpha q' : \sigma' \cdot q' \in q(\sigma)\} \cup \\ & \{[\alpha, !t] \cdot (\rho \parallel q') : [\alpha, !t] \cdot q' \in q(\sigma)\} \cup \\ & \{c \cdot \rho \triangleright_\alpha q' : c \cdot q' \in q(\sigma) \ \ for \ \ c \neq [\alpha, !t]\} \cup \\ & \{c \cdot \lambda\beta\tau.\rho \triangleright_\alpha f(\beta)(\tau) : c \cdot f \in q(\sigma)\} \ ) \end{aligned}$$

The function $\mathcal{D}[\![\cdot]\!] : Goal \to Proc \to Succ \to Fail \to \mathbb{P}$, giving a denotational meaning to the language $\mathcal{L}_2$, resembles the corresponding function for $\mathcal{L}_1$ to a large extent. We again take $Succ = Fail \to \mathbb{P}$ and $Fail = \mathbb{P}$. Notice that we use the effect function as defined in the transition system for $\mathcal{L}_2$, and remember that in equation (v) the process identifier β results from applying the effect function.

Let $\sigma = (\theta, s, i)$, $R_0 = \lambda\rho.\rho$ and $F_0 = \delta$.

$\mathcal{L}_2$

(i) $\mathcal{D}[\![a]\!]\alpha RF = \lambda\sigma.\sigma(a)(\alpha)\,defined \rightarrow \{\sigma(a)(\alpha)\cdot RF\}, F\sigma$

(ii) $\mathcal{D}[\![m(t)]\!]\alpha RF = \lambda\sigma.\{\sigma(m(t))(\alpha)\cdot\mathcal{D}[\![b\nu_{\alpha mi(\alpha,m)}(t\theta_\alpha)]\!]\alpha RF\}$
for $m \leftarrow b$ in D_α

(iii) $\mathcal{D}[\![g_1; g_2]\!]\alpha RF = \mathcal{D}[\![g_1]\!]\alpha(\mathcal{D}[\![g_2]\!]\alpha R)F$

(iv) $\mathcal{D}[\![g_1 \Box g_2]\!]\alpha RF = \mathcal{D}[\![g_1]\!]\alpha R(\mathcal{D}[\![g_2]\!]\alpha RF)$

(v) $\mathcal{D}[\![O :: new(c(t))]\!]\alpha RF =$
$\lambda\sigma.\{\sigma^\star\cdot(RF \parallel \mathcal{D}[\![c(s_{obj(\alpha)}(t)\theta_\alpha)]\!]\beta R_0F_0)\}$
with $\sigma^\star = \sigma(O :: new(c(t)))(\alpha)$

(vi) $\mathcal{D}[\![O!m(t)]\!]\alpha RF = \lambda\sigma.\{[\alpha, Q :: (O!m(s_{obj(\alpha)}(t)))\theta_\alpha]\cdot\mathcal{D}[\![Q?]\!]\alpha RF\}$
for a fresh variable Q

(vii) $\mathcal{D}[\![accept(m_1, ..., m_n)]\!]\alpha RF = \lambda\sigma.\{[\alpha, \overline{m}_i]\cdot f_i : 1 \le i \le n\}$
with $f_i = \lambda\beta t.RF \rhd_\beta \mathcal{D}[\![m_i(t); !t \Box !\delta]\!]\beta R_0F_0$

(viii) $\mathcal{D}[\![Q?]\!]\alpha RF = \lambda\sigma.\{[\alpha, Q\theta_\alpha?]\cdot f\}$
with $f = \lambda\beta t.\mathcal{D}[\![eval(Q?, !t)(\sigma)(\alpha,\beta)]\!]\alpha RF$

(ix) $\mathcal{D}[\![!t]\!]\alpha RF = \lambda\sigma.\{[\alpha, !t]\cdot RF\}$
with $f = \lambda\beta t'.\mathcal{D}[\![\overline{eval}(t'?, !t)(\sigma)(\beta,\alpha)]\!]\alpha RF$

The equation for the *accept* statement shows that a process for evaluating the method call and for returning the result is prepared, to become an actual process when a process identifier and the actual parameters of the method call are provided. The meaning of the resumption statement $Q?$ is a process that effects the binding of the communicated solution while undoing it when it is forced into its failure continuation. When no more answers are available the failure continuation is taken directly.

Definition 8.3.2 $\mathcal{M}[\![< D \mid g >]\!] = \mathcal{D}[\![g]\!]\alpha_0R_0F_0$ *for some initial process* α_0

8.3.3 Equivalence between operational and denotational semantics

We state our equivalence result.

Theorem 8.3.3 $\mathcal{O}[\![< D \mid g >]\!] = \pi \circ \mathcal{M}[\![< D \mid g >]\!]$ *for a suitable projection* π

The proof is along the same lines as the one for $\mathcal{L}_1$, but as an extra complexity we must now deal with (syntactic) process continuations. As an outline of the proof we put

$$\begin{aligned}\mathcal{O}[\![< D \mid g >]\!] &= \mathcal{T}[\![\{< \alpha_0, g; \surd : \Delta >: \Xi\}]\!] \text{ by definition 8.3.1}\\ &= \pi \circ \mathcal{G}[\![\{< \alpha_0, g; \surd; \Delta >: \Xi\}]\!] \text{ by corollary 8.3.7}\\ &= \pi \circ \mathcal{F}[\![g; \surd : \Delta]\!]\alpha_0 \text{ by definition 8.3.4}\\ &= \pi \circ \mathcal{D}[\![g]\!]\alpha_0 R_0 F_0 \text{ by definition 8.3.4}\\ &= \pi \circ \mathcal{M}[\![< D \mid g >]\!] \text{ by definition 8.3.2}\end{aligned}$$

We use a function $\mathcal{G} : \mathcal{P}(ProcCo) \to \mathbb{P}$, taking sets of process continuations to (semantic) processes, a function $\mathcal{C} : ProcCo \to \mathbb{P}$ that maps a process continuation into $\mathbb{P}$, and the functions $\mathcal{F} : FailCo \to Fail$ and $\mathcal{R} : SuccCo \to Succ$.

Definition 8.3.4

a. $\mathcal{R}[\![\surd]\!]\alpha = \lambda\rho.\rho$

b. $\mathcal{R}[\![g; R]\!]\alpha = \mathcal{D}[\![g]\!]\alpha\mathcal{R}[\![R]\!]\alpha$

c. $\mathcal{F}[\![\Delta]\!]\alpha = \delta$

d. $\mathcal{F}[\![R : F]\!]\alpha = \mathcal{R}[\![R]\!]\alpha\mathcal{F}[\![F]\!]\alpha$

e. $\mathcal{C}[\![\Xi]\!] = \delta$

f. $\mathcal{C}[\![< \alpha, F >: C]\!] = \mathcal{C}[\![C]\!] \rhd_\alpha \mathcal{F}[\![F]\!]\alpha$

g. $\mathcal{G}[\![\{C_1, ..., C_n\}]\!] = \mathcal{C}[\![C_1]\!] \parallel ... \parallel \mathcal{C}[\![C_n]\!]$

Intuitively, the equation $\mathcal{C}[\![< \alpha, F >: C]\!] = \mathcal{C}[\![C]\!] \rhd_\alpha \mathcal{F}[\![F]\!]\alpha$ states that the process resulting from evaluating C is inserted in the process arising from evaluating F for α at the point that α is willing to communicate its first result.

Lemma 8.3.5 *If* $(\Gamma, \sigma) \longrightarrow (\Gamma', \sigma)$ *then* $\mathcal{G}[\![\Gamma]\!]\sigma = \mathcal{G}[\![\Gamma']\!]\sigma$

Not surprisingly by now, the key step in the proof $\mathcal{O} = \pi \circ \mathcal{M}$ consists of showing that $\pi \circ \mathcal{G}$ is a fixed point of the operator that characterizes the operational meaning of a program.

We use a projection π similar to the one we used for $\mathcal{L}_1$, but redefine for ρ non-empty

$$rem(\rho)(\sigma) = \rho(\sigma) \backslash (\{c \cdot \rho' : c \cdot \rho' \in \rho(\sigma)\} \cup \{c \cdot f : c \cdot f \in \rho(\sigma)\})$$

in order to remove all unresolved communication intentions.

Lemma 8.3.6 $\Psi(\pi \circ \mathcal{G}) = \pi \circ \mathcal{G}$

Proof: We extend the complexity measure given for $\mathcal{L}_1$ to syntactic process continuations by stating

$$c(< \alpha, F >: C) = c(F) + c(C) \quad \text{and} \quad c(\Xi) = 0$$

It is easy to establish that the required property of c stating that if $(\Gamma, \sigma) \rightarrow (\Gamma', \sigma)$ then $c(\Gamma) > c(\Gamma')$ holds.

The proof is now straightforward. We leave the various cases, with reference to section 6.5.4, to the reader.

Corollary 8.3.7 $\mathcal{T} = \pi \circ \mathcal{G}$

Part III

Implementation

9

An implementation model for DLP

- But if what we desire is to increase our knowledge rather than cultivate our sensibility, we should do well to close all those delightful books; for we shall not find any instruction there upon the questions which most press upon us -
George Santayana, *The Sense of Beauty*

Having dealt with the design and semantics of DLP we are ready to look at the implementation of our language. In this chapter we will give an introductory account of the implementation model employed. The model that we will sketch covers all the constructs introduced in chapter 3. It is more general than the computation model presented in part II. A noticeable difference is that we allow nested accept statements, whereas in giving the semantics for DLP_2 we required accept statements to occur in the constructor process, which prevents such nesting. See section 3.9 for a more detailed discussion.

The basic notions that we deal with are, again: *objects*, encapsulating data; *processes*, created to evaluate goals; *communication* between processes; and *inference* by which the evaluation of goals takes place.

We will restrict ourselves here to a treatment of active objects, and communication by rendez-vous. We will not discuss inheritance, since inheritance, because of its static nature, does not influence the behavior of an object in any dynamic way. An overview of the prototype implementation is given in section 9.5.2. We have also included a description of the implementation language in section 9.5.1. In chapter 11 we will present a much more detailed description, including passive objects, inheritance and communication over channels.

For our prototype implementation we have chosen to use a Prolog interpreter derived from a formal continuation semantics for Prolog, given in [Allison, 1986]. We describe this interpreter in chapter 10. We have not used the semantics given in the previous part for implementing DLP, simply because at the time we did not have any of these. The semantics given in part II have been developed afterwards to establish the soundness of the language. We must, however, remark that the semantics we have used covers only the Prolog inference part. It may be replaced by a more efficient Prolog interpreter without affecting the structure of the prototype in any significant way.

9.1 Objects

In DLP objects are given by a declaration such as

ctr

```
object ctr {
var n=0.

ctr() :-    accept(any), ctr().

inc() :-   n :=   n + 1.
value(N) :-   N = n.
}
```

Each instance of such an object is uniquely identified by an *instance number*. Each instance has a private copy of the non-logical variables and (conceptually) of the clauses declared for the object.

Active objects In addition, each active object has a number of attributes, invisible to the programmer, that contain the *state* of the object determining the acceptance of method calls.

These attributes are

- the *accept list* — that contains the accept expressions by which it is decided whether a method call is acceptable,
- the *accept queue* — that contains the method calls for which the evaluation is suspended, and
- the *process stack* — that records the processes for which an accept statement is evaluated.

A stack of processes is maintained since accept statements may occur in a nested fashion. Apart from the attributes mentioned, a boolean variable *locked* is kept, to indicate whether an object is willing to receive any new requests for engaging in a rendez-vous.

object (*ctr*,*i*)	
variable	n = 0
constructor	ctr() :- *accept*(any),\n ctr().
methods	inc() :- n := n + 1. value(N) :- N = n.

state information	
accept list	ctr
accept queue	*empty*
process stack	*empty*
locked	*true*

constructor

In the figure above we have pictured the creation of a new active instance of the object declared above. The accept list is initially set to the constructor of the object. Both the accept queue and the process stack are initially empty. As soon as the constructor process is created the newly created object is locked and remains locked until it is notified of an accept statement.

The protocol by which method calls are handled will be illustrated by an example. We represent the state of an instance of the counter object by a tuple

state

(*n*, *accept list*, *accept queue*, *process stack*, *locked*)

where *n* is the non-logical variable of a counter. Suppose that we have as a goal

?- C = new(ctr()), C!inc(), C!value(X).

Evaluating the atom C = new(ctr()) results in an object (*ctr*, 1) for which we have

(1) (0, *ctr*, *empty*, *empty*, *true*)

as the state. On reaching the statement *accept*(any) the state becomes

(2) (0, *any*, *empty*, *constructor*, *false*)

in order to enable the object to accept a method call. The call C!inc() will now be accepted, and during the evaluation of inc() the state of the counter object will become

(3) (1, *any*, *empty*, *constructor*, *true*)

After the evaluation of inc() the state becomes

(4) (1, *any*, *empty*, *empty*, *true*)

to enable the constructor to continue. When the constructor then reaches the statement *accept*(any), after a recursive call to ctr(), the state becomes

(5) (1, *any*, *empty*, *constructor*, *false*)

enabling the acceptance of the call value(X). We have summarized these changes of state in the table below.

	(1)	(2)	(3)	(4)	(5)
n	0	0	1	1	1
accept list	*ctr*	*any*	*any*	*any*	*any*
accept queue	*empty*	*empty*	*empty*	*empty*	*empty*
process stack	*empty*	*constructor*	*constructor*	*empty*	*constructor*
locked	*true*	*false*	*true*	*true*	*false*

When an accept statement occurs in a process that is not the constructor process a similar procedure is followed. The process evaluating the accept statement is suspended and pushed on the process stack.

As the example above illustrates, if the accept queue contains no request satisfying an acceptance condition, the object is unlocked and waits for a method call. The object will consider requests for a method call only if it is not locked. If it then receives a request that does not satisfy the acceptance conditions this request is put in the accept queue. For an example of an object where this may happen look at the semaphore presented in section 3.3. When notified of an accept statement, the object first inspects the accept queue to see if there are any requests satisfying the new acceptance conditions. When no such request is available the object becomes unlocked, and waits for a method call.

Acceptance of method calls is determined by the accept expressions contained in the accept list. For a simple accept expression, just naming the method, it suffices to check the predicate name of the call. Conditional accept expressions require a more involved procedure to decide whether a call may be accepted. Recall that a conditional accept expression is of the form

method : *guard* → *goal* (see section 3.5)

To be accepted, a method call must unify with *method* and the *guard* must hold. The process created to establish this has to return a single result, recording the bindings of the variables in *method* and *guard*. If the test is successful, these bindings are taken over by the process created to evaluate the *goal*. The bindings resulting from the test and the bindings resulting from the evaluation of the goal are communicated to the process in which the accept statement occurred. If the evaluation of the goal fails this process is sent only the bindings that result from unifying the call with *method* and evaluating the *guard*. The process that called the method receives only the answer substitution, that is the bindings of the variables uninstantiated at the time of the call. Only the bindings of these variables are undone when backtracking occurs. The bindings of the variables in the accept statement are committed to when the test succeeds.

Fairness Method calls are accepted when they satisfy one of the expressions occurring in the accept list. If a method call does not satisfy any acceptance condition it is put in the accept queue to await a change of the acceptance conditions. The procedure sketched above guarantees a fair treatment of method calls, since incoming requests are either granted or stored in the accept queue in the order that they are received. No call has to wait indefinitely long under favorable acceptance conditions. Cf. [America, 1989b].

9.2 Processes

A process is created for each request to an object to evaluate a goal. The evaluation of a goal is done by a (more or less standard) Prolog inference engine. Each such inference is, in other words, accompanied by a so-called *evaluation process* taking care of communicating with the environment, if necessary. The evaluation process also serves to administrate where to cut off the search and to communicate interactively with the user.

Each process refers to an object, from which it derives its functionality. When a process is created, it is given a pointer to the object for accessing non-logical variables and to delegate the evaluation of the accept statement.

State To keep track of the whereabouts of the evaluation of the goal, a process has an attribute *state* that may have one of the following values:

BUSY — the inference is still going on,

PEND — an answer has been produced, but not necessarily the last answer,

WAIT — the last answer has been produced, and

STOP — the last answer has been sent to the caller.

Apart from the state attribute, we use two attributes to store the resulting answers:

- *result* — to store the most recent answer,
- *solutions* — which contains all the answers that have been produced.

In order to deliver the proper resumption, the evaluation process has an attribute:

- *goal* — for storing the initial goal

that is used to create a resumption when the process is asked for an answer.

Resumptions A *resumption* is an ordinary Prolog goal that must be executed by the caller of a method to effect the bindings produced by evaluating the call.

What resumption is returned depends on the *state* of the process and the contents of the *result* attribute. Assuming that we have an appropriate translation of the values of the attributes *goal*, *result* and *solutions* to Prolog terms, resumptions may take the following form:

- *fail* — the failing resumption

which is delivered when the state parameter indicates WAIT and the *result* is empty,

- *goal* = *result* — the unifying resumption

which is delivered when the state indicates either PEND or WAIT and the *result* is not empty, and

- *member*(*goal*, *solutions*) — the backtracking resumption

which is delivered when the state indicates STOP.

The failing resumption, when executed by the process requesting an answer, results in failure, evidently. Both the unifying and the backtracking resumption bind the variables occurring in *goal* to their instantiations in respectively *result* and *solutions*. The latter resumption, moreover, backtracks over all solutions generated. Backtracking resumptions may be delivered when goals occur in between a call and a resumption request.

Recall that a synchronous method call of the form *O*!*G*, where *O* refers to an object and *G* to a goal literal may be regarded as implemented by the clause

O!G

```
O!G :-   Q = O!G, Q?.
```

Hence when a method is called in DLP, a resumption request of the form *Q*? is dynamically inserted to replace the call. The variable *Q* is bound to the evaluation process handling the call.

To enable the calling process to backtrack repeatedly over these solutions, the evaluation process created to answer the method call stores the last solution found (in the variable *result*) as well as all the solutions produced thus far (in the variable *solutions*). As long as new solutions are produced the evaluation process returns the last solution stored in *result* to the calling process. When no more solutions can be generated and the calling process asks for another solution then the resumption request *Q*? initially fails. If the resumption request immediately follows the method call as is the case with a synchronous method call, this is the end of the story. However, when the calling process successfully backtracks over a goal in between the method call and the resumption request, as may be the case for goals of the form

?- Q = O!m(t), B, Q?,...

then calling the resumption request $Q?$ will result in trying all the solutions generated. These solutions will be handed over to the calling process by a *backtracking resumption.* This is only possible, of course, when the number of solutions is finite.

With $A\&B$ defined by

A&B

```
A&B :-  Q = O!B, A, Q?.
```

this mechanism enables us to get all the solutions to a goal $A\&B$, whereas otherwise we would have to face the situation that $A \,\&\, B \neq A, B$. See also section 3.6.

9.3 Communication

Communication between processes occurs on the occasion of calling a method and returning an answer. In the part dealing with the semantics of DLP we have described the synchronization that takes place between processes during such a rendez-vous. See sections 6.5.1 and 7.3.

Accepting a method call When a process encounters an accept statement, control is delegated to the object to which the process refers. The process itself is pushed on what we have called the *process stack* of the object. When a method call, satisfying the acceptance conditions, is accepted, a new process is created to evaluate the call. The process calling the method receives a pointer to this newly created evaluation process and states a resumption request to wait for an answer.

The evaluation process receives a pointer to the process in which the accept statement occurred. When the evaluation process comes in state PEND or WAIT the accepting process is told to continue. By then it has been popped from the process stack.

Returning an answer When an answer has been produced, the evaluation process waits for a request to return a resumption. The kind of resumption that is returned depends on the state of the evaluation process and the result that is produced. After sending the resumption, its changes its state into BUSY if it was in state PEND and to STOP if it was in a WAIT state. The process requesting the resumption checks whether the evaluation process was in state PEND when sending the resumption. If so, then the resumption executed by the requesting process will be of the form $(R; Q?)$, where R is the resumption received, to allow backtracking over alternative answers. In case the evaluation process was not in a PEND state, the resumption will simply be R.

9.4 Inference

Goals are evaluated using a sequential Prolog interpreter. The object, on behalf of which the evaluation occurs, creates an evaluation process to handle the inference.

To deal with backtracking, the evaluation process (conceptually) possesses a copy of the clauses declared for the object to which it refers.

For our prototype implementation of DLP we have chosen to employ a technique for compiling clauses, derived from a formal continuation semantics originally given in [Allison, 1986]. Our compilation scheme has proven its usefulness, in particular in the implementation of inheritance.

Alternative implementations are described in [Nilsson, 1982]. [Campbell, 1984] and [Cohen, 1985]. See also [Warren, 1977] and [Warren, 1983] for the description of an efficient abstract machine for Prolog. Further, [Lusk and Overbeek, 1980] and [Lusk et al, 1982] discuss implementation techniques for general resolution-based inference mechanisms.

9.5 The prototype

In the next chapter we will show how we derived the code for the sequential Prolog interpreter from the continuation semantics given in [Allison, 1986]. In chapter 11 we will discuss the implementation of the prototype in detail. Here, however, we wish to give an overview of the structure of our prototype implementation of DLP. But first, we will devote some attention to the implementation language that we have used for developing the prototype.

9.5.1 The implementation language

For the implementation of the prototype we have used a syntactic variant of the parallel object oriented language POOL-X as defined in [America, 1989]. We will use the name *POOL** for our dialect. We wish to remark that our variant conforms to the restrictions imposed in [Beemster, 1990].

Since our language DLP has partly been inspired by the language POOL, a forerunner of POOL-X, described in [America, 1987], the obvious similarities between these languages should come as no surprise.

Those familiar with POOL-X should have no trouble reading the code fragments presented when taking into account that we use lower case keywords and curly brackets { and } instead of BEGIN and END. Moreover, since we do not like to speak of routines, we have also replaced the keyword ROUTINE by the keyword *fn*, to indicate a function definition. Another difference with POOL-X is that we have allowed ourselves the use of an adapted version of the C-preprocessor.

For those not familiar with POOL-X we explain the main features of our implementation language. The most interesting aspect of *POOL** is that it allows to create dynamically an indefinite number of active objects that may communicate with each other by means of a synchronous method call, resembling the Ada rendez-vous.

Objects are taken to be instances of a class. A class declaration generically describes the behavior of each object that is an instance of that class. The language *POOL** is strongly typed, in the sense that each entity, including integers and strings, must be an instance of some class.

Class declarations in *POOL** have the following form, with keywords written in italic:

declaration

```
class name
var instance variables
newpar(new parameters)
init initialization part tini
functions
methods
body body part ydob
end name
```

Each class has a name that must start with a capital. A class declaration may specify a number of instance variables. In the following we will speak of instance variables as the attributes of an object, since instance variables contain the private data of an object, that may be accessed and modified by the methods defined for that class of objects. The new parameters are a special kind of instance variables. They may not be modified after being initialized. When creating a new instance of a class, the value for such a parameter must be given as an argument. Apart from the new parameters, an initialization part may be specified that will be executed, when creating a new object, before the body containing the own activity of the object will start to execute. Each class declaration may contain a number of function definitions. These functions cannot access the instance variables of objects belonging to the class. The class merely acts as the scope within which the function is known. In contrast, the methods defined for a class do have access to the local data of an object as stored in the instance variables. In effect methods are the exclusive way to access and modify the encapsulated data. Finally, we may encounter the specification of the own activity of an object in the body part of a class declaration. We remark that in an actual class declaration not all of the components listed above need to occur.

As an example of a class declaration in *POOL** consider the definition of a semaphore. See section 3.3 for the declaration of a semaphore in DLP.

Sema

```
class Semaphore
var n:Integer
newpar(n1:Integer)
init n := n1 tini
method v():Sema { n := n + 1; result self }
method p():Sema { n := n - 1; result self }
body do
 if n = 0 then answer(v) else answer(p, v) fi
od ydob
end Semaphore
```

The declaration of class *Sema* shows all the aspects of a class declaration mentioned, except the definition of functions.

Statements in *POOL** have a Pascal-like syntax. The keyword *result* indicates what to return as a result of applying a method. The expression *self* represents the object to which the method is applied. The statement *do ... od*in the body part may be read as *while true do ... od*. The statements *answer*(v) and *answer*(p, v) are like the accept statements in DLP. When executing such a statement, the execution of own activity of the semaphore object will be interrupted, to await the call for a method allowed by the answer statement.

Creating a new instance of *Sema* is, having a variable x of type *Sema*, achieved by stating

$$x := \; Sema.new(1)$$

which calls the function *new* of *Sema*, as implicitly defined by the new parameters and the initialization part. We may then subsequently call the methods p and v of the newly created object by stating respectively $x!p()$ and $x!v()$.

Function definitions in $POOL^\star$ are given as in the example below

```
fn max(i,j:Integer):Integer
{
if i > j then result i else result j fi
}
```

Such a function definition must occur within a class declaration, say of a class X. The function may then be called as, for example, $X.max(3, 7)$.

Another, in effect rather essential, feature of our implementation language is the possibility to define functions dynamically, as illustrated by the statement

```
inc := fn (i:Integer):Integer { result i + n }
```

where we assume that n is an integer variable declared in the environment surrounding the statement. The result of assigning the function definition to the variable *inc* is a function that increments an integer with the value that n had at the moment of defining the function.

Temporary variables may be used in both function definitions and method definitions. As an example consider the function definition

```
inc := fn (i:Integer):Integer temp x:Integer { x := i; result x + n }
```

that stores its argument i first in the temporary variable x, declared by the keyword *temp*, before returning its result. Temporary variables may also be directly initialized to a value.

Special methods are provided when instance variables are annotated. For instance, the declaration

```
class F
var f put get : String
...
end F
```

implicitly declares the methods

```
method put_f(s:String):F { f :=  s; result self }
method get_f():String { result f }
```

that may be used to modify and access the value of the instance variable f.

As syntactic sugar *POOL** provides the notation x@f with, for x a variable of type F, the meaning x!put_f(s) if x@f occurs on the left-hand side of an assignment, as in x@f := s , and x!get_f() otherwise. These abbreviations may also be used when the corresponding methods are declared explicitly.

Global objects and functions may be declared by using the keyword *global* as in

global knot := Knot.new()

that stores an instance of class Knot in the global variable *knot*.

Pragmas of the form (* ALLOC at n *), for some integer n, are used to handle the allocation of instances of classes to processor nodes. The statement

O := O.new() (* ALLOC at n *)

where n is an integer variable defined in the environment, results in the creation of a new instance of class O allocated at processor node n.

Units provide an additional scoping mechanism in *POOL** . Each unit may contain a number of class declarations. The prototype implementation has been partitioned in the units listed in section 9.5.2.

In addition to the language features discussed we use, in the next two chapters, conditional expressions of the form $b \rightarrow e_1 . e_2$ with the meaning *if* b *then* e_1 *else* e_2. This construct is not part of *POOL** .

We wish to stress the fact that, apart from the commands for macro definitions and file inclusion, *POOL** is a strict subset of POOL-X. We have not used exceptions, tuple-types or any of the esoteric syntactic sugar announced in [America, 1989a].

From a *POOL** program we obtain a POOL-X program as indicated in the diagram below.

*POOL** ⟶ [*preprocessor*] ⟶ POOL-X

In its turn the POOL-X program is compiled to C by using the compiler described in [Beemster, 1990].

Concluding the description of our implementation language, we will note some of the differences between DLP and the implementation language *POOL** . First of all DLP is untyped, whereas *POOL** is strongly typed. Secondly, *POOL** does not allow inheritance, while DLP supports inheritance by code-sharing. In the third place, the notion of an object and a process are identical for *POOL** . For DLP, on the other hand, multiple processes may be active concurrently for a single object. And as a fourth, perhaps the major, difference between the two languages, DLP supports backtracking over the answers produced in a rendez-vous, whereas *POOL** , because of its imperative character, naturally does not.

9.5.2 The implementation of the prototype

The prototype is subdivided in $POOL^{\star}$ units, as listed below. In chapter 11 we will describe the functionality of each of these units.

- *Types and abbreviations*: We have collected the definition of the types used throughout the program in this unit. Some of the types are defined as abbreviations.

- *Terms*: Since terms are the primary data structure on which the functions defined in the program operate we have devoted a separate unit to them. Both objects and processes may be represented by DLP terms. The unit contains definitions for *constructors*, to make terms, *selectors* to access the constituent parts of a term, and *tests* to be able to perform a case analysis on a term.

- *The sequential Prolog interpreter*: In the next chapter we will describe in detail how we have derived the sequential Prolog interpreter from a continuation semantics for a Prolog-like language. There is no need to say that, in terms of efficiency, we could significantly improve on the execution speed by using a high performance Prolog implementation. Cf. [Warren, 1983].

- *Objects*: This unit defines the functionality of objects with respect to the acceptance of method calls. It also defines the attributes of DLP objects, such as the list of non-logical variables and the inheritance lists. In addition it contains the functions effecting inheritance and the initialization of DLP objects.

- *Processes*: The evaluation of goals requires some global administration, and a facility to access the declaration of objects. Also, an evaluation process must be able to handle commands to consult a file. To the tasks of an evaluation process belong moreover, the communication with other objects and processes during a rendez-vous, the handling of cuts, and to report trace information to the user.

- *Non-logical variables and channels*: Together with the definition of non-logical variables, this unit contains the protocol governing synchronous communication over channels.

- *The initial database*: The simplification function defined in this unit, is in particular important for the treatment of special forms used for the creation of objects and processes. This unit also contains our interpretation of the equality predicate and assignment. In addition the DLP system predicates are defined here. Part of these are included for compatibility with Prolog. Others are used as primitives for communication over channels and for engaging in a rendez-vous.

- *Utilities*: We have collected here a number of auxiliary definitions. Also this unit provides the low level term manipulation functions to support the handling of terms.

We have omitted a description of the units for reading in and parsing DLP programs.

10

Deriving a Prolog interpreter

- The question is the story itself, and whether or not it means something is not for the story to tell. -
Paul Auster, *The New York Trilogy*

The use of formal semantics may vary from checking whether the constructs for a particular language are well-defined, in that they allow a consistent interpretation, to being a guideline for the correct implementation of the language. In developing DLP we have taken the semantics of a subset of what turned out to be the final language as a starting point for developing additional constructs, illustrating yet another usage of semantics.

To implement our Prolog interpreter we have developed a compilation scheme for converting clauses to functions by adapting a continuation semantics for Prolog (without cut) given in [Allison, 1986]. Using function composition to combine the functionality of separately compiled objects, we were able to implement inheritance in a rather elegant way. In this chapter we will present our adapted version of the semantics given in [Allison, 1986], and illustrate how to derive the code from the semantic equations.[1] Since our primary intention here is to elucidate the transition from semantic equations to code, we have only indicated how to provide a mathematical justification, without going into details.

[1]The requirement imposed on the implementation language by the semantics we employed is that it must be possible to treat functions as first class objects. Although the use of such features definitely does not give the most efficient coding, in this stage of development conciseness is to be preferred to enable experimentation and to understand what has been done. See section 9.5.1 for a description of the implementation language used.

Terms lie at the basis of the implementation of DLP. We use an extended notion of terms to include, apart from constants, logical variables and applicative terms, also *atoms* (in a Prolog sense), *goals* and *clauses*. We define terms $t \in T$ by

$$t ::= \varepsilon \mid v \mid f(t_1, t_2)$$

where ε is called the empty term, v is an element of the set of logical variables V and f is an arbitrary function symbol from a set A. Constants may be considered to be terms of the form $f(\varepsilon, \varepsilon)$. A term with one argument is written as $f(t_1, \varepsilon)$. An n-ary function term is represented as $f(t_1, (t_2, (..., t_n)))$, where the arguments $t_2, ..., t_n$ are represented as a compound term with a comma as a function symbol, written infix. Our definition of terms reflects the definition of terms used in the actual implementation. Algorithms on terms are simplified by this encoding, since recursion on subterms can be written out directly, without being mediated by lists of argument terms. We stress the fact that the set of function terms A we use for extended terms includes connectives such as the comma, predicate symbols that we may encounter in atoms and ordinary function symbols.

The definition of terms given above allows us to represent atoms a defined by

$$a ::= p(t_1, ..., t_n) : p \text{ a predicate symbol, } n \geq 0$$

as terms. Similarly, goals g defined by

$$g ::= \varepsilon \mid a, g$$

may be represented by terms, simply by taking the conjunctive comma as a special function symbol. Finally, (lists of) clauses cl defined by

$$cl ::= \varepsilon \mid (a :\!-\, g); cl$$

are also clearly representable as terms.

A program is a fixed list of clauses, represented by $\overline{cl}$.

Renaming and substitutions We use *environments* $e \in E = V \rightarrow V$ to rename variables. Each logical variable is initially represented by a natural number indicating the position in which it first occurs in a clause. In effect, we take $V = N$ for N the set of natural numbers. Since logical variables are local to the clause in which they occur, it suffices to keep track of the number of variables in use and raise this count with the number of different variables occurring in the clause that is tried to solve a goal. Given a renaming function e, the renaming is effected by using a map of type $E \rightarrow T \rightarrow T$ to apply e to a term t, which we write as $\hat{e}(t)$. For determining the (maximum) number of variables in a term, we define a *norm* function that delivers the maximum of the variable numbers occurring in a term, be it a goal or a clause. The notation for applying the norm function is $\mid t \mid$.

A *substitution* is a function of type $S = V \rightarrow T$ that returns a term for a variable. Only for finitely many variables is the term different from the variable itself. Given a substitution $s \in S$, we write $\hat{s}(t)$ to denote the application of s to a term t.

10.1 Evaluation

Suppose that we have a goal, say $p(X)$, and that we have a program consisting of the following clauses:

```
p(1).
p(2).
```

Then, when stating $p(X)$ as a goal, we expect the answers $X = 1$ and $X = 2$, obviously. What we are interested in are the answer substitutions given for, in this case, the goal $p(X)$. The terms $p(1)$ and $p(2)$ may also represent the possible answer substitutions for $p(X)$, with respect to the program given above. Below, we will represent answer substitutions by instantiated terms.

Before giving a more detailed description of the semantics on which we based the implementation we wish to give an outline of the components involved, and a characterization of the type structure of the functions used.

As the result domain of the function $\mathcal{E}$, that we use for evaluating goals, we take $R = T^{\omega} \cup T^{\infty}$, the set of finite and infinite sequences over T. We will stick to the use of ε to denote the empty term, since we do not need an explicit notation for the empty sequence of terms.

As a metric on R we use the standard metric on sequences, defined by

$$d(w_1, w_2) = 2^{-sup\{n \mid w_1(n)=w_2(n)\}}$$

where $w(n)$ denotes the prefix of length n in case the length of w exceeds n and w otherwise. See section 6.1.1.

We introduce an operator $\cdot : R \times R \rightarrow R$ that concatenates sequences of terms. We remark that for contractivity to hold we cannot ignore the empty term ε occurring in a sequence; however, informally we use the convention that $\varepsilon \cdot w = w = w \cdot \varepsilon$.

The function $\mathcal{E}[\![\cdot]\!]$ decomposes a non-empty goal t into an atom a and the remainder of the goal g. It then calls the database $\mathcal{C}[\![\overline{cl}]\!]k_0d_0$, compiled from the program $\overline{cl}$, to evaluate the atom a, after having prepared a suitable continuation to evaluate the remainder g. See section 10.2 for a characterization of $\mathcal{C}[\![\overline{cl}]\!]k_0d_0$.

We use continuations of type

$$C = N \times S \rightarrow R$$

to store the computation needed to evaluate the remainder of a goal. A typical continuation c is called as $c(n, s)$, where n is a natural administrating the highest variable number in use and s a substitution of type $V \rightarrow T$ that records the substitution computed while evaluating the goal.

The function $\mathcal{E}[\![\cdot]\!]$ has a type structure as expressed in

$$\mathcal{E}[\![\cdot]\!] : T \rightarrow C \rightarrow N \rightarrow S \rightarrow R$$

Apart from a goal t to evaluate we need to provide $\mathcal{E}[\![\cdot]\!]$ with a continuation $c \in C$ and parameters $n \in N$ and $s \in S$ to be used, possibly modified, for calling the continuation c.

Database functions are of type

$$D = T \times C \times N \times S \rightarrow R$$

analogous to the type of $\mathcal{E}[\![\cdot]\!]$. As will be seen in section 10.2, functions $d \in D$ are the result of compiling (a list of) clauses.

For a clause $a{:}{-}g$, such a function replaces a goal atom a' unifying with a by the goal g, in effect by recursively calling $\mathcal{E}[\![g]\!]$ with the appropriate continuation parameters, while modifying the substitution according to the unifier of a and a'. In section 10.3 we will discuss how we deal with unification in our continuation semantics.

To illustrate the use of the function $\mathcal{E}$ we may remark that, ignoring empty terms,

$$\mathcal{E}[\![p(X)]\!]cns_0 = p(1) \cdot p(2)$$

where we assume that c is the initial continuation $\lambda ns.\hat{s}(p(X))$, n $(= 1)$ the number of variables in $p(X)$ and s_0 the initial substitution, that acts as the identity on all variables.

The equations defining $\mathcal{E}[\![\cdot]\!]$ reflect the previous discussion.

$\mathcal{E}$

$$\mathcal{E}[\![\cdot]\!] : T \to C \to N \to S \to R \text{ for goals, with}$$

$$\mathcal{E}[\![\varepsilon]\!] = \lambda cns.c(n, s)$$

$$\mathcal{E}[\![a, g]\!] = \lambda cns.\overline{d}(a, c', n, s)$$
$$\text{where } c' = \lambda ns.\mathcal{E}[\![g]\!]cns \text{ and } \overline{d} = \mathcal{C}[\![\overline{cl}]\!]k_0 d_0$$

An empty goal simply results in calling the continuation. For non-empty goals the continuation argument c is modified to take care of the remainder of the goal.

The definition of the function *eval*, in its turn, reflects the equations for $\mathcal{E}$ in an obvious manner.

eval

```
fn eval(t:T,c:C,n:N,s:S):R
{
if t = ε then c(n,s)
elsif t = (a,g) then
      dotail := fn (n1:N, s1:S) { result eval(g,c,n1,s1) };
      result d̄(a,dotail,n,s)
}
```

The code straightforwardly results from converting the lambda terms occurring in the equations for $\mathcal{E}$ to the format imposed by our implementation language. We assume that the database corresponding to the program $\overline{cl}$ is stored in a global function $\overline{d}$. We remark that if t does not conform to the syntactic conventions for goals we may consider the result undefined.

10.2 Compilation

We have now arrived at the point where we may look more closely at the procedure by which clauses are compiled to what we have called a database function. As a preparation, look at the empty database d_0, that we define as

$$d_0 = \lambda tcns.\varepsilon$$

which delivers the empty term, irrespective of its actual parameters.

Having a clause of the form $a :- g$, the database resulting from compiling this clause must deliver whatever evaluating g delivers, assuming that we have a goal atom a' that unifies with a. To effect this, we have defined a unification function

$$\mathcal{U}[\![\cdot]\!][\![\cdot]\!] : T \to T \to C \to N \to S \to R$$

that takes two terms (in the case sketched above, the goal atom and the head of a clause), a continuation containing the computation for evaluating the body of the clause, a variable count and a substitution. Now suppose that, in compiling a list of clauses, we have arrived at a clause $a :- g$. In the general case we may, for a goal t, have tried clauses occurring before this particular clause; and likewise clauses may follow that contribute to the solutions for this (sub) goal. Just assume that we have stored the effect of the preceding clauses in a database function d, then the resulting database d' will be like

$$d' = \lambda tcns.(d(t, c, n, s) \cdot \mathcal{U}[\![t]\!][\![a]\!]c'n's)$$

for some continuation c' and variable count n'. Note that backtracking is taken care of by appending the result of using a clause to the result of the database encoding all previous clauses. When failure occurs the empty term ε is delivered, which consequently disappears. When trying an alternative clause the substitution need not be changed.

To deal with the clauses following the clause $a :- g$ we need an auxiliary continuation of type

$$K = D \to D$$

to compute the combined database function. When compiling a list of clauses $(a :- g); cl$, assuming that we already have compiled the clauses preceding $a :- g$ into a function d, we create a continuation $k \in K$ for compiling the clauses cl taking d', that is d augmented with the functionality of $a :- g$, as a parameter.

It is obvious that initially we must take as a continuation

$$k_0 = \lambda d.d$$

that acts as the identity on database functions. We list the equations for $\mathcal{C}$ below.

$\mathcal{C}$

$\mathcal{C}[\![\cdot]\!] : T \rightarrow D \rightarrow K \rightarrow D$ for clauses, with

$$\mathcal{C}[\![\varepsilon]\!] = \lambda dk.k(d)$$

$$\mathcal{C}[\![(a :\!- g); cl]\!] = \lambda dk.\ k'(\lambda tcns.(d(t,c,n,s) \cdot \mathcal{U}[\![t]\!][\![\hat{e}(a)]\!]c'n's))$$

where

$$c' = \lambda ns.\mathcal{E}[\![\hat{e}(g)]\!]cns$$
$$n' = n + \mid a :\!- g \mid, e = \lambda v.v + n$$
$$k' = \lambda d'.\mathcal{C}[\![cl]\!]d'k$$

Naturally, the renaming of variables must be taken care of, as has been done above.

The equations for $\mathcal{E}$, $\mathcal{C}$ and $\mathcal{U}$ are mutually recursive. To establish that these functions are mathematically well-defined, we must investigate whether a contractivity argument of the kind introduced in chapter 6 applies.

As we will illustrate below, compiling a program results in a series of attempts to unify the head of a clause with a particular goal, in the order in which the clauses occur. Applying the unification function results in either the empty term or in the results of applying $\mathcal{E}$ to the body of the clause. Since we start with d_0, delivering the empty term ε for any goal, each application of $\mathcal{C}$ adds a term to the result, thus ensuring contractivity.

To provide some intuition we will illustrate how this scheme works for the example with which we started section 10.1. As clauses, we have the unit clauses $p(1)$ and $p(2)$ that we write as

$p(1) :\!- \varepsilon.$
$p(2) :\!- \varepsilon.$

We start with the initial database $d_0 = \lambda tcns.\varepsilon$ and the initial continuation $k_0 = \lambda d.d$ to compute the database $\mathcal{C}[\![(p(1) :\!- \varepsilon); ((p(2) :\!- \varepsilon); \varepsilon)]\!]d_0 k_0$.

Compiling $p(1) :\!- \varepsilon$ results in

$$d_1 = \lambda tcns.d_0(t,c,n,s) \cdot \mathcal{U}[\![t]\!][\![p(1)]\!](\mathcal{E}[\![\varepsilon]\!]c)ns$$

which, informally, we take to be equivalent to

$$\lambda tcns.\mathcal{U}[\![t]\!][\![p(1))]\!](\mathcal{E}[\![\varepsilon]\!]c)ns$$

since $d_0(t,c,n,s)$ evaluates to ε. The continuation arguments c, n and s remain unmodified because $p(1) :\!- \varepsilon$ does not contain any variables.

To compile the clauses $(p(2) :\!- \varepsilon); \varepsilon$ we have created the continuation

$$k' = \lambda d'.\mathcal{C}[\![(p(2) :\!- \varepsilon); \varepsilon]\!]d'k_0$$

which may be written as

$$k' = \lambda d'.\lambda tcns.(d'(t,c,n,s) \cdot \mathcal{U}[\![t]\!][\![p(2)]\!](\mathcal{E}[\![\varepsilon]\!]c)ns)$$

Hence, since $\mathcal{E}[\![\varepsilon]\!]c$ is equivalent to c, we may write the database function that is the result of compiling the program $(p(1) :\!- \varepsilon); ((p(2) :\!- \varepsilon); \varepsilon)$ as

$$\lambda tcns.\mathcal{U}[\![t]\!][\![p(1)]\!]cns \cdot \mathcal{U}[\![t]\!][\![p(2)]\!]cns$$

which, in other words, successively tries to unify a goal t with $p(1)$ and $p(2)$. Of course, the unification function is defined such that it delivers ε whenever t does not unify with either $p(1)$ or $p(2)$.

Again, the code for the compilation function may be derived from the equations given above in a rather straightforward way. In our presentation, we will first treat the part where we deal with a single clause $a :- g$, while assuming that we have a database function d containing the functionality of the clauses preceding the currently inspected clause. We dynamically define a function *newd* in the way pictured below.

newd

```
newd := fn ( t:T, c:C, n:N, s:S):R
        temp n1:N
        {
        n1 :=  n + | a :- g |;
        e  :=  fn (v:V):V { result v + n };
        body := fn (n2:N, s2:S):T
                {
                result eval(q, ê(g), c, n2, s2)
                };
        result append( d(t,c,n,s), unify(t, ê(a), body,n1,s) )
        }
```

First of all we need to take care of renaming variables according to the variable count n, given as a parameter. We then create a continuation for evaluating the (renamed) body of the clause. We append the result of evaluating the goal t by d and the result of unifying t with the (renamed) head of the clause, taking the evaluation of the body of the clause as a continuation. We can now define the function *compile*.

compile

```
fn compile(t:T, d:D, k:K):D
{
if t = ε then result k(d)
elsif t = (a :- g); cl then
          dotail := fn (d1:D) { result compile(cl, d1, k) };
          [newd];
          result dotail( newd )
}
```

The picture must be completed by replacing $\boxed{newd}$ by the definition of the function *newd* given above.

10.3 Unification

Finally, we arrive at defining the unification function

$$\mathcal{U}[\![\cdot]\!][\![\cdot]\!] : T \rightarrow T \rightarrow C \rightarrow N \rightarrow S \rightarrow R$$

that performs the unification of a goal atom and the head of a clause, to call the continuation evaluating the body of the clause if the unification succeeds.

If two terms are syntactically equal the unification results in calling the continuation.

Unifying two terms may result in a substitution, modifying the already given substitution by binding variables to terms. For a variable v that becomes bound to a term t, the modification of a substitution s is effected by creating a substitution s' given as

$$s' = \lambda v'.v = v' \rightarrow t, s(v')$$

that is a variant of s with respect to v. Binding a variable to a term is allowed only when the variable is unbound, otherwise the term must be unified with the substitution value of the variable. This condition is expressed in the definition of θ as

$$\theta = \lambda vt.s(v) = v \rightarrow c(n, s'), \mathcal{U}[\![s(v)]\!][\![t]\!]cns$$

where s' is the substitution s modified to bind v to t. The function $\mathcal{U}$ is given by the equations below.

$\mathcal{U}$

$\mathcal{U}[\![\cdot]\!] : T \rightarrow T \rightarrow C \rightarrow N \rightarrow S \rightarrow R$ for pairs of terms, with

$$\mathcal{U}[\![t_1]\!][\![t_2]\!] = \lambda cns. \begin{cases} c(n, s) & \text{if } t_1 = \varepsilon = t_2 \\ \theta(v, t_2) & \text{if } t_1 = v \\ \theta(v, t_1) & \text{if } t_2 = v \\ \mathcal{U}[\![t_{11}]\!][\![t_{21}]\!]c'ns & \text{if } t_1 = f(t_{11}, t_{12}) \\ & \text{and } t_2 = f(t_{21}, t_{22}) \\ \varepsilon & \text{otherwise} \end{cases}$$

where $\theta = \lambda vt.s(v) = v \rightarrow c(n, s'), \mathcal{U}[\![s(v)]\!][\![t]\!]cns$

and $s' = \lambda v'.v = v' \rightarrow t, s(v')$

and $c' = \lambda n's'.\mathcal{U}[\![t_{12}]\!][\![t_{22}]\!]cn's'$

For function terms with identical function symbols the unification is applied to their first arguments, taking as a continuation the unification of their second arguments.

If the attempt at unification fails, the empty term ε is delivered. In agreement with other implementations of Prolog we have omitted the occur-check.

We leave it to the reader to define the function $unify(t_1, t_2 : T, c : C, n : N, s : S) : R$ implementing the equations for $\mathcal{U}$. See section 11.3.3.

10.4 Initialization

Summarizing our description thus far, we have defined a function $\mathcal{E}$ to evaluate goals as making use of database functions compiled from the program by the function $\mathcal{C}$. As an auxiliary function we have defined the unification function $\mathcal{U}$ to compute a most general unifier and to continue the computation accordingly. For a goal g we must create an initial continuation

$$c_g = \lambda ns.\hat{s}(g)$$

and we may then evaluate g by calling $\mathcal{E}[\![g]\!]c_g n s_0$, where n is the maximum variable number occurring in g.

Processes In defining the functions $\mathcal{E}$, $\mathcal{C}$ and $\mathcal{U}$ we have proceeded from the assumption that we have a fixed program $\overline{cl}$. In the context of DLP, however, we may encounter a collection of objects, each having a list of clauses. Moreover, for each object, a multiplicity of processes may be active in evaluating a goal.

In order to extend the functionality of the interpreter, we have introduced evaluation processes q of type Q that accompany the evaluation of a goal. Such a process is given as a parameter to the function *eval* and the database functions resulting from compiling clauses.

- Evaluation processes store the database function used in evaluating goals. The stored database function combines the functionality of an object with the functionality of the objects it inherits. In the function *eval*, the database $\overline{d}$ must be replaced by the call $q@d$, that delivers the database stored in the attribute d of q.

- Another usage of evaluation processes, as will be explained in detail in the next chapter, is to keep a record of the occurrence of cuts and to cut off the search accordingly.

- More importantly, however, evaluation processes play an intermediary role in communicating the answer substitutions that result from evaluating a goal to the process that requested the evaluation. The initial continuation for a goal g must then be of the form $\lambda ns.q!yes(\hat{s}(g))$, in order to notify the process q of the computed answer substitution. We have sketched the protocol by which this takes place in the previous chapter, when discussing the computation model underlying DLP. In the next chapter we will deal with the details of the implementation of this protocol.

10.5 Composition

Enlarging our scope by introducing objects, each containing a list of clauses, that may inherit each other's functionality, the question arises how to combine the functionality of these objects.

The naive approach would be, for objects O_1 and O_2 with lists of clauses cl_1 and cl_2, to compile the concatenated list $cl_1; cl_2$ to arrive at the proper database function, in case O_1 inherits O_2.

However, composition $\circ : D \times D \rightarrow D$ is easily defined by

$$d_1 \circ d_2 = \lambda tcns.d_1(t, c, n, s) \cdot d_2(t, c, n, s)$$

which allows to compile the clauses of objects separately. We observe that composition is associative and $(D, \circ, d_0)$ a monoid, satisfying $d_0 \circ d = d$ and $d \circ d_0 = d$.

Alternatively, we may define a variant of composition where the functionality of one component may be overwritten as in

$$d_1 \hat{\circ} d_2 = \lambda tcns.d_1(t, c, n, s) = \varepsilon \rightarrow d_2(t, c, n, s), d_1(t, c, n, s)$$

Overwriting d_2 with d_1 results in a function that tries to evaluate a goal t by using d_1 first, and only if this results in ε then d_2 will be used. When using the function $d_1 \circ d_2$ instead, the results of applying d_2 are appended to the results of applying d_1, irrespective what these results are.

With regard to the declarative semantics of DLP we have chosen to employ the first variant, since we may then regard inheritance in DLP as a mechanism to extend a logical theory in a monotonic way.

11

The implementation of the prototype

- 'Then maybe you will understand this', she said, leading me over to the deep-freeze, and opening it. Inside was nothing but cats; stacks of frozen, perfectly preserved cats, dozens of them. -
Truman Capote, *Music for cameleons*

Having a global impression of the computation model underlying DLP, and an understanding of the interpreter supporting the Prolog-like base language, we are prepared to inspect the prototype in more detail. In describing the prototype we follow the outline given in section 9.5.

Some aspects, such as the representation of terms, the interpreter and the way cuts are dealt with, are relevant only to the current implementation. Other aspects, such as the implementation of objects and processes, and our treatment of inheritance are of a more general concern, since they will be handled likewise in alternative implementations of DLP.

11.1 Types and abbreviations

As basic types we use strings, booleans and integers, which are abbreviated by respectively A, B and N. Logical variables are represented by integers; nevertheless we use type V to indicate explicitly that variables are expected as arguments. Several other types of entities play a role in the DLP system. We list them, together with the basic types just mentioned:

- A for strings,
- B for booleans,
- N for integers,
- V for logical variables ($= N$),
- O for objects (in the sense of DLP),
- Q for evaluation processes , and
- X for non-logical variables and channels.

In describing the interpreter we will use the type abbreviations:

- $E = V \to V$ for environments or renaming functions,
- $S = V \to T$ for substitutions,
- $C = N \times N \times S \to T$ for continuations,
- $D = Q \times T \times C \times N \times N \times S \to T$ for database functions, and
- $K = D \to D$ for (clause) continuations,

where a function type of the form $N \times N \times S \to T$ must be read as *fn* $(N, N, S) : T$. The types introduced here are similar to the types employed in the previous chapter, when characterizing the interpreter. There are some differences, however. First of all, we take a sequence of terms to be a (compound) term itself; and so we have replaced the result type R by T. Secondly, we have introduced an additional integer parameter in the types C and D, to be able to handle cuts. See section 11.3. And in the third place, database functions of type D are enriched with a parameter of type Q in order to provide a pointer to the process accompanying an inference, as announced in section 10.4.

11.2 Terms

The language DLP is term-oriented. Terms may represent objects, processes and channels as well as goals and clauses. For this reason the term type T must include constants (that is strings) of type A, logical variables of type V ($= N$), function terms of type $A \times T \times T$, objects of type O, processes of type Q and non-logical variables and channels of type X. From entities of these types a term can be created by using one of the following constructors:

- *Con* $: A \to T$ for creating constants,
- *Var* $: V \to T$ for creating logical variables,
- *Fun* $: A \times T \times T \to T$ for creating function terms,
- *Obj* $: O \to T$ for converting an object into a term,

- $Prc : Q \rightarrow T$ for converting a process into a term, and
- $Chv : X \rightarrow T$ for converting a non-logical variable or channel into a term.

As an inverse to these constructors there are the selector functions

conof, varof, funof, objof, prcof, chvof

of obvious types.

With each term is associated a tag that indicates the type of a term. A tag is one of the following constants

CON, VAR, FUN, OBJ, PRC, CHV

that for arbitrary term t is obtained by calling $tagof(t)$. These tags allow to inspect the type of a term in a case analysis on the structure of the term. For this purpose also the tests

iscon, isvar, isfun, isobj, isprc, ischv

all of type $T \rightarrow B$, can be used.

Compound terms A function term is represented as a function-symbol with two argument terms. For function terms with only one argument we make the second argument *nil*, which is an expression denoting undefined in our implementation language. This representation allows to write many algorithms with a direct recursion on the subterms of a term, but necessitates coding the argument list of a term as a term itself whenever the arity exceeds two.

The following functions are used for dealing with function terms. Let t be a term with base type $A \times T \times T$, then:

$fc(t)$ delivers the function symbol of t,

$a_1(t)$ delivers the first argument of t, and

$a_2(t)$ delivers the remaining arguments of t.

When the arity of a function term exceeds two, the second subterm will be a function term of the form (t_1, t_2). We call a function term with a comma as a function-symbol a *compound* term. The test $isc(t)$ decides whether a term is a compound term, the constructor $mkc(t_1, t_2)$ makes a compound term of two terms. Function terms (and hence compound terms) are left-justified. The first argument of such a term will be non-compound, while the second may be compound. This is reflected in the definition of the function *length*, given by

$$length(t) = \quad if \;\; isc(t) \;\; then \;\; 1 + length(a_2(t)) \;\; else \;\; 1$$

which delivers the number of components of a term. The definition

$$argsof(t) = \quad if \;\; a_2(t) \equiv nil \;\; then \;\; a_1(t) \;\; else \;\; mkc(a_1(t), a_2(t))$$

allows then to define the arity of a term by

$$arity(t) = length(argsof(t))$$

We will treat some auxiliary functions to manipulate terms in section 11.8. One of these functions is the function *maxvar* that gives us the maximum variable number occurring in a term.

Representing clauses Terms may be used to represent clauses. A clause of the form

```
p(X) :-  q(X,Y), p(Y).
```

is, in our format, converted to a term by the expression

```
Fun(":-",Fun("p",Var(1),Nil), mkc(Fun("q",Var(1),Var(2)), Fun("p",Var(2),Nil)))
```

where *Nil* is the empty term, that is taken as an abbreviation for *Con*("[]"). We may access any part of the term by using the appropriate selectors. For example, the predicate name of the first atom of the body of the clause is obtained by

$$fc(a_1(a_2(t)))$$

where t is the term representing the clause. We represent lists of clauses as clauses connected by a comma. When t_1 and t_2 represent clauses, the term $mkc(t_1, t_2)$ represents the list containing these clauses. In such a case we may use the test $isc(t)$ to determine whether t represents a list of clauses.

In the following sections we will use a function *append* that is like *mkc* except that it ignores empty terms. For searching whether a term occurs in a list of terms, we use a function *member*. The test $isempty(t)$ is used to decide whether t is the empty term.

11.3 The sequential Prolog interpreter

In chapter 10 we have outlined the structure of our interpreter by giving a continuation semantics from which we derived the functions *eval*, *compile* and *unify* that constitute our interpreter. We will repeat the description of these functions here, but with the inclusion of the code implementing the interaction with the accompanying inference process, needed for tracing, handling cuts, and the communication with other processes.

Tracing has been implemented according to the box-model described in [Clocksin and Mellish, 1981]. We notify the user of both the *call* entry for a goal atom, that is when the evaluation of the atom is started, and of the *exit* entry, when the evaluation resulted in a solution. We have omitted the *redo* entry, but indicate successful backtracking by reporting *exit* each time a solution is found. In addition we report *fail* in case of failure. To distinguish between traces for separate evaluation processes, each entry is preceded by an identification of the evaluation process.

Cuts are dealt with by the process accompanying an inference. The idea is that on encountering a cut in *eval*, a counter that indicates the depth of the derivation with respect to the nesting of cuts is increased by one. The system database function (described in the section on the initial database) notifies the evaluation process of the depth at which the cut takes effect. The database function, delivered by *compile*, takes care that before a clause is tried a check is made whether a cut has taken effect, and if so results in failure.

Renamings and substitutions (Cf. section 10.) For renaming variables we use environments e of type E, that are typically defined as

```
e := fn (v:V):V { result v + n }
```

where n is the number of variables already in use. Recall that V equals N. To effect a renaming we use a function *mape* and write $mape(e,t)$ to apply the environment e to the term t. See section 11.8.2 for the code of *mape*.

Substitutions, binding a variable v to a term t, may be created by statements of the form

```
s1 := fn (v1:V):T { result v = v1 → t, s(v1) }
```

that defines a substitution $s1$ that delivers t as a value if the actual parameter $v1$ equals the variable v and $s(v1)$ otherwise, for s the given substitution. We write $maps(s,t)$ to apply a substitution to a term. See also section 11.8.2 for the definition of *maps*.

11.3.1 Evaluation

In defining the *eval* function below, we assume that goals t are either empty, or consist of an atom a and a remainder g.

Empty goals result in the continuation. If we have a compound goal, it is decomposed in an atom a and a remainder g. We apply the given substitution s to the atom a and create a continuation for g. Before evaluating a by the database function stored in the process q, we simplify a as described in section 11.7.1. Note that we have apart from q an additional parameter m, that we use for dealing with cuts.

eval

```
fn eval(q:Q,t:T,c:C,m,n:N,s:S):T
temp a,g:T
{
if isempty(t) then c(m,n,s)
else a := maps(s,a1(t)); g := a2(t);
     dotail := fn (m1,n1:N, s1:S)
               {
               q!trace("exit",maps(s1,a));
               if iscut(a) then mct := m1 + 1 else mct := m1;
               result eval(q,g,c,mct,n1,s1)
               };
     q!trace("call",a);
     result q@d(q,simplify(q,a),dotail,m,n,s)
}
```

When creating a continuation, a check is made whether the goal atom a is a cut by the test *iscut*(a). If this is the case then the depth-counter is increased by one, relative to the depth with which the continuation *dotail* is provided as an argument. When reporting *exit* of the evaluation of a, we apply the then current substitution $s1$, to show the binding that resulted from evaluating a.

11.3.2 Compilation

The compilation procedure given below differs from the one given in section 10.2 by the incorporation of statements for handling cuts. We refer to that section for the code of *compile*, which remains unaffected. Here we will treat the definition of the function *newd* that corresponds to compiling a single clause.

When compiling a clause of the form a :- g, assuming that we have already constructed a database d for the clauses preceding that clause, we insert a test for checking whether a cut is active:

r := d(q,t,c,m,n,s); if checkcut(q,t,m) then result r else ...

We store the result of evaluating a goal t by the database d in r. If a cut is active we return r as the result; otherwise we proceed by unifying the goal with the head of the clause and creating a continuation for evaluating its body. See section 11.5.3 for the definition of *checkcut*. The creation of *newd* is pictured below. We have used the notation 'a :- g' to represent the clause that is compiled; and write a for a_1('a :- g') and g for a_2('a :- g').

newd

```
newd := fn ( q:Q, t:T, c:C, m,n:N, s:S):T
        temp m1, n1:N
        {
        r := d(q,t,c,m,n,s);
        if checkcut(q,t,m) then result r
        else
            m1 := m+1; n1 := n + maxvar('a :- g');
            e := fn (v:V):V { result v + n };
            body := fn (m2,n2:N, s2:S):T
                    {
                    result eval(q, mape(e, g), c, m2, n2, s2)
                    };
            result append( r, unify(t, mapcut(m, fc(a),
                                       mape(e,a)), body,m1,n1,s))
        }
```

When creating the continuation for the body of the clause the cuts occurring therein are replaced by a special predicate *cuton*(m,p), where m is the depth at which the clause is invocated and p the predicate name of the head of the clause. This is effected by the function *mapcut* that is defined as

mapcut

```
fn mapcut(m:N,p:A,t:T):T
{
if isc(t) then result mkc( mapcut(m,p,a1(t)), mapcut(m,p,a2(t)))
elsif iscon(t) & conof(t) = "!" then result Cuton(m,p)
else result t
}
```

where *Cuton*(m,p) makes a predicate *cuton*(m,p) that stores, when evaluated, the predicate name p and the depth m in the evaluation process q. See section 11.7.3. This information is used by the process q when *checkcut*(q,t,m') is called to determine whether a cut is active.

11.3.3 Unification

Unification may result in modifying the given substitution, by binding variables to terms. The definition of the function updating a substitution s with respect to a variable v and a term t, as given below, refers to a continuation c and integers m and n, that come from the environment in which the function definition must be placed.

update

```
update := fn (v:V, t:T):T
          {
          news := fn(v1:V):T { result v = v1 → t . s(v1) };
          result unbound(v,s) → c(m,n,news),
                                unify( s(v), t, c,m,n,s)
          }
```

When the test *unbound*(v,s) succeeds, the newly created substitution is handed as a parameter to the given continuation; otherwise the term t is unified with the substitution value of v. This definition is used in the function *unify* as depicted below.

unify

```
fn unify(t1,t2:T,c:C,m,n:N,s:S):T
{
[update];
if isvar(t1) then result update(varof(t1),t2)
elsif isvar(t2) then result update(varof(t2),t1)
elsif isfun(t1) & isfun(t2) then
      if fc(t1) = fc(t2) then
                  doargs := fn (m1,n1:N, s1:S):T
                              {
                              result unify(a2(t1),a2(t2),c,m1,n1,s1)
                              };
                  result unify(a1(t1),a1(t2), doargs, m,n,s)
                  else result Nil
else result t1 = t2 → c(m,n,s) , Nil
}
```

For function terms, having identical function symbols, the first arguments are unified with as continuation the unification of their remaining arguments.

11.3.4 Initialization

To enable an evaluation process to communicate the results of an inference to another process, we must take care to store the initial goal in the evaluation process and to report the instantiation of the goal (by the current substitution) each time a solution is found. This is effected by creating an initial continuation in the following manner.

yes

```
fn yes(q:Q,t:T):C
{
c := fn(m,n:N, s:S):T { q@result := maps(s,t); result maps(s,t) };
q@goal := t;
result c
}
```

Before returning the initial continuation c, that reports the instantiation of t with respect to the then current substitution s, the process q is called to store t in its *goal* attribute. Cf. sections 9.2 and 11.5. We may then start up an inference for a goal t by calling

eval(q,t,yes(q,t),0,maxvar(t),starts)

where *starts* is the initial substitution given by

fn starts(v:V):T { result Var(v) }

and *maxvar(t)* represents the maximum variable number occurring in t.

For evaluating a goal t we may also spawn off an inference process by calling

infer(q,t,yes(q,t),0,maxvar(t),starts)

The function *infer* is similar to the function *eval*, except that a $POOL^\star$ process is created to do the evaluation. The communication of the result is then mediated by the accompanying process q.

11.3.5 Composition

As described in section 10.5, we deal with inheritance by composing database functions. The function *compose*, defined as

compose

```
fn compose(d1,d2:D):D
{
d :=  fn (q:Q,t:T,c:C,m,n:N,s:S):T
          {
          result append(d1(q,t,c,m,n,s), d2(q,t,c,m,n,s));
          }
result d
}
```

merely appends the results of the composed databases.

To be able to report *fail* on failure, we put the combined database of each DLP object in composition with the database *fail* defined as

fail

```
fn fail(q:Q,t:T,c:C,m,n:N,s:S):T { q!trace("fail",t); result Nil }
```

Apart from notifying q of failure, this database adds nothing to the result.

11.4 Objects

Objects, in the sense of DLP, are implemented by instances of the *POOL** class *O*. In section 9.1 we have sketched the attributes and behavior of active objects. We will now also pay attention to the behavior of passive objects, that do not have own activity but instead allow multiple method calls to be active simultaneously.

We distinguish between four groups of attributes. The first three attributes are needed to identify (an instance of) a (DLP) object and to keep account of the number of evaluation processes created for it:

- *name* — the name of the object,
- *instance* — the instance number of the object, and
- *process number* — records the number of evaluation processes created for the object.

When a copy is made the instance number is raised by one and its process number is set to zero.

The second group of attributes stores the functionality of the (DLP) object, the clauses and its inheritance relations:

- *use list* — the names of the objects from which clauses are inherited,
- *isa list* — the names of the objects from which non-logical variables are inherited,
- *nlvars* — the list of non-logical variables,
- *clauses* — the clauses declared for the object, and
- *d* — the database function compiled from the clauses.

Each instance receives a copy of these attributes. Alternatively, we could have stored this information in a data structure shared by all instances of an object.

The next two attributes are needed to distinguish between active and passive objects:

- *active* — that determines whether mutual exclusion between method calls is necessary, and
- *locked* — a boolean, that indicates whether the object is locked, that is unable to receive any requests for evaluating a method call.

The last group determines the dynamic behavior of active objects with respect to the acceptance of method calls:

- *accept list* — that contains the current acceptance conditions,
- *accept queue* — containing the requests that are waiting for a rendez-vous, and
- *process stack* — containing the processes for which an accept statement is evaluated.

11.4.1 The protocol

Passive objects display full internal concurrency, in that multiple method calls may be evaluated simultaneously. Active objects, on the other hand, refuse to grant a request as long as there are method calls waiting to be evaluated.

If the object is *locked* then only the methods safe with respect to the acceptance of method calls may be answered. These methods are collected in the constant *SAFE*. Otherwise any call may be answered, including the methods *accept* and *request* for respectively evaluating an accept statement and a (DLP) method call.

The body below implements this behavior.

protocol

```
body do if locked then answer(SAFE) else answer(any) fi od ydob
```

11.4.2 Acceptance

When a process evaluating a goal encounters an accept statement, it calls the method *accept*, that we may characterize as below. Note that the method *accept* refers to the instance variables of the ($POOL^*$) object, written in italic. We have omitted the result parameter because we are not interested in the result.

accept

```
method accept(q:Q, t:T)
{
suspend the process q and put it in the process stack
set the accept list to t,
and check the accept queue to see whether it contains an
acceptable call, otherwise unlock
}
```

The accept queue contains pairs of the form (q, t), for q a process and t the call to be evaluated. Whether a call is acceptable depends on the accept expressions contained in the accept list. Simple accept expressions require merely to check the predicate name of the call.

For accept expressions of the form

$$method : guard \rightarrow goal$$

and a call mc, we create a test goal t by

$$t := mkc(Fun(" = ", mc, method), guard);$$

and, having created an evaluation process q referring to the object for which the test is made, we evaluate the test by stating *infer(q,t,yes(q,t),0,maxvar(t),starts)*

We then ask for the resumption r by

r := *q!resume();*

and if r is not *fail* we modify *goal* by

goal := *mkc(r,goal);*

in order to effect the bindings that result from the evaluation of t before evaluating *goal.* The modified *goal* is then evaluated as an ordinary (accepted) method call. The bindings contained in the resumption r must further be communicated to the process for which the accept statement was evaluated.

11.4.3 Method calls

How a method call is treated depends on whether an object is active or not. For passive objects, a method call t results in immediately spawning off an inference process by calling

infer(q,t,yes(q,t),0,maxvar(t),starts)

For an active object, it must first be determined whether the call is acceptable, as depicted in the definition of the method *request.* The result of calling *request* is an evaluation process created to accompany the evaluation of the goal.

request

```
method request(t:T):Q
{
q :=  "a new evaluation process for the object";
if ¬ active then
        infer(q,t,yes(q,t),0,maxvar(t),starts);
elsif acceptable(t) then
        lock();
        infer(q,t,yesQ(q,t),0,maxvar(t),starts);
else
        put (q,t) in the accept queue and suspend q
fi;
result q
}
```

If the goal is acceptable then the object becomes *locked* and an inference process will be created, otherwise the pair (q,t), containing the goal and the accompanying evaluation process, is put in the accept queue to await further treatment. In that case the process q is suspended.

11.4.4 Inheritance and compilation

An object may inherit non-logical variables and clauses from other objects. Multiple inheritance is allowed. Objects inherited by an inherited object are inherited. We have a simple algorithm to deal with possible cycles in the inheritance graph, illustrated in the definition below.

inherit

```
method inherit(x:T,had:T)
{
if isc(x) then inherit(a1(x), had); inherit(a2(x), had)
elsif ¬ member(x,had) then
      copy the non-logical variables of x and add x to had
fi
}
```

If x is compound, a recursive call is made to inherit from the components of x. Otherwise, copies of the non-logical variables of x are added to the list of non-logical variables of the object, and x is added to the *had* list.

For compiling the clauses of an object the function *compile* defined in section 11.3.2 is used. The compiled databases of the inherited objects are then put in composition with the own database of the object, following a similar procedure as outlined for the inheritance of non-logical variables. The combined database is stored in the attribute d, and given as a parameter to the evaluation processes created for the object.

11.5 Processes

A DLP program consists of a number of object declarations. To execute a program, the system needs to keep a record of the declared objects (in the sense of DLP) in order to create new instances.

A global *supervisor* is created to handle input from the user, and to create new instances of objects.

Each evaluation of a goal is accompanied by a so-called evaluation process. Its major tasks are to keep track of when a cut becomes active, to report the trace information to the user and to engage in communication with another process in order to deliver the answer substitutions resulting from the evaluation of a goal.

11.5.1 Global information

The global $POOL^{\star}$ object *knot* maintains the

- *object list* — a list in which the declared objects (in the sense of DLP) are kept.

When reading in a program, each time an object declaration is encountered a new entry is created in the *object list*. Instances of objects do not give rise to a new entry.

11.5.2 Object and command management

User input is directed to the global $POOL^\star$ object *supervisor*, that deals with the declaration of new objects.

For each top level goal that is evaluated, a copy of the supervisor is created, to handle the creation of instances of objects, using the information contained in the global *knot*.

11.5.3 Evaluation processes

Each inference process is accompanied by an evaluation process, referring to the object for which the goal is being evaluated. Evaluation processes are used for reporting trace information, for dealing with options, for keeping track of cuts, and more importantly for communicating to the invoking process the resumptions encoding the answer substitutions resulting from the evaluation of a goal.

Evaluation processes are implemented as instances of the $POOL^\star$ class Q. Among the attributes of class Q we have:

- *name* — the name of the process to be used in tracing,
- *obj* — the object to which the process refers, and
- *d* — the database that is initially given to the process.

The name of the process is derived from the name, instance number and process number of the object to which the process refers. The object pointer is given to enable the process access to the non-logical variables of the object. The database stored in d is initially the database of the object. However, when clauses are dynamically asserted or retracted, the changes affect only the database stored in d, and not the database of the object.

Cuts are handled by the process accompanying an inference. We maintain a dynamic record of the positions in the derivation at which a cut occurs and check when evaluating a particular goal atom whether a cut is active, that is whether the derivation must be cut off.

For doing this we need the attribute:

- *cut* — that stores the current cut level or cut *depth*,
- *cms* — that stores the current (*depth*, *predicate*) pair, and
- *cutlist* — a stack of previous (*cut*, *cms*) values.

The cut level stored in *cut* is a number indicating the depth at which a cut is active. When a goal is evaluated at a depth below *cut* then necessarily this means that backtracking has occurred. In the Prolog context, encountering a cut means that on backtracking failure occurs, and moreover that no other clauses will be tried for the predicate that is the head of the clause in the body of which the cut occurs. For this reason, the *cms* attribute records the predicate name of the head of the clause that contains the cut as well as the depth at which the clause is tried. Whenever the depth of the evaluation becomes less than the depth stored in the *cms* attribute, backtracking may occur again, in this case the *cutlist* is popped to restore *cut* and *cms* to the values previously held.

The function *checkcut*, that is called in the database function produced by compiling a clause, summarizes this procedure. Cf. section 11.3.2.

checkcut

```
fn checkcut(q:Q,t:T,m:N):B
{
k := q@cut;
(k0,p) := q@cms;
result m > k → false,
        m ≤ k & m ≠ k, → true,
        m = k0 & fof(t) = p → true,
        checkcut(q!cutit(),t,m)
        }
```

When the last alternative is tried, that is when the actual depth of evaluation is lower than the depth of the current *cms* attribute the method *cutit*() is called, which amounts to popping the *cutlist* and resetting *cut* and *cms* to their appropriate value, as expressed by the definition

cutit

```
method cutit() { cut := m'; cms := (m,p); cutl := rest; }
```

where we assume that *cutlist* is of the form $(m', (m, p)) \cdot rest$.

Upon encountering a cut, that is when the system predicate *cuton*(m, p), as introduced in the compilation, is evaluated by the system database, the method *cuton* is called, as in $q!cuton(m', m, p)$, to update the values of *cut*, *cms* and *cutlist*. The argument m' represents the depth at which the goal *cuton*(m, p) is actually encountered, which is not necessarily equal to m.

The method *cuton* is defined as

cuton

```
method cuton(m',m:N,p:A)
{
cutlist := (cut, cms) · cutlist; cut := m'; cms := (m,p);
}
```

thus modifying the appropriate attributes in a straightforward way.

Returning answer substitutions As we have explained in section 9.2, answer substitutions requested by the process that invoked the method call are returned in the form of a resumption that must be executed by that process to effect the answer substitutions.

We use an attribute

- *state* — that may take the values BUSY, PEND, WAIT and STOP

to determine whether the process is willing to answer a request for a resumption, and if so what resumption will be returned.

The attribute

- *goal* — initialized when creating the initial continuation

is used to store the initial goal, and the attributes

- *result* — to store the most recent answer, and
- *solutions* — to store all answers that have been produced,

contain instantiations of (the variables of) the initial goal.

To be able to suspend a process a boolean *locked* is used, that may be changed by calling the methods *lock* and *unlock*. A process is locked, either when an accept statement is evaluated, or when it must await the acceptance of a method call.

The protocol governing the communication of resumptions is contained in the body of Q. Below we assume that *ME* represents all methods except *resume* and *unlock*.

protocol

```
body do
    if locked then answer(unlock)
    elsif state = BUSY then answer(ME)
    else answer(resume)
    fi
od ydob
```

The request for a resumption may obviously only be answered if the process is not BUSY evaluating a goal, that is when it has produced an answer, or cannot produce any further answers.

Dependent on the state, either a failing, a unifying or a backtracking resumption is created, as explained in section 9.2. The code for the method *resume* now looks as follows.

resume

```
method resume():T
{
if state = WAIT & isempty(result) then result 'fail'
elsif state = PEND then result 'goal = result'
else result 'member(goal,solutions)'
}
```

The quoted terms must be read as Prolog terms, constructed as explained in section 11.2.

11.6 Non-logical variables and channels

When executing a DLP program, two kinds of special objects may come into existence, non-logical variables and channels. Non-logical variables are typically created when an instance of a DLP object is created. Channels are created dynamically by asking for a new channel.

11.6.1 Non-logical variables

Non-logical variables have as attributes a *name* and a *value*. This value can be initialized when creating a non-logical variable. There are no restrictions on accessing the value of a non-logical variable other than those imposed by the behavior of the object to which it belongs.

11.6.2 Channels

Channels mediate the unification of terms that belong to different processes. Such a transfer takes place when both an input side and an output side are present, provided that the terms put on either side on the channel are unifiable. Communication over channels allows backtracking on the input side when the input term and output term do not unify.

The attributes of a channel are:

- *free* — indicates whether an output term is present,
- *confirmed* — indicates whether new input terms are allowed,
- *store* — stores the most recent input term, and
- *message* — stores the most recent output term.

These attributes, together with the protocol described below, enforce the desired behavior of the channel.

protocol

```
body do
        if ¬ confirmed & ¬ free then answer(read, confirm, force)
        elsif ¬ free & confirmed then answer(receive)
        else answer(any)
od ydob
```

Initially the channel is free, in that no output term is present. While the channel has not received an output term it may accept anything.

When it first receives an input term, by a call to *read*, it waits until the attribute *message* is given a value, by a call to *write*.

read

```
method read(t:T):T
{
store := t;
while isempty(message) do answer(write) od;
result message
}
```

When another call to *write* is still active, the channel must wait for a call to *read*.

write

```
method write(t:T)
{
while ¬ isempty(message) do answer(read) od;
message := t; free := false; confirmed := false;
}
```

When the message is unifiable with the input term the process evaluating the input statement calls for the method *confirm* that sets the attribute *confirmed* to true.

confirm

```
method confirm() { confirmed := true; }
```

The output side, by calling the method *receive*, then merely has to collect the input term as stored in the attribute *store*, to unify this with its message. Cf. section 11.7.3.

receive

```
method receive():T
{
free := true; confirmed := false;
message := nil; result store;
}
```

When the message is not unifiable with the input term then another input term must be provided. Since the attribute *message* already has a value the unification of the input term and output term is then tried immediately.

When the channel first receives an output term it must wait for a call to *read*, or a call to the method *force*, that has a similar effect as the method *confirm*, but for the fact that the value delivered results in a failure on the output side.

11.7 The initial database

For the evaluation of the special forms by which DLP extends Prolog, simplification is applied in order to replace symbolic terms referring to objects, processes, non-logical variables or channels by a pointer or a value. Simplification is also used to provide a special interpretation to equality and assignment. Apart from the system database, that contains primitives for dealing with cuts and communication, we will discuss also the DLP object *boot*, in which a number of standard Prolog connectives are defined.

11.7.1 Simplification

Simplification is performed by the function

fn simplify(q:Q,t:T):T

When a term is simplified, non-logical variables are replaced by their values, except when the non-logical variable occurs on the left hand side of assignment. In that case the name of the variable is replaced by a pointer to allow subsequent assignment of the value on the right hand side.

Simplification is also applied to terms with the function symbol *new*. For instance, a term of the form *new*($c(t)$) is replaced by an active object, as shown in the code below.

new($c(t)$)

```
o := knot!obj('c')!cpy();
o@acceptlist := 'c'; o@active := true;
o!request('c(t)');
result o;
```

Somewhat informally, we use $'c'$ and $'c(t)'$ to represent the object name c and the constructor term $c(t)$. After creating a copy of the object c, as known to the global *knot*, the accept list of the newly created object o is set to c and the object is made active. Then o is requested to evaluate the constructor. Finally, the object o is returned to replace the term $new(c(t))$.

As another simplification, we wish to mention the replacement of arithmetic expressions like $'1+2'$ by their (standard) interpretation, $'3'$ in this case.

11.7.2 Equality and assignment

The interpretation of equality and assignment takes place by the function

fn assign(q:Q, t:T, c:C, m,n:N, s:S):T

Having a goal of the form $O = new(c(t))$, the term $new(c(t))$ is replaced by an object, as described above, and the logical variable O is bound to this object.

Goals of the form $Q :: O!m(t)$ are evaluated as depicted in the code below.

```
q := objof('O')!request('m(t)');
result unify('Q',Prc(q),c,m,n,s);
```

$Q = O!m(t)$

The notation $'O'$ and $'Q'$ is used to represent the terms containing the variables O and Q. We request the object to which O is bound to evaluate the goal $'m(t)'$ and unify the variable Q with the term $Prc(q)$, where q is the result of the request, with the continuation parameters c, m, n and s as originally given.

11.7.3 The system database

The evaluation of a number of system primitives is handled by the database function

fn system(q:Q, t:T, c:C, m,n:N, s:S):T

When a goal of the form $cuton(m',p)$, for a natural m and a predicate name p, is encountered the method *cuton* is called for the process q, given as a parameter to the system database, as in $q!cuton(m,m',p)$ for m the current cut level.

Accept statements of the form $accept(t_1,...,t_n)$ are handed over to the object to which q refers. If we have an accept statement containing conditional accept expressions, the result of processing the accept statement may be a non-empty goal that must be evaluated in order to effect the bindings resulting from the evaluation of the guard.

A synchronous call of the form $'O!m(t)'$ is rewritten into the sequence $'Q = O!m(t)'$, for a fresh variable Q, and evaluated by calling *assign*. The code below shows how to create a fresh variable. Cf. section 11.2.

```
g := mkc(Fun("=",Var(n+1),t), Fun("?",Var(n+1),Nil));
result assign(q,g,c,m,n+1,s);
```

$O!m(t)$

The evaluation of g by *assign* results in binding the variable $Var(n+1)$ to the process evaluating $m(t)$ so as to be able to ask for the resulting resumptions.

If the goal atom is of the form $Q?$ then a resumption is asked for and evaluated, as shown below.

$Q?$

```
r := prcof('Q')!resume();
if prcof('Q')@state ≠ BUSY then r := Fun(";",r,t) fi;
result eval(q,r,c,m,n,s);
```

The test if the process Q is $BUSY$ is to determine whether backtracking must occur to ask for any alternative resumptions.

Goals of the form $C!t$ and $C?t$, with C bound to a channel are interpreted as respectively an output statement and an input statement.

An output statement is evaluated as follows, for C the channel and t the output term:

$C!t$

```
chvof('C')!write(t);
r := chvof('C')!receive();
result unify(t,r,c,m,n,s);
```

After the term t is written on the channel, an input term must be waited for. See section 11.6.2.

An input statement, for channel C and input term t, is dealt with as depicted below:

$C?t$

```
r := chvof('C')!read(t);
g := mkc(Fun("=",t,r), Fun("confirm",'C',nil));
result eval(q,g,c,m,n,s);
```

Evaluating the goal $'t = r, confirm(C)'$ amounts to unifying the input term t with the output term r, and to evaluate $confirm(C)$ if the unification succeeds. In case the unification does not succeed, backtracking takes place over the alternatives contained in the continuation c. The evaluation of $confirm(C)$ results in calling the method *confirm*() for the channel C.

11.7.4 Booting

In the object *boot* we have defined, among others, the predicate *true*, negation by failure, the disjunctive connective of Prolog and the Prolog conditional. Also, we have defined the and-parallel connective of DLP treated in section 3.6, and the predicates *member* and *append*.

boot

```
object boot {
true.
not(A) :-  A,!,fail.
not(A).
A;_ :- A.
_;B :- B.
A → B :-  A, !, B.
A&B :-  Q = self!A, B, Q?.
member(X,[ X | _ ]).
member(X,[ _ | T ]) :-  member(X,T).
append([],L,L).
append([H|T],L,[H|R]) :-  append(T,L,R).
}
```

The object *boot* is by default inherited by all DLP objects.

11.8 Utilities

We have collected here a variety of abbreviations and function definitions that support the definitions given in the previous sections.

11.8.1 Auxiliary definitions

In the actual prototype we have defined a number of options and system parameters, such as the maximum number of objects that may be in existence, the amount of debugging and tracing information that must be given, and the symbols that are recognized as keywords of DLP (see sections 12.2 and 12.2).

11.8.2 Term manipulation functions

The representation of terms used enables us to formulate the functions for manipulating terms by a direct recursion on the subterms. We will give three examples. The first example is the function *maxvar*, determining the maximum variable number occurring in a term.

maxvar

```
fn maxvar(t:T):N
{
if isvar(t) then result varof(t)
elsif isfun(t) then result max(maxvar(a1(t)),maxvar(a2(t)))
else result 0
}
```

The second is the function for applying a renaming function e of type E to a term.

mape

```
fn mape(e:E,t:T):T
{
case tagof(t)
VAR then result Var(e(varof(t))
FUN then result Fun( fc(t), mape(e, a1(t)), mape(e, a2(t)) )
otherwise result t
esac
}
```

And the last example, following a similar pattern, is the function for applying a substitution.

maps

```
fn maps(s:S,t:T):T
{
case tagof(t)
VAR then result isbot(s(varof(t))) → t, maps(s,s(varof(t)))
FUN then result Fun( fc(t), maps(s, a1(t)), maps(s, a2(t)) )
otherwise result t
esac
}
```

In all these cases, dealing with a function term gives rise to creating a function term with arguments appropriately modified.

12

Conclusions and future work

- If someone is looking for something and perhaps roots around in a certain place, he shows that he believes that what he is looking for is there. -
Ludwig Wittgenstein, *On Certainty*

Now that we have completed the description of the various aspects of our language, we wish to spend some time evaluating our efforts, and the route taken to arrive at our results. Also, we wish to indicate some lines of future research.

The research reported in this book covers the design, semantics and implementation of DLP, a language for distributed logic programming.

Design Design is a delicate issue. The, in our view, most distinguishing feature of our language DLP is that it offers a kind of *backtrackable rendez-vous*. Combining logic programming, object oriented features and parallelism, it allows to employ message-based computation without sacrificing the opportunities of search by backtracking. Characterizing our language, we may say that DLP extends Prolog with features for parallel object oriented programming. The difference with respect to other parallel object oriented extensions of logic programming languages is precisely that we did not wish to sacrifice the backtracking offered by Prolog. We have expended considerable effort to arrive at a notion of objects compatible with the demands of search-based programming. We have defended our decisions with respect to the way (distributed) backtracking takes place, the mutual exclusion provided between method calls, and the protection of non-logical variables in chapter 5.

From the point of view of a declarative reading of DLP programs, non-logical variables, by which objects may be assigned a persistent state, form an impediment to formulating a natural declarative semantics. The *conditional accept* statement, introduced in section 3.5, however, obviates the need for non-logical variables. We may remark that this feature has been developed relatively late, when our study of the semantics of the language was in full progress. We think that it deserves a thorough semantic study. Such a study may well influence the design of the language. Nonetheless, eliminating non-logical variables altogether might make inheritance an infeasible feature, since basing inheritance on behavioral notions is far more difficult than basing it on code-sharing.

Semantics Semantics may guide the design of a language. The formal semantics elaborated in part II encourages us to believe that we have developed a sound language. Apart from being a rather entertaining enterprise, developing a formal semantic description is a good way of checking that the features included in the language are sensible, that is well-defined and non-trivial. For the designer of a language, to afford a formal semantics reduces the probability of errors. We disagree with the opinion that semantic amenability is the only criterion for the usefulness of a language construct. In our case, working on a semantic description helped in demarcating the core of our language. In proving our operational and denotational semantics equivalent we have restricted ourselves to the most important features, leaving out those that did not seem worth the trouble. Encouraging indeed was the fact that the operational description of the interplay between backtracking and message passing turned out to be rather concise and elegant, much more than we expected. Finding a suitable denotational (that is mathematical) compositional characterization equivalent to our operational description strengthened our conviction that we have hit on a solid (language) construct.

Implementation Implementing a prototype proved to be very fruitful in designing the language. Having a (modifiable) prototype available allowed us to experiment with different language features and to test our intuition by actual examples. Shortcomings could easily be corrected, giving full chance to a healthy exchange between practical experience and formal scrutiny.

The prototype, described in the previous chapters, is written in *POOL** (a variant of POOL-X) which is in its turn compiled to C by using the compiler described in [Beemster, 1990]. In developing the prototype we have taken benefit from the constructs for process creation and communication available in our implementation language. From the point of view of language design one could even view DLP as lifting a parallel object oriented (POOL-like) language to the level of logic programming. Nevertheless, in order to implement distributed backtracking we had to write code for object and process management, since it requires a distinction to be made between (DLP) objects and processes.

We have few experimental figures to illustrate the adequacy of our implementation with respect to performance and the utilization of parallelism. We did, however, compare the performance of our system with the performance of C-Prolog, under Unix, on a 12 MB Sparc workstation, for a sequential version of the *quicksort* program described in section 3.6. We varied the length of the lists to be sorted from 10 to 70. With the list of 70 elements our system ran into memory problems and gave up. Compared with the slight increase in execution time of Prolog, when increasing the length of the lists, the increase in time for DLP was rather dramatic. Memory usage obviously is the problem.

Further, we tried to measure the speed-up obtained for the parallel quicksort program described in section 3.6. Unfortunately, the parallel interpreter we had at our disposal also ran into memory problems.

We were able to check the adequacy of our allocation primitives. With a DLP program that merely created processes, distributing them evenly over the available processors, we obtained a speed-up proportional to the number of processes created. We must remark that what is actually measured, by using a parallel interpreter for POOL-X, is not the amount of parallelism in DLP but the parallelism displayed by its underlying implementation. We did not pursue this line of research, since efficiency and speed-up have not been our primary concern. Nevertheless, at this stage we begin to consider performance as an important issue, and we will make some recommendations aimed at improving the efficiency of the system.[1]

Although we have repeatedly stated that our language is logic based, we have not paid any attention to the declarative semantics of our language. Concluding our book, we will try to come up with an inventory of the problems posed by our language, and some of the possible directions of research.

12.1 Improving the efficiency of DLP

A breakthrough in the execution speed of sequential Prolog has been achieved with the introduction of the Warren Abstract Machine. See [Warren, 1977] and [Warren, 1983]. Since Prolog is the base language of DLP, an obvious improvement in performance would come about by replacing our Prolog interpreter, as described in chapter 10, by an interpreter based on the Warren Abstract Machine.

An extended version of the Warren Abstract Machine has also been the basis of a parallel implementation of Prolog. See [Hermenegildo, 1986] and [Hermenegildo and Nasr, 1986]. Although our needs are somewhat different, since we do not aim at realizing implicit parallelism, we may well profit from the primitives for process creation and communication developed in [Hermenegildo, 1986].

Performance would also definitely be improved by using compilation techniques for implementing the access to non-logical variables.

With regard to our choice of the implementation model for DLP, we may remark that the use of sequential Prolog as the base language of objects allows us to apply all the optimizations developed for Prolog. Our communication mechanism (which employs resumptions – goals that facilitate computation of the results) provides an efficient solution to deal with incompatible variable bindings. In contrast, the computation and communication models of concurrent logic programming languages preclude such optimizations. Cf. [Shapiro, 1989]. See also the discussion in [Hermenegildo, 1986] in which a similar view is put forward.

[1] Recently, we developed Active C++, an extension of C++ with active classes and communication by rendez-vous [Eliëns and Visser, 1992]. We are now in the process of implementing DLP in Active C++.

12.2 Declarative semantics for distributed logic programming

Although we did provide a mathematical denotational semantics for DLP in part II, we did not give a declarative semantics in the sense this phrase is commonly understood. Cf. [Apt et al, 1987]. Our denotational semantics may be understood as characterizing the flow of control of our language in a mathematical way, rather than providing a characterization of the logical meaning of the language.

Model-theoretically, a Horn clause program may be given a meaning by assigning it a subset of the Herbrand base, the set of ground atoms over the signature of the language. Such an interpretation, that is a subset of the Herbrand base, is usually obtained as the fixed point of a consequence operator, delivering the atoms that logically follow from a given interpretation. The least fixed point of such an operator is commonly called the success-set, containing all atoms that are valid with regard to the program characterized by the operator. For pure Horn clauses, a completeness result is known, stating that every atom in the success-set may be derived as a goal using SLD resolution. See section 2.1.1, [van Emden and Kowalski, 1976], [Apt and van Emden, 1982] and [Lloyd, 1987]. This result can be extended to simple distributed logic programs, consisting of a number of modules (containing Horn clauses) that cooperate in finding a solution to a goal, as proved in [Ramanujam, 1989].

Leaving the realm of pure Horn clause programs such a completeness result become more difficult to obtain. For instance, mechanisms encountered in Concurrent Prolog or Parlog, such as the commit operator that realizes *don't care* non-determinism controlled by guards, and input constraints, on which the synchronization of *and*-processes is based, enforce a reduction of the success set. Cf. [de Boer et al, 1989].

More drastic repairs are necessary for most of the languages that we have studied in section 5.2. As a preliminary investigation into the declarative semantics of DLP, we will study the adaptations needed to deal with features such as objects with states, contexts in which a derivation takes place, and the synchronization due to explicit communication.

States The most characteristic property of an object, from a logical point of view, is that whatever functionality an object may provide, this functionality is dependent on its state. In [Chen and Warren, 1988] it is proposed to consider objects as *intensions*, that is as functions from states to values. It is observed that, operationally, each object has a closed past with respect to its current state, and an open future. An update to an object will determine the values delivered in the next state. The approach taken in [Chen and Warren, 1988] is to extend the semantics of first order logic programming by the notion of intensions, representing the behavior of objects that may change in time. Since there is a temporal dependence between the values of an object in consecutive states, we may adopt a frame assumption stating that the values of an object remain the same as in the last state, unless they have explicitly been updated.

Contexts Another way to view objects is as providing a context determining the meaning of a particular predicate. In [Monteiro and Porto, 1988] this aspect of objects is treated by introducing context-dependent predicate definitions. A possible worlds declarative semantics is given for a language for, what they call, contextual logic programming. Method calls may be given meaning in this framework as a change of context for evaluating the call, that is as the transition to another world. A somewhat similar approach for dealing with modular features of logic programming has been sketched in [Miller, 1986].

Synchronization Finally, the question remains how to deal with communication in a declarative way. Work in this area has been reported in [Monteiro, 1984], that provided a semantic foundation for Delta Prolog. Cf. [Pereira and Nasr, 1984]. The idea is, roughly, that the validity of a goal is made dependent on the history of communication events.

A rather different approach is contained in [Falaschi et al, 1984], where an operational, model-theoretic and fixed-point semantics is given for Horn clauses extended with a synchronization operator. The extended Horn clause logic presented there resembles the languages of Logical Objects and Communicating Prolog Units, described in section 5.2.

Our explorations thus far indicate that we need to include a dynamic aspect in the declarative semantics of DLP — to account for the dynamic creation of objects, the changes that result from the assignment to non-logical variables, the rendez-vous between objects, and the dynamically changing acceptance conditions of objects. Such a declarative semantics is beyond the scope of this book and left as future research.

Appendices

Appendix A: Syntax

An overview of the syntax and the informal semantics of DLP is given in section 3.8 and table A.1. For clarity we will here provide a more detailed description of the syntax of DLP by means of BNF-grammar rules.

Keywords The following keywords are used in DLP:

- *object* — to start an object declaration,
- *var* — to declare non-logical variables,
- *use* — to indicate the inheritance of clauses,
- *isa* — to inherit non-logical variables,
- *new* — to create new objects,
- *accept* — to indicate the willingness to engage in a rendez-vous,
- *deterministic* — to disallow backtracking over answers,

BNF grammar rules The rules describing the syntax of DLP programs are quite similar to those for Prolog programs as given in section 2.1.3. In addition we have rules describing object declarations and the special forms by which DLP extends Prolog.[2]

DLP is term-oriented. A term is either a constant, a variable or a compound term. We distinguish between compound terms that are constructed from a function symbol *name* and a possibly empty list of argument terms, and expressions built from an (arithmetical) operator and one or two sub-terms.[3]

term

term ::= *constant* | *variable* | *compound*

compound ::= *name*(*arguments*) | *expression*

arguments ::= *empty* | *term-list*

expression ::= *term*+*term* | ...

[2] As before, terminal symbols are written bold-face.

[3] A *name* is a special constant, namely a sequence starting with a lower case letter followed by an arbitrary number of letters or digits.

Table A.1: DLP — an overview

non-logical variables	$v := t$	assigns the term t to the non-logical variable v
object creation	$O = new(c)$	creates a passive instance of object c
	$O = new(c(t))$	creates an active instance of object c
allocation	$O = new(c@N)$	creates a passive instance of object c allocated at node N
	$O = new(c(t)@N)$	creates an active instance of object c, allocated at node N
channels	$C = new(channel)$	creates a new channel
	$C!t$	output statement for term t over channel C
	$C?t$	input statement for term t over channel C
process creation	$Q = O!G$	requests the evaluation of G by the object to which O refers
resumptions	$Q?$	requests the results of a remote goal evaluation
synchronization	$accept(e_1, ..., e_n)$	accepts any call satisfying an accept expression e_i
Abbreviation		Definition
synchronous rendez-vous	$O!G$	O!G :- Q = O!G, Q?.
and-parallel operator	$A \& B$	A&B :- Q = self!B, A, Q?.
allocating goals	$G@N$	G@N :- O = new(self@N), O!G.

Given a syntactical unit we define a list of such units as consisting of one such item possibly followed by other items, separated from each other by a comma. In such a fashion we define lists of terms, literals and clauses.

list

term-list ::= *term* | *term*, *term-list*

literal-list ::= *literal* | *literal*, *literal-list*

clause-list ::= *clause* | *clause*, *clause-list*

Among the special forms by which DLP extends Prolog is a *new*-statement. The objects created are passive or active dependent on the descriptor given to the new-statement. Both passive and active objects may be allocated to a particular processor. The other forms provide statements to request the (remote) evaluation of a goal and statements to synchronize the acceptance of a method call and the communication of the results of accepted method calls.

form

form ::= *new-statement* | *request* | *sync*

new-statement ::= *new* (*descriptor allocator*)

descriptor ::= *name* | *name*(*arguments*)

allocator ::= *empty* | @ *term*

request ::= *term*!*literal* | *variable*=*term*!*literal*

sync ::= *variable*? | *accept-statement*

For an active object, acceptance of a method call is determined by the occurrence of either a template as an argument of the accept statement or an accept-expression. An accept-expression is built from a template, a guard and a method-body that is evaluated when the guard succeeds.

acceptance

accept-expr ::= *template* | *template* : *guard* → *method-body*

template ::= *name* | *name*(*arguments*)

guard ::= *literal* | (*literal-list*)

method-body ::= *literal* | (*literal-list*)

acceptance-list ::= *accept-expr* | *accept-expr* , *acceptance-list*

accept-statement ::= **accept** (*acceptance-list*)

An atom is a predicate with or without arguments. Syntactically, a predicate without arguments conforms to the constraints imposed on names. A test is a predicate-expression involving an arithmetical comparison operator. A literal is either an atom, a test, a special form or a cut (written as an exclamation mark).

literal

```
atom ::= predicate | predicate(arguments)
test ::= term < term | ...
literal :: atom | test | form | !
```

A clause is either a fact, a rule or a goal. A fact is a rule without a body and is written as an atom followed by a dot. The head of a rule is an atom and the body of a rule is a list of literals. A goal is also a list of literals, just as the body of a rule.

clause

```
fact ::= literal.
rule ::= head:-body.
head ::= literal
body ::= literal | literal,body
goal ::= ?-body.
clause ::= fact | rule | goal
```

When declaring the non-logical variables of an object, these may be given an initial value. Such an initialization takes the form of an equation with the name of the variable on the left-hand side and the initializing value on the right-hand side. An objectdeclaration may also specify the objects from which non-logical variables or clauses are inherited.

declarations

```
init ::= neme | name=term
var-decl ::= empty | var init-list .
isa-decl ::= empty | isa name-list .
use-decl ::= empty | use name-list .
options-decl ::= empty | option init-list .
name-list ::= name | name, name-list
init-list ::= init | init, init-list
```

An object declaration may specify from which objects it inherits non-logical variables and clauses. Further it may specify the non-logical variables of the objects, additional inheritance information, and clauses embodying the constructor and the methods that the object supports.

object

object-decl ::= *object name inheritance-decl* {
instance-decl constructor methods }
inheritance-decl ::= *empty* | : *name-list*
instance-decl ::= *var-decl use-decl isa-decl options-decl*
constructor ::= *empty* | *clause-list*
methods ::= *empty* | *clause-list*

Reading-in declarations Clauses represent either facts, rules or goals. Goals encountered when consulting a file or reading-in an object declaration are interpreted as a command.

As an alternative to the way specified above, object declarations in DLP may also be read in as a sequence consisting of goals and program clauses.

For ordinary object declaration a preprocessor takes care of the appropriated conversion as sketched below.

As an example, the declaration

object a {		object(a).
var k, n=1.	corresponds to	var(k, n=1).
...	the sequence	...
}		end_object.

The clauses and goals are read-in one by one, by the global object io, and sent to the global supervisor. For unit clauses, it is tested whether they must be interpreted as a command. Each newly declared DLP object is then added to the object list of the global knot. As a remark, the parser we used allows brackets to be omitted in a number of cases. However, brackets may always be used.

Appendix B: Extensions to DLP

The DLP system contains a number of features not described in parts I, II and III. For example, options and defaults have not been treated, since they are not of importance from a conceptual point of view. Nevertheless, for actually using the system such features are of importance.

A quite different consideration is that the language DLP is still evolving. We have included a description of these extensions, to provide a starting point for further experiments and research.

Options may be set for an object by a unit clause of the form

- set name = value.

which sets the option name to value. A value may be either on or off, or a number. When no value is specified, the value given is assumed to be on. Each process created for each instance of the object is initialized with the options as set for the object.

Options may also be set dynamically, by a goal of the form

- option(name) := value

which sets the option name to value for the process evaluating the goal.

If we do not explicitly mention what values an option may take, the value is either on or off. Unless explicitly set by the user, the value of an option is zero or off. We have the following options:

- trace — with possible values 0, 1, 2 or 3 to determine the amount of tracing.
- nosimplify — to enforce that no automatic simplification of arithmetic expressions and the like takes place.
- eager — to effect that all solutions are computed and communicated at the first resumption request.
- sol — to determine the number of solutions that must be produced. When sol has value 0 then all solutions will be generated. When sol is 1 then the behavior of the object will be deterministic. Otherwise, a call will result in no more solutions than indicated by the value of sol.

- override — if set the overriding mode of composition is used in combining the databases of the inherited objects; in other words, inherited predicates can only be redefined instead of being extended.

- copy — to initialize the process created for evaluating a method call to the options of the invoking process, instead of to the options of the object to which the call was addressed.

- branch — determines the branching degree of the (imaginary) tree of processors, as used in the allocation primitives described in section 3.7. The default is 2, when branch is zero.

- width — determines the width of the (imaginary) matrix of processors. See also section 3.7. The default is 4, when width is zero.

- nproc — determines the number of processors assumed to be available. The default is 10, when nproc is zero.

Further, we have three options aux1, aux2 and aux3, that may be used for other purposes.

To inspect the value of an option the expression option(name) may be used, which will be replaced by the value of the option name unless the expression occurs on the left hand side of an assignment.

For debugging purposes the goals debug and nodebug may be used, that respectively turn on and switch off debugging globally.

Defaults may be used for the initialization of objects with respect to inheritance and the values of options. As an example, the command

- :- default(use(boot,system),set(trace)).

effects that all declared objects will inherit the objects boot and system, and will have their trace option set.

Context switches with respect to the functionality of a process may be effected by manipulating a stack of databases. For each evaluation process, clauses that are asserted or retracted take effect only for the evaluation performed by the process itself. Such modifications do not affect the functionality of the object to which the process refers. The state of a process, that is the clauses that are active, may be saved or restored in the following way. When clauses have been asserted, the goal

- push()

effects that the current database of the process is pushed onto a stack.

The goal

- pop()

restores the old situation by popping the stack.

Process splitting is allowed, in addition to creating a new process when asking an object to evaluate a goal. A copy of the current process can be made by using the expression new(*this*) or new(*this*@N) that simplify to a copy of the current process, in the latter case allocated at the processor node denoted by N.

Such a process may be asked to evaluate a goal. For instance, when we wish to use the functionality of a particular process, we may state the goal

- new(*this*)!G

to have G evaluated by a copy of the current process.

Object-to-process conversion takes place when asking an active object for a resumption. The goal sequence

- O = new(c(t)), O?

results in creating an object for which the constructor c(t) is evaluated, that is subsequently asked for the resumption resulting from evaluating c(t). The request to the object O is simply redirected to the constructor process for O.

Accessing non-logical variables is facilitated by expressions of the form

- O@name

denoting the non-logical variable name of the object O. Cf. chapter 4. We allow goals of the form

- O@name := t

to assign t as a value to the non-logical variable name of the object O.

Global non-logical variables may be declared by unit clauses of the form

- global name.

in the same way as ordinary non-logical variables. These variables may also be initialized when declared. A global non-logical variable may be accessed by using an expression of the form global(name). When such an expression occurs on the left-hand side of an assignment, the (global) non-logical variable name is assigned the value on the right-hand side.

Clashes between names of objects, non-logical variables, globals and options may be resolved by using the expressions

- obj(name)
- val(name)
- global(name)
- option(name)

indicating that respectively an object, a non-logical variable, a global non-logical variable or an option value must be delivered.

Hiding names local to an object may be done by indicating which names are private, with a declaration of the form

- *private* f1, f2.

which results in post-fixing the function symbols f1 and f2 with the name of the object in which the declaration occurs. The *private* list may contain arbitrary function symbols. even for instance the function symbol ';' provided that it is quoted.

Allocation of objects and processes is handled by *node-expressions*. See section 3.7. We allow the following node-expressions:

- () — allocation is left to the system.
- N1,...,N_{n} — selects one of the processor nodes N1,...,N_{n} .
- T:N — delivers the node on the N-th branch following the tree T (as explained in section 3.7).
- N1 # N2 — delivers a process from the (imaginary) matrix of processors (as explained in section 3.7).
- [N|T] — is just another notation for T:N.
- here — allocates the object or process to the same processor.

The parameters of both the (imaginary) tree and the (imaginary) matrix of processors may be modified by setting the appropriate options, as discussed above.

Bibliography

[Aikins, 1980] J.S. AIKINS, *Prototypes and Production Rules: A knowledge representation for consultations*, Report STAN-CS-80-814 (1980) Stanford

[Ait-Kaci and Nasr, 1986] H. AIT-KACI AND R. NASR, *LOGIN: A logic programming language with built-in inheritance*, Journal of Logic Programming, 3 (1986) pp. 185-215

[Agha, 1986] G. AGHA, *Actors: A Model of Concurrent Computation in Distributed Systems*, (MIT Press, 1986)

[Akama, 1986] K. AKAMA, *Inheritance hierarchy mechanism in Prolog*, in: Proc. Logic Programming '86, E. Wada (ed.), Lecture Notes in Computer Science 264, Springer (1986) pp. 12-21

[Allison, 1986] L. ALLISON, *A practical introduction to denotational semantics*, Cambridge Computer Science Texts 23, (1986)

[America, 1987] P. AMERICA, *POOL-T: a parallel object oriented language*, in: [Yonezawa and Tokoro, 1987]

[America, 1987a] P. AMERICA, *Inheritance and subtyping in a parallel object oriented language*, in: Proc. ECOOP 87, Paris, J. Bezivin, J.M. Hullot, P. Cointe and H. Lieberman (eds.), Lecture Notes in Computer Science 276, Springer (1987) pp. 234-242

[America and de Bakker, 1988] P. AMERICA AND J.W. DE BAKKER, *Designing equivalent models for process creation*, Theoretical Computer Science, 60 (2) (1988) pp. 109-176

[America, 1989] P. AMERICA, *Language definition of POOL-X*, Doc. Prisma 0350, Philips Research Laboratorium, Eindhoven (1989)

[America, 1989a] P. AMERICA, *Changes in POOL-X for Release 2.0*, Doc. Pooma 0104, Philips Research Laboratorium, Eindhoven (1989)

[America, 1989b] P. AMERICA, *Issues in the design of a parallel object oriented language*, Doc. DOOM 452, Philips Research Laboratorium, Eindhoven (1989), also in [America and Rutten, 1989a]

[America et al, 1989] P. AMERICA, J.W. DE BAKKER, J.N. KOK AND J.J.M.M. RUTTEN, *Denotational semantics of a Parallel Object Oriented Language*, Information and Computation, 83 (2) (1989) pp. 152-205

[America and Rutten, 1989a] P. AMERICA AND J.J.M.M. RUTTEN, *A parallel object-oriented language: design and foundations*, Joint Ph.D. thesis, Vrije Universiteit Amsterdam (1989)

[America and Rutten, 1989b] P. AMERICA AND J.J.M.M. RUTTEN, *Solving reflexive domain equations in a category of complete metric spaces*, Journal of Computer and System Sciences, 39 (1989) pp. 343-375

[America and Rutten, 1991] P. AMERICA AND J.J.M.M. RUTTEN, *A layered semantics for a parallel object-oriented language*, in: Foundations of Object-Oriented Languages, J.W. de Bakker, W.P. de Roever and G. Rozenberg (eds.), Lecture Notes in Computer Science 489, Springer (1991) pp. 91-123

[Andrews and Schneider, 1983] G.R. ANDREWS AND F.B. SCHNEIDER, *Concepts and notations for concurrent programming*, ACM Computing Surveys, 15(1) (1983) pp. 3-43

[Apt and van Emden, 1982] K. APT AND M. VAN EMDEN, *Contributions to the theory of logic programming*, Journal of the ACM, 29 (3) (1982) pp. 841-862

[Apt et al, 1987] K. APT , H. BLAIR AND A. WALKER, *Towards a theory of declarative knowledge*, in: Foundations of Deductive Databases and Logic Programming J. Minker (ed.) Morgan Kaufmann, Los Altos (1987)

[Armstrong et al, 1986] J.L. ARMSTRONG, N.H. ELSHIEWY AND R. VIRDING, *The Phoning Philosophers Problem or Logic for Telecommunications*, in: Proc. Symp. of Logic Programming, Salt Lake City, IEEE (1986) pp. 28-35

[Bal et al, 1989] H. BAL, J. STEINER AND A. TANENBAUM, *Programming languages for distributed systems*, ACM Computing Surveys, 21 (3) (1989) pp. 262-322

[de Bakker and Zucker, 1982] J.W. DE BAKKER AND J.I. ZUCKER, *Processes and the denotational semantics of concurrency*, Information and Control 54 (1982) pp. 70-120

[de Bakker et al, 1984] J.W. DE BAKKER, J.A. BERGSTRA, J.W. KLOP AND J.-J. CH. MEYER, *Linear time and branching time semantics for recursion with merge*, Theoretical Computer Science 34 (1984) pp. 135-156

[de Bakker et al, 1986] J.W. DE BAKKER, J.N. KOK, J.-J.CH. MEYER, E.-R. OLDEROG AND J.I. ZUCKER, *Contrasting themes in the semantics of imperative concurrency*, in: Current Trend in Concurrency: Overviews and Tutorials, J.W. de Bakker, W.P. de Roever and G. Rozenberg (eds.), Lecture Notes in Computer Science 224, Springer (1986) pp. 51-121

[de Bakker et al, 1988] J.W. DE BAKKER, J.-J.CH. MEYER, E.-R. OLDEROG AND J.I. ZUCKER, *Transition systems, metric spaces and ready sets in the semantics of uniform concurrency*, Journal of Computer and System Sciences 36 (1988), 158-224 [de Bakker and Meyer] J.W. DE BAKKER AND J.-J.CH. MEYER. *Metric semantics for concurrency*. BIT 28 (1988) pp. 504-529

[de Bakker, 1989] J.W. DE BAKKER, *Designing concurrency semantics*, in: Proc. 11th World Computer Congress, G.X. Ritter (ed.), North Holland (1989) pp. 591-598

[de Bakker et al, 1990] J.W. DE BAKKER, W.P. DE ROEVER AND G. ROZENBERG (EDS.), *Foundations of Object Oriented Languages*. (REX School/Workshop 1990), Lecture Notes in Computer Science 489, Springer (1990)

[de Bakker, 1991] J.W. DE BAKKER, *Comparative semantics for flow of control in logic programming without logic*, Information and Computation 91 (1991) pp. 123-179

[de Bakker and de Vink, 1991] J.W. DE BAKKER AND E.P. DE VINK, *CCS for OO and LP*, in: Proc. Theory and Practice of Software Development '91, Vol. 2, S. Abramsky and T.S.E. Maibaum (eds.), Lecture Notes in Computer Science 494, Springer (1991) pp. 1-28

[Beck and Cunningham, 1989] K. BECK AND W. CUNNINGHAM, *A laboratory for teaching object-oriented thinking*, in: Proc. OOPSLA '89, N. Meyrowitz (ed.), Sigplan Notices 17 (4) (1989) pp. 1-6

[Beemster, 1990] M. BEEMSTER, *POOL±X*, Doc. P0522, Philips Research Laboratorium, Eindhoven (1990)

[Black et al. 1987] A. BLACK, N. HUTCHINSON, E. JUL AND L. CARTER, *Distribution and abstract types in Emerald*. IEEE Transactions Software Engineering SE-13 (1) (1987) pp. 65-76

[Blaschek et al, 1989] G. BLASCHEK, G. POMBERGER, A. STRITZINGER, *A comparison of object oriented programming languages*, Structured Programming (1989) 10/4:187-197

[Bobrow, 1984] D.G. BOBROW, *If Prolog is the answer, what is the question?*, in: Proc. Conf. 5th Gen. Comp. Systems ICOT (1984) pp. 139-145

[de Boer et al, 1989] F.S. DE BOER, J.N. KOK, C. PALAMIDESSI AND J.J.M.M. RUTTEN, *Semantic models for a version of Parlog*, in: Proc. of the sixth Conf. on Logic Programming, Lisboa, G. Levi and M. Martelli (eds.), MIT Press (1989) pp. 621-636 (extended version to appear in Theoretical Computer Science)

[de Boer et al, 1989a] F.S. DE BOER, J.N. KOK, C. PALAMIDESSI AND J.J.M.M. RUTTEN, *Control flow versus logic: a denotational and a declarative model for guarded Horn clauses*, Report CS-R8952, Centre for Mathematics and Computer Science, Amsterdam (1989)

[de Boer et al, 1990] F.S. DE BOER, J.N. KOK, C. PALAMIDESSI, J.J.M.M. RUTTEN, *From failure to success: Comparing a denotational and a declarative semantics for Horn Clause Logic*, in: Proc. International BCS-FACS Workshop on

Semantics for Concurrency. M.Z. Kwiatkowska. M.W. Shields and R.M. Thomas (eds.). Workshops in Computing, Springer (1990). pp. 38-60

[Booch, 1986] G. BOOCH, *Object-oriented development*, IEEE Transactions on software engineering SE-12 (2) (1986) pp. 211-221

[Booch and Vilot, 1990] G. BOOCH AND M. VILOT, *The design of the C++ Booch components*, in: Proc. ECOOP/OOPSLA '90, N. Meyrowitz (ed.), ACM (1990) pp. 1-11

[Booch, 1991] G. BOOCH, *Object oriented design with applications*, Benjamin Cummings (1991)

[De Bosschere, 1989] K. DE BOSSCHERE, *Parallelism in Logic Programming*, Report DG 89-02 Lab. voor Electronica en Meettechniek. Gent (1989)

[Bratko, 1990] I. BRATKO, *Prolog Programming for Artificial Intelligence*, Addison Wesley (1990) (2nd edition)

[van Breugel, 1991] F. VAN BREUGEL, *Comparative semantics for a real-time programming language with integration*, in: Proc. Theory and Practice of Software Development '91 S. Abramsky and T.S.E. Maibaum (eds.) vol. 1, Lecture Notes in Computer Science 493, Springer (1991) pp 397-411

[Browne, 1986] J.C. BROWNE, *Framework for the formulation of parallel computation structures*, Parallel Computing 3 (1986) pp. 1-9

[de Bruin, 1986] A. DE BRUIN, *Experiments with continuation semantics: jumps, backtracking, dynamic networks*, Ph.D. thesis, Vrije Universiteit, Amsterdam (1986)

[Buchanan and Shortliffe, 1984] B.J. BUCHANAN AND E.H. SHORTLIFFE (EDS.), *Rule Based Expert Systems*. Addison-Wesley (1984)

[Budd, 1991] T. BUDD, *An introduction to object-oriented programming*, Addison Wesley (1991)

[Butler Cox, 1983] *Expert Systems*, Report no 37, Butler Cox Foundation (1983)

[Butler and Karonis, 1988] R.M. BUTLER AND N.T. KARONIS, *Exploitation of parallelism in prototypical deduction problems*, in: Proc. CADE-9, E. Lusk and R. Overbeek (eds.), Lecture Notes in Computer Science 310, Springer (1988) pp. 333-343

[Butler et al. 1986] R. BUTLER, E. LUSK, W. MCCUNE AND R. OVERBEEK, *Parallel logic programming for numeric applications*, in: Proc. CADE-8, J.H. Siekman (ed.), Lecture Notes in Computer Science 230, Springer (1986) pp. 375-388

[de Bruin and de Vink, 1989] A. DE BRUIN, E.P. DE VINK, *Continuation semantics for PROLOG with cut*, in: Proc. Theory and Practice of Software Development '89, Vol I, J. Diaz and F. Orejas (eds.), Lecture Notes in Computer Science 351, Springer (1989) pp. 178-192

[Campbell, 1984] J.A. CAMPBELL. *Implementations of Prolog*, Ellis Horwood (1984)

[Cardelli, 1984] L. CARDELLI. *A semantics of multiple inheritance*, in: Semantics of Data Types, G. Kahn, D.B. MacQueen and G. Plotkin (eds.), Lecture Notes in Computer Science 173, Springer (1984) pp. 51-68

[Cardelli and Wegner, 1985] L. CARDELLI AND P. WEGNER, *On understanding types, data abstraction and polymorphism*, Computing Surveys 17(4) (1985) pp. 472-522

[Chambers et al, 1984] F.B. CHAMBERS, D.A. DUC AND G.P. JONES (EDS.), *Distributed Computing*, Academic Press (1984)

[Chen and Warren, 1988] W. CHEN AND D.S. WARREN, *Objects as intensions*, in: Proc. 5th Int. Conf. on Logic Programming, Seattle (1988) pp. 404-419

[Clark and Tarnlund, 1984] K.L. CLARK AND S.A. TARNLUND (EDS.), *Logic Programming*, Academic Press (1982)

[Clark and Gregory, 1986] K.L. CLARK AND S. GREGORY, *PARLOG: Parallel programming in Logic*, ACM TOPLAS 8 (1) (1986) pp. 1-49

[Clocksin and Mellish, 1981] W.F. CLOCKSIN AND C.S. MELLISH, *Programming in Prolog*, Springer (1981)

[Coad and Yourdon, 1990] P. COAD AND E. YOURDON, *Object oriented analysis*, Yourdon Press, Englewood Cliffs, NJ (1990)

[Cohen, 1985] J. COHEN, *Describing Prolog by its interpretation and compilation*, Communications of the ACM (Dec 1985) pp. 1311-1324

[Cointe, 1987] P. COINTE, *Metaclasses are first class: the ObjVLisp Model*, in: Proc. OOPSLA'87, N. Meyrowitz (ed.), ACM Sigplan Notices 22 (12) (1987) pp. 156-167

[Cook, 1990] W.R. COOK, *Object oriented programming versus abstract data types*, in: [de Bakker et al, 1990]

[Conery, 1987] J.S. CONERY, *Parallel execution of logic programs*, Kluwer (1987)

[Conery, 1988] J.S. CONERY, *Logical Objects*, in: Proc. Int. Conf. on Logic Programming, Seattle (1988) pp. 420-434

[Conklin, 1987] J. CONKLIN, *Hypertext: An Introduction and Survey*, IEEE Computer 20 (9) (1987) pp. 17-41, originally MCC STP-356-86, Rev. 2

[Cook and Palsberg, 1989] W. COOK AND J. PALSBERG, *A denotational semantics of inheritance and its correctness in: Proc. OOPSLA '89, N. Meyrowitz (ed.), Sigplan Notices 17 (4), pp. 433-443*

[Cook et al, 1990] , W. Cook, W. Hill and P. Canning, *Inheritance is not subtyping*, in: Proc. ACM Symp. on Principles of Programming Languages (1990)

[Dahl and Nygaard, 1966] O.J. DAHL AND K. NYGAARD, *Simula – an Algol-based simulation language*, Communications of the ACM, 9 (1966) pp. 671-678

[Davis, 1980] R. DAVIS, *The Contract Net Protocol: High Level Communication and Control in a Distributed Problem Solver*, IEEE Transactions on Computing C-29 (12) (1980) pp. 1104-1113

[Davison, 1989] A. DAVISON, *Polka: A Parlog object oriented language*, Ph.D. thesis, Dept. of Computing, Imperial College, London (1989)

[Davison, 1989a] A. DAVISON, *Design issues for logic programming-based object oriented languages*, Report Dept. of Computing, Imperial College, London (1989), also in: [Davison, 1989]

[Ducournau and Habib, 1988] R. DUCOURNAU AND M. HABIB, *On some algorithms for multiple inheritance in object oriented programming*, in: Proc. ECOOP 1987, J. Bezivin, J.M. Hullot, P. Cointe and H. Lieberman (eds.), Lecture Notes in Computer Science 276, Springer (1988) pp. 243-252

[Debray and Mishra, 1988] S.K. DEBRAY AND P. MISHRA , *Denotational and Operational Semantics for Prolog*, Journal of Logic Programming, 5 (1988) pp. 61-91

[Dowling and Gallier, 1984] W.F. DOWLING AND J.H. GALLIER, *Linear time algorithms for testing the satisfiability of propositional Horn formulae*, Journal of Logic Programming, 3 (1984) pp. 267-284

[DeGroot, 1984] D. DEGROOT, *Restricted and-parallelism*, in: Proc. Future Generation Computer Systems, ICOT (1984) pp. 471-478

[DoD, 1982] US DEPARTMENT OF DEFENSE, *Reference manual for the Ada programming language*, (1982)

[Dijkstra, 1971] E.W. DIJKSTRA, *Hierarchical ordering of sequential processes*, Acta Informatica, 1 (1971) pp. 115-138

[Eliëns, 1989] A. ELIËNS, *Extending Prolog to a parallel object oriented language*, in: Proc. IFIP W.G. 10.3 Working Conference on Decentralized Systems, Lyon (1989), M. Cosnard and C. Girault (eds.), Elsevier (1990)

[Eliëns, 1991a] A. ELIËNS, *Distributed Logic Programming for Artificial Intelligence*, AI Communications, 4 (1) (1991) pp. 11-21

[Eliëns, 1991b] A. ELIËNS, *Comparative semantics of a backtrackable rendez-vous*, in: Proc. CSN'91/SION, Utrecht, Mathematisch Centrum, Amsterdam (1991)

[Eliëns and de Vink, 1991] A. ELIËNS AND E.P. DE VINK, *Asynchronous rendez-vous in the presence of backtracking*, in: ISLP'91 Workshop on Asynchronous Communication, San Diego (November 1991)

[Eliëns and Visser, 1992] A. ELIËNS AND C. VISSER, *Active C++ — active classes and communication by rendez-vous*, Technical Report Vrije Universiteit (to appear)

[Ellis and Stroustrup, 1990] M. ELLIS AND B. STROUSTRUP, *The Annotated C++ Reference Manual*, Addison-Wesley (1990)

[van Emden and Kowalski, 1976] M.H. VAN EMDEN AND R.A. KOWALSKI, *The semantics of predicate logic as a programming language*, Journal of the ACM 21 (4) (1976) pp. 733-742

[van Emden and de Lucena Filho, 1982] M.H. VAN EMDEN AND G.J. DE LUCENA FILHO, *Predicate logic as a language for parallel programming*, in: [Clark and Tarnlund, 1984] pp. 189-199

[Fahlman, 1985] S.F. FAHLMAN, *Parallel processing in Artificial Intelligence*, Parallel Computing, 2 (1985) pp. 283-285

[Falaschi et al, 1984] M. FALASCHI, G. LEVI AND C. PALAMIDESSI, *A synchronization logic: Axiomatics and formal semantics of generalized Horn clauses*, Information and Control 60 (1984) pp. 36-69

[Fox, 1981] M. FOX, *An organizational view of distributed systems*, IEEE Transactions on Systems, Man, and Cybernetics 11 (1) (1981) pp. 70-80

[Fukunaga and Hirose, 1986] K. FUKUNAGA AND S. HIROSE, *An experience with a Prolog-based Object Oriented Language*, in: Proc. OOPSLA '86, N. Meyrowitz (ed.), SIGPLAN Notices 21 (11) (1986) pp. 224-231

[Gehani and Roome, 1986] N. H. GEHANI AND W.D. ROOME, *Concurrent C*, Software – Practice and Experience 16 (9) (1986) pp. 821-844

[Gehani and Roome, 1988] N. H. GEHANI AND W.D. ROOME, *Concurrent C++ : Concurrent programming with classes*, Software – Practice and Experience 18 (12) (1988) pp. 1157-1177

[Gelernter et al, 1986] D. GELERNTER, S. AHUJA AND N. CARRIERO , *Linda and friends*, Computer 19 (8) (1986) pp. 26-34

[Goguen, 1984] J.A. GOGUEN, *Parametrized Programming*, IEEE Transactions on software engineering 10 (1984) pp. 528-543

[Goldberg and Robson, 1983] A. GOLDBERG AND D. ROBSON, *Smalltalk-80: The language and its implementation*, Addison Wesley (1983)

[Gomez and Chandrasekaran, 1981] F. GOMEZ AND B. CHANDRASEKARAN, *Knowledge Organization and Distribution for Medical Diagnosis*, IEEE Transactions on Systems, Man, and Cybernetics 11 (1) (1981) pp. 34-42

[Gorlen et al, 1990] K. GORLEN, S. ORLOW AND P. PLEXICO, *Dat abstraction and object-oriented programming in C++*, Wiley (1990)

[Halbert and O'Brien, 1987] D. HALBERT AND P. O'BRIEN, *Using types and inheritance in object oriented programming*, IEEE Software 4 (5) (1987) pp. 71-79

[Hasegawa and Amamiya, 1984] R. HASEGAWA AND M. AMAMIYA, *Parallel Execution of Logic Programs based on Dataflow Concept*, in: Proc. Fifth Generation of Computer Systems, ICOT, (1984) pp. 507-516

[Hayes-Roth, 1985] F. HAYES-ROTH, *Rule Based Systems*, Communications of the ACM 28 (9) (1985) pp. 921-932

[Helm et al, 1990] R. HELM, I.M. HOLLAND AND D. GANGOPADHYAY, *Contracts: Specifying behavioral compositions in object oriented systems*, in: Proc. ECOOP/OOPSLA'90, N. Meyrowitz, ACM (1990) pp. 169-180

[van den Herik and Henseler, 1986] H.J. VAN DEN HERIK AND J. HENSELER, *Control mechanisms in the parallel knowledge based system HYDRA*, Report 86-36 Universiteit Delft (1986)

[Hermenegildo and Nasr, 1986] M.V. HERMENEGILDO AND R. NASR, *Efficient management of backtracking in and-parallelism,* in: Proc. Third Int. Conf. on Logic Programming, E. Shapiro (ed.), Lecture Notes in Computer Science 225, Springer (1986) pp. 40-55

[Hermenegildo, 1986] M.V. HERMENEGILDO, *An abstract machine based execution model for computer architecture design and efficient implementation of logic programs in parallel*, Ph.D. thesis, TR-86-20, University of Texas at Austin (1986)

[Hewitt, 1977] C. HEWITT, *Viewing Control Structures as Patterns of Passing Messages*, Artificial Intelligence (1977) pp. 323-364

[Hoare, 1978] C.A.R. HOARE, *Communicating Sequential Processes*, Communications of the ACM 21 (8) (1978) pp. 666-677

[Hoare, 1987] C.A.R. HOARE, *An overview of some formal methods for program design*, IEEE Computer (September 1987) pp. 85-91

[Houtsma and Balsters, 1988] M.A.W. HOUTSMA AND H. BALSTERS, *Formalizing the Data and Knowledge Model*, Memorandum INF-88-23, Universiteit Twente (1988)

[Hynynen and Lassila, 1989] J. HYNYNEN AND O. LASSILA, *On the use of object oriented paradigm in a distributed problem solver*, AI Communications, 2 (3/4) (1989) pp. 142-151

[Iline and Kanoui, 1987] H. ILINE AND H. KANOUI, *Extending Logic Programming to Object Programming: The system LAP*, in: Proc. 10th IJCAI, Vol. 1 (1987) pp. 34-39

[Inmos, 1984] INMOS LTD, *The Occam Programming Manual*, Prentice Hall (1984)

[Ishikawa and Tokoro, 1986] Y. ISHIKAWA AND M. TOKORO, *A concurrent object oriented knowledge representation language Orient84/K: Its features and implementation*, in: Proc. OOPSLA 86, N. Meyrowitz (ed.), ACM Sigplan Notices 21 (11) (1986) pp. 232-241

[Jacquet and Monteiro] J.-M. JACQUET & L. MONTEIRO, *Comparative Semantics for a Parallel Contextual Programming Language.* in: Proc. North-American Logic Programming Conf., S. Debray and M. Hermenegildo (eds.), MIT Press (1990) pp. 195-214.

[Jones and Mycroft, 1984] N. JONES AND A. MYCROFT, *Stepwise development of operational and denotational semantics for Prolog*, in: Proc. Int. Symp. on Logic Programming, Atlantic City (1984) pp. 281-288

[Jones, 1985] G. JONES, *Programming in Occam*, Technical Report TM PRG-43, Oxford (1985)

[Kahn et al, 1986] K. KAHN, E. TRIBBLE, M. MILLAR, D. BOBROW, *Objects in concurrent logic programming languages*, OOPSLA 86, N. Meyrowitz (ed.), SIGPLAN Notices Vol. 21, No. 11, 1986 pp. 242-257

[Karam, 1988] G.M. KARAM, *Prototyping Concurrent systems with Multilog*, Technical Report Dept. of Systems and Computer Engineering Carleton University (1988)

[Karam, 1988a] G.M. KARAM, C.M. STANCZYK AND G.W. BOND, *Critical races in ADA Programs*, TR SCE-88-15 Carleton University Ottawa (1988)

[Karam, 1989] G.M. KARAM, *Mlog: A language for prototyping concurrent systems*, electronic news

[Kim and Lochovsky, 1989] W. KIM AND F. LOCHOVSKY (EDS.), *Object oriented concepts, databases and applications*, Addison Wesley, 1989

[King, 1989] R. KING, *My cat is object oriented*, in: [Kim and Lochovsky, 1989], pp. 23-30

[Klint, 1985] P. KLINT, *A study in string processing languages*, Lecture Notes in Computer Science 205, Springer (1985)

[Klint, 1986] P. KLINT, *Modularization and reusability in current programming languages*, Report CS-R8635, Centre for Mathematics and Computer Science, Amsterdam (1986)

[Kok, 1988] J.N. KOK, *A compositional semantics for Concurrent Prolog*, in: Proc. 5th Annual Symp. on Theoretical Aspects of Computer Science, Bordeaux, February 1988, R. Cori and M. Wirsing (eds.), Lecture Notes in Computer Science 294, Springer (1988) pp. 373-388

[Kok and Rutten, 1988] J. KOK AND J. RUTTEN, *Contractions in comparing concurrency semantics*, in: Proc. Automata, Languages and Programming, T. Lepisto and A. Salomaa (eds.), Lecture Notes in Computer Science 317, Springer (1988) pp. 317-332

[Kok and Rutten, 1990] J. KOK AND J. RUTTEN, *Contractions in comparing concurrency semantics*, Theoretical Computer Science 76 (1990) pp. 180-222

[Kornfield and Hewitt, 1981] W. KORNFELD AND C.E. HEWITT, *The scientific community metaphor* , IEEE Transactions on Systems, Man, and Cybernetics 11 (1) (1981)

[Kowalczyk, 1990] W. KOWALCZYK, *Introduction to Prolog*, Dept. Mathematics and Computer Science, Vrije Universiteit, Amsterdam (1990)

[Kowalczyk and Treur, 1990] W. KOWALCZYK AND J. TREUR, *On the use of a formalized generic task model in knowledge acquisition*, in: Proc. EKAW 90, IOS Press (1990) pp. 198-220

[Kowalski, 1979] R. KOWALSKI, *Logic for problem solving*, North Holland (1979)

[Knuth, 1983] D. KNUTH, *Literate programming*, Computer Journal, 27 (2) (1984) pp. 97-111

[Krasner, 1984] G. KRASNER, *Smalltalk-80 Bits of history, words of advice*, Addison Wesley, 1984

[Lassez and Maher, 1983] J.-L. LASSEZ, M.J. MAHER, *The denotational semantics of Horn clauses as production-systems*, in: Proc. Am. Nat. Conf. on A.I., Washington (1983)

[Lieberherr and Holland, 1989] K. LIEBERHERR AND I. HOLLAND, *Assuring good style for object oriented programs*, IEEE Software 6 (5) (1989) pp. 38-48

[Linton et al, 1989] M. LINTON, J. VLISSIDES AND P. CALDER, *Composing user interfaces with Interviews*, IEEE Computer 22 (2) (1989) pp. 8-22

[Lipovski and Hermenegildo, 1985] G.J. LIPOVSKI M.V. HERMENEGILDO, *B-log: A branch and bound methodology for the parallel execution of logic programs*, in: IEEE Proc. Int. Conf. on Par. Processing (1985) pp.560-567

[Lloyd, 1987] J.W. LLOYD, *Foundations of Logic Programming*, Symbolic Computation, Springer (1984) 2nd edn.

[Lucas, 1986] P.J.F. LUCAS, *Knowledge representation and inference in rule based systems*, Report CS-R8613, Centre for Mathematics and Computer Science, Amsterdam (1986)

[Lusk and Overbeek, 1980] E.L. LUSK AND A.R. OVERBEEK, *Data-structures and Control-architectures for the implementation of theorem-proving programs*, in: Proc. 5th Conf. on Automated Deduction, Lecture Notes in Computer Science 87, Springer (1980) pp. 232-249

[Lusk et al, 1982] E.L. LUSK, W. MCCUNE AND A.R. OVERBEEK, *Logic Machine Architecture: inference mechanisms*, in: Proc. 6th Conf. on Automated Deduction, Lecture Notes in Computer Science 138, Springer (1982) pp. 85-97

[Lusk and Overbeek, 1984] E.L. LUSK AND R.A. OVERBEEK, *Parallelism in automated reasoning systems*, Report, Argonne National Laboratory (1984)

[Malenfant et al, 1989] J. MALENFANT, G. LAPALME AND J. VAUCHER, *ObjVProlog: Metaclasses in Logic*, in: Proc. ECOOP'89, Cambridge University Press (1989) pp. 257-269

[Manthey and Bry, 1988] R. MANTHEY AND F. BRY, *SATCHMO: A theorem prover implemented in Prolog*, in: Proc. CADE-9, E. Lusk and R. Overbeek (eds.), Lecture Notes in Computer Science 310, Springer (1988) pp. 415-434

[McArthur et al, 1982] D. MCARTHUR, R. STEEB AND S. CAMMARATA, *A framework for distributed problem solving*, in: Proc. Conf. AAAI (1982) pp. 181-184

[Mello and Natali, 1986] P. MELLO AND A. NATALI, *Programs as collections of communicating Prolog units*, in: Proc. ESOP 86, B. Robinet and R. Wilhelm (eds.), Lecture Notes in Computer Science 213, Springer (1986) pp. 274-288

[Meltzer, 1982] B. MELTZER, *Prolegomena to a theory of efficiency of proof procedures*, Machine Intelligence (1982) pp. 15-33

[Meyer, 1988] B. MEYER, *Object-oriented software construction*, Prentice Hall, 1988

[Meyer, 1990] B. MEYER, *Tools for the new culture: Lessons from the design of the Eiffel libraries*, Communications of the ACM 33 (9) (1990) pp. 69-88

[Meyrowitz, 1986] N. MEYROWITZ, *Intermedia: The architecture and construction of an object oriented hypermedia system and applications framework*, in: Proc. OOPSLA '86, N. Meyrowitz (ed.), ACM (1986) pp. 186-201

[Miller, 1986] D. MILLER, *A theory of modules for logic programming*, in: IEEE Symp. on Logic Programming, IEEE (1986) pp. 106-114

[Monteiro, 1981] L. MONTEIRO, *An extension to Horn clause logic allowing the definition of concurrent processes*, in: Proc. Int. Coll. on Formalization of Programming Concepts, J. Diaz and I. Ramos (ed.), Lecture Notes in Computer Science 107, Springer (1981) pp. 401-407

[Monteiro, 1984] L. MONTEIRO, *A proposal for distributed programming in logic*, in: [Campbell, 1984] pp. 329-340

[Monteiro and Porto, 1988] L. MONTEIRO AND A. PORTO, *Contextual Logic Programming*, Report UNL-50/88, University Lisboa (1988)

[Mundie and Fisher, 1986] D.A. MUNDIE AND D.A. FISHER, *Parallel processing in Ada*, IEEE Computer 19 (8) (1986) pp. 20-25

[Nelson, 1991] M. NELSON, *Concurrency and object oriented programming*, ACM Sigplan Notices, 26 (10) (1991) pp. 63-72

[Nilsson, 1982] J.F. NILSSON, *Formal Vienna definition method models of Prolog*, in: [Campbell, 1984]

[OOPSLA 91] *Proceedings OOPSLA '91*, A. Paepcke (ed.), Sigplan Notices 26 (11), ACM (1991)

[Ohsuga and Yamauchi, 1985] S. OHSUGA AND H. YAMAUCHI, *Multi-layer logic - A predicate logic including data-structure as knowledge representation language,* New Generation Computing 3 (1985) pp. 403-43

[Padawitz, 1988] P. PADAWITZ, *Computing in Horn Clause Theories,* EATCS Monographs 16, Springer (1988)

[Parsay et al, 1989] K. PARSAYE, M. CHIGNELL, S. KOSHAFIAN AND H. WONG, *Intelligent databases : Object-oriented, deductive and hypermedia technologies,* Wiley (1989)

[Pelaez, 1989] E. PELAEZ, *Parallelism: Performance or Programming,* Computers & Society, 19 (4) (1989)

[Pereira and Nasr, 1984] L.M. PEREIRA AND R. NASR, *Delta Prolog: A distributed logic programming language,* in: Proc. FGCS, ICOT (1984) pp. 283-231

[Pereira et al, 1986] L. PEREIRA, L. MONTEIRO, J. CUNHA, J. AND J. APARICO, *Delta Prolog: a distributed backtracking extension with events,* in: Lecture Notes in Computer Science 225 (1986) pp. 69-83

[Perrott, 1987] R. PERROTT, *Parallel Programming,* Addison-Wesley (1987)

[Plotkin, 1983] G.D. PLOTKIN, *An operational semantics for CSP,* in: Formal Description of Programming Concepts II, D.Bjorner (ed.), North Holland, Amsterdam (1983) pp. 199-223

[Pokkunuri, 1989] B. POKKUNURI, *Object Oriented Programming,* Sigplan Notices 24 (11) (1989) pp. 96-101

[Pope, 1991] S. POPE (ED.), *The Well-Tempered Object: Musical applications of Object-Oriented Software Technology,* MIT Press (1991)

[Rabin, 1974] M.O. RABIN, *Theoretical impediments to Artificial Intelligence,* IFIP (1974) pp. 615-619

[Ramakrishnan, 1986] R. RAMAKRISHNAN, *Annotations for Distributed Programming in Logic,* in: Proc. ACM POPL, St. Petersburg (1986) pp. 255-262

[Ramanujam, 1989] R. RAMANUJAM, *Semantics of distributed definite clause programs,* Theoretical Computer Science 68 (2) (1989) pp. 203-220

[Ringwood, 1988] G.A. RINGWOOD, *Parlog86 and the dining logicians,* Communications of the ACM, 31 (1) (1988) pp. 10-25

[Rizk et al, 1989] A. RIZK, J-M. FELLOUS AND M. TUENI, *An object oriented model in the concurrent logic programming language Parlog,* Report No 1067, INRIA (1989)

[Robinson, 1965] J.A. ROBINSON, *A machine oriented logic based on the resolution principle,* Journal of the ACM 12 (1965) pp. 23-41

[Rodet and Cointe, 1991] X. RODET AND P. COINTE, *FORMES: Composition and scheduling of processes*, in: [Pope, 1991] pp. 64-82

[Rutten, 1990] J.J.M.M. RUTTEN, *Semantic correctness for a parallel object-oriented language*, SIAM Journal on Computing 19, 1990, pp. 341-383

[Saunders, 1989] J. SAUNDERS, *A survey of object oriented programming languages*, Journal of Object Oriented Programming March/April (1989) pp. 5-11

[Shapiro and Takeuchi, 1983] E. SHAPIRO AND A. TAKEUCHI, *Object-oriented programming in Concurrent Prolog*, New Generation Computing, Vol. 1, No. 2 (1983) pp. 5-48

[Shapiro, 1984] E. SHAPIRO, *Systolic programming: a paradigm of parallel processing*, in: Proc. FGCS, ICOT (1984) pp. 458-470

[Shapiro, 1986] E. SHAPIRO, *Concurrent Prolog: Progress Report*, IEEE Computer, 19 (8) (1986) pp. 44-59

[Shapiro, 1989] E. SHAPIRO, *The family of concurrent logic programming languages*, ACM Computing Surveys, 21 (3) (1989) pp. 414-510

[Shatz and Wang, 1987] S.M. SHATZ AND J-P. WANG, *Introduction to distributed software engineering*, IEEE Computer (October 1987) pp. 23-31

[Shriver and Wegner, 1987] B. SHRIVER AND P. WEGNER (EDS.), *Research directions in object-oriented programming*, MIT Press, Cambridge MA, 1987

[Smith and Davis, 1981] R.G. SMITH AND R. DAVIS, *Frameworks for Cooperation in Distributed Problem Solving*, IEEE Transactions on Systems, Man, and Cybernetics 11 (1) (1981) pp. 61-69

[Snyder, 1986] A. SNYDER, *Encapsulation and inheritance in object oriented programming languages*, in: Proc. OOPSLA 1986, N. Meyrowitz (ed.), ACM (1986) pp. 31-45 (extended version in: [Shriver and Wegner, 1987], pp. 165-188)

[Stefik and Bobrow, 1986] M. STEFIK AND D.G. BOBROW, *Object Oriented Programming: Themes and Variations*, AI Magazine, 10 (4) (1986) pp. 40-62

[Sterling, 1986] L. STERLING, *Expert System = Knowledge + Meta-Interpreter*, Report, The Weizman Institute of Science, Israel

[Stroustrup, 1986] B. STROUSTRUP, *The C++ programming language*, Addison Wesly (1986)

[Stroustrup, 1988] B. STROUSTRUP, *What is "Object-Oriented Programming"?*, IEEE Software, 5 (3) (1988) pp. 10-20

[Stroustrup, 1991] B. STROUSTRUP, *The C++ Programming Language*, Addison Wesley (1991) 2nd edn.

[Subrahmanyam, 1985] P.A. SUBRAHMANYAM, *The Software Engineering of Expert Systems: Is Prolog appropriate?*, IEEE Transactions on software engineering 11 (1985) pp. 1391-1400

[Talukdar et al, 1986] S.N. TALUKDAR, E. CARDOZO, L. LEAO, R. BANARES AND R. JOOBBANI, *A system for distributed problem solving,* in: Coupling symbolic and numerical computing in expert systems, J.S. Kowalik (ed.), (1986)

[Tello, 1989] E.R. TELLO, *Object Oriented Programming for Artificial Intelligence,* Addison Wesly (1989)

[Thomsen, 1987] K. S. THOMSEN, *Inheritance on processes, exemplified on distributed termination detection,* International Journal of Parallel programming, 16 (1) (1987) pp.17-51

[Touretzky. 1986] S. TOURETSKY , *The mathematics of inheritance systems,* Pitman London (1986)

[Tsujino et al. 1984] Y. TSUJINO, M. ANDO, T. ARAKI AND N. TOKURA, *Concurrent C: A programming language for distributed systems,* Software Practice and Experience 14 (11) (1984) pp. 1061-1078

[Ungar and Smith, 1987] D. UNGAR AND R.B. SMITH. *Self: The power of simplicity,* in: Proc. OOPSLA'87, N. Meyrowitz (ed.), ACM Sigplan Notices 4 (8), ACM (1987) pp. 227-242

[de Vink, 1989] E.P. DE VINK, *Comparative semantics for Prolog with cut,* Science of Computer Programming 13 (1990) pp. 237-264

[de Vink, 1990] E.P. DE VINK, *Comparative semantics for Prolog with cut,* Science of Computer Programming 13 (1990), pp. 237-264

[Warren, 1977] D. WARREN, *Implementations of Prolog: Compiling Predicate Logic Programs,* Report, Dept. of Artificial Intelligence, Univ. of Edinburgh (1977)

[Warren, 1983] D. WARREN, *An abstract Prolog instruction set,* Technical Note 309, SRI International (1983)

[Webster, 1988] D. WEBSTER, *Mapping the Design Information Representation Domain,* IEEE Computer (December 1988) pp. 8-23

[Wegner, 1987] P. WEGNER, *Dimensions of Object-Based Language Design,* in: Proc. OOPSLA87, N. Meyrowitz (ed.), Orlando Florida, ACM (1987) pp. 168-182

[Wegner and Zdonik, 1988] P. WEGNER AND S. ZDONIK, *Inheritance as an Incremental Modification Mechanisms or what Like Is and Isn't Like,* in: Proc. ECOOP'88, S. Gjessing and K. Nygaard (eds.), Lecture Notes in Computer Science 322, Springer (1988) pp. 56-77

[Wiener and Pinson, 1988] R.S. WIENER AND J.P. PINSON, *An Introduction to Object-Oriented Programming and C++,* Addison-Wesley (1988)

[Wirfs-Brock, 1989] R. WIRFS-BROCK, *Object oriented design: a responsibility-driven approach,* in: Proc. OOPSLA'89, N. Meyrowitz (ed.), ACM (1989) pp. 71-75

[Wirfs-Brock et al, 1990] R. WIRFS-BROCK, B. WILKERSON AND L. WIENER, *Designing object-oriented software*, Prentice Hall (1990)

[Wirth, 1983] N. WIRTH, *Programming in Modula-2*, Springer (1983)

[Wos et al, 1984] L. WOS, R. OVERBEEK, E. LUSK AND J. BOYLE, *Automated Reasoning: Introduction and applications*, Prentice Hall (1984)

[Yokoi, 1986] S. YOKOI, *A Prolog based object oriented language SPOOL and its compiler*, in: Proc. Logic Programming 86, Tokyo, E. Wada (ed.), Lecture Notes in Computer Science 264, Springer (1986) pp. 116-125

[Yonezawa and Tokoro, 1987] A. YONEZAWA AND M. TOKORO (EDS.), *Object oriented concurrent systems*, MIT Press, 1987

[Zaniolo, 1984] C. ZANIOLO, *Object oriented programming in Prolog*, in: Proc. Int. Symp. on Logic Programming, Atlantic City, IEEE (1984) pp. 265-270

Index